Pitch, Tweet, or Engage on the Street

Pitch, Tweet, or Engage on the Street offers a modern guide for how to practice public relations and strategic communication around the globe. Drawing upon interviews with public relations professionals in over 30 countries as well as the author's own experience as a global public relations practitioner in the United Nations and in U.S. President Barack Obama's administration, this book explains how to adapt public relations strategies, messages, and tactics for countries and cultures around the globe. The book begins by explaining key cultural differences which require practitioners to adapt their approaches, before discussing how to build and manage a global public relations team and how to practice global public relations on behalf of corporations, non-profit organizations, and governments. Then, the book takes readers on a tour of the world, explaining how to adapt their campaigns for Asia-Pacific, Europe, the Middle East, the Americas, and Sub-Saharan Africa. Along the way, readers are introduced to practitioners around the globe and case studies of particularly successful campaigns—from a public relations "siege" that successfully ended an epidemic of violence in Kenya to the remarkable P.R. strategy adopted by Bordeaux wineries in China that led to a staggering 26,900 percent increase in sales.

Dr. Kara Alaimo is Assistant Professor in the Department of Journalism, Media Studies, and Public Relations at Hofstra University in New York.

Pitch, Tweet, or Engage on the Street

How to Practice Global Public Relations and Strategic Communication

Kara Alaimo

Routledge
Taylor & Francis Group

NEW YORK AND LONDON

First published 2017
by Routledge
711 Third Avenue, New York, NY 10017

and by Routledge
2 Park Square, Milton Park, Abingdon, Oxon, OX14 4RN

Routledge is an imprint of the Taylor & Francis Group, an informa business

© 2017 Taylor & Francis

Library of Congress Cataloging-in-Publication Data
Names: Alaimo, Kara, author.
Title: Pitch, tweet, or engage on the street : how to practice global
    public relations and strategic communication / Dr. Kara Alaimo.
Description: New York : Routledge, 2016. | Includes index.
Identifiers: LCCN 2016002020 (print) | LCCN 2016017290 (ebook) |
    ISBN 9781138916043 (hardback) | ISBN 9781138916050 (pbk.) |
    ISBN 9781315689869 (ebk) | ISBN 9781315689869 (Ebook)
Subjects: LCSH: Public relations. | Social media. | High technology
    industries—Public relations.
Classification: LCC HM1221 .A483 2016 (print) | LCC HM1221
    (ebook) | DDC 659.2—dc23

ISBN: 978-1-138-91604-3 (hbk)
ISBN: 978-1-138-91605-0 (pbk)
ISBN: 978-1-315-68986-9 (ebk)

Typeset in Goudy
by Apex CoVantage, LLC

For my students

Contents

Note from the Author

If you are reading this book, you likely have some interest in practicing global public relations. In my opinion, you could not be selecting a more exciting career or choosing this profession at a more opportune time. Today, demand for public relations professionals is expanding around the globe. The field grew by more than 7 percent in 2014 and 11 percent in 2013 and is now a $13 billion industry (Holmes Report, 2015).

There is also greater need than ever before for professionals who can craft and implement international and intercultural public relations campaigns. In our modern, globalized world, the boundaries between people and countries are continuing to break down. Today, in order to stay competitive, companies increasingly must pursue overseas markets to produce and sell their goods. Countries are not only seeking to lure foreign tourists and business investment, but also taking to social media to try to win hearts and minds in the war on global terrorism. And non-profit organizations need to cross national and regional borders in order to effectively address modern challenges—from poverty and hunger to global health pandemics and climate change. Professionals who can effectively communicate and build relationships across countries and cultures are invaluable to such organizations.

My own career in global public relations has taken me around the world many times over—from the Toronto Film Festival to a meeting with a Saudi prince in Riyadh to a mangrove farm in Togo, West Africa. I began my career as a spokesperson for the City of New York, where I helped promote the city globally as a location for film production and business investment. Later, I worked at the United Nations, where I liaised with the global media to build support for efforts to eradicate extreme poverty and achieve sustainable development. In 2011, I was appointed by U.S. President Barack Obama as Spokesperson for International Affairs in the Treasury Department, where I promoted U.S. economic diplomacy initiatives. I also traveled around the globe with World Bank President Jim Yong Kim to build international support for his candidacy to lead the world's premier development institution. I then returned to the U.N.

In my travels around the world, I was regularly confronted with situations that tested and, frankly, caught me completely off guard. For example, in Cote d'Ivoire, I set up an interview for the U.S. Deputy Treasury Secretary with Vox Africa, a pan-African satellite television station. After conducting but before airing the interview, the reporter emailed me to explain that he was not paid for his work at Vox Africa—a situation that is not uncommon in parts of Africa, where reporters in such situations will attempt to sell stories directly to the people whom they interview. The reporter asked me for the Deputy Secretary's help getting a job at the African Development Bank. Although we ethically could not help, we also worried about the treatment the reporter would give us in the story if we declined.

On a trip to Tunisia, I landed to read a Reuters story in which a Tunisian government minister was quoted announcing that the United States had agreed to give Tunisia a loan guarantee of more than $500 million. In fact, the U.S. government had not officially decided to do so. I immediately (and, as I later discovered, wrongly) assumed that the minister was trying to force our hand by making us either deliver the loan guarantee or publicly disavow support to a post-Arab-Spring ally in media interviews I had set up for later in the day. As it turns out, I had completely overestimated the Tunisian government's strategy. In fact, my boss was later told that Tunisia's ambassador in Washington had mistakenly informed his government that we had approved the loan guarantee after it was proposed by a Senate sub-committee. Apparently, the ambassador did not fully understand how a bill becomes a law in the United States!

During Jim Kim's campaign for the World Bank Presidency, we visited South Korea, his family's country of origin. I should have better anticipated the reception he would face in the country, because when he was nominated for the job, it felt like every reporter in Korea called me to request an interview; by the time we departed Washington, I had nearly lost my voice! Still, when we landed in Seoul, I told President Kim that if reporters were waiting for us at the airport, he should not speak, since I wanted his first statement in the country to be from the Blue House (the official residence of South Korea's head of state, which is akin to the White House in the United States). Had I fully appreciated the excitement with which he would be greeted in the country, I would have arranged in advance for him to make a statement in the airport when we landed so that reporters would have been waiting for him in a designated room. Instead, when we arrived, we were surrounded and absolutely mobbed by reporters and paparazzi pushing and shoving to get to the center of the scrum, in a scene reminiscent of the days of Princess Diana. When we somehow managed to safely escape the airport, President Kim told me that he thought the reporters were going to reach down his throat and pull out the words that I had told him not to utter. There was no question that my public relations plan had put my colleagues and me in danger.

I would have been better prepared for each of these situations if I had a deeper understanding of the media systems of the countries in which I was working and our local partners. (Of course, all of this was complicated by the fact that, in my position in the Obama administration, I often traveled to more than one country in a single day; when I returned home after President Kim's campaign, I realized that I had not slept in a bed for an entire week! If you plan to work in global public relations, I do hope you have lots of energy and highly recommend taking your vitamins.) However, this book will give you the tools and skills you need to adapt your public relations strategies for different countries and cultures.

To be sure, cultures and media outlets will continue to evolve; the social media platforms that are hot today may not even exist in a few years. This book is therefore designed, above all, to explain *how* to identify salient cultural differences and adapt your public relations strategies accordingly. These skills are timeless. Yet I won't pretend that applying them is easy. Cultures are complicated constructs, and much of what defines them is not identifiable on the surface level, which is why I strongly recommend working with local partners (and will teach you how to do so in Chapter 3). In addition to local knowledge, it also takes a creative spark to come up with a strategy and messaging that will resonate with your audiences. However, if you can learn how to deeply understand your target audiences and find fresh, sophisticated ways to apply the tools of the public relations trade, I am confident that you will be successful in your practice.

I wrote this book because I could no longer subject my students to the alternatives. Although the goal of this book is to bridge theory and practice, unlike other authors, I will not subject you to long histories of how public relations was practiced in the past in various nations, or how public relations education has evolved in different countries. Rather, I have searched the global literature on public relations and strategic communication, interviewed more than seventy-five top practitioners from around the world, and drawn on my own experience to craft a modern guide to practicing public relations across countries and cultures. Similarly, I have not relegated an obscure chapter on ethics to the back of this book. Ethical principles have infused every sentence.

Do you have more advice to offer about the public relations strategies, messages, and tactics that work best in your country or culture—or have things changed since I wrote this? I would be happy to consider your ideas for the next edition of this book. I love hearing from my readers and can be reached at Kara.S.Alaimo@hofstra.edu. I also invite you to follow my Twitter handle, @karaalaimo, where we can continue this conversation.

Please also be sure to visit the companion website for this book, www.rout ledge.com/cw/alaimo, where you can access more resources for practicing your craft globally.

Finally, as one of the last U.S. government officials to leave our embassy in Tunisia before it was breached and torched in 2012, I feel the need to offer one last piece of advice to you before we begin: When traveling in different countries, be sure to exercise prudence and plan ahead to ensure your safety. Keep track of any travel warnings or advisories issued by governments and make sure that you get needed vaccinations and travel visas in advance. (When I worked for the U.S. government, I had three different passports—needed in part because some Arab states won't let you enter their countries if you have an Israeli stamp on your passport—but, even still, they weren't always enough to get all the visas I needed in advance of travel. I once had to abandon my team on an overseas trip because my visa for Libya couldn't be overnighted to me in time). Also, when it comes to your safety, don't assume that other people know more than you do or have better judgment than you do. For example, on September 11, 2012—when the U.S. ambassador to Libya was killed in Benghazi—I was in Beirut with a U.S. Treasury official who ran programs targeting terrorist assets. One of my colleagues in Washington had argued that we should announce our trip to the press in advance, assuring me that it would not be rational for the terrorist group Hezbollah to try to kill us in Lebanon. I told him that I wouldn't be counting on the rationality of a terrorist group on the anniversary of the September 11, 2001, terrorist attacks to keep myself alive and I would issue the media advisory once we landed in the country, thank you very much. Follow your gut every time and don't rely on others to keep you safe. As long as you always use your best judgment, I think global public relations can be one of the most exciting jobs in the world.

I wish you all the very best in your career and hope that this book will be useful to you.

Warmest wishes,

Kara S. Alaimo

Kara Alaimo, Ph.D.

1 Global and Local Approaches to International Public Relations

Defining International Public Relations

Copyright: Maksim Kabakou

What is international public relations? Curtin and Gaither (2007, p. 4) describe public relations as "a form of strategic communication directed primarily toward gaining public understanding and acceptance and the process of creating a good relationship between an organization and the public, especially with regard to reputation and to communication of information." International public relations is "a title that denotes the practice and study of public relations across international boundaries and cultures" (Curtin & Gaither, 2007, p. 19). The key distinction is that the *practice* must occur across national borders. For example, a person from Benin who moves to Brazil to work for a Brazilian firm is not practicing international public relations unless (s)he is interacting on behalf of the firm with publics outside of Brazil. When an organization and the publics with which it attempts to build relationships are located in different countries, then the organization's public relations activities are said to be international (Wakefield, 2008, p. 140). The key difference between local and international public relations campaigns is that international campaigns must take account of cultural differences. Banks (1995, p. 42) defines effectiveness in multicultural public relations as "the successful negotiation of multiple meanings that result in positive outcomes in any communicative activity."

Scholars disagree about how much of modern public relations can be said to be international. Sriramesh (2009a, p. xxxv) suggests that the terms international public relations and global public relations are becoming tautologies "because even 'domestic' publics are becoming multinational and multicultural due to globalization." By this account, nearly all public relations practice can be considered to be global or international. By contrast, Wakefield (2008, p. 139) argues that domestic public relations practice continues to exist because "practitioners who represent school districts or private schools, small to mid-size cities, hospitals and medical centers, high school or small university sports programs, local nonprofit agencies, and myriads of other organizations most likely never practice . . . *international public relations*." While Wakefield is correct that some practitioners remain cloistered in their communities, this is becoming increasingly uncommon. Furthermore, practitioners at such supposedly local firms cannot safely assume that they will remain disconnected from the broader international community—as local hospitals in Madrid, Spain, and Dallas, Texas, in the United States of America discovered in 2014 when patients arrived with Ebola, a virus that originated in West Africa. The global media was soon at their doorsteps.

The increased practice of global public relations is due to globalization, which Stiglitz (2002, p. 9) defines as the

> closer integration of the countries and people of the world which has been brought about by the enormous reduction of costs of transportation and communication, and the breaking down of artificial barriers to the flows of goods, services, capital, knowledge, and to a lesser extent people across borders.

As a result of these forces, Friedman (2005) famously argues that today "the world is flat." People of different countries and cultures are interacting and collaborating more than ever before. In addition to increased global communication, Sharpe and Pritchard (2004) argue that the expansion of public relations practice globally has also been driven by social interdependence— the increased recognition that global cooperation is necessary to solve modern problems—as well as by the spread of democracy, because when the people exercise control over their governments, public opinion takes on greater importance.

It has therefore become essential for the modern public relations practitioner to understand how to build relationships and communicate with stakeholders in other countries and cultures. This book will give you the skills and knowledge to do so.

International vs. Global Public Relations Campaigns

Copyright: hobbit

In 2012, the Swedish furniture company IKEA faced a dilemma in the Saudi market. Its popular catalogs showcasing the company's merchandise featured some pictures of women. However, in Saudi Arabia, it is inappropriate for a woman to appear in public without her face and body covered. The company therefore decided to airbrush the women out of the version of the catalog it would use in Saudi Arabia. When the Swedish version of the newspaper *Metro* broke the story about what the company had done, the incident quickly provoked outrage. The trade minister of Sweden—a country globally renowned for its efforts to advance the role of women in society—responded by arguing that "it is impossible to retouch women out of reality." IKEA quickly apologized (Paterson, 2012). However, the incident illustrates a dilemma that every international public relations practitioner faces. On the one hand, it is necessary to develop culturally specific communication products and messages that are appropriate for local audiences. On the other hand, it is also important to project a coherent global identity and values—especially in our modern, globalized world in which messages intended for a particular audience often spread far beyond their intended reach. Pretending that women do not exist is unlikely to foster a positive global reputation.

One of the first questions you will need to answer when you work in international public relations is whether you will implement a single, global strategy around the world or craft different approaches for different markets. Anderson (1989, p. 413) defines international public relations practice as one in which practitioners "implement distinctive programs in multiple markets, with each program tailored to meet the often acute distinctions of the individual geographic market." Proponents of this approach argue that different countries

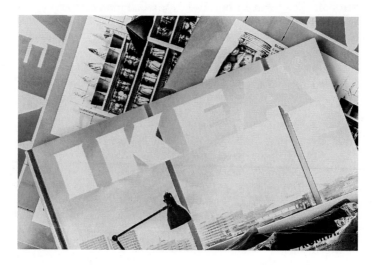

IKEA ignited a firestorm after cropping women out of their catalogs for Saudi Arabia.
Copyright: OlegDoroshin

and cultures are so different that they require strategies that are specifically designed to respond to local opportunities and challenges. The benefit of adopting a strictly local approach is that you are completely unencumbered by concepts that do not make sense for your target audience. Because you focus single-mindedly on the country or culture at hand, you are more likely to arrive at an approach that will be effective in its target market.

However, the cost of starting from scratch in every new environment will often prove to be prohibitive for many organizations. Additionally, a major disadvantage to such an approach is that your client will lack a coherent global identity. In fact, as the IKEA debacle illustrates, an approach too narrowly designed for one market may actually offend and alienate key stakeholders in other locations. Another significant downside to a strictly local approach is that an organization does not benefit from the range of creative ideas it can generate when its entire global public relations team comes together to brainstorm on a unified strategy.

The opposite of a local, or international, approach to public relations is adopting a single global strategy. Anderson (1989, p. 413) defines **global public relations** practice as one that "superimposes an overall perspective on a program executed in two or more national markets, recognizing the similarities among audiences while necessarily adapting to regional differences." Practitioners who apply this approach believe that there are certain best practices and messages that are generally successful across countries and cultures. For example, Hofstede, Hofstede, and Minkov (2010, p. 6) note that part of human nature—which we all inherit in our genes—is "the human ability to feel fear, anger, love, joy, sadness, and shame; the need to associate with others and to play and exercise oneself; and the facility to observe the environment and to talk about it with other humans." Therefore, global messages can appeal to these common experiences. Chris Nelson, Crisis Lead for the Americas at the global public relations agency FleishmanHillard, explains that

> there are certain universals—survival, hunger, fear, greed, love, pride— that we share as a species. Operating on a global stage, I can start by understanding how a situation plays into those universal elements, and then I can find people who can help me understand the local culture.

Practitioners who adopt a global approach also typically believe that their organizations benefit from having a consistent global brand identity. Michael Morley (2002, pp. 30–31), former Deputy Chairman of Edelman Public Relations—the world's largest public relations firm—argues that speaking with a global voice is now a "corporate necessity" because news travels rapidly around the world and "governments, consumer protection organizations, non-governmental organizations (NGOs) and pressure groups of all kinds are making it their business to discover inconsistencies in multinational concerns." He (2002, p. 32) also says that there is often a degree of "local anarchy" in business practices around the globe, and so "taking the first steps in this quest to establish a global voice can serve a different and valuable purpose—as a catalyst in the process of defining 'the reality.'" These days, organizations are increasingly embracing integrated marketing communications, which focuses on communicating a consistent brand identity across both public relations and marketing efforts.

Another advantage of establishing common public relations practices at the global level is that it allows you to enforce universal ethical principles. As the IKEA example evinces, local conduct is often judged by global standards— especially in an era in which news travels faster than ever before via social media. For example, as I will discuss in the coming chapters, in many parts of the world, it is common to offer reporters "brown envelopes" (full of cash) for media coverage. If you work for a Fortune 500 company and one of your practitioners in Nigeria is exposed for following this customary local practice, all of a sudden, your organization will have a global reputation for corruption and bribery. One way that practitioners get around paying journalists in places where reporters are truly not compensated by news organizations for their stories is by offering meals at events and press briefings. You can also help with transportation. When I worked for the U.S. Treasury and one of our officials addressed the Parliament in Togo, the embassy's communication officer drove around the capital city of Lomé in a van picking up reporters to attend his speech, because otherwise they would have had no way of getting there!

It is clearly advisable to set and enforce a global set of standards for ethics and professional conduct in your organization's public relations practice. Members of the International Public Relations Association (IPRA) adopted a Code of Conduct in 2011 that commits practitioners to promote dialogue; be honest, open, transparent, and truthful; avoid and disclose conflicts of interest;

protect confidential information; not smear the reputations of other practitioners; avoid poaching clients; and not "give any financial or other inducement to public representatives or the media, or other stakeholders" (IPRA, 2015a). The IPRA has also adopted a Charter on Media Transparency, which indicates that practitioners may not pay reporters for editorial coverage; paid promotions must be identified as such; and samples provided to journalists should be returned after use (IPRA, 2015b). Both codes are printed here for your reference. These provide helpful guidelines that you can use as a starting point for establishing your own global practices.

The International Public Relations Association Code of Conduct

Adopted in 2011, the IPRA Code of Conduct is an affirmation of professional and ethical conduct by members of the International Public Relations Association and recommended to public relations practitioners worldwide.

The Code consolidates the 1961 Code of Venice, the 1965 Code of Athens and the 2007 Code of Brussels.

(a) RECALLING the Charter of the United Nations which determines "to reaffirm faith in fundamental human rights, and in the dignity and worth of the human person";

(b) RECALLING the 1948 "Universal Declaration of Human Rights" and especially recalling Article 19;

(c) RECALLING that public relations, by fostering the free flow of information, contributes to the interests of all stakeholders;

(d) RECALLING that the conduct of public relations and public affairs provides essential democratic representation to public authorities;

(e) RECALLING that public relations practitioners through their wide-reaching communication skills possess a means of influence that should be restrained by the observance of a code of professional and ethical conduct;

(f) RECALLING that channels of communication such as the Internet and other digital media, are channels where erroneous or misleading information may be widely disseminated and remain unchallenged, and therefore demand special attention from public relations practitioners to maintain trust and credibility;

(g) RECALLING that the Internet and other digital media demand special care with respect to the personal privacy of individuals, clients, employers and colleagues;

In the conduct of public relations practitioners shall:

1 Observance

Observe the principles of the UN Charter and the Universal Declaration of Human Rights;

2 Integrity

Act with honesty and integrity at all times so as to secure and retain the confidence of those with whom the practitioner comes into contact;

3 Dialogue

Seek to establish the moral, cultural and intellectual conditions for dialogue, and recognise the rights of all parties involved to state their case and express their views;

4 Transparency

Be open and transparent in declaring their name, organisation and the interest they represent;

5 Conflict

Avoid any professional conflicts of interest and to disclose such conflicts to affected parties when they occur;

6 Confidentiality

Honour confidential information provided to them;

7 Accuracy

Take all reasonable steps to ensure the truth and accuracy of all information provided;

8 Falsehood

Make every effort to not intentionally disseminate false or misleading information, exercise proper care to avoid doing so unintentionally and correct any such act promptly;

9 Deception

Not obtain information by deceptive or dishonest means;

10 Disclosure

Not create or use any organisation to serve an announced cause but which actually serves an undisclosed interest;

11 Profit

Not sell for profit to third parties copies of documents obtained from public authorities;

12 Remuneration

Whilst providing professional services, not accept any form of payment in connection with those services from anyone other than the principal;

13 Inducement

Neither directly nor indirectly offer nor give any financial or other inducement to public representatives or the media, or other stakeholders;

14 Influence

Neither propose nor undertake any action which would constitute an improper influence on public representatives, the media, or other stakeholders;

15 Competitors

Not intentionally injure the professional reputation of another practitioner;

16 Poaching

Not seek to secure another practitioner's client by deceptive means;

17 Employment

When employing personnel from public authorities or competitors take care to follow the rules and confidentiality requirements of those organisations;

18 Colleagues

Observe this Code with respect to fellow IPRA members and public relations practitioners worldwide.

IPRA members shall, in upholding this Code, agree to abide by and help enforce the disciplinary procedures of the International Public Relations Association in regard to any breach of this Code.

Source: *International Public Relations Association*

The International Public Relations Association Charter on Media Transparency

IPRA members observe the IPRA code of conduct. IPRA members expect editorial providers to observe the following:

Editorial. Editorial appears as a result of the editorial judgement of the journalists involved, and not as a result of any payment in cash or in kind, or barter by a third party.

Identification. Editorial which appears as a result of a payment in cash or in kind, or barter by a third party will be clearly identified as advertising or a paid promotion.

Solicitation. There should be no suggestion by any journalist or members of staff of an editorial provider, that editorial can be obtained in any way other than through editorial merit.

Sampling. Third parties may provide samples or loans of products or services to journalists where it is necessary for such journalists to test, use, taste or sample the product or service in order to articulate an objective opinion about the product or service. The length of time required for sampling should be agreed in advance and all loaned products or services should be returned after sampling.

Policy statement. Editorial providers should prepare a policy statement regarding the receipt of gifts or discounted products and services from third parties by their journalists and other staff. Journalists and other staff should be required to read and sign acceptance of the policy. The policy should be available for public inspection.

Source: *International Public Relations Association*

The downside of a strictly global approach to public relations, however, is that it runs the risk of imposing strategies that work in certain circumstances in contexts in which they are inappropriate and/or ineffective. In practice, many global public relations strategies today are developed in global head-quarters in New York or London, where practitioners are often wholly unfamiliar with the principles of successful public relations practice in Lagos or New Delhi. The trick to crafting a global public relations strategy that can be successful globally is soliciting input as you develop it from practitioners around the world who know what will—and will not—work in local countries and cultures. As Paulo Henrique Soares, Head of Communications for Vale, one of the world's largest mining companies, explains, "once a global strategy is developed, there is not a lot of room for adaptation, so what we have learned is that it is nice if a strategy is built together. A global strategy will only be global if it starts with global inputs."

Jennifer Stapper, Chief of Communications for United Nations Volunteers, also recommends making sure that key messages developed at the global level will translate well into the local languages in which your campaign will be implemented. "You should ask at the outset how your ideas will look and feel in different languages," she says. "There are a lot of things that are simply not going to work in other languages, so it doesn't make sense to create a global campaign and worry about translating your messages later." For example, for years, communication professors have told their students that the Chevy car called the Nova sold poorly in Spanish-speaking countries because the name translates literally in Spanish as "it doesn't go." As it turns out, the vehicle actually sold well in Mexico and surpassed Chevy's expectations in Venezuela. Nevertheless, it is not a strategy you will want to emulate. Launched in 2006, Clairol's "Mist Stick" (a name that translates literally into German as manure) curling iron unsurprisingly fared poorly in the German market (Smith, 2011).

R. P. Kumar, Executive Vice President and Global Director of Strategic Planning for the global public relations agency Ketchum, says that any time you have a message translated into a different language, you should have a different translation company "back translate" the translated version into its original language in order to be sure that the meaning has not changed in translation. Kumar says that he once crafted a message for a large consumer products company in India promising that a laundry detergent contained "Extra Lather! Extra Power!" When he had the message translated from Hindi into other Indian languages, the "back translations" came back promising consumers "Extra Lather, Extra Powder!"—though the product did not, of course, contain extra powder. "Only when I saw the back translation did I see how close we were to a major lawsuit and to the entire agency getting fired," Kumar remembers.

Today, most organizations craft some type of global approach to public relations that they attempt to modify in local contexts. For example, when I worked at the United Nations headquarters in New York, I often drafted global press releases that we sent to regional and national hubs called U.N. Information Centres around the world for adaptation and translation at the local level. Some of the changes that organizations make to adapt their global strategies to local markets are drastic; others are quite minor. When May Hauer-Simmonds worked as an account executive for the global public relations firm Burson-Marsteller in Guayaquil, Ecuador, she was responsible for adapting a global strategy developed by executives in Miami, Florida for the Ecuadorian market in order to launch a new Sony product. While Miami-based executives recommended planning a local launch event with a set program in order to garner media coverage, as I explain in Chapter 2, Latin Americans tend to have a "polychronic" view of time, in which punctuality is not a major priority. For this reason, instead of hosting an event in Ecuador that started at an exact time, the agency organized an open house so that, regardless of when journalists arrived, they could still participate.

Indeed, differences in attitudes towards time are one of the most important dimensions on which cultures differ. Chapter 2 will explain how to identify relevant cultural differences when working in a new place. An understanding of such cultural and national differences should form the basis of your decisions about whether and how to adapt a global strategy for a local audience.

Another approach to making global strategies work at the local level is developing different local communication products around central themes. For example, Fabio Cavalcanti Caldas, Director of External Affairs in Latin America for the energy company Shell, says that while the company has developed global campaigns around topics such as innovation, sustainability, and biofuels, he has enjoyed freedom to develop different films on these topics for different countries. In Brazil, for example, Shell's films have employed humor, been informal, and attempted to convey passion and emotion—characteristics that resonate strongly with Brazilians.

A scene from a film in which Shell unveils a soccer stadium in Brazil that is powered by energy from the players' footsteps. Courtesy of Shell

Verčič, Grunig, and Grunig (1996, p. 36) have proposed an influential theory advocating a middle ground between crafting different public relations strategies for every market and crafting a single public relations strategy applied universally around the globe, which they call the generic/specific theory. They argue that there are nine generic principles of good public relations practice "applicable across cultures and political/economic systems" and that, in applying these principles, international public relations practitioners must take account of five dimensions along which societies differ. They argue that, across the world, the following principles of good practice apply:

1   Public relations practitioners must be involved in their organization's strategic planning process, so that they develop plans to reach internal and external stakeholders who represent risks and opportunities for them. This helps an organization reach its goals. According to Verčič et al. (1996, p. 37),

> when public relations helps the organization build relationships, it saves the organization money by reducing the costs of litigation, regulation, legislation, pressure campaigns, or boycotts that result from bad relationships with publics. . . . It also helps the organization make money by cultivating relationships with donors, consumers, shareholders, and legislators.

2   The most senior public relations professional in an organization should be part of the organization's dominant coalition: "the power-elite group of managers that makes strategic decisions for the organization" (Verčič et al., 1996, p. 37). Otherwise, managers without expertise in public relations may make wrong-headed decisions.

3 All public relations practitioners should be located in the same department or otherwise coordinate with one another so that they can act strategically.

4 A public relations department should be its own separate entity, not a subsidiary of a different department. Otherwise, practitioners will not be able to easily re-allocate resources in order to focus their attention on reaching their most important stakeholders.

5 Every organization should have a public relations professional who is responsible for conceptualizing and managing public relations programs. If an organization's public relations staff only handles technical work, such as writing publications, then important decisions will be made by senior managers who lack public relations expertise.

6 Practitioners should practice **two-way symmetrical** communication, which requires that an organization foster genuine dialogue with their key stakeholders and be open to changing themselves as a result of such exchanges, rather than attempting to simply persuade or impose their point of view on others. Verčič et al. (1996, p. 39) advocate this model in contrast to three other models: the **asymmetrical** model of communication, which strives to change the views or behaviors of publics while the organization itself is unwilling to adapt; the **press agentry** model, which "strives only for favorable publicity in the mass media, often in a deceptive way," and the **public information** model, which entails simply distributing information to the media.

Grunig and White (1992, p. 46) argue that

> excellent organizations realize that they can get more of what they want by giving publics some of what they want. Reciprocity means that publics, too, will be willing to give up some of what they want to the organization. The logic of reciprocity breaks down, however, when one actor (such as an organization) has more power than another (such as a public).

They (1992, p. 57) argue that this reciprocity also ensures that the practice is ethical.

Numerous scholars have noted that it is unrealistic to expect multinational corporations, for example, to give up their power advantages to ensure that their stakeholders all communicate with them on an equal footing (Wakefield, 2011, p. 175). In reality, there will almost certainly be power differentials between your organization and its stakeholders. However, you should never use them as an opportunity to take advantage of people. This is not only unethical, but, over the long term, such heavy-handed tactics will almost certainly be ineffective.

7 Public relations departments should be decentralized so that professionals enjoy autonomy and engage in symmetrical communication with their employers.

8 Public relations practitioners should have professional training and knowledge of the field.

9   Public relations departments should be diverse, because they are responsible for communicating with diverse groups of stakeholders.

Based upon the results of my research for this book, I would add an additional generic principle:

10   Public relations strategies, tactics, and messages should be tailored to be
culturally appropriate.

While Verčič et al. (1996) argue that the above principles apply universally, they indicate that societies differ along five dimensions which have a
major impact on local public relations practice. It will be critical for you to
learn about each of these dimensions before determining whether and how to
implement a public relations strategy in a new market:

Some scholars believe that public relations can be properly practiced only in a democracy. Copyright: Niyazz

1 Political-Economic System: Sriramesh and Verčič (2009, pp. 5–7) argue
that in political systems that do not place importance on public opinion, public relations practice tends to be unsophisticated and propagandistic. Additionally, in some emerging democracies, "alternative views may be encouraged
in theory but not in practice, resulting in various forms of covert and overt
forms of self-, social, and government censorship."

De Beer and Mersham (2004, p. 322) argue that "public relations, as it is
defined today on the basis of an open communication process, can only exist in
democratic societies" because authoritarian regimes are not open to true public
debate in order to resolve issues. Sriramesh (2004, p. 5) likewise argues that

> public relations thrives on public opinion, which leads one to conclude
> that only pluralistic societies offer an environment that is conducive to

practicing strategic public relations . . . in societies where public opinion is not valued, the nature of public relations tends to be one-way and propagandistic in nature. Democracy, then, is the primary underpinning on which strategic public relations thrives.

You will want to keep close tabs on political developments and the stability of countries in which you work by reading local and global media and monitoring any advisories, such as travel warnings, issued by other governments. You can learn more about the political systems of different countries by reading country profiles on the U.S. Central Intelligence Agency (CIA) World Factbook, available at www.cia.gov.

However, it is not only the country's political system that will be an important factor in your public relations campaign, but also the country's diplomatic relationship with your organization's country of origin. For example, following Russia's annexation of Crimea in 2014, numerous countries announced sanctions against Russia, including the United States, European Union, Canada, and Japan. Russia followed suit, banning food imports from the United States, European Union, Canada, Australia, and Norway.

A country's economic system will also be a key factor in your public relations strategy. Sriramesh and Verčič (2009, p. 8) report that

strategic public relations generally thrives in developed countries because the more developed an economy is, the greater the number of organizational players and the higher the level of competition among organizations. These multiple suppliers of goods and services obviously need to compete for public attention, approval, and support—a prime reason to employ public relations professionals as in-house staff or consultants.

By contrast, Sriramesh (2010, p. 701) reports that "developing economies usually foster public relations aimed at national development and nation building, with government communication taking the bulk of the attention." Sriramesh (2012, p. 14) notes that other economic factors that influence the way public relations is practiced in a country include

the predominant objective that drives a nation's economy, the roles of liberty, equality, harmony, and community in the economy, the extent to which the economy is open to the outside world, the extent to which the economy is in transition, and the extent to which "winners" and "losers" exist in the economy and the dynamics of the relationship between these groups.

Additionally, a country's legal system provides the framework within which professionals practice. Sriramesh and Verčič (2009, p. 9) note that "whereas legal codes tend to be explicit in Western democracies, the legal structure may appear to be more nebulous and embedded in the social or religious codes in many other regions of the world."

The World Bank publishes an annual "Doing Business" report, available at www.doingbusiness.org, that ranks and explains the ease of doing business in countries around the world, based upon how difficult it is to do everything from obtain electricity to enforce contracts. This will be a valuable resource as you prepare to work in a new country for the first time. Additionally, you can learn about the level of corruption in individual countries on Transparency International's website, www.transparency.org.

2 Culture: Ting-Toomey (2005, pp. 71–72) defines culture as

> a learned system of meanings that fosters a particular sense of shared identity and community among its group members. It is a complex frame of reference that consists of patterns of traditions, beliefs, values, norms, symbols, and meanings that are shared to varying degrees by interacting members of a community.

Correctly understanding culture is *the* key to practicing international public relations successfully. As Curtin and Gaither (2007, p. 12) put it, "cultural constructs don't affect public relations practice; they are the essence of public relations practice." Chapter 2 will explain how to identify salient cultural differences so that you can adapt your public relations strategies accordingly.

Levels of activism vary widely by country. Copyright: Seita

3 Extent of Activism: The level of activism in a local market will impact the degree of opposition your organization will need to overcome in order to operate successfully. Kim and Sriramesh (2009, p. 92) note that "societies that have pluralistic political systems, free or at least partly free media systems, and greater individualism among the populace, are more likely to foster high levels of activism requiring more symmetrical or strategic approaches to public relations practice." You will usually be able to gain some sense of the level of activism in a new environment from reading local media and from visiting the websites of international and local advocacy organizations. Your local partners should also have their fingers on the pulse of local activist communities. Chapter 3 will explain how to find your local partners.

4 Level of Development: A country's level of economic development affects its literacy rate and communication infrastructure, which determine how public relations practitioners can reach their target audiences (Sriramesh & Verčič, 2009, p. 8). For example, in parts of Asia and Africa with high illiteracy rates, it is common for public relations practitioners to utilize folk media such as dances, songs, and plays. In countries with high rates of literacy and Internet penetration, traditional and social media are more common tools of the trade. On the World Bank's website, www.worldbank.org, you can find detailed reports on individual economies. Additionally, the CIA World Factbook offers a trove of country-specific economic data.

Understand the level of media control, diffusion, and access before working in a new country. Copyright: Brian A Jackson

5 Media System: Although the definition of public relations has expanded beyond media relations to include all management of an organization's relationships with important publics, the use of traditional and new media remains at the heart of public relations practice in much of the world. Therefore, a country's media system has an important influence on local public relations practice. Sriramesh and Verčič (2009), drawing upon a model first developed by Sriramesh, note that three factors are particularly critical. First, the level of *media control* describes who owns media outlets and how they control editorial content. Sriramesh and Verčič (2009, p. 16) note that although media ownership is concentrated in the hands of a small elite around the world, in developing countries, political elites often also own or monitor and control the media. Such officials, of course, have an interest in maintaining the status quo (Sriramesh, 2004, p. 19). Second, the level of *media diffusion* describes how much of a population the media reaches. In many developing countries, poverty, illiteracy, and lack of infrastructure mean that newspapers, television shows, and other forms of media reach only a small elite (often in urban areas). Third, the level of *media access* describes how easy it is for members of society to convince the media to disseminate their messages—a preeminent goal of most public relations practitioners (Sriramesh & Verčič, 2009, pp. 15–18).

A good resource for learning more about media systems in particular countries is the website of Freedom House, www.freedomhouse.org, which provides data on press freedom in individual countries that is updated in an annual report. Additionally, the CIA World Factbook offers country-specific data on the penetration of telephone lines, mobile phones, Internet hosts, Internet users, and broadcast media.

These five dimensions offer a helpful framework for you to consider as you adapt public relations strategies to different local contexts. However, the problem with Verčič et al.'s theory is that it was developed by extending a literature review published in 1992, which Wakefield (2000, p. 65) notes was "supported by research in the USA and the UK, but . . . remained relatively untested across other national boundaries." The assumption that what is found to work well in a few rich, Western nations will be best for the rest of the world is unfortunately commonplace in modern international public relations scholarship, which Sriramesh (2009b, p. 58) notes continues to be characterized by "extreme ethnocentricity." Public relations textbooks written by U.S. scholars are predominant globally, and most of these texts remain squarely focused on U.S. practice (Bardhan & Weaver, 2011, p. 6). You will read more about other theories of public relations—including the European concept of reflective public relations, the Latin American school of public relations, and African communitarian approaches—in the chapters to follow. For now, it is clear that, while Verčič et al.'s principles are sound, they are not sufficient to inform public relations practice.

Based upon the results of my interviews with more than seventy-five practitioners from Argentina, Australia, Brazil, Canada, Chile, China, Ecuador, Egypt, France, Germany, Ghana, India, Indonesia, Israel, Italy, Japan, Jordan, Kenya, Malaysia, Mexico, New Zealand, Nigeria, Russia, Saudi Arabia, South Africa, South Korea, Spain, Sweden, the United Arab Emirates, the United Kingdom, and the United States of America, at least two additions should be made to Verčič et al.'s list of dimensions on which public relations practice differs between cultures. They are:

6 Social Expectations: The practitioners who you will hear from throughout this book discuss how expectations of organizations differ dramatically in countries and cultures throughout the world. For example, in Chapter 11, Serge Giacomo, Head of Communications and Institutional Relations for GE in Latin America, explains that, in local communities in Latin America, citizens expect companies to assume responsibility for actions totally unrelated to their businesses, such as building roads and schools. By contrast, in the U.S., such activities would be seen as falling strictly within the province of the government. As will be discussed in Chapter 12, communities in Sub-Saharan Africa likewise have high expectations for corporate social responsibility. You will want to understand such expectations *before* beginning to operate in a new culture. Once again, your local partners (to be discussed in Chapter 3) should be able to explain these expectations to you.

In the United States, stories written by the traditional media are most influential on Twitter, while in China, the most influential content is written by influencers who do not write for the traditional press. Copyright: Blan-k

7 Influencers: While in the past public relations practitioners were the main evangelizers for their brands and organizations, today, we increasingly rely upon others to evangelize for us. We call these people influencers, of course. Another important factor you must therefore understand is *who* is influential in a particular society. For example, as I will discuss in Chapter 7, in the U.S., much of the content that gets re-tweeted and goes on to "trend" on Twitter is generated by the traditional U.S. media, such as *The New York Times*, CNN, and ESPN, which covers sports (Asur, Yu, & Huberman, 2011). By contrast, Chen Liang, Account Executive for the global public relations firm Ruder Finn, says that, in China, many people do not view the traditional media as a reliable source of news, and therefore turn to public figures such as actors, independent journalists, professors, and writers who have garnered reputations for sharing reliable information on social media. Once again, you will rely upon your local partners to give you a sense of who is influential in local cultures.

Like academic researchers, when practitioners develop global public relations strategies, they too often draw upon the principles that are typical in Western practice and then simply work to adapt them locally. However, the universe of global public relations is *so much* broader, richer, and more diverse. In surveying how public relations is practiced in nations around the world, this book therefore seeks to not only highlight how to practice the art and science of public relations in such nations and cultures, but also how lessons and best practices from countries around the world can help to inform a more universal international public relations theory and richer, more effective global public relations strategies. I believe that global public relations practitioners will be most effective if they employ a modified generic/specific approach: one that begins with an awareness of the *full range* of public relations strategies practiced around the world and then selects from the best among them in order to craft global approaches to be adapted locally. This book will help you do just that. So let's get started!

Overview of this Book

Copyright: Digital Storm

I have defined international and global public relations and discussed the merits of each. Now, let's focus on *how* to craft campaigns tailored to specific countries and cultures.

Chapter 2 will discuss the specific dimensions on which cultures differ. It is essential to identify relevant cultural attributes before beginning to craft a public relations strategy in a new environment so that you can adapt your strategy accordingly.

Chapter 3 will discuss how to build and manage a global public relations team and evaluate your outputs. In particular, it will discuss how to hire staff (including the merits of hiring employees, freelancers, local public relations firms, and global public relations firms) and how to manage a multicultural team of people who have very different workplace practices and expectations.

Chapter 4 will discuss how to craft global public relations campaigns on behalf of corporations, while Chapter 5 will explain how to practice on behalf of non-profit organizations and Chapter 6 will discuss how to practice global public relations on behalf of governments. You'll find snapshot boxes at the end of each chapter discussing global public relations tactics that can be used by any organization.

Chapter 7 will describe and explain how to work with key global media outlets and social media platforms around the world.

Finally, we will explore how the practice of public relations differs around the world. We will start in Asia in Chapter 8, before traveling to Europe in Chapter 9, the Middle East and North Africa in Chapter 10, the Americas in Chapter 11, and Sub-Saharan Africa in Chapter 12. Within these chapters, I will describe the ten "cultural clusters" identified as part of the GLOBE study—a ten-year study of more than 17,000 managers in 62 societies conducted by 170 researchers—that groups the world's people by cultural similarities. We will discuss how public relations is practiced within each of these clusters. Along the way, we will meet practitioners who will share their own experiences of working in public relations in these regions, and explore case studies of particularly successful public relations campaigns. Because there was limited previous research on what works best in different countries and cultures, in addition to the extant literature, these sections also rely heavily on my interviews with top practitioners around the globe. I hope they will be useful to you in crafting your own public relations strategies for the cultures within these regions.

References

Anderson, G. (1989). A global look at public relations. In B. Cantor & B. Burger (Eds.), *Experts in action: Inside public relations* (2nd ed.) (pp. 412–422). New York, NY: Longman.

Asur, S., Yu, L., & Huberman, B. A. (2011, August 21). What trends in Chinese social media. Paper presented at the SNAKDD Workshop, San Francisco, CA.

Banks, S. P. (1995). *Multicultural public relations: A social-interpretive approach.* Thousand Oaks, CA: Sage.

Bardhan, N., & Weaver, C. K. (2011). Introduction: Public relations in global cultural contexts. In N. Bardhan & C. K. Weaver (Eds.), *Public relations in global cultural contexts: Multi-paradigmatic perspectives* (pp. 1–28). New York, NY: Routledge.

Curtin, P. A., & Gaither, T. K. (2007). *International public relations: Negotiating culture, identity, and power.* Thousand Oaks, CA: Sage.

De Beer, A. S., & Mersham, G. (2004). Public relations in South Africa: A communication tool for change. In D. J. Tilson & E. C. Alozie (Eds.), *Toward the common good: Perspectives in international public relations* (pp. 320–340). Boston, MA: Pearson.

Friedman, T. (2005). *The world is flat.* New York, NY: Farrar, Straus and Giroux.

Grunig, J. E., & White, J. (1992). The effect of worldviews on public relations theory and practice. In J. E. Grunig (Ed.), *Excellence in public relations and communication management* (pp. 31–64). Hillsdale, NJ: Lawrence Erlbaum Associates.

Hofstede, G., Hofstede, G. J., & Minkov, M. (2010). *Cultures and organizations: Software of the mind*. (3rd ed.) New York, NY: McGraw Hill.

International Public Relations Association (IPRA). (2015a). The IPRA charter on media transparency. Retrieved from http://www.ipra.org/programmes/ipra-charter-on-media-transparency

International Public Relations Association (IPRA). (2015b). IPRA codes. Retrieved from http://www.ipra.org/about/ipra-codes

Kim, J. N., & Sriramesh, K. (2009). Activism and public relations. In K. Sriramesh & D. Verčič (Eds.), *The global public relations handbook: Theory, research, and practice* (2nd ed.) (pp. 79–97). New York, NY: Routledge.

Morley, M. (2002). *How to manage your global reputation: A guide to the dynamics of international public relations*. New York, NY: Palgrave.

Paterson, T. (2012, October 2). Ikea airbrushes women from its Saudi catalogue. *The Independent*. Retrieved from http://www.independent.co.uk/news/world/middle-east/ikea-airbrushes-women-from-its-saudi-catalogue-8193204.html

Sharpe, M. L., & Pritchard, B. J. (2004). The historical empowerment of public opinion and its relationship to the emergence of public relations as a profession. In D. J. Tilson & E. C. Alozie (Eds.), *Toward the common good: Perspectives in international public relations* (pp. 14–36). Boston, MA: Pearson.

Smith, D. (2011, October 26). Lost in translation: Nokia Lumia, and the 5 worst name oversights. *International Business Times*. Retrieved from http://www.ibtimes.com/lost-translation-nokia-lumia-5-worst-name-oversights-361866

Sriramesh, K. (2004). Public relations practice and research in Asia: A conceptual framework. In K. Sriramesh (Ed.), *Public relations in Asia: An anthology* (pp. 1–28). Singapore: Thomson Learning.

Sriramesh, K. (2009a). Introduction. In K. Sriramesh & D. Verčič (Eds.), *The global public relations handbook: Theory, research, and practice* (2nd ed.) (pp. xxxiii–xl). New York, NY: Routledge.

Sriramesh, K. (2009b). The relationship between culture and public relations. In K. Sriramesh & D. Verčič (Eds.), *The global public relations handbook: Theory, research, and practice* (2nd ed.) (pp. 47–61). New York, NY: Routledge.

Sriramesh, K. (2010). Globalization and public relations: Opportunities for growth and reformulation. In R. L. Heath (Ed.), *The SAGE handbook of public relations* (2nd ed.) (pp. 691–707). Thousand Oaks, CA: Sage.

Sriramesh, K. (2012). Culture and public relations: Formulating the relationship and its relevance to the practice. In K. Sriramesh & D. Verčič (Eds.), *Culture and public relations: Links and implications* (pp. 9–24). New York, NY: Taylor & Francis.

Sriramesh, K., & Verčič, D. (2009). A theoretical framework for global public relations research and practice. In K. Sriramesh & D. Verčič (Eds.), *The global public relations handbook: Theory, research, and practice* (2nd ed.) (pp. 3–21). New York, NY: Routledge.

Stiglitz, J. E. (2002). *Globalization and its discontents*. New York, NY: W.W. Norton & Company.

Ting-Toomey, S. (2005). The matrix of face: An updated face-negotiation theory. In W. B. Gudykunst (Ed.), *Theorizing about intercultural communication* (pp. 71–92). Thousand Oaks, CA: Sage.

Verčič, D., Grunig, L. A., & Grunig, J. E. (1996). Global and specific principles of public relations: Evidence from Slovenia. In H. M. Culbertson & N. Chen (Eds.), *International public relations: A comparative analysis* (pp. 31–65). Mahwah, NJ: Lawrence Erlbaum Associates.

Wakefield, R. I. (2000). World-class public relations: A model for effective public relations in the multinational. *Journal of Communication Management, 5*(1), 59–71.

Wakefield, R. I. (2008). Theory of international public relations, the internet, and activism: A personal reflection. *Journal of Public Relations Research, 20*(1), 138–157.

Wakefield, R. (2011). Critiquing the generic/specific public relations theory: The need to close the transnational knowledge gap. In N. Bardhan & C. K. Weaver (Eds.), *Public relations in global cultural contexts: Multi-paradigmatic perspectives* (pp. 167–194). New York, NY: Routledge.

2 Culture Is the Key

Copyright: Arthimedes

The management expert Peter Drucker famously said that "culture eats strategy for breakfast." (PWC, 2015). If your public relations strategies, tactics, and messages and your workplace behavior are not adapted for the cultures in which you work, you are almost certain to fail. This chapter will begin by discussing the meaning of culture, before exploring the key dimensions on which cultures differ and questions you should ask when working in a new culture. Then, I will discuss resources you can use to identify important cultural differences when developing international and intercultural public relations campaigns. While an ignorance of cultural differences may be the best way to destroy your public relations campaign, at the same time, a campaign that is right on cultural code gives you your very best chance of success. Here's how to identify key cultural differences so that you can adapt your public relations strategies accordingly.

The Meaning of Culture

When I was a spokesperson in the U.S. government, I traveled to Brazzaville, the capital of the Republic of the Congo, for a meeting between U.S. government officials and the Chief of Staff to the President of the Congolese Republic. In the middle of the meeting, a man entered the room and offered us all drinks. My colleagues and I politely declined. Afterwards, the U.S. embassy official who was our local escort on the trip informed my colleagues and me that our refusal of the drinks was a personal affront to the official with whom we had met. If you ever work in the Republic of the Congo, it turns out that, when offered a drink, you should accept an alcoholic beverage if you wish to signal that you are particularly excited about the way things are going, or a soft drink to indicate that you are merely pleased. Confused, one of my colleagues noted that the U.S. Ambassador to the Republic of the Congo (who presumably understood local customs) had also declined the offer of a drink. *Of course* he did, we were told. Once the most senior U.S. official in the room had refused a drink, the rest of us were obligated to follow his lead.

When you work in international public relations, you'll want to learn such customs *before* engaging with local audiences and partners. As I discussed in Chapter 1, understanding the culture in which you work is not just critical to your practice. It is the very heart of international public relations. As I also discussed in Chapter 1, culture is one characteristic of a country—along with its political-economic system, extent of activism, level of development, media system, local expectations and influencers—that it is essential to understand before crafting a public relations strategy. However, culture is both the most important and the hardest of these characteristics to understand.

Understanding the cultures in which you work will be essential to your practice for two reasons. First, you will need to understand the audiences you seek to reach and adapt your strategies, messages, and tactics accordingly. Second, you will need to understand the expectations of the colleagues and partners with whom you work. Livermore (2011, pp. xii, 5) argues that your level of cultural intelligence—which he defines as your "capacity to function effectively across a variety of cultural contexts"—is more important in our modern globalized world than even your intellect and professional experience. He stresses that cultural intelligence requires not just understanding other cultures, but also the ability to problem solve and adapt effectively in different cultural environments.

Although there is no universal definition of culture that is accepted by all scholars, in Chapter 1, I defined culture as "a learned system of meanings that fosters a particular sense of shared identity and community among its group members" (Ting-Toomey, 2005, pp. 71–72). Hofstede, Hofstede, and Minkov (2010, p. 6) note that "culture consists of the unwritten rules of the social game. It is *the collective programming of the mind that distinguishes the members of one group or category of people from others.*" All cultures have codes, which Banks

(1995, p. 36) defines as "systematically organized sets of signals that cultural groups use for eliciting meaning and assigning meaning to phenomena"—such as, for example, language, gestures, clothing, rituals, and forms of art.

As my experience in the Republic of the Congo illustrates, cultural differences are typically obvious and taken for granted by a member of a culture—and often totally surprising and even baffling to an outsider. The reason why cultural attributes can be so difficult for a foreigner to fully understand is that, as Hofstede, Hofstede, and Minkov (2010, p. 5) explain,

> the sources of one's mental programs lie within the social environments in which one grew up and collected one's life experiences. The programming starts within the family; it continues within the neighborhood, at school, in youth groups, at the workplace, and in the living community.

In other words, such experiences are imbued over a lifetime of living in a culture—and not easily picked up by a foreign public relations practitioner who parachutes in from headquarters for a few days. In fact, the vast majority of a culture cannot be easily observed, which is why many scholars use the metaphor of an iceberg to convey the concept that most aspects of a culture are not visible at the surface level. For example, if you came to New York City, you would quickly observe that New Yorkers can be gruff and are always in a hurry. As someone who lived in the City for more than a decade, however, I know that, beneath the surface, New Yorkers are actually quite moral and kind. I have almost never taken a suitcase on the subway without someone stopping to help me carry it; although I have met genuinely lovely people all over the world, if I am ever to have an emergency that requires help from strangers, I truly hope that it happens in Manhattan.

Culture is like an iceberg. The majority is visible only below the surface. Copyright: Niyazz

Another reason why it is hard to understand a culture is that members of a culture may not *themselves* be consciously aware of the characteristics that distinguish it. For example, Clotaire Rapaille (2006, pp. 14–16), a French anthropologist who has consulted for half of the world's Fortune 100 companies on how to position their products in different cultures, claims that "the only effective way to understand what people truly mean is to ignore what they say." This is because Rapaille believes that human beings do not ourselves understand the reasons behind many of our own actions, which are heavily guided by instincts that are imprinted unconsciously in our brains by the culture in which we grow up. For example, if you ask a person what (s)he looks for when purchasing an automobile, the person may claim that safety and gas mileage are important—but may actually select a car because it appears aggressive and sexy. Therefore, in order to understand what appeals to people in particular cultures, Rapaille uses strategies such as asking people to describe their earliest memories of a product—or pretending to be a visitor from another planet and asking people to describe an item and the emotions it provokes.

Third, culture is dynamic—it is constantly evolving—and so it can never be fully mastered. Indeed, understanding how a culture is changing will often give you particularly creative ideas for how to craft messages that will especially resonate with local people. Learning about a culture, therefore, always requires investing in ongoing effort.

Fourth, cultures themselves are not homogeneous. Think about your own family members and friends: they are likely very different from one another. It can therefore be dangerous to rely too heavily on stereotypes about a particular group. Banks (1995, p. 10) notes that within a single group, other differences, or subcultures, can always be identified—such as generations, social classes, and genders, to name a few (Hofstede, Hofstede, & Minkov, 2010, p. 46). Yet, even within a subculture, human beings will still vary. As Banks (1995, p. 35) reminds us, "any social action is based in part on voluntary motives and decisions. Because humans are creative beings, communicative action is not wholly mechanistic or based on predictable responses to environmental stimuli." In other words, human beings have agency and so their behavior can never be completely predicted in advance. Additionally, an organization's internal culture often exerts a significant influence on the behavior of its employees or members.

Fifth, it is important not to confuse a culture with a country. For example, Mateus Furlanetto, Head of Institutional Relations for the Brazilian Association for Business Communication, known as Aberje, says that a public relations professional from São Paulo or Rio de Janeiro—Brazil's largest cities—would literally be considered a foreigner if (s)he attempted to implement a campaign in the Brazilian countryside. Single nations often contain many different ethnic, linguistic, and religious groups and have major regional differences; therefore, numerous cultures often coexist within a country. Indeed, Anderson (2006) calls nations "imagined communities." For example, within the country of Papua New Guinea, 836 different indigenous languages are spoken (CIA, 2015). At the same time, a single culture may cross national borders. Today, members of the global wealthy elite arguably have more in common with the elite on other continents than with poor people in their own nations (Clegg, 2005, p. 44). For this reason, it is critical that you are clear and specific about the audience(s) you wish to reach in your public relations strategy.

Yet, even despite the difficulty of understanding a culture and the diversity to be found within a single culture, learning about cultural differences remains one of the key ways—in fact, I would argue it is the most effective way—for you to successfully adapt your public relations strategies for international audiences. Therefore, this chapter will explain the key differences between cultures and then discuss how you can pinpoint those differences when working in a new culture.

Cultural Dimensions

There are a number of classic ways in which cultures differ from one another. Being cognizant of such differences will help you tailor your public relations strategies and workplace behaviors to be appropriate and effective in your host cultures.

The seminal study of cultural dimensions was published by Geert Hofstede in his 1980 book *Culture's Consequences*, based upon surveys of IBM employees around the world. Hofstede has since expanded his cultural dimensions in his most recent (2010) book *Cultures and Organizations: Software of the Mind*, published with Gert Jan Hofstede and Michael Minkov.

They find that cultures differ along these key dimensions:

1 **Power Distance:** Cultures with high power distance, such as Russia, China, and Mexico, are more hierarchical. Children are expected to show respect and obedience towards their parents and teachers. In the workplace, subordinates are expected to follow orders from their bosses. Status symbols are valued and the gap between salaries at the top and bottom of an organization is large. Such societies often have just one political party; scandals in government are regularly covered up. By contrast, cultures with low power distance, such as Sweden, Norway, and Denmark, are more egalitarian. In the workplace, managers are more approachable; subordinates are expected to actively voice their ideas and opinions, and it is even acceptable to question one's boss. Subordinates are typically consulted before managers make final decisions. Status symbols are suspect and salary gaps are narrower (Hofstede, Hofstede, & Minkov, 2010, pp. 57–78).

The level of power distance in a society will impact not only your public relations messages, but also how you interact with your colleagues. Meyer (2014, pp. 117, 122, 125, 133) notes that, in hierarchical cultures such as Japan, Korea, Nigeria, and Saudi Arabia, subordinates call their bosses by formal titles and will not skip layers of management to communicate with those too far above or below them. There are formal rules about who sits where in a business meeting and whose hands should be shaken first, based upon seniority. If a boss from a culture with lower power distance attempts to upend these rules—such as, for example, by sitting in a cubicle next to his or her subordinates rather than in a fancy corner office—(s)he may be seen as a weak leader and an embarrassment to the team. By contrast, in egalitarian cultures such as Denmark, the Netherlands, and Sweden, a boss is expected to act and dress like other members of the team, it is okay to disagree openly with one's superior, and subordinates have more latitude to take action without approval from their bosses (Meyer, 2014, pp. 115, 125, 131).

Do not confuse decision-making processes with power distance. Meyer (2014, pp. 150, 154) reports, for example, that the United States of America generally has lower power distance, but decisions tend to ultimately be made by one person, whereas countries such as Germany and Japan have high power distance but decisions are usually made by consensus.

The degree to which you can disagree with colleagues also differs. Meyer (2014, p. 200, 207) notes that, "in more confrontational cultures, it seems quite natural to attack someone's position without attacking that person. In avoid-confrontation societies [such as in Latin America and the Middle East], these two things are tightly interconnected."

A danger of societies with high power distance is that public relations practitioners may not be included in dominant coalitions if they are not senior enough within their organizations (Sriramesh, 1992, pp. 205–206). Furthermore, Sriramesh and White (1992, p. 610) report that cultures with high power distance tend to practice one-way, rather than two-way, communication (see also Sriramesh, 1992, p. 206). In his study of how culture affects public relations practice in India, Sriramesh (1992, p. 204) reports that

> senior executives of class-oriented societies believe that they possess the faculty to decide what is good for the public. Therefore, they use communication only to publicize the 'good' activities of the organization. These senior executives will be less inclined to seek information from their publics because they do not intend to shape the organizational activities to the needs of their environment.

Kent and Taylor (1999) find that, in high power distance societies, governments tend to exert significant control on society, and therefore, for public relations practitioners,

> close relationships with key decision-makers are necessary in order to minimize government regulation, secure government approval, and ensure positive press coverage. Successful international public relations

professionals may want to recruit individuals with prestige to seek out relationships with key leaders. Personal influence with key decision-makers
rather than public influence needs to be recognized and incorporated into
the public relations strategy if organizations wish to be successful at reaching key constituencies.

However, high power distance cultures may sometimes react to a crisis more
swiftly. Taylor (2000, p. 282) argues that

organizations from low power distance cultures may not see a need to
communicate with local governments about a particular situation. Organizations from high power distance . . . nations may take the opposite
approach and communicate directly with governments during a crisis to
secure their support.

Taylor (2000), for example, studied how different European nations reacted
when children in Belgium fell ill after drinking Coca-Cola in 1999. She found
that those cultures with high power distance—Belgium, France, and Spain—
banned the sale of Coca-Cola, while those with lower power distance—
Denmark, Norway, and Sweden—did not (although, as will be discussed in
Chapter 8, other cultural factors have historically caused practitioners in high
power distance Asian countries not to be transparent during crises). Furthermore, Taylor (2000, p. 282) notes that, in a high power distance culture, "people will be able to blame the powerful for their ills."

2 Individualism vs. Collectivism: Hofstede, Hofstede, and Minkov (2010,
pp. 90–128) note that individualistic cultures stress the importance of the
individual, while collectivist societies place greater importance on the
group to which one belongs. They (2010, p. 92) define collectivist societies
(which constitute the majority of the world's cultures) as "societies in which
people from birth onward are integrated into strong, cohesive in-groups,
which throughout people's lifetime continue to protect them in exchange
for unquestioning loyalty." Equality is a core value in such societies. Thus, in
collectivist societies, such as China, South Korea, Pakistan, and Venezuela,
people tend to grow up with members of their extended family, who share
resources such as their salaries. Hofstede, Hofstede, and Minkov (2010,
p. 107) note that "in the collectivist family, children learn to take their
bearings from others when it comes to opinions. Personal opinions do not
exist: opinions are predetermined by the group." Furthermore, silence is not
considered to be uncomfortable; "in a collectivist culture, the fact of being
together is emotionally sufficient; there is no compulsion to talk unless there
is information to be transferred" (Hofstede, Hofstede, & Minkov, 2010,
p. 108). Individuals will often not speak up in a classroom or workplace
environment unless specifically called upon to do so. In the workplace, it

is normal to hire one's relatives. Hofstede, Hofstede, and Minkov (2010, p. 120) note that *nepotism?*

> the relationship between employer and employee is seen in moral terms. It resembles a family relationship with mutual obligations of protection in exchange for loyalty. Poor performance of an employee in this relationship is no reason for dismissal: one does not dismiss one's child.

A person who does not act according to group expectations will feel ashamed. Managers do not give negative feedback directly, as this may lead to loss of **face** (Hofstede, Hofstede, and Minkov, 2010, p. 110). Kent and Taylor (2011) note that the concept of face entails avoiding embarrassment and maintaining one's sense of pride and dignity, but also ensuring that one's actions do not cause another person to lose face. They (2011, p. 66) explain that

> to help another person to maintain face is actually more valued than retaining one's own face in many cultures. When we prevent another person from being embarrassed or ridiculed this both allows the person being put on the spot to maintain face, as well as helping the person who challenged the other's face to maintain his or her own face by not appearing unkind. "Face management," and face needs vary in different cultures. Thus, in some cultures (like the mainstream United States), being perceived as clever for making a witty comment in a public situation, thereby embarrassing someone else or making him or her look foolish, is sometimes seen as being socially acceptable. In high face cultures, however, embarrassing someone else with a snide comment both makes the recipient of the comment look bad, and the person who made the comment look worse.

By contrast, in individualistic societies, such as the U.S., Great Britain, Australia, and Canada, people see their identities as distinct from those of others. People in individualistic cultures tend to grow up in nuclear families, consisting of two parents and their children, though there is an increasing percentage of single-parent households. In such societies, "the ties between individuals are loose: everyone is expected to look after him- or herself and his or her immediate family" (Hofstede, Hofstede, and Minkov, 2010, p. 92). People are generally expected to leave their family and live on their own once they go to college. Furthermore, individuals are expected and encouraged to develop and voice their own personal opinions:

> Telling the truth about how one feels is characteristic of a sincere and honest person. Confrontation can be salutary; a clash of opinions is believed to lead to a higher truth. The effect of communications on other people should be taken into account, but it does not, as a rule, justify changing the facts. Adult individuals should be able to take direct feedback constructively (Hofstede, Hofstede, & Minkov, 2010, p. 107).

In individualistic societies, people see their identities as distinct from those of others.
Copyright: bikeriderlondon

Thus, managers give direct feedback in performance reviews and employment relationships are contractual; it is perfectly acceptable for a supervisor to fire an employee for poor performance or for an employee to leave an organization if (s)he receives a better offer elsewhere. Preferential treatment to one's family is considered unacceptable in the workplace or elsewhere in society; rules and laws are expected to apply equally to all. However, in social situations, silence is considered to be uncomfortable and is therefore typically filled with "small talk." When an individual does not live up to expectations, he or she typically feels guilt, rather than shame. Education in individualistic cultures tends to focus on how to adapt to new situations, rather than how to be a good member of one's group. Freedom is prized over equality.

The GLOBE study (which, as discussed in Chapter 1, was a ten-year study of more than 17,000 managers in 62 societies conducted by 170 researchers) divided this dimension into two measures. The GLOBE researchers describe cultures based upon whether they exhibit **institutional collectivism**, which they define as "the degree to which organizational and societal institutional practices encourage and reward collective distribution of resources and collective action," and **in-group collectivism**, which they describe as "the degree to which individuals express pride, loyalty, and cohesiveness in their organizations or families" (House & Javidan, 2004, p. 12).

As will be discussed repeatedly throughout this book, the level of collectivism of a society will significantly impact whether your messages should stress individual or group benefits.

3 Masculinity vs. Femininity: Hofstede's third continuum names countries as either masculine or feminine. According to this definition, in a masculine society, such as Japan, Italy, and Great Britain, "emotional gender roles are clearly distinct: men are supposed to be assertive, tough, and focused on material success, whereas women are supposed to be more modest, tender, and concerned with the quality of life." Societies characterized as masculine place importance on individual salaries, recognition, advancement, hard work, and challenges. Money is prized over leisure time. Individuals are expected to talk up their accomplishments in situations such as job interviews. There is often a divide in families between men, who are employed outside of the home, and women, who take care of the home. Males are expected to fight and compete, but not to cry, while females are expected to be cooperative. Homosexuality and the subject of sex are more taboo; there is a double standard in that women, but not men, are expected to be chaste before marriage and there is a stronger taboo on male nudity than on female nudity. People purchase more status objects, such as fancy jewelry. Conflicts are resolved through fighting, the strongest win, and politics are adversarial. Governments prize growth and performance over values such as environmental protection and helping the needy. Immigrants are expected to assimilate into their host country's culture (Hofstede, Hofstede, & Minkov, 2010, pp. 140–180).

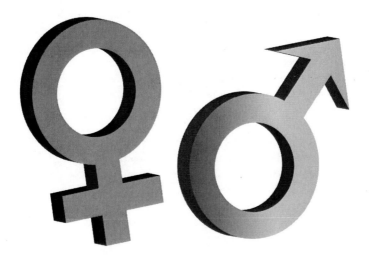

Copyright: Polarpx

A feminine culture, such as Norway, Sweden, and the Netherlands, is one in which "emotional gender roles overlap: both men and women are supposed to be modest, tender, and concerned with the quality of life." Feminine cultures prize relationships and quality of life. Leisure time is prized over money. Individuals are more modest—even in situations such as job interviews; bragging is considered to be a negative quality, and people even under-rate their own skills and performances. Individuals are comfortable with being marked as average, as opposed to the best, at what they do. Both men and women are expected to be emotionally intelligent, to have equal options to work outside the home, and to do an equal amount of housework. Homosexuality and the subject of sex are less taboo; the same standards apply to female and male nudity. Conflicts are resolved through negotiation and compromise. There is emphasis on helping the needy and values such as environmental preservation; immigrants are expected to integrate rather than to assimilate (Hofstede, Hofstede, & Minkov, 2010, pp. 140–180).

The GLOBE researchers call this dimension **gender egalitarianism**, which they define as "the degree to which an organization or a society minimizes gender role differences while promoting gender equality" (House & Javidan, 2004, p. 12).

Once again, these differences will significantly impact how you frame your messages in different cultures.

4 Uncertainty Avoidance: Uncertainty avoidance refers to "the extent to which the members of a culture feel threatened by ambiguous or unknown situations" (Hofstede, Hofstede, & Minkov, 2010, p. 191). Cultures with high uncertainty avoidance, such as Greece, Portugal, and Russia, exhibit greater levels of stress anxiety (Hofstede, Hofstede, & Minkov, 2010, pp. 192, 203). As Hofstede, Hofstede, and Minkov (2010, p. 196) explain, "anxious cultures tend to be expressive cultures. They are the places where people talk with their hands and where it is socially acceptable to raise one's voice, to show one's emotions, and to pound the table"—though they note that the uncertainty-avoiding but less expressive Japanese are an exception to this rule!

More people in cultures with high uncertainty avoidance feel unhappy, and they have more worries about money and their health. People tend to be more neurotic and less agreeable. Circumstances or luck—as opposed to one's own ability—are believed to be the causes of events. Such cultures have more stringent rules for children on what is "dirty and taboo." People are hesitant to try new technology and other products. People tend to be more conservative with their financial investments. Experts such as teachers are expected to know everything, so advertisers use experts to bolster their claims. People have an "emotional need" for rules, and keep them even when they do not work; there is a high desire for formalization, precision, and technical solutions. People tend to work for the same employer for longer periods of time and to have a harder time achieving work-life balance. In such cultures, "there is an emotional need to be busy and an inner urge to work hard"; managers are involved in daily operations. People in such cultures believe that "time is money" and are very punctual. Such hard-working cultures are actually not as good at innovating, because creative people are held back by all the rules; however, they are excellent at implementing ideas. There are more self-employed people. Individuals are motivated by security and tend to be more politically conservative and to desire law and order; however, people tend to be less interested in politics overall, less trusting of politicians and government officials, and less likely to participate in voluntary associations (Hofstede, Hofstede, & Minkov, 2010, pp. 197–223).

Outsiders also believe there is higher corruption in high uncertainty-avoiding cultures. Extreme ideas are repressed. There is more ethnic prejudice and xenophobia, less tolerance for accepting refugees, and people may be aggressively nationalistic. There is also a higher degree of ideological, political, and religious fundamentalisms and intolerance and a tendency towards grand theories to explain the world. Fictional stories deal with rules and truth (Hofstede, Hofstede, & Minkov, 2010, pp. 223–231).

By contrast, in cultures with low uncertainty avoidance, such as Great Britain and the U.S., the unknown is met with curiosity rather than anxiety. Stress and emotions are internalized rather than exhibited openly; "people who behave emotionally or noisily meet with social disapproval." Fewer people are unhappy, and fewer people worry about money and their health. Results are believed to be attributable to a person's individual ability. People tend to be more agreeable; they less strictly proscribe what is "dirty and taboo." People tend to consume higher amounts of caffeine and alcohol. Ethical considerations influence the purchasing decisions of people in such cultures more than in cultures with high uncertainty avoidance, and people search for convenience when they shop. People will take greater risks with their financial investments. Experts may admit that they do not "have all the answers." Advertisers tend to make humorous appeals. Rules are made only when necessary; there is a greater acceptance of chaos and ambiguity, and people rely on common sense and generalists as opposed to the experts who high uncertainty-avoiding cultures prefer (Hofstede, Hofstede, & Minkov, 2010, pp. 194–217).

In low uncertainty avoidance cultures, time is "a framework in which to orient oneself but not something one is constantly watching." (Of course, this is a good example that not all general characteristics of a category apply to every country within it. For example, the U.S. ranks as relatively low on uncertainty avoidance, and yet time is incredibly important in this country). Overall, in such cultures, "people like to relax." People tend to work for a single employer for shorter periods of time. People work hard only when it is actually necessary to do so; managers focus on strategy rather than daily operations. Such cultures are wonderful at innovating, but not as good at implementing new ideas, because they focus less on detail; there are fewer self-employed people. People are motivated by achievement rather than security. People tend to be more politically liberal and tend to volunteer more to improve their communities. There is greater tolerance of ideas, even if they are extreme, and greater tolerance for people of different ethnicities and countries. Refugees are more

In cultures with low uncertainty avoidance, the unknown is met with curiosity rather than anxiety. Copyright: Lightspring

likely to be admitted. People do not attempt to impose their religions or views on others, and may be friends with people who have different beliefs. Fictional stories are often set in fantasy worlds (Hofstede, Hofstede, & Minkov, 2010, pp. 208–231).

Hofstede, Hofstede, and Minkov (2010, p. 197) explain that these characteristics explain why people from strong uncertainty avoidance cultures may come across to others as busy, fidgety, emotional, aggressive, or suspicious and why people from weak uncertainty avoidance countries may give the impression to others of being dull, quiet, easygoing, indolent, controlled, or lazy.

In her study of how different European countries responded to the tainted Coca-Cola in 1999, Taylor (2000, p. 282) likewise argues that "low uncertainty avoidance organizations may not view isolated incidents as constituting a crisis and thus may do little to communicate to publics about the situation." Taylor (2000, p. 284) reports that "Coca-Cola reacted to these claims as a . . . low uncertainty avoidance organization" and, accordingly, their chief executive officer did not acknowledge the problem for nine days. If you are working in a low uncertainty avoidance culture, you will likely need to work extra hard to ensure that signs of possible problems are addressed seriously and urgently.

5 Long-Term Orientation: Not originally part of Hofstede's four dimensions, the concept of long-term orientation was later pinpointed by other research and is now considered by Hofstede to be one of the five main dimensions on which cultures differ. Hofstede, Hofstede, and Minkov (2010, p. 239) define long-term orientation as

> the fostering of virtues oriented toward future rewards—in particular, perseverance and thrift. Its opposite pole, short-term orientation, stands for the fostering of virtues related to the past and present—in particular, respect for tradition, preservation of "face," and fulfilling social obligations (House & Javidan, 2004, p. 12).

The GLOBE researchers call this dimension **future orientation**.

Copyright: Jane0606

Cultures with high long-term orientations include the countries of "Confucian Asia" discussed in Chapter 8, including China, Japan, and South Korea. In such cultures, people are careful to preserve resources. They are willing to work hard over extended periods of time for results that come slowly and to subordinate themselves in the service of a larger purpose. Children are rewarded for their education and development. Marriage is viewed as a pragmatic arrangement, and it is common for couples to live with their spouse's parents. Such cultures value the elderly. Situations are viewed in light of the circumstances, and a premium is placed on personal adaptation. People learn to be humble and feel shame when they do not live up to social expectations (Hofstede, Hofstede, & Minkov, 2010, pp. 242–243). In the business world, accountability, honesty, learning, and self-discipline are valued. Leisure time is less important, and businesses focus on long-term, rather than short-term, profits. Major economic and social differences are considered to be detrimental, and managers and their employees share the same goals. People build life-long relationships with business associates as part of their personal networks. People are concerned with being virtuous, and believe that the difference between good and evil depends on the circumstances; common sense and pragmatism are prized. Therefore, they are less bothered by cognitive inconsistencies. Results are attributed to effort, rather than to luck, and knowledge and education are valued (Hofstede, Hofstede, & Minkov, 2010, pp. 251, 275).

Cultures with long-term orientations also tend to exhibit what Minkov (2007) has named "flexhumility" (Hofstede, Hofstede, & Minkov, 2010, p. 259). In such cultures, such as in India and East Asia, people tend to see their identities as more "fluid and flexible" and to be more humble and cooperative (Minkov, 2007, p. 20). As a result, they have an easier time adapting to other cultures.

By contrast, people living in cultures with a short-term orientation, such as the U.S., Great Britain, Australia, Nigeria, and the Philippines, feel social pressure to spend money, rather than save it, and expect to see more rapid results from their efforts. They are concerned with maintaining "face" and meeting their social obligations. Children are rewarded for fun and out of love, rather than for their education and development. Marriage is considered to be a moral, rather than pragmatic, arrangement, and couples do not live with their in-laws. Old age is an unhappy, rather than a happy, phase of one's life, and therefore it is considered to start later in cultures with short-term orientations. People have respect for traditions, rather than circumstances, and a premium is placed on personal stability (Hofstede, Hofstede, & Minkov, 2010, pp. 239–243). In the business world, achievement, freedom, rights, and thinking for oneself are valued. Leisure time is considered to be important, and people focus on immediate profits, rather than long-term prospects. The workplace is a meritocracy, in which people are rewarded based upon their abilities, and managers and their employees are "psychologically in two camps." Relationships with business associates change based upon business needs. People are concerned with truth, rather than virtue, and the culture has clear guidelines delineating what is good and what is evil. People desire cognitive consistency and are bothered by disagreements (Hofstede, Hofstede, & Minkov, 2010, p. 251). Results are attributed to luck, rather than to effort, and folk wisdom may be valued more than formal education (Hofstede, Hofstede, & Minkov, 2010, p. 275).

Cultures with short-term orientations also tend to exhibit what Minkov (2007) calls "monumentalism," as opposed to flexhumility (Hofstede, Hofstede, & Minkov, 2010, p. 275). Minkov (2007, p. 19) says that in "monumentalist" cultures such as North America and the Arab world, people are believed to have a "single stable identity" and to be more prideful and competitive.

Again, an understanding of these differences will help you to adapt your public relations messages appropriately.

6 Indulgence vs. Restraint: In their 2010 book, Hofstede, Hofstede and Minkov added a sixth cultural dimension: indulgence vs. restraint. They (p. 281) explain that

> indulgence stands for a tendency to allow relatively free gratification of basic and natural human desires related to enjoying life and having fun. Its opposite pole, restraint, reflects a conviction that such gratification needs to be curbed and regulated by strict social norms.

In countries that rank high on indulgence—such as Venezuela, Mexico, Puerto Rico, El Salvador, Columbia, Trinidad, Sweden, and New Zealand—people tend to be more happy, extroverted, and optimistic about the future and to feel healthier. They tend to believe that they have control over their lives, place importance on leisure and friends, have more positive attitudes, and have higher birthrates. They tend to be more open to foreign sources of entertainment such as movies and music, to be more actively involved in sports, to consume more soft drinks and beer, and to have higher rates of obesity. They also tend to have less strict gender divides and fewer moral regulations against behavior such as casual sex. They place greater importance on freedom of speech and democracy. They also smile more (Hofstede, Hofstede, & Minkov, 2010, pp. 282–297).

Copyright: wavebreakmedia

By contrast, in countries that show greater restraint—such as Pakistan, Egypt, and Eastern European countries such as Latvia, Ukraine, Albania, and Belarus—people tend to be more neurotic, less optimistic about the future, and to have fewer children. They tend to believe that they have less control over their lives, place less importance on leisure and friends, be more cynical and pessimistic, feel less healthy, and have lower birthrates. They place greater importance on thrift and moral discipline, value the maintenance of order, and have more police officers (Hofstede, Hofstede, & Minkov, 2010, pp. 285–296).

7 Performance Orientation: The GLOBE study identified an additional cultural dimension of performance orientation, which Javidan (2004, p. 239) defines as "the extent to which a community encourages and rewards innovation, high standards, and performance improvement." Cultures with high levels of performance orientation—such as Confucian Asia, Germanic Europe, and the Anglo culture—value assertiveness, competitiveness, development, financial rewards, taking initiative, training, and materialism. They measure results, expect challenges and feedback so that they can improve, and reward performance and achievement. They have a "can-do" attitude, believe that individuals are "in control," believe that education leads to success, and believe that, with hard work, anyone can succeed. People are valued for what they do rather than for who they are. On the job, promotions are based on performance rather than age. People in such cultures tend to be low-context communicators and to have a monochronic approach to time (two other cultural dimensions which will be described below) (Gupta & Hanges, 2004, p. 193; Javidan, 2004, p. 245).

Copyright: alphaspirit

By contrast, cultures with low performance orientation—such as in Latin America and Eastern Europe—value attending the "right school," belongingness (including family and societal relationships), experience, harmony with (rather than control over) the environment, loyalty, seniority, sympathy, tradition, and quality of life. They reward cooperation, integrity, and loyalty and believe that feedback can be uncomfortable and it is inappropriate to be assertive or to be motivated by financial rewards. People are valued for who they are rather than for what they achieve; age is an important factor in decisions to promote people at work; and they believe that merit pay may destroy harmony. People in such cultures tend to be high-context communicators and to have a polychronic approach to time (both of which are described below) (Gupta & Hanges, 2004, p. 193; Javidan, 2004, p. 245).

8 Humane Orientation: The GLOBE researchers also identified the cultural dimension of humane orientation, which they define as "the degree to which individuals in organizations or societies encourage and reward individuals for being fair, altruistic, friendly, generous, caring, and kind to others" (House & Javidan, 2004, p. 13). Cultures that rank highly on humane orientation—such as in Southern Asia and Sub-Saharan Africa—believe that other people are important. People in such cultures have a greater desire for belonging and affiliation. They value altruism, benevolence, generosity, kindness, and love, and tend to have fewer psychological problems. People in such cultures also tend to believe that members of society—rather than the state—are responsible for the well-being of others. Members of cultures with high humane orientation provide emotional and material support to people in their close circles and show concern for all people. Children are expected to be obedient, paternalistic and patronage relationships are common, and people are sensitive to racial discrimination (Gupta & Hanges, 2004, p. 193; Kabasakal & Bodur, 2004, p. 570).

Copyright: Kosobu

By contrast, cultures with low humane orientation—such as in Latin and Germanic Europe—value comfort, material possessions, pleasure, power, self-enjoyment, and self-interest. There are higher levels of psychological problems. People are generally expected to solve their own problems. Children are expected to be autonomous and do not have the same obligations as those in cultures with high humane orientation to take care of their parents as they age; people in such cultures tend to be less sensitive to racial discrimination (Gupta & Hanges, 2004, p. 193; Kabasakal & Bodur, 2004, p. 570).

9 Context: The cultural dimension of context is among those that I consider to be most critical for public relations practitioners to understand. In a low-context culture—such as the U.S., Canada, Australia, the Netherlands, Germany, and the United Kingdom—people say what they mean directly (Meyer, 2014, p. 34).

By contrast, in a high-context culture, messages are conveyed less directly and more subtly, and it is critical to pick up on cues which can include the circumstances of the situation, the relationship between the communicators, and the history of the subject being discussed (Hall, 1976, p. 79). Samovar, Porter, McDaniel, and Roy (2013, p. 254), for example, note that in the high-context Korean culture, "instead of asking a subordinate to work on a project over the weekend, a Korean manager may say, 'the success of this project is important to the company, and we cannot miss the deadline.'" In other words, in high-context cultures, you must focus on the deeper, rather than literal, meaning of what is being said. As one cross-cultural expert explains, "in Chinese culture, children are taught not to just hear the explicit words but also to focus on *how* something is said, and on what is *not* said" (Meyer, 2014, pp. 48, 50). High-context cultures include Asian cultures such as China, India, Indonesia, Iran, and Japan, as well as many African cultures, and to a lesser extent Latin American countries (Meyer, 2014, p. 31).

Guth and Marsh (2012, p. 433) likewise explain that, in Japanese culture, the concept of *nemawashi* prizes consensus building, and therefore a Japanese person is unlikely to say no outright to a colleague. If a Japanese colleague says "yes" to you, however, it does not necessarily mean that (s)he agrees with you. As Liswood (2010, p. 119), explains,

> it simply means: "I heard you. I acknowledge that you just spoke." Or— the individual takes in a deep breath, and says "yes." You have actually just been told very loudly that the answer is indeed *no*. The deal is *not* done.

This cultural difference can be the source of significant cross-cultural mis-understandings. For example, Beatriz Alegría Carrasco, a corporate communications consultant from Madrid, Spain, says that

> in Spain, some people mistakenly think Americans are simple-minded because you need to explain everything to them. For example, Americans write that coffee may be hot on their coffee cups. For Spanish people, this is common sense, and [they] wonder, who doesn't know that? Of course, in America, companies write these messages to avoid being sued. But in Spain, you would never sue a company for not telling you that coffee is hot, because everyone knows that.

By contrast, people from high-context societies can "perceive a low-context communicator as inappropriately stating the obvious ('You didn't have to say it! We all understood!'), or even as condescending and patronizing ('You talk to us like we are children!')" (Meyer, 2014, p. 42). For example, one of my former students, who is originally from Mexico but now works in the U.S., told me that she genuinely thought that her manager in the U.S. must consider her to be very dumb since her boss constantly explained things that were so obvious to her, until she learned about this cultural dimension in my class! In addition to impacting our workplace behavior, this dimension and other cultural norms also impact how we frame our public relations messages. For example, Alegría Carrasco says that

> in the United States, public relations practitioners use superlatives. Everything is expected to be awesome, or great, or amazing. In Spain, people would assume that you are not worth it if you need to use those words. We don't want people to feel that we are pushing a product. We try to convince more subtly. I would never say that my product is the best.

Jennifer Stapper, the Bonn, Germany-based Chief of Communications for United Nations Volunteers, likewise explains that

> in the United States, if you organize an event to raise money for a cause, you make a direct ask at the event. In England and Germany, that is out

of context. It is not appropriate to make the ask right there at the event. Instead, a whole follow-up mechanism needs to be in place.

Meyer (2014, pp. 95–109) argues that there are three key ways that people of different cultures persuade. In applications-first cultures such as Australia, Canada, New Zealand, the United Kingdom, and the U.S., people get right to the point with their arguments. In principles-first cultures such as Belgium, France, and Russia, people are expected to provide more information about how they reached their conclusions before advancing their arguments. Meanwhile, in Asia, people focus more on background, whereas in Western Europe and the United States, people believe that individuals and issues can be separated from their environments and examined in isolation. Meyer (2014, p. 111) explains,

> a typical example is that Westerners may think that the Chinese are going all around the key points without addressing them deliberately, while East Asians may experience Westerners as trying to make a decision by isolating a single factor and ignoring significant interdependencies.

Obviously, you will need to be aware of these differences so you can craft your messages accordingly.

10 Time: When I worked for the U.S government, my colleagues and I once flew from Washington to Africa to meet with a head of state. When we arrived for the scheduled meeting, we discovered that the President had gone off to meet with the head of a neighboring country and was not in the office. My boss was furious that no one had been in touch with us to reschedule the meeting once it became clear that the President would not be there, though eventually the meeting did happen. Of course, what this boils down to is different approaches to time.

In **monochronic** cultures, such as in Germanic, Anglo-Saxon, and Northern European countries, it is expected that people will be prompt and deadlines will be met (Meyer, 2014, p. 227). By contrast, in **polychronic** cultures, such as in Latin America and the Middle East, "appointments just don't carry the same weight. . . . Things are constantly shifted around. Nothing seems solid or firm, particularly plans for the future, and there are always changes in the most important plans right up to the very last minute" (Hall, 1976, p. 15). Wealthier countries and more populated cities have a faster pace of life, while there tends to be a slower pace of life in more tropical climates (Levine, 1997, pp. 9, 16, 17). One study found that adjusting to local concepts of time is the second hardest adjustment to make when living in a new culture, after mastering the language (Levine, 1997, p. 5).

Levine (1997, pp. 193–201) recommends that, when working in a new culture, you learn to "translate" appointment times (How many minutes count

Copyright: liseykina

as being late and is it socially acceptable to run late?); the boundary between work and play time (How many hours are you expected to work? How much socializing are you expected to do with your colleagues while at work?); "the rules of the waiting game" (Who waits for whom? When and how long?); what pauses, silences, and "doing nothing" mean (Is appearing busy respected or pitied?); and the order of sequences (Is there a mid-day siesta? How long are you expected to socialize before business commences?). Also determine whether people are on "clock time" (following set schedules) or "event time" (accommodating unexpected developments and doing more than one thing at a time).

11 Value Orientations: Kluckhohn and Srodtbeck (1961) argue that societies differ along five value orientations. The first value orientation entails how people perceive *human nature*. Some cultures believe that human nature is inherently good, others that it is neutral, others that it is a mixture of good and evil, and others that human nature is essentially evil. Kent and Taylor (2011, p. 64) note that these views impact the level of trust that people of a society have in one another and in organizations—which is useful information for us as public relations practitioners, since we are often tasked with building or regaining trust on behalf of our clients.

Second, cultures differ on how they understand *man's relationship to nature*. Some cultures believe that human beings are subjugated to nature, others that nature should be mastered by human beings, and still others that people should live in harmony with nature.

The third orientation involves the degree of importance that a culture places on the *past, present, and future*. Cultures that value the past tend to

Copyright: Rudchenko Liliia

place greater import on tradition, while cultures that value the future are par-ticularly open to change.

Fourth, cultures vary on human *activity*. In cultures with a "doing" orienta-tion, there is "a demand for the kind of *activity* which results in accomplish-ments that are measurable by standards conceived to be external to the acting individual." In cultures with a "being orientation," activity is more spontane-ous and not focused on the person's development. In societies with a "being-in-becoming" orientation, emphasis is placed on "that kind of *activity* which has as its goal the development of all aspects of the self as an integrated whole" (Kluckhohn & Srodtbeck, 1961, p. 17).

Fifth, and finally, cultures vary on their *relational orientations*. This dimen-sion is similar to Hofstede's distinction between individualistic and collectivist societies. Under Kluckhohn and Srodtbeck's formulation, in "individualistic" societies, individual goals are paramount, whereas in "collateral" societies, group goals have primacy. In "lineal" societies group goals also have primacy, but these cultures also place emphasis on continuity of the group over time and on the hierarchical positions that people hold within them.

Again, all of these cultural dimensions are, ultimately, stereotypes, and therefore problematic. Many scholars disagree profoundly that they accurately and/or adequately describe the differences among people. Gerhart and Fang (2005) argue that the differences between people within the same country are greater than the differences between people of different countries and that organizational differences are a greater determinant of cultural values than differences between countries. McSweeney (2002) has questioned Hofstede's methodology. As previously discussed, people of the same culture are very different, and you therefore cannot assume that they will uniformly exhibit the country's average score on these dimensions. Still, the dimensions provide the best framework we have for identifying the types of cultural differences that we need to account for in our public relations strategies, and in my own practice I have found them to be remarkably insightful. Even if it is unfair to assume that every person in Latin America will always run late, for example, knowing that the a country has an overall polychronic approach to time and therefore deciding to hold an open house, as opposed to an event with a specific start time, as May Hauer-Simmonds described in Chapter 1, is just plain smart.

Manifestations of Cultural Differences

Hofstede, Hofstede, and Minkov (2010) note that cultural differences become manifest in four ways:

- **Symbols** may be "words, gestures, pictures, or objects." They "carry a particular meaning that is recognized as such only by those who share the culture. The words in a language or jargon belong to this category, as do dress, hairstyles, flags, and status symbols" (Hofstede, Hofstede, & Minkov, 2010, p. 8).

- **Heroes** "are persons, alive or dead, real or imaginary, who possess characteristics that are highly prized in a culture and thus serve as models for behavior." Cultural heroes have included "even Barbie, Batman, or, as a contrast, Snoopy in the United States, Asterix in France, or Ollie B. Bommel (Mr. Bumble) in the Netherlands" (Hofstede, Hofstede, & Minkov, 2010, p. 8).

Asterix is a "cultural hero" in France. Copyright: meunierd

- **Rituals** "are collective activities that are technically superfluous to reach desired ends but that, within a culture, are considered socially essential. They are therefore carried out for their own sake." Rituals can "include ways of greeting and paying respect to others, as well as social and religious ceremonies" (Hofstede, Hofstede, & Minkov, 2010, p. 9).

- **Values** "are broad tendencies to prefer certain states of affairs over others." Some cultures, for example, place particularly high importance on values such as their views of safety, cleanliness, and morality (Hofstede, Hofstede, & Minkov, 2010, p. 9).

Studying a culture's symbols, heroes, rituals, and values can offer you important insight on the types of stories and messages that are culturally relevant.

Other Questions to Ask About Culture

In addition to these major dimensions, there are a variety of other aspects of culture that you need to understand before attempting to practice public relations in a new environment. I recommend that you start by asking these questions:

- **What's taboo?** In every culture, certain topics of conversation are taboo. For example, while it might be considered polite in some countries to inquire how a colleague's family is doing, in Saudi Arabia, it would be considered offensive. In the U.S., it would generally not be appropriate to argue about politics in the workplace, while in Europe, such debates can be commonplace (Samovar et al., 2013, p. 251).
- **What's being communicated nonverbally?** Samovar et al. (2013, p. 271) define nonverbal communication as "all those nonverbal stimuli in a

communication setting that are generated by both the source and his or her use of the environment, and that have potential message value for the source and/or receiver." Importantly, nonverbal communication includes both messages that the sender intends to convey as well as messages that are unintentional. Because different cultures have different ways of communicating nonverbally, there is significant potential for confusion. For example, when U.S. troops fighting in Iraq were greeted by schoolchildren giving them the "thumbs up" sign, they mistakenly perceived it as a sign of approval. In Iraq, however, the signal is a profanity, akin to the "middle finger" in U.S. culture (Samovar et al., 2013, p. 267). Similarly, shaking one's head from side to side is meant to convey the word "no" in the United Kingdom, but "yes" in India (Samovar et al., 2013, p. 283).

Likewise, because I am from the U.S., when someone tries to avoid eye contact, I tend to assume that (s)he has something to hide. However, in many parts of Asia, the Caribbean, and Latin America, people avoid eye contact as a mark of respect. In some cultures, the rules are more granular; for example, women and men in Arab countries such as Egypt and Saudi Arabia who do not know each other are expected to avoid eye contact, while in India, people avoid eye contact with those from other socioeconomic classes (Samovar et al., 2013, p. 287).

- **What types of emotion are expected?** When executives from the Japanese carmaker Toyota testified before the U.S. Congress to discuss a recall, the executives were perceived by members of Congress as not remorseful because they did not show outward signs of emotion. However, in Asian cultures such as China, Japan, and Korea, it is considered inappropriate to display strong feelings and emotions outwardly (Samovar et al., 2013, p. 284). By contrast, as will be discussed in Chapter 10, emotions are an important part of communication in the Arab world.

Copyright: Fotovika

- **What is considered ethical and unethical in this culture?** As Lewis (2006, pp. 5–6) notes,

  the American calls the Japanese unethical if the latter breaks a contract. The Japanese says it is unethical for the American to apply the terms of the contract if things have changed. Italians have very flexible views on what is ethical and what is not, which sometimes causes Northern Europeans to question their honesty.

  So, you must find out what is considered to be ethical and appropriate before working in a new culture.

- **What meanings do particular words, numbers, colors, and other symbols convey?** Different phrases have different connotations in different cultures.

  In the United States, for instance, the phrase 'we are on a parallel course' is used to indicate that you agree with the other party's proposal. However, in Japan, it means that the proposal will never be accepted because parallel lines never meet (Samovar et al., 2013, pp. 261–262).

  Samovar et al. (2013, p. 262) also warn that humor does not usually translate properly across cultures.

  Colors convey divergent and often contradictory connotations in different cultures, so you will want to select the colors of your communication materials carefully. For example, the color blue, which is favored by top global brands, is associated with warmth in Holland, but cold in Sweden; evil in East Asia, but purity in India and death in Iran; masculinity in the United States, but femininity in Holland. Red, the second most favored color by top global brands, is perceived as lucky in Argentina, China, Denmark, and Romania—but unlucky in Chad, Germany, and Nigeria. Hindus and Buddhists consider the color orange to be sacred, while some Zambians do not even consider orange to be a discrete color (Aslam, 2005, pp. 2–3; Marketo, 2014). Table 2.1 lists additional regional differences.

  Numbers often have different—and sometimes extremely significant—connotations in different cultures. For example, the number eight is so auspicious in the Chinese culture that the Beijing Olympics began on August 8, 2008 (8/8/2008) at 8:00 pm. As the case study in (coincidentally) Chapter 8 discusses, one way in which the French winemaker Chateau Lafite Rothschild won popularity in the Chinese market was by etching the Chinese symbol for the number 8 on the bottles of its 2008 vintage.

  Also, even if you will be communicating in your native language, I recommend learning a few words of the local language to demonstrate that you are willing to make the effort. Download a language podcast to listen to on the airplane.

Table 2.1 Meaning of Colors by Culture

Color	Anglo-Saxon	Germanic	Latin	Nordic	Slavic	Chinese	Japanese	Korean	ASEAN
White	Purity Happiness	—	—	—	—	Death Mourning	Death Mourning	Death Mourning	Death Mourning
Blue	High quality Corporate Masculine	Warm Feminine	—	Cold Masculine	—	High quality Trustworthy	High quality Trustworthy	High quality Trustworthy	Cold Evil (Malaysia)
Green	Envy Good taste	—	Envy	—	—	Pure Reliable	Love Happy	Pure Adventure	Danger Disease (Malaysia)
Yellow	Happy Jealousy	Envy Jealousy	Envy Infidelity	—	Envy	Pure Good taste Royal Authority	Envy Good taste	Happiness Good taste	—
Red	Masculine Love Lust Fear Anger	Fear Anger Jealousy	Masculine	Positive	Fear Anger Jealousy	Love Happiness Lucky	Love Anger Jealousy	Love Adventure Good taste	—
Purple	Authority Power	—	—	—	Anger Envy Jealousy	Expensive Love	Expensive Sin Fear	Expensive Love	—
Black	Expensive Fear Grief	Fear Anger Grief	Fear Anger Grief	—	Fear Anger	Expensive Powerful	Expensive Powerful	Expensive Powerful	—

Source: Aslam, M. M. (2006). Are you selling the right colour? A cross-cultural review of colour as a marketing cue. *Journal of marketing communications*, 12(1), 15–30.

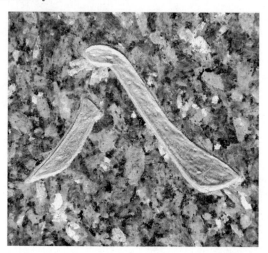

The number eight is hugely auspicious in Chinese culture. Copyright: JEEPNEX

- **What types of personal contact are expected?** How should you greet a local business partner? If you are in Syria or Mexico, you will probably embrace. In India and Japan, people bow. In Japan, you should bow even if your partner extends his or her hand. Guth and Marsh (2012, p. 432) explain that

  > you can flatter your Japanese guest by bowing first. In Japan, the person who initiates a bow is acknowledging the high social status of the other person. If you exchange business cards with your Japanese visitor, bow slightly and extend yours with both hands. You should accept your visitor's card in the same manner and look at it respectfully after receiving it.

Copyright: Jennifer Lam

In the U.S., Spain, and Zambia, people shake hands upon ⸳ however, in Zambia, the left hand should support the right as and in Spain you may also pat your partner on the back. Furtl Islamic countries such as Pakistan and Saudi Arabia, it is generally con-sidered inappropriate for a man to shake hands with a woman (Guth & Marsh, 2012, p. 431–432; Samovar et al., 2013, p. 23). In the Arab world, never touch someone with your left hand (that's for the bathroom) or show the sole of your shoe—an insult "because it is on the ground and associated with the foot, the lowest part of the body" (Gammell, 2008).

- **What types of exchanges will be expected by my associates?** In some cultures, such as some East Asian nations, it would be considered rude not to offer a gift at the beginning of a business meeting (Curtin & Gaither, 2007, p. 240). Organizations in other cultures have strict rules about what their employees may accept, which are designed to prevent corruption and bribery. When I worked in the Obama administration, sometimes when I attended meetings with heads of state or other high-level officials in other countries, staffers from both countries would actu-ally discuss ahead of time whether gifts would be exchanged (a practice I found to be gauche!) and gifts given to officials could not be brought back on government planes, just in case someone had tampered with such a "gift." Customs also vary about how you should react to a gift. For exam-ple, "in Arab cultures gift recipients are expected to be profuse in offer-ing thanks, whereas, in English culture recipients are expected to offer restrained thanks because too much exuberance is considered offensive" (Samovar et al., 2013, p. 17).

Copyright: elisekurenbina

- **What business practices are prevalent in this culture?** In countries such as China, India, and Brazil, for example, great importance is placed on established business relationships, and therefore if you wish to approach a potential partner—such as, for example, a local public relations agency—you should ask for an introduction from your country's Department of Trade or Commerce or perhaps from the country's public relations federation (to be discussed in Chapter 3). On the other hand, in countries such as the U.S., it would be perfectly acceptable to approach a potential partner directly. You should also be aware of how negotiations are conducted in different cultures. For example, when negotiating with a potential partner in China,

> the host side will first describe themselves—who they are, what they do—with many statistics. They will then expect the guests to do the same. None of this has any real bearing on the issue being negotiated, but this form is important (Samovar et al., 2013, p. 327).

Molinsky (2013, pp. 14–15) argues that six dimensions . . . capture the expectations that others have for our behavior in a foreign setting:

- Directness: How straightforwardly am I expected to communicate in this situation?
- Enthusiasm: How much positive emotion and energy am I expected to show to others in this situation?
- Formality: How much deference and respect am I expected to demonstrate in this situation?
- Assertiveness: How strongly am I expected to express my voice in this situation?
- Self-promotion: How positively am I expected to speak about my skills and accomplishments in this situation?
- Personal disclosure: How much can I reveal about myself in this situation?

I would also add that you should determine what constitutes appropriate attire for your meetings and other engagements and how much small talk is expected before business commences.

- **How do members of this culture build trust?** As Sriramesh (2009, p. 56) notes, "trust is a key ingredient that gives credibility to a source in any communication. . . . There can be little doubt that the strategies of developing and maintaining interpersonal trust are culture-specific."

  Meyer (2014, p. 168) explains that there are two types of trust. In countries such as the U.S. and Switzerland, people rely on "cognitive trust," which is gained through knowledge of a person's skills and accomplishments. By contrast, other cultures, such as China and Brazil, also value "affective trust" which "arises from feelings of emotional closeness, empathy, or friendship." To gain this, you must build a deeper relationship with a person. Meyer suggests being yourself, letting your hair down, and investing in relationship building through meals together. In countries such as China, Japan, Korea, and Thailand, it is also customary to drink together. This brings us to the next, related question.

- **How important is it to build relationships before getting down to business?** Culbertson (1996, p. 6) notes that

  in China, Japan, and other Oriental societies, as well as in Latin America and Saudi Arabia, great emphasis is placed on personal interaction to establish a sense of trust, mutual understanding, and loyalty among those engaged in almost any shared undertaking.

Copyright: lenetstan

The public relations model that accounts for this cultural difference in known as the **personal influence model**. It was identified by Grunig, Grunig, Sriramesh, Huang, and Lyra (1995) in their study of public relations practitioners in India, Greece, and Taiwan. Under this model, "practitioners try to establish personal relationships—friendships, if possible—with key individuals in the media, government, or political and activist groups."

- **What are the values of my stakeholders, and how should this influence how I engage them?** For example, in many Asian and African cultures, the elderly are revered. By contrast, in the U.S., youth is revered. Rapaille (2006, p. 31) argues that this helps explain why American businesses are famous for creating and exporting "the trappings of adolescence: Coca-Cola, Nike shoes, fast food, blue jeans, and loud, violent movies." This clearly makes a difference in how you craft your messages to appeal to local audiences.

- **Do I need to be sensitive to the religion of my employees, business partners, and audiences and how will this impact how I frame my messages?**

An individual's religion—or secularism, a belief that answers about the universe are to be found in science—affects his or her ethical code of conduct and beliefs about how the world works, his or her place in the world, and the very meaning of life. Different religions espouse very different practices: Muslims pray five times per day, many Christians go to church on Sundays, and many observant Jews observe the Sabbath on Friday nights and Saturdays. Be cognizant of the religious practices of your colleagues. For example, it would be offensive to ask a colleague in Italy—where more than 80 percent of the population is Christian—to participate in a conference call on Christmas Day (Pew, 2012, p. 47). It would likewise be inappropriate to invite a Muslim colleague, whose religion proscribes drinking alcohol, to a bar after work, or to lunch during the holy month of Ramadan, when Muslims fast.

- **To what other organizations do my stakeholders belong, and what can this tell me about their values and how my messages will be received?** In addition to religion, other social organizations have a major influence on culture. One of the most critical such institutions is the family. For example, whereas individuals in the U.S. tend to live as part of nuclear families—parents and children (notwithstanding high rates of divorce and single parenthood)—in other cultures across Africa, Asia, the Arab world, and Latin America, people grow up in extended families and even consider people who are not blood relations to be part of their families (Samovar et al., 2013, pp. 80–82). Another membership that has a major influence on people of different cultures is their nationality and relationship to the country in which they live.

- **What historical background will influence how my messages are received?** Historical events have a lasting impact on cultures. For example, Russia's long history of invasion by the Mongols, Germans, Turks, Poles, Swedes, French, Japanese, and English has, rather understandably, inculcated a suspicion of foreigners that continues to this day (Samovar et al., p. 96). Similarly, the work ethic and belief in progress of the first European settlers to arrive in the U.S. continues to be reflected in the entrepreneurialism of its businesses (Samovar et al., 2013, pp. 92–94).

- **Are my business partners trying to adapt their own behavior to my culture?** If you are both attempting to adapt to one another's culture, this will be a recipe for confusion—and a few laughs.

Cracking Cultural Codes

Now that you understand the cultural differences for which you should be on the lookout and the additional questions you should ask when you work in a new culture, where can you find the answers? Your local partners (to be discussed in the next chapter) are a good place to start and will be critical sources of information for you. Below are additional valuable resources you can use to learn about different cultures:

Copyright: cybrain

1 **Hofstede's invaluable website**, http://geert-hofstede.com, allows you to look up how countries around the world rank on core cultural dimensions.

2 **The findings of the GLOBE study** are reported in a 2004 book called *Culture, Leadership, and Organizations: The GLOBE Study of 62 Societies*, edited by R. J. House, P. J. Hanges, M. Javidan, P. W. Dorfman, and B. Gupta.

3 **Public opinion surveys**. The World Values Survey has surveyed people in nearly 100 countries on their views on everything from money to God. Other sources of public opinion research are the Pew Research Center Global Attitudes and Trends reports and Gallup.

4 **Market research reports**. Check out available research from companies such as Mintel and Ipsos.

5 **Transparency International Country Profiles** offer intelligence on the level of corruption in countries around the globe, at www.transparency.org.

6 **The Edelman Trust Barometer**, available at www.edelman.com, annually measures the level of trust that people have in institutions in countries around the world.

7 **Freedom House** offers country-level data on freedom of the press around the globe, at www. Freedomhouse.org.

8 **The World Bank's Doing Business report**s, available at www.doingbusiness.org, provide country-level data on the business climate in economies around the globe.

9 **Export.gov**, a website of the U.S. government, provides country-level business information, geared towards U.S. businesses interested in exporting abroad but useful in other contexts, as well.

10 **The U.S. Central Intelligence Agency's World Factbook**, available at www.cia.gov, provides detailed country-level data in the following

categories: geography, people and society, government, economy, energy, communications, transportation, military, and transnational issues.

11 **Local media.** Start consuming as much local media as possible to begin to learn about the country and how its media organizations cover the news. Read local blogs. Also, watch local movies and read local literature. As Hofstede, Hofstede and Minkov (2010, p. 156) explain, "mainstream movies are modern myths—they create hero models according to the dominant culture of the society in which they are made."

12 **Books and academic journal articles.** Google Scholar is a good resource for searching academic journal articles. If you have a subscription to a library that has access to the article(s) you want, you can obtain them for free; otherwise, you can purchase individual articles from their publishers.

13 **Local public relations campaigns of other organizations and your competitors.** What messages, strategies and tactics are they (and are they not) using?

14 **Primary research.** You can commission local interviews, focus groups, ethnographies, surveys, and other studies to help figure out what will— and won't—work in the local culture.

Of course, simply learning about different cultures is not enough; you will also need to understand how people view *your organization and/or product* in local cultures. Ideally, you will conduct research such as focus groups, interviews, or surveys in each market to generate insights to inform your local public relations strategy. For example, Rowan Benecke, Chair of the Global Technology Practice at the global public relations firm Burson-Marsteller, says that when one client—a leading global consumer electronics company headquartered in Asia—developed a smart watch, Burson-Marsteller conducted local research in order to develop their public relations strategy for Europe. The agency found that European consumers largely purchase smart watches to give to other people as gifts. "The insight was that the competition wasn't Apple—it was chocolate and flowers," Benecke says. Burson-Marsteller therefore developed a public relations campaign for Europe presenting smart watches as ideal gifts. "You need to generate data that will give you insights to inform your campaigns," Benecke says. "Be creative, but back up your strategy with a big idea."

The above resources should begin to help you understand the culture(s) in which you work more deeply, which is the first step. Chapters 8–12 will also provide detailed guidance on how to adapt your public relations strategies, tactics, and messages for each of the world's major cultural groups. First, however, the next chapter will discuss how to effectively build and manage a global public relations team comprised of people who exhibit such vast cultural differences.

References

Anderson, B. (2006). *Imagined communities: Reflections on the origin and spread of nationalism.* New York, NY: Verso.

Aslam, M. (2005). Are you selling the right colour? A cross-cultural review of colour as a marketing cue. In I. Papasolomou (Ed.), *Developments and trends in corporate and marketing communications: Plotting the mindscape of the 21st century: Proceedings of the 10th International Conference on Corporate and Marketing Communications* (pp. 1–14). Cyprus: School of Business Administration.

Banks, S. P. (1995). *Multicultural public relations: A social-interpretive approach*. Thousand Oaks, CA: Sage.

Central Intelligence Agency (CIA) (2015). World factbook. Retrieved from https://www.cia.gov/library/publications/the-world-factbook/

Clegg, A. (2005, October 20). A word to the worldly-wise. *Marketing Week*, 43–48.

Culbertson, H. M. (1996). Introduction. In H. M. Culbertson & N. Chen (Eds.), *International public relations: A comparative analysis* (pp. 1–13). Mahwah, NJ: Lawrence Erlbaum Associates.

Curtin, P. A., & Gaither, T. K. (2007). *International public relations: Negotiating culture, identity, and power*. Thousand Oaks, CA: Sage.

Gammell, C. (2008, December 15). Arab culture: The insult of the shoe. *The Telegraph*. Retrieved from http://www.telegraph.co.uk/news/worldnews/middleeast/iraq/3776970/Arab-culture-the-insult-of-the-shoe.html

Gerhart, B., & Fang, M. (2005). National culture and human resource management: Assumptions and evidence. *International Journal of Human Resource Management*, 16(6), 971–986.

Grunig, J. E., Grunig, L. A., Sriramesh, K., Huang, Y. H., & Lyra, A. (1995). Models of public relations in an international setting. *Journal of Public Relations Research*, 7(3), 163–186.

Gupta, V., & Hanges, P. J. (2004). Regional and climate clustering of societal clusters. In R. J. House, P. J. Hanges, M. Javidan, P. W. Dorfman, & V. Gupta (Eds.), *Culture, leadership, and organizations: The GLOBE study of 62 societies* (pp. 178–218). Thousand Oaks, CA: Sage.

Guth, D. W., & Marsh, C. (2012). *Public relations: A values-driven approach*. New York, NY: Allyn & Bacon.

Hall, E. T. (1976). *Beyond culture*. Garden City, NY: Doubleday.

Hofstede, G. (1980). *Culture's consequences: International differences in work related values*. Beverly Hills, CA: Sage.

Hofstede, G., Hofstede, G. J., & Minkov, M. (2010). *Cultures and organizations: Software of the mind*. (3rd ed.) New York, NY: McGraw Hill.

House, R. J., & Javidan, M. (2004). Overview of globe. In R. J. House, P. J. Hanges, M. Javidan, P. W. Dorfman, & B. Gupta (Eds.), *Culture, leadership, and organizations: The GLOBE study of 62 societies* (pp. 9–28). Thousand Oaks, CA: Sage.

Javidan, M. (2004). Performance orientation. In R. J. House, P. J. Hanges, M. Javidan, P. W. Dorfman, & B. Gupta (Eds.), *Culture, leadership, and organizations: The GLOBE study of 62 societies* (pp. 239–281). Thousand Oaks, CA: Sage.

Kabasakal, H., & Bodur, M. (2004). Humane orientation in societies, organizations, and leader attributes. In R. J. House, P. J. Hanges, M. Javidan, P. W. Dorfman, & B. Gupta (Eds.), *Culture, leadership, and organizations: The GLOBE study of 62 societies* (pp. 564–601). Thousand Oaks, CA: Sage.

Kent, M. L., & Taylor, M. (1999). When public relations becomes government relations. *Public Relations Quarterly*, 44(3), 18–22.

Kent, M., & Taylor, M. (2011). How intercultural communication theory informs public relations practice in global settings. In N. Bardhan & C. K. Weaver (Eds.), *Public* relations in global cultural contexts: Multi-paradigmatic perspectives (pp. 50–76). New York, NY: Routledge.

Kluckhohn, F. R., & Srodtbeck, F. L. (1961). *Variations in value orientations*. Westport, CT: Greenwood Press.

Levine, R. (1997). *A geography of time: The temporal misadventures of a social psychologist, or how every culture keeps time just a little bit differently*. New York, NY: Basic Books.

Lewis, R. E. (2006). *When cultures collide: Leading across cultures*. Boston, MA: Nicholas Brealey International.

Liswood, L. (2010). *The loudest duck: Moving beyond diversity while embracing differences to achieve success at work*. Hoboken, NJ: John Wiley & Sons.

Livermore, D. A. (2011). *The cultural intelligence difference: Master the one skill you can't do without in today's global economy*. New York, NY: American Management Association.

Marketo. (2014). True colors: What your brand colors say about your business. Retrieved from https://www.marketo.com/infographics/true-colors-what-your-brand-colors-say-about-your-business-infographic/

McSweeney, B. (2002). Hofstede's model of national cultural differences and their consequences: A triumph of faith-a failure of analysis. *Human Relations, 55*(1), 89–118.

Meyer, E. M. (2014). *The culture map: Breaking through the invisible boundaries of global business*. New York, NY: PublicAffairs.

Minkov, M. (2007). Monumentalism versus flexhumility. Paper presented at the SIE-TAR Europa Congress, Sofia, Bulgaria.

Molinsky, A. (2013). *Global dexterity: How to adapt your behavior across cultures without losing yourself in the process*. Boston, MA: Harvard Business Review Press.

Pew Research Center (2012, December). The global religious landscape: A report on the size and distribution of the world's major religious groups as of 2010. Retrieved from http://www.pewforum.org/files/2014/01/global-religion-full.pdf

PWC (2015, March 31). Culture eats strategy for breakfast webinar. Retrieved from http://www.strategyand.pwc.com/media/file/Katzenbach-Center_Webinar_Culture-Eats-Strategy-for-Breakfast.pdf

Rapaille, C. (2006). *The culture code: An ingenious way to understand why people around the world live and buy as they do*. New York, NY: Broadway Books.

Samovar, L. A., Porter, R. E., McDaniel, E. R., & Roy, C. S. (2013). *Communication between cultures* (8th ed.). Boston, MA: Cengage Learning.

Sriramesh, K. (1992). Societal culture and public relations: Ethnographic evidence from India. *Public Relations Review, 18*(2), 201–211.

Sriramesh, K. (2009). The relationship between culture and public relations. In K. Sriramesh & D. Verčič (Eds.), *The global public relations handbook: Theory, research, and practice* (2nd ed.) (pp. 47–61). New York, NY: Routledge.

Sriramesh, K., & White, J. (1992). Societal culture and public relations. In J. E. Grunig (Ed.), *Excellence in public relations and communication management* (pp. 597–614). Hillsdale, NJ: Lawrence Erlbaum Associates.

Taylor, M. (2000). Cultural variance as a challenge to global public relations: A case study of the Coca-Cola scare in Europe. *Public Relations Review, 26*(3), 277–293.

Ting-Toomey, S. (2005). The matrix of face: An updated face-negotiation theory. In W. B. Gudykunst (Ed.), *Theorizing about intercultural communication* (pp. 71–92). Thousand Oaks, CA: Sage.

3 Building, Managing, and Evaluating Your Global Public Relations Team

Copyright: EDHAR

When I first started working at the United Nations, I would often ask my colleagues around the world whether they could meet my proposed deadlines for particular deliverables, and they would invariably say yes. Then, when the deadlines came and I did not receive what I expected them to send, I would be genuinely confused and upset. Finally, my boss had to explain to me that my colleagues in some of our national offices would consider it to be inappropriate to say no to me, and therefore they would always say yes to anything I asked, regardless of whether they had any intention of ever fulfilling my requests. If I wanted to actually obtain what I needed, I would need to find a different way of communicating with my team.

This chapter explains how to manage and work as part of such a cross-cultural public relations team. First, I will explain how to hire the local experts you will need to craft and implement campaigns at the regional, national, or sub-national level and discuss the merits of four types of hiring options: freelancers, full-time staff, local public relations agencies, and global public relations agencies. Next, I will discuss how to adapt your workplace behavior in order to successfully lead a team comprised of people who exhibit the array of cultural differences discussed in the previous chapter. Finally, I will offer guidelines for measuring the success of your global public relations campaigns.

Hiring Staff and Agencies

You know by now that, in order to successfully implement public relations campaigns in different countries and cultures, you will need help on the ground from locals who speak the language fluently, understand the culture and its unspoken assumptions, and are skilled in the practice of public relations. As you will hear repeatedly from public relations professionals around the globe in the chapters to follow, even among people who speak the same language, local dialects, phrases, senses of humor, and approaches to life often differ dramatically. These differences can be significant not just between people of different countries, but often between people of different regions or communities in the *same* country. And while this would make it difficult to do any type of work globally, pinpointing nuances in language and culture is at the very heart of how we craft public relations campaigns that truly connect with people. Clearly, we need local help.

Of course, there is another reason why you will want to hire a diverse team: it will make your public relations strategies more creative. Surowiecki (2005, p. 28) notes that cognitive diversity gives a team a competitive edge because it spurs creative thinking. He argues that "the more similar [people] are, the more similar the ideas they appreciate will be. . . . By contrast, if they are diverse, the chances that at least someone will take a gamble on a radical or unlikely idea obviously increases."

> Diversity also allows a group to better distinguish good ideas from bad ideas, because homogeneous groups, particularly small ones, are often victims of what the psychologist Irving Janis called "groupthink." . . . [They] become more cohesive more easily than diverse groups, and as they become more cohesive they also become more dependent on the group, more insulated from outside opinions (Surowiecki, 2005, p. 36).

In fact, Bloomberg founder Michael Bloomberg (1997, p. 172) admits that he hopes his competitors practice discrimination, because his team's diversity gives his business a competitive edge! The downside is that a multicultural group can be slower, because it is more time-consuming to manage (Meyer, 2014, p. 114). However, if you are working in global public relations, you will certainly need to work with diverse colleagues.

When hiring local public relations practitioners, you first need to decide whether to hire individuals or public relations firms. Rich Kylberg, Vice President of Corporate Communications and Global Marketing for Arrow Electronics, a company that provides electronic and information technology products and services to businesses around the world, finds that which option is more cost effective generally depends upon the workload of the project for which he is hiring. "If you do have a 40 hour workweek, it is probably less expensive to have your own staff, but there are hidden management costs to consider, such as human resources costs," he says. "It's also easier to separate from independent people and firms who are underperforming than from full-time employees." Kylberg also notes that business cycles go up and down, and when companies are struggling, public relations departments are one of the first places where they cut costs. He never brings people onto his payroll as full-time staffers unless he is confident that he will have the budget to keep them over the long term. When this is not the case, Kylberg recommends hiring freelancers or outside agencies.

A benefit of working with agencies over individuals is that they can often bring fresher ideas to the table. Capozzi (2015, p. 363) explains that

> even in the largest internal departments, the same few people are usually charged with developing creative ideas and angles for promoting the interests of the organization. Because consulting firms are larger collections of people, and because people can be brought in who do not regularly work on one particular client, new perspectives can be brought to bear and fresh ideas emerge.

If you work with a well-respected agency, their recommendations can also serve as useful ammunition for you during internal battles within your organization. Capozzi (2015, p. 363) notes that "the input of external advisors often carries weight internally, especially when other staff functions—such as the lawyers—bring in their own 'experts' to advise management."

On the other hand, Glenn Goldberg, Chief Executive Officer of the Parallel Communications Group, a global agency that specializes in business-to-business communications, says that he prefers to hire individual freelancers instead of working with agencies because "usually, they have much more flexibility in terms of time and fee structure. Large agencies will bill for everything—conference calls, writing, research, etc. Freelancers are the much more productive and cost-effective avenue."

If you do decide to hire individuals, you will need to decide whether to hire full-time staff members or freelancers. Goldberg says that he hires staff as freelancers as opposed to as full-time employees because hiring full-time staff subjects a business to often cumbersome labor and tax regulations of the employees' home countries. The qualities he looks for when hiring are "someone who is a self-starter and accountable, and has a sense of investment in what we are doing as a public relations firm." Goldberg says that he finds all of his local freelancers through searching mutual contacts on LinkedIn (a platform which will be discussed in Chapter 7) and by asking his business contacts for recommendations. "If someone works in this industry, they are going to know certain editors, and we are going to have connections in common," Goldberg says. "So reverse social networking is a pretty reliable way to find candidates."

Goldberg says that one of the tricks to successful hiring is making expectations clear from the start. For example, he says that when he hires freelancers in Europe, he finds that many practitioners are accustomed to having budgets to pay for editorial coverage in the trade press and speaking engagements at industry conferences—a practice that is unusual and considered to be unethical in the United States of America. He needs to be certain that his freelancers will be willing and able to place editorial coverage without "paying to play." While you will obviously hire local staff around the world precisely for their local knowledge and practices, it is also important for you to ensure that they will understand and abide by your firm's global compliance standards (Judd, 2013, p. 29).

Gary Weaver, Executive Director of the Intercultural Management Institute at American University, says that another trait to select for when hiring members of a global team is tolerance for ambiguity, because people who succeed when working in different cultures tend to be unflappable and flexible. However, he notes that you ultimately must adapt your hiring criteria to each individual position. For example, "in the U.S., we like people who get things done, are well-organized and are intolerant of ambiguity. That kind of person could be a disaster in the Middle East, where meetings start late and relationships are so important" (Judd, 2013, pp. 17–18).

Finally, when hiring local staff members, consider carefully how they will be perceived by stakeholders (both internally and externally) in their work locations. For example, Judd (2013, p. 17) notes that

> in some cultures, a foreigner might succeed, while in others the hire would be perceived as a troubling signal. In Asia, for instance, deploying a Singaporean to mainland China could be a recipe for problems. That's because some Chinese perceive Singaporeans as arrogant and may balk at such a reporting arrangement.

Similarly, in Chapter 11, Serge Giacomo, Head of Communications and Institutional Relations for GE in Latin America, explains that he decided not to hire a regional spokesperson in Argentina because he did not believe that Colombian journalists would "be able to engage in a positive conversation" with an Argentinian. Fair or not, these stereotypes and prejudices will impact your work, so you must avoid viewing regions as monolithic and astutely evaluate how people of different cultures can and will interact with one another.

If you choose to go the agency route, you will need to determine whether to hire a single global agency or different local agencies. Kylberg has found that there are not necessarily differences in the level of talent that local and global agencies possess. "What matters is who is doing the work," he says. He explains that

> you're looking for experienced, talented people, and they aren't all at the big agencies. A lot of these people have hung out a shingle and are doing their own thing. If I'm going into a market where I don't know people, I end up paying a premium to work with a global agency because I don't know people and undoubtedly the big agency has done that vetting for me, so it's a risk reduction to go with them. But there's no particular inherent guarantee of success, because they have a range of talent, as anyone else does. If you have operations in that market, you can also ask your

internal staff in other departments to make good referrals of local firms who they've worked with in the past.

If you have a consumer product that is similar in different markets around the world, Goldberg says that it may make sense to hire a global agency to implement a unified strategy with adaptations in different markets. Kylberg concurs that

> if you work with a big firm, there's a better chance that the agency will communicate out a consistent brand message. Otherwise, I have to explain my brand message to a larger group of people, but really, that's my job anyway.

However, if you work in a niche or business-to-business industry, Goldberg says that it is likely that you will be better served by a local agency that specializes in your subject matter and has real expertise and contacts in the local industry. Goldberg explains,

> if you are working for Coca Cola, which sells products through supermarkets around the world that people consume in the same way all over the world, you can hire a global agency that can bombard mainstream publications around the world to reach a consumer market. But if you're Cisco and you sell network technology, you have different competitors, resellers, and sales cycles in different markets, so you need people with highly specific expertise in your particular market. You can always find a local one- or two-person shop in a country that specializes in your industry, but it's not reasonable to expect a global agency to have that high level of expertise.

Kylberg says that the best local agencies also have the local media contacts that are especially critical when an organization is challenged. He explains,

> if you're only working with a big agency, you're incredibly vulnerable when local media is coming after you and you don't have the local resources to deal with it until it becomes a bigger problem. Then you have a larger problem than necessary on your hands. It's not that all global agencies don't have those local contacts, but it's harder for them to manage the media at that smaller level, and so they're variable and inconsistent.

However, Kylberg says that an advantage of working with big firms is that "they have a lot of bodies and are fast to execute, so if you have a big initiative and need to scale up quickly, you'll want to go with a bigger firm over a smaller local one." On the other hand, he says, "if you just have a little project, you'd be a fool to put a big global firm on it, because they won't be interested and it will be incredibly expensive to execute." Kylberg says that both global and local agencies tell him "all the time" that they will be able to take on projects when in reality they are not well equipped to deliver the results he is looking for. The trick is for you to assess the size, capabilities, strengths, and weaknesses of different firms. "You've got to apply the right partners in the right places," Kylberg says.

For example, Kylberg has internal managers for the regions of Asia-Pacific, the Americas, and Europe who are responsible for hiring and overseeing the work of numerous agencies in their respective markets in order to implement communications campaigns in about seventy-five countries. His managers work with global agencies such as Ogilvy PR and FleishmanHillard, who have been contracted by the company's headquarters in the U.S., but they also have the freedom to hire local agencies.

If you do decide to work with a global agency, Appelbaum, Belmuth, and Schroeder (2011, p. 253) note that you should "demand a 'bulk purchase' discount." Table 3.1 lists the top 250 public relations agencies in the world by revenue. If you need help finding a local firm, table 3.2 lists the names of national and regional associations of public relations professionals around the world. Contact a local association in the area in which you seek to hire to request recommendations of agencies (or practitioners). Of course, with any firm you consider, you will want to ask whether they are already working for any of your direct competitors before sharing proprietary information.

Table 3.1 World's Largest Public Relations Firms by Revenue

Edelman	USA
Weber Shandwick	USA
FleishmanHillard	USA
Ketchum	USA
MSLGroup	France
Burson-Marsteller	USA
Hill+Knowlton Strategies	USA
Ogilvy PR	USA
Golin	USA
Havas PR	France
Brunswick	UK
FTI Consulting	USA
Cohn & Wolfe	USA
BlueFocus (BlueDigital)	China
Media Consulta International	Germany
Porter Novelli	USA
APCO Worldwide	USA
Grayling	UK
Waggener Edstrom Worldwide, Inc.	USA
Finsbury	USA/UK
FSB Comunicacoes	Brazil
InVentiv Health 1	USA
W2O Group	USA
Ruder Finn, Inc.	USA
Vector Inc.	Japan
Res Publica (National PR)	Canada
Public Systeme Hopscotch	France
Lewis PR	UK

PMK*BMC	USA
Kreab 2	UK/Sweden
Text100 Corporation	USA
MWW	USA
Instinctif Partners 4	UK
Finn Partners	USA
fischerAppelt	Germany
ICR	USA
Bell Pottinger Private	UK
We Are Social	UK
CYTS-Linkage Public Relations Consulting Co., Ltd	China
Freud Communications	UK
Dentsu Public Relations Inc 5	Japan
DeVries Global	USA
DKC Public Relations	USA
PRAP Japan, Inc.	Japan
Marina Maher Communications	USA
Zeno Group	USA
Hering Schuppener	Germany
Allison+Partners	USA
Citizen Relations	USA
Blue Rubicon	UK
Citigate Dewe Rogerson	UK
Kyodo PR	Japan
Global Strategy Group	USA
Mikhailov & Partners	Russia
PadillaCRT	USA
PPR	Australia
Llorente & Cuenca	Spain
Iris Worldwide	UK
Prain Global	Korea
Maquina Public Relations	Brazil
Racepoint Global	USA
Four Communications Group plc	UK
MHP Communications	UK
iMARS Group	Russia
GCI Health	USA
Hotwire Public Relations	UK
G&S Business Communications	USA
AGT Communications Group	Russia
The Outcast Agency	USA
Oliver Schrott Kommunikation	Germany
SPN Communications	Russia
Coyne PR	USA
Tonic Health	UK

(*Continued*)

Table 3.1 (Continued)

Taylor	USA
Newgate Communications	UK
ICF Mostra	Belgium
Geelmuyden.Kiese Group	Norway
Olson Engage	USA
SEC	Italy
Prosek Partners	USA
Hunter Public Relations	USA
Barabino & Partners	Italy
Farner Consulting	Switzerland
Strategic Public Relations Group	Hong Kong
5W Public Relations	USA
The Red Consultancy	UK
Adfactors PR	India
CROS	Russia
Interel	Belgium
Peppercomm	USA
M Booth	USA
French/West/Vaughan	USA
Fishburn	UK
Fahlgren Mortine	USA
Shift Communications Inc.	USA
Lansons	UK
Serviceplan PR Group	Germany
Levick Strategic Communications	USA
SparkPR	USA
Atrevia 6	Spain
Jackson Spalding	USA
Mitchell Communications Group, LLC	USA
Haberlein & Mauerer	Germany
PR One	South Korea
Maitland	UK
Cooney/Waters Group	USA
Brands2Life	UK
TRACCS	Saudi Arabia
achtung!	Germany
LaunchSquad	USA
Motiv Communication Group	Russia
Faktor 3	Germany
TVC Group	UK
Makovsky	USA
ROI Communication	USA
Rasky Baerlein	USA
ergo Kommunikation	Germany

A&B One	Germany
Rowland	Australia
RF Binder	USA
AMI Communications	Czech Republic
Action Global Communications	Cyprus
First House	Norway
Miltton	Finland
Grupo CDI—Comunicacao e Marketing	Brazil
Brodeur Partners 7	USA
Eric Mower + Associates	USA
F&H Porter Novelli	Germany
Bite Communications 8	USA
Nelson Bostock Group	UK
Max Borges Agency	USA
Kaplow	USA
Hanover	UK
Approach	Brazil
M&C Saatchi Sport & Entertainment	UK
Wellcom	France
Davies	USA
Singer Associates	USA
Frank PR	UK
Catalyst	USA
The Hoffman Agency	USA
Merritt Group, Inc.	USA
Sobytie Communications	Russia
Veritas	Canada
Jeschenko MedienAgentur	Germany
Pegasus	UK
Exponent	USA
Eastwick	USA
3 Monkeys Communications	UK
124 Communications Consulting	Thailand
Advice A/S	Denmark
InkHouse	USA
TBWA/Corporate	France
M&C Saatchi PR	UK
Red Door Communications	UK
Lift World	Portugal
ReviveHealth	USA
Kwittken	USA
KPR & Associates	South Korea
Apple Tree Communications	Spain
Highwire	USA
Podesta Group	USA

(*Continued*)

Table 3.1 (Continued)

Spectrum	USA
FoodMinds	USA
PAN Communications	USA
JeffreyGroup	USA
Murphy O'Brien	USA
EMG	The Netherlands
Gregory FCA	USA
SenateSHJ	New Zealand
Octopus	UK
Airfoil Group	USA
Horn Group	USA
Enzaim Health	Republic of Korea
451 Marketing	USA
Dodge Communication	USA
Marco de Comunicacion	Spain
Nebo	USA
Lambert, Edwards & Associates	USA
Bliss Integrated Communications	USA
McNeely Pigott & Fox Public Relations	USA
Lou Hammond & Associates	USA
Bateman Group	USA
Englander Knabe & Allen	USA
Krichhoff Consult	Germany
salt	UK
Talk PR	UK
Imagem Corporativa	Brazil
360 Public Relations	USA
Excel Communications Management	Turkey
Narva	Sweden
Mischief	UK
RBB Public Relations, LLC	USA
Public Integrated Communications	USA
komm.passion	Germany
Eulogy!	UK
Fink & Fuchs Public Relations	Germany
Shine	UK
CP/compartner	Germany
Diplomat Communications	Sweden
LDWWgroup	USA
akkanto sa	Belgium
Yjoo	Switzerland
London Communications Agency	UK
W Communications	UK
Magna Carta	South Africa

Akima Media	Germany
Creative Crest	India
Threepipe Communications Limited	UK
Saxum	USA
Integral PR Services Pvt Limited	India
Seven Hills	UK
Cerrell Associates	USA
Just:Health	UK
Tangerine PR	UK
Bersay Communications Group	Turkey
Berkeley PR International	UK
All Channels	Bulgaria
Story Partners	USA
CooperKatz & Company, Inc.	USA
LC Williams & Associates	USA
cirkle	UK
Harvard	UK
Pretty Green	UK
Trigger Oslo	Norway
Rumeur Publique	France
Pro-Vision Communications	Russia
ikp	Austria
PLMR	UK
Het PR	Netherlands
RMA Comunicacao	Brazil
RockOrange	USA
GroundFloor Media	USA
Djembe Communications	UAE
The Whiteoaks Consultancy	UK
Hope&Glory	UK
Meropa Communications	South Africa
Bellenden	UK
Cambre Associates	Belgium
Lane	USA
Standing Partnership	USA
Intermarket Communications	USA
Walker Sands	USA
Tact Intelligence-conseil	Canada
Crossroads	USA
Whyte Corporate Affairs	Belgium
Agenda	USA
Cap & Cime PR	France
JMW kommunikation	Sweden
Rose	Russia

List courtesy of the Holmes Report.

Table 3.2 Regional and National Public Relations Associations

Country/Region	Organization
Africa	The African Public Relations Association (APRA)
Australia	Public Relations Institute of Australia
Austria	Public Relations Association of Austria/Public Relations Verband Austria (PRVA)
Bangladesh	Bangladesh Public Relations Association (BPRA)
Belgium	Belgium Association of Public Relations Consultancies (BGPRA)/Association Belge des Conseils en Relations Publiques
Brazil	Brazilian Public Relations Association/Associaçao Brasileira de Relacoes Publicas (ABRP)
Canada	Canadian Public Relations Society Inc. (CPRS)
China	Shanghai Public Relations Association
China	China International Public Relations Association (CIPRA)
Croatia	Croation Public Relations Association (HUOJ)
Cuba	National Committee of Public Relations from the Cuban Association of Social Communicators
Denmark	Danish Association of Communication Professionals
Denmark	Danish Association of Public Relations Consultancies (BPRV)
Estonia	Estonian Public Relations Association (EPRA)
Europe	European Public Relations Confederation (CERP)— Belgium
Europe	European Public Relations Education and Research Association (EUPRERA)—Belgium
Finland	ProCom, Finnish Association of Communications Professionals
France	SYNTEC Public Relations Consultants Organisation
France	Information Press & Communication
Germany	German Public Relations Consultancies Association (GPRA)
Germany	German Public Relations Society (DPRG)
Greece	Hellenic Association of Advertising-Communications Agencies
Gulf Cooperation Council Countries: Kuwait, Qatar, Bahrain, Oman, United Arab Emirates and Saudi Arabia	International Public Relations Association—Gulf chapter
Hong Kong, China	Hong Kong Public Relations Professionals' Association
Hungary	Hungarian Public Relations Association
Iceland	Public Relations Association of Iceland
India	Public Relations Consultants Association of India (PRCAI)
Indonesia	Public Relations Association of Indonesia (PERHUMAS)
Ireland	Public Relations Consultants Association of Ireland
Ireland	Public Relations Institute of Ireland (PRII)

Country/Region	Organization
Israel	Israel Public Relations Association
Kenya	Public Relations Society of Kenya (PRSK)
Latvia	Latvian Public Relations Association
Luxembourg	National Association of Public Relations of Luxembourg
Malaysia	Institute of Public Relations Malaysia
Netherlands	Logeion, Assocation for Communication
Netherlands	Netherlands Association of Public Relations Consultants (VPRA)
New Zealand	Public Relations Institute of New Zealand (PRINZ)
Norway	The Norwegian Communication Association
Philippines	Public Relations Society of the Philippines
Poland	Polish Public Relations Association
Poland	Polish Public Relations Consultancies Association
Puerto Rico	Association of Public Relations Professionals of Puerto Rico
Republic of Korea	Korea Public Relations Association (KPRA)
Russian Federation	Russian Public Relations Association (RPRA)
Serbia	Public Relations Society of Serbia
Singapore	Institute of Public Relations of Singapore
Slovak Republic	Association of Public Relations of the Slovak Republic
Slovenia	Public Relations Society of Slovenia
South Africa	Public Relations Institute of Southern Africa (PRISA)
Spain	Spanish Association of Communicators (DIRCOM)
Spain	Association of Public Relations Consultancies
Swaziland	Swaziland Public Relations Association (SPRA)
Sweden	Public Relations Consultancies in Sweden (PRECIS)
Sweden	Swedish Public Relations Association
Switzerland	Swiss Public Relations Association (SPRG)
Switzerland	Swiss Public Relations Institute
Taiwan, China	The Foundation for PR Research & Education
Taiwan, China	Chinese Public Relations Association
Thailand	Public Relations Association of Thailand
Trinidad & Tobago	Public Relations Association of Trinidad & Tobago
Turkey	Public Relations Consultancies Association (HDD)
Turkey	Turkish Public Relations Association (HID)
Uganda	Public Relations Association of Uganda (PRAU)
Ukraine	Ukrainian PR League (UPRL)
United Kingdom	Chartered Institute of Public Relations (CIPR)
United Kingdom	Public Relations Consultants Association (PRCA)
Uruguay	Uruguayan Association of Public Relations
USA	Arthur W. Page Society
USA	Council of Public Relations Firms
USA	Hispanic Public Relations Association
USA	Institute for Public Relations (IPR)
USA	National Schools Public Relations Association
USA	Public Relations Society of America (PRSA)
Zimbabwe	Zimbabwe Institute for Public Relations

List courtesy of the International Public Relations Association.

In short, there is no single answer for whether freelancers, full-time staff, local agencies, or global agencies will work best for you. You'll need to consider your budget, timeframe, workload, and goals carefully, and do your best to match them with the capabilities of a range of possible local partners.

Managing Your Global Team

Copyright: Dean Drobot

The previous section discussed how to hire your global team. Once you do, you'll need to manage them. One of the (many, many) challenges of managing a global public relations team is that sometimes your organization's communication staffers will not actually report to you. For example, when I worked for the United Nations Millennium Campaign, I worked for our organization's global Head of Communications in New York. However, communicators in the Campaign's country and regional offices around the globe reported to the heads of their local offices, rather than to the head of global communications. This meant that local priorities often prevailed. Under such circumstances, it takes extra skill to persuade your colleagues to provide the inputs you need at the global level and to coordinate with other communicators around the globe.

As the previous chapter discussed, people of different cultures around the world think and act very differently. Managing a global communication team therefore requires adapting much more than just your public relations strategies and messages. You also need to learn how to effectively lead, motivate, and provide feedback to people with extraordinarily different workplace practices and expectations. Here are some principles to help:

1 Use language that everyone can understand. Goldberg, of the Parallel Communications Group, says that it is important to ensure that you use inclusive language when speaking with your team. He explains that

> you want to be careful not to use local phrases that people in other countries may not understand—for example, saying that you struck out, which is a metaphor from baseball in the United States that people in other countries may or may not know.

Depending upon the level of fluency of the entire group in the language in which you are communicating, you also may need to speak more slowly and simplify your words (without being patronizing). For example, Samovar, Porter, McDaniel, and Roy (2013, p. 261) explain that speaking in a non-native language

> may require the second language speaker to mentally convert the received message into his or her native language, prepare a response in the native language, and then cognitively translate that response into the second language. If their second language vocabulary is limited, the cognitive demands are even greater. This difficulty is increased if the second language speaker is unfamiliar with the native speaker's accent.

This process can also be exhausting! Be cognizant of this if you are speaking in your native language to a non-native speaker.

2 Ask everyone for their ideas and offer multiple ways for them to submit their ideas to you. Liswood (2010, p. 50) notes that, in the U.S., the aphorism "the squeaky wheel gets the grease" implies that if a person speaks up at work, (s)he will get noticed and rewarded. By contrast, the Japanese say that "the nail that sticks out gets hit on the head," while in China it is said that "the loudest duck gets shot." Likewise, a Thai proverb states that "a wise man talks a little, an ignorant one talks much" (Samovar et al., 2013, p. 46). Therefore, Liswood (2010, p. 69) reports that

> in some cultures, people have to be asked to give their ideas, because this is what is considered the norm for them. They will respond with their ideas and thoughts once asked—but not before. This means that a manager cannot just let a discussion flow in a way that they view as natural; otherwise, the dominant groups will command all of the attention. The person leading a meeting, for example, needs to be aware of what is going on, and not immediately assume the others have nothing to say. They must act like a traffic cop, and say, "Let's hear from A; now let's hear from B; and hold on,

C, D, do you have anything to add?" This is an invitation to speak, and most will respond positively to it. If this approach isn't taken, however, the manager may unconsciously credit the dominant speakers with all of the good ideas. Then, when promotion time comes, the continually aggressive speaker has the advantage—even though they may not actually have the best ideas.

However, Liswood (2010, p. 71) also notes that, in some cultures, it is inappropriate to make off-the-cuff comments without deeply thinking about the question—so you should give people notice in advance of a meeting in which they will be called upon, so that they have time to prepare their ideas.

Still, not everyone will be comfortable speaking up in a meeting at all. Jennifer Stapper, the Bonn, Germany-based Chief of Communications for United Nations Volunteers, says that one of the first things she learned when she began leading her global communications team was that she needed to give people multiple ways of providing input. "Brainstorming is very important in communications, because it's not like accounting; you don't start with numbers," she says. She explains that

> I was very American in my approach when I first started. I had a flip chart and I would ask people to start shouting ideas out. I got silence. Eventually people started to warm up, but I realized that in order to get the full spectrum of different people's really good ideas, I needed to give them different outlets for sharing them with me. I would still do the conversation, but I would also tell people to feel free to put their ideas in writing or stop by. People who had said nothing in the brainstorming session would write novels of incredible ideas. You just have to remember to give them a deadline.

In her excellent book *The Culture Map: Breaking Through the Invisible Boundaries of Global Business*, Meyer (2014, p. 140) also suggests that, if you are working with a team of people who will not criticize the ideas of their boss, you ask your team to meet and brainstorm without you first and then report back on their ideas so that they do not defer to your proposals. Another option, which one IBM manager calls "popcorning," is to have everyone write their ideas on post-its and put them all on a board. Gilbert (2014) argues that "when you give voice to more people, the best ideas win, not the loudest ones."

3 Use low-context processes. As discussed in the previous chapter, high-context communicators leave much unspoken, while low-context communicators are more explicit. Meyer (2014, pp. 55–59) reports that the most misunderstandings occur not between high and low-context communicators, as we might expect, but rather between people from different high-context cultures—because they each assume that others are picking up on different subtle clues that are in fact foreign to them! She says that high-context communication works well when people are of the same culture, but when they're not, people simply cannot pick up on implicit meanings. Therefore, "there is just one easy strategy to remember: *Multicultural teams need low-context processes.*" Meyer recommends summarizing the key takeaways from each meeting and everyone's next steps, both orally and in writing. However, because high-context communicators may feel that you do not trust them (or believe they are very smart!) if you are so explicit, Meyer says that it is critical for you to explain the reason why you are doing so.

As for my U.N. colleagues who would not say no to me even when they had no intention of doing what I asked, Richard Lewis, founder of Richard Lewis Communications, advises,

> the way to handle this when you make your proposal is to point out to them that you understand that they wish to avoid negativity and, at the same time, you ask them to state clearly what their intentions are. I find this always works and they are grateful for your consideration.

4 Provide assignments with the level of background that your employees expect. Meyer (2014, p. 112) explains that

> in a *specific* culture when managing a supplier or team member, people usually respond well to receiving very detailed and segmented information about what you expect of each of them. If you need to give instructions to a team member from a specific culture, focus on what that person needs to accomplish. . . . In *holistic* cultures if you need to motivate, manage, or persuade someone, you will be more influential if you take the time to explain the big picture and show how all the pieces fit together.

5 Agree on your team's level of hierarchy. As discussed in the previous chapter, one of the big dimensions on which cultures differ is power distance. In a low power distance environment, it is acceptable to speak directly to a subordinate without approaching his or her boss, and in fact approaching the person's boss may send the signal that you do not trust him or her. By contrast, in a more hierarchical culture, it would be an affront to the boss not to be copied on emails to his or her subordinates. As with all other cultural differences, if you have a team of people from cultures with different levels of power distance, Meyer (2014, pp. 160, 239) advises discussing and agreeing upon protocols in advance.

6 Understand differences in how cultures set goals so that you can set and manage expectations accordingly. Judd (2013, p. 31) explains that

> "failure" is one term that is viewed differently depending upon the nationality of the speaker. In Asia, for instance, "failure" has very negative connotations. "In the U.S.," says . . . Fleming Voetmann [Head of Public

Affairs and Leadership Communication for the global manufacturer Danfoss], "people try to be very, very ambitious. It's not unusual to set yourself bold targets like going to the moon or Mars." Americans realize that "even if we don't go to Mars, it's a bold ambition, and a lot of good stuff might come out of it," he says. Different attitudes prevail elsewhere in the world. "In Asia, no one would make going to Mars a success criteria unless they were 100 percent sure they could get there," says Voetmann. "In some Asian cultures, you're not allowed to fail."

Be aware of whether members of your team are speaking in terms of aspirational or realistic goals. You will likely want to set a global standard for the whole team to follow.

7 Explain your style of providing feedback, provide feedback explicitly, and be sure to give the same amount of feedback to all team members. Liswood (2010, pp. 77, 143) advises that you should give each member of your staff opportunities to share his or her accomplishments and career goals with you. While this will likely influence your assessments of your colleagues, keep in mind that, as discussed in Chapter 2, cultural norms vary widely; in some cultures, people downplay their accomplishments to appear modest, while people from other cultures will sell themselves strongly in such situations. Do not let these cultural differences color your honest evaluations of the members of your team.

When evaluating your staff, be cognizant of the fact that different cultures have very different norms for how feedback should be provided. As Meyer (2014, p. 65) explains,

> the Chinese manager learns never to criticize a colleague openly or in front of others, while the Dutch manager learns always to be honest and to give the message straight. Americans are trained to wrap positive messages around negative ones, while the French are trained to criticize passionately and provide positive feedback sparingly.

If you come from a culture that provides feedback bluntly, doing so can be devastating to a colleague who is accustomed to more indirect messages. On the other hand, Meyer (2014, p. 78) says that the American approach to trying to provide positive feedback alongside the negative in order to take some of the sting out of it "to the French, Spanish, Russians, Dutch, and Germans . . . comes across as false and confusing."

Meyer therefore recommends explaining your style of communication before giving feedback to a colleague from a different culture. For example, a French manager might explain to an American employee, "When I say 'okay,' you should hear 'very good.' And when I say 'good,' you should hear 'excellent'" (Meyer, 2014, p. 82).

Overall, Meyer (2014, p. 81) recommends giving feedback explicitly and trying to give an even amount of positive and negative feedback over time.

However, she (2014, p. 72) warns that, if you are speaking to someone who is from a culture that provides more direct feedback than your own,

> *don't try to do it like them*. Even in the countries farthest to the direct side . . . it is still quite possible to be *too* direct. If you don't understand the subtle rules that separate what's appropriately frank from what is callously insensitive in [a particular] culture, then leave it to someone from that culture to speak directly. If you try to do it like them, you run the risk of getting it wrong, going too far, and making unintended enemies.

If you are giving feedback to a colleague who is not accustomed to receiving it directly, Meyer (2014, pp. 83–84) says that another strategy is "*blurring the message*" which involves providing "*the feedback slowly, over a period of time, so that it gradually sinks in.*" You can also focus on the positives, and hopefully your colleague will get the message that the areas or items that were not praised were not liked. For example, as one professional explained to Meyer (2014, p. 86),

> a while back, one of my Indonesian colleagues sent me a set of four documents to read and review. The last two documents he must have finished in a hurry, because they were very sloppy in comparison to the first two. When he called to ask for my reaction, I told him that the first two papers were excellent. I focused on these documents only, outlining *why* they were so effective. I didn't need to mention the sloppy documents, which would have been uncomfortable for both of us. He got the message clearly, and I didn't even need to bring up the negative aspects.

In particular, in collectivist societies, do not give feedback—positive or negative—in front of a group, as this would be humiliating to the recipient (Meyer, 2014, p. 83)—though, as Chapter 10 explains, in the Arab world, giving positive public feedback is generally appreciated, while it would hurt a person's pride to be given negative feedback publicly.

Of course, if you yourself are working for a manager who is from a culture that provides more direct feedback than your own, "accept their direct criticism in a positive manner. It is not meant to offend you" (Meyer, 2014, p. 73).

Finally and critically, be sure to give the same amount of feedback to all members of your team, because such information is vital to a staff member's ability to improve and advance in his or her career. Liswood (2010, pp. 84–85) reports that managers may subconsciously give less feedback (particularly less negative feedback) to people from other cultures, since

> critical feedback is especially tricky because we are telling someone potentially negative information. A manager tends to be fairly comfortable giving critical feedback to someone who is very much like him or her. This might mean that the manager can break the ice, find commonalities, or provide reassurance that will be appreciated, understood, and heard the way the manager intended. But that same person will feel awkward, uncomfortable,

and less skilled at providing feedback to a person who doesn't look like her, [and] dress like her. It is easy to understand this. If you are like the other, you are pretty sure you know how they will react—because you can imagine yourself in the situation and envision how you might respond. . . . If a manager is speaking to someone . . . who is *not* like them, however . . . The manager may be uncomfortable, or even worried. He could be asking himself whether the person sitting opposite him will misinterpret his comments, think he is sexist, racist, or has a beef with the employee's religion.

However, this is one of the challenges we must overcome in order to work as part of a cross-cultural team. Hopefully, using the strategies discussed here will help you become more comfortable with providing feedback to people whose approaches may differ from your own.

8 Provide everyone on your team with equal access to you and avoid favoring those who are similar to you. Liswood (2010, p. 142) explains that

while it is fine to play basketball with your employees and colleagues, be conscious of the fact that spending hours outside of the office with certain people means you will naturally get to know them well—while *not* getting to know the other members of your team. You will feel comfortable with your sports buddies, and when the next opportunity comes up, you may be inclined to put that companion forward for a promotion— possibly over someone better qualified whom you know less well, or with whom you have fewer common bonds. To keep the playing field level, the skilled manager needs to find ways to learn about the other members of the team so that an equal level of comfort and knowledge exists with the people who aren't naturally like you.

This is especially important—and will take some extra effort—when some members of your team work in different locations from you. Avoid favoring those who work in your own office simply because it is easier to get to know them better.

Also, avoid favoring those who are most similar to you. Liswood (2010, p. 95) warns that there may be less mentoring between people who are different from one another, because mentors don't immediately identify with such potential mentees. "If the mentor sees a version of himself when he was young in his new mentee, then he will react with more tolerance and enthusiasm," she explains. Don't fall into this trap.

Hyun and Lee (2014, p. 69) offer this advice for connecting with a colleague who appears to be dissimilar:

• Connect with a trait, communication pattern, or cultural dimension that you share.
• Search for a common interest, be it your shared love of music, sports, the arts, your alma mater, or the mission of the company.
• Discover a shared experience.

9 Find ways of building relationships and communicating that work for everyone. Weaver, of the Intercultural Management Institute, explains that "in the U.S. and northern Europe, we're visually oriented and we like words." Therefore, "we have a tendency to think that things should be put in writing as quickly as possible, and we don't hesitate to communicate in email or texting." By contrast, people in non-Western countries often communicate verbally rather than in writing. "They want to see and hear you, and be physically present so they can develop trust," he says. "This means that you have to spend a lot more face time together. And if you start putting things into written words too early, it raises alarms."

I learned this the hard way at the U.N., when my lengthy emails were met with radio silence by many of my foreign colleagues. Try to meet your colleagues in person as often as possible, and during such encounters make sure that there is "down time" for things like coffee or tea, rather than overscheduling your time with formal meetings. When you are not in person, Evan Kraus, an Executive Director at the global public affairs firm APCO, says that using video conferences rather than telephone calls can help foster connectedness and teambuilding (Judd, 2013, pp. 25–27).

10 Keep careful track of time zones and alternate coming in early or staying late for global conference calls. If your team is truly global, you will never all be in the office at the same time. For example, at 9:00 a.m. in New York, it will be 9:00 p.m. in Beijing. Therefore, the mere time of day that you schedule conference calls has power dimensions. Don't schedule them so that they are always convenient for the team at headquarters but have other colleagues consistently up early or in the office late. Instead, alternate the timing to shoulder the burden of early and late calls equally. This will demonstrate your respect for your team and inculcate the feeling that, when it comes to overcoming the challenges of working globally, you are all in it together.

Finally, this may appear to be rather obvious advice, but you will also need to be diligent to keep your time zones straight. I once lost out on an interview opportunity with the South African Broadcasting Corporation because the reporter, who was in the Central African Republic, told me to call her at a certain time, and I mistakenly looked up Central Africa Time. It turns out that the Central African Republic is not on Central Africa Time; by the time I called in, I was an hour late and had missed the program. Similarly, keep in mind that the number of hours of time difference between countries may actually change during the year, because not all countries observe daylight savings time. Double and triple check your time zone differences so that you don't miss important appointments.

11 Coordinate the timing of your messages. Keep careful track of when different local offices are planning to make announcements so that you can project a unified global identity and avoid competing with or sabotaging one another. For example, you will not want your team in India to announce a large number of layoffs on the same day that you announce the appointment of your new Chief Executive Officer from London, because the bad news will overshadow your big announcement. Likewise, you will want to time out dates on which you will communicate the same message or theme everywhere around the globe. Consider building a content calendar on a globally accessible intranet or shared drive.

12 Agree in advance how crises will be handled. As will be discussed in the chapters that follow, there are very different cultural approaches to handling crises. For example, Yu and Wen (2003, p. 54) explain that, in Chinese culture, people try to avoid "risky communication" because they "believe that talking about their problems may bring them even more problems in the future, so they are socialized to 'keep their mouths shut.'" This has led to cover-ups of major crises, which only further damages organizational reputations.

Harlan Loeb, Global Chair of Crisis and Risk Practice at Edelman, explains that "you need to create a context for interacting long before a crisis when you are dealing with conflicts of mindsets and backgrounds. Precisely the wrong time is when you're in panic mode." Agree with your team in advance on how potential future crises will be handled. Loeb advises that, when you are trying to convince a colleague or client to handle a crisis in a manner that goes against his or her natural inclinations, it helps to "find examples of past crises that mirror as closely as possible their circumstances, ideally in their country" and illustrate why the principles you are advocating for or against are sound.

Measuring and Evaluating Your Global PR Campaigns

Copyright: Jirsak

Finally, you will need to continually evaluate the impact of your team's work so that you can learn and improve. Measuring the impact of public relations efforts is notoriously difficult. As Gregory (2014) notes, assets such as relationships and reputations are intangible and therefore cannot be quantified. Furthermore, Grunig (2008, p. 110) reminds us that

> relationships save money by preventing costly issues, crises, regulation, litigation, and bad publicity. It is not possible, however, to determine the cost of something that *did not happen* or even to know that the negative event or behavior *would have happened* in the absence of excellent public relations.

Although the subject of public relations measurement and evaluation requires a book unto itself (I recommend *Evaluating Public Relations: A Guide to Planning, Research and Measurement* by Tom Watson and Paul Noble), here is a quick crash course:

Setting Your Objectives

Of course, before you begin any public relations activity, you should identify your objectives so that they guide your work and so that you can later measure your impact against them. Ideally, your objectives should be informed by research on current stakeholder attitudes towards your organization or on your issue (which you can measure through polls, surveys, interviews, or focus groups). Stacks and Bowen (2011, p. 2) note that, in contrast to a goal, which is "a broad idea of what you would like to happen," an objective "is a clearly defined statement that includes an action statement (a verb), a timeline and a measurable outcome (usually expressed as a percentage)." For example, your objective may be to increase awareness of your product by 15 percent in a specified region by the end of the year. Watson and Noble (2014, pp. 127–128) advise that your objectives should be SMARRTT: **S**pecific, **M**easurable, **A**chievable, **R**ealistic, **R**elevant to the task at hand, **T**argeted to the audiences you seek to reach, and **T**imed.

Evaluating the Outcomes of Your Programs

Grunig (2008, pp. 105–106) notes that you can use five measures to evaluate the impact of your communication programs: **Exposure** indicates your reach. For example, how many people visited your website, read an article, or attended your event? This can be measured through website analytics, surveys of readers, or attendance numbers, for example. Of course, equally important when assessing your exposure is whether you are reaching the *right* people. As a practitioner, you will have multiple stakeholders whom you seek to influence. If you work for a company, these publics may include your customers, the people in the communities in which you operate, suppliers, employees (and even potential staffers), shareholders, investors, government regulators, consumer and other social advocates, and perhaps a board of directors. If you work for a government, your intended audiences will include not just the domestic citizens who (hopefully) elect their leaders, but also the international business community that will decide whether or not to invest in your country, foreign governments that will determine whether or not to provide you with aid or cooperate with you on global issues, and people around the world who you want to lure to visit your country, pumping valuable dollars (or yuan, or rupees) into your tourism industry. Are your messages reaching *these* people?

The second measure, **retention of messages**, indicates whether people remember what you tried to convey. Third, **cognition** indicates whether people understand and learn from your messages. Fourth, **attitude** refers to whether your audience not only hears and understands your message, but also views it favorably and intends to act in a manner that is consistent with your message. Finally, **behavior** indicates whether your stakeholders are behaving differently as a result of your message. The latter four indicators can be measured using surveys or questionnaires. Consider pre-testing your messages to learn whether they will be effective on these last four dimensions before using them.

In the past, clips of media coverage were often used to measure public relations impact. The Barcelona Declaration of Media Principles, adopted by the International Association for the Measurement and Evaluation of Communication in 2010, affirmed that advertising value equivalencies (a heavy-handed attempt to calculate what earned media would have cost if it were paid for as advertising) emphatically "do not measure the value of public relations" (AEMC, 2012). To evaluate the impact of media coverage, you will need to conduct a content analysis of the coverage. Watson and Noble (2014, pp. 77–78) note that, in a media content analysis, when selecting criteria for evaluation, you can use a mnemonic called IMPACT:

Influence or tone
Message communicated
Prominence
Audience reached
Consultant/ spokesman quoted
Type of article

In order of importance, the letters could be reorganized as M (Message communicated), A (Audience reached), T (Type of article), C (Consultant/ spokesman quoted), I (Influence or Tone), and P (Prominence).

Still, as discussed, you would need to conduct primary research to determine whether the messages conveyed in the media coverage were actually read by and impacted your target audience, since

> press clippings and broadcast monitor reports, all available from commercial services . . . indicate only what is being printed or broadcast, *not* what is read or heard. And they *do not* measure whether or not the audiences learned or believed message content (Watson & Noble, 2014, p. 53).

Finally, when evaluating your social media impact, Watson and Noble (2014, pp. 147–154) advise focusing on four measures: First, **exposure**, **reach**, and **impressions** indicate who you are reaching. Walter and Gioglio (2014, p. 130) note that you can look at the "virality" of your Facebook posts on the platform's page analytics—or calculate this yourself by taking the number of likes, comments, and shares garnered by a particular post and dividing the sum by the total impressions the post received. Walter and Gioglio (2014, p. 130) also advise that you can measure your impact on Twitter by computing "the number of replies and retweets divided by your number of followers that day multiplied by 100." When using data from a site, make sure that you understand how it is being calculated. For example, Cassandra Olivos, Senior Social Media Account Analyst at Driven Local, a New York-based firm that develops social media campaigns, says, "it's important to remember that the way a video 'view' is counted on Facebook is not equivalent to a 'view' on YouTube, because each platform tallies things differently. Different amounts of seconds count as a play."

Second, **engagement**, **sentiment**, and **tone** focus on how people are responding to your messages and communicating about your organization on social media. Paine (2011, p. 79) notes that

> engagement is a way to determine whether you are having a dialog, or you are just yelling ever more loudly. . . . Engagement produces brand advocates, the proverbial "people like me" (PLM), that these days have much more influence and credibility than corporations. These are the folks who broadcast their enthusiasm for your brand to their friends.

Watson and Noble (2014, p. 150) offer some examples:

> Examples of low level engagement include Facebook likes, Twitter followers, and clicks on "read more" links. Equivalent medium-level engagement examples are Facebook comments, Twitter retweets, and time spent viewing content. Finally, high level engagement is exemplified by Facebook shares (including e-mail), Twitter @mentions or #hashtags, and downloads.

The third set of social media metrics, **influence**, **respect**, and **relevance**, focus on whether and what key influencers are communicating about your organization on social media. Finally, **action**, **impact**, and **value** focus on the financial impact of the engagement you have achieved.

Evaluating Your Relationships

Of course, the ultimate goal of public relations practice is cultivating positive relationships with your stakeholders. Hon and Grunig (1999, pp. 18–20) report that you can use four indicators to measure your relationships with key constituencies: **Control mutuality** refers to "the degree to which parties agree on who has rightful power to influence one another." Hon and Grunig (1999, p. 18) explain that "for the most stable, positive relationship, organizations and publics must have some degree of control over the other." **Trust** refers to "one party's level of confidence in and willingness to open oneself to the other party." **Satisfaction** refers to "the extent to which one party feels favorably toward the other because positive expectations about the relationship are reinforced." Finally, **commitment** refers to "the extent to which one party believes and feels that the relationship is worth spending energy to maintain and promote." You can use research methods including interviews, focus groups, and surveys to identify how your stakeholders perceive your organization on these dimensions.

Evaluating Your Reputation

Because the concept of reputation is so amorphous, it is perhaps the hardest to evaluate. One way to do it is to ask people—in interviews, focus groups, or surveys—"what comes to mind when they hear the name of" your organization (Grunig, 2008, p. 109).

Now that you're prepared to hire, manage, and evaluate your team, you're ready to get to work! The next three chapters will discuss how to conduct global public relations on behalf of three very different types of clients: corporations, non-profit organizations, and governments.

References

Appelbaum, L., Belmuth, G. S., & Schroeder, K. (2011). Global corporate communication. In J. Doorley & H. F. Garcia (Eds.), *Reputation management: The key to successful public relations and corporate communication* (2nd ed.) (pp. 228–257). New York, NY: Routledge.

Bloomberg, M. (1997). *Bloomberg by Bloomberg.* New York, NY: John Wiley & Sons.

Capozzi, L. (2015). Public relations consulting: Consulting and corporate communication— the nexus. In J. Doorley & H. F. Garcia, *Reputation management: The keys to successful public relations and corporate communication* (3rd ed.) (pp. 357–376). New York, NY: Routledge.

Gilbert, P. (2014, December 7). Hearing every voice in the room. *The New York Times.* Retrieved from http://www.nytimes.com/2014/12/07/jobs/how-ibm-brings-ideas-forward-from-its-teams.html?_r=0

Gregory, A. (2014). Foreword. In T. Watson & P. Noble (Eds.), *Evaluating public relations: A guide to planning, research and measurement* (3rd ed.). Philadelphia, PA: Kogan Page.

Grunig, J. E. (2008). Conceptualizing quantitative research in public relations. In B. Van Ruler, A. Tkalac Verčič, & D. Verčič (Eds.), *Public relations metrics: Research and evaluation* (pp. 88–119). New York, NY: Routledge.

Hon, L. C., & Grunig, J. E. (1999). *Guidelines for measuring relationships in public relations.* Institute for Public Relations. Retrieved from http://www.instituteforpr.org/wp-content/uploads/Guidelines_Measuring_Relationships.pdf

Hyun, J., & Lee, A. S. (2014). *Flex: The new playbook for managing across differences.* NewYork, NY: Harper Business.

International Association for Measurement and Evaluation of Communication (AMEC) (2012, June 20). Barcelona declaration of measurement principles. Retrieved from http://amecorg.com/2012/06/barcelona-declaration-of-measurement-principles/

Judd, E. (2013). *Building and managing a global public affairs function.* Washington, DC: Foundation for Public Affairs. Retrieved from http://pac.org/wp-content/uploads/Building-and-Managing-a-Global-PA-Function.pdf

Liswood, L. (2010). *The loudest duck: Moving beyond diversity while embracing differences to achieve success at work.* Hoboken, NJ: John Wiley & Sons.

Meyer, E. M. (2014). *The culture map: Breaking through the invisible boundaries of global business.* New York, NY: PublicAffairs.

Paine, K. D. (2011). *Measure what matters: Online tools for understanding customers, social media, engagement, and key relationships.* Hoboken, NJ: John Wiley & Sons.

Samovar, L. A., Porter, R. E., McDaniel, E. R., & Roy, C. S. (2013). *Communication between cultures* (8th ed.). Boston, MA: Cengage Learning.

Stacks, D. W., & Bowen, S. A. (2011). The strategic approach: Writing measurable objectives. In *Charting your PR measurement strategy* (pp. 2–4). Institute for Public Relations. Retrieved from http://www.instituteforpr.org/wp-content/uploads/Master-PR-Tactics-document-08–10–16.pdf

Surowiecki, J. (2005). *The wisdom of crowds.* New York, NY: Anchor Books.

Walter, E., & Gioglio, J. (2014). *The power of visual storytelling: How to use visuals, videos, and social media to market your brand.* New York, NY: McGraw Hill Education.

Watson, T., & Noble, P. (2014). *Evaluating public relations: A guide to planning, research and measurement.* Philadelphia, PA: Kogan Page.

Yu, T. H., & Wen, W. C. (2003). Crisis communication in Chinese culture: A case study in Taiwan. *Asian Journal of Communication, 13*(2), 50–64.

4 Global Public Relations for Corporations

Chris Nelson, Crisis Lead for the Americas at FleishmanHillard, once worked with a client that needed to recall the batteries in millions of mobile phones worldwide. It was one of the largest consumer electronics recalls in history. In India, where those phones were many people's only means of telecommunications, consumers lined up down the street to swap out their batteries, despite the fact that the batteries posed an almost immeasurably small risk of overheating. At one Indian store, when consumers learned that it would be a week or more before a new shipment of batteries arrived, they rioted and eventually attacked and killed the phone manufacturer's store manager.

"I have spent a career being paid to anticipate scenarios and how crises will unfold, but in this situation it never occurred to me that someone—let alone a company employee—might end up dead," Nelson recalls. "That is why it's critical to understand cultural nuances in any market in which you're delivering sensitive messages and to fully appreciate the experiences of those affected by a crisis in the context of that culture."

Hopefully this story convinces you of the need for culturally appropriate corporate messages. This chapter discusses how to practice global public relations on behalf of corporations. First, I will discuss how to engage meaningfully with local peoples before you begin operating in a new location. Second, I will explain how to conduct a local public relations audit in order to assess the factors you will need to take into account when crafting a public relations strategy in a new market. Third, I will discuss how to practice global corporate social responsibility. Fourth, I will review how to position your brand in new markets, depending upon how local people perceive your brand, product category, and the ideals associated with your product, as well as the mood of the nation. Finally, I will explain two global public relations tactics that work particularly well for corporations: harnessing global events and issuing global reports.

Listening Before You Leap

Before your company begins doing business in a new environment, you will need to introduce your organization to the community. The first thing that you absolutely must do before beginning your operations is sit down and listen to members of the community. Eunice Lima, the São Paulo, Brazil-based Director

of Communications and Government Affairs for the global aluminum company Novelis, says that "companies are used to talking more than listening, and that's when you see the problems. For a company to do business here, the first action is to listen to relevant stakeholders."

Keep in mind that different communities have very different expectations for how you should engage with them. As Motion, Haar, and Leitch (2012, p. 57) explain,

> identifying how to communicate and engage with indigenous people may . . . be challenging for those who are unaccustomed to stepping outside Western cultural perspectives. Common problems may be as basic as not being able to identify whom to communicate with or how indigenous cultural groups are organised. For example, during a public policy engagement process, public relations practitioners wishing to communicate with Maori [the indigenous people of New Zealand] will not find one single individual who represents the community. Depending upon the issue involved, they will need to engage with a number of social groupings including traditional tribal affiliations, community groups, urbanised individuals or members of indigenous organisations and corporations.

Your best bet is therefore to work with someone who has experience engaging with the local community and can act as an ambassador for you. For example, David Lian, General Manager of the Zeno Group in Malaysia, helps businesses working in Malay communities form relationships with local peoples. Lian says that, in Malay communities, it is important to engage with the head of the Kampung, or village. "Being Asian, we respect our elders," Lian says. "The head villager is usually 60 or 70 years old, so he commands a lot of respect in his community. Normally, you come with a gift, accept his hospitality, and then make the ask."

Lian says that when he and his colleagues promoted a telecommunications company in a local village, they often organized a *jamuan*—a Malay word for a feast—by inviting about ten villagers to dinner at a local restaurant. "In exchange for the food you give them, they sit down and answer your questions," he says. After learning more about one village, his agency organized a carnival on behalf of their telecommunications client, in order to introduce their brand to local people at the event. Lian recalls that "the insight was that, being a village, they didn't have a lot of entertainment and they enjoy the simple things of life, like a carnival."

Of course, Lian gained this insight by listening. You will need to resist the urge to use such consultations to try to build support for decisions that you have already made. First of all, such efforts to engage superficially are usually rather transparent. As Motion, Haar, and Leitch (2012, p. 59) explain, in the case of New Zealand's indigenous people, "consultation has not always been a positive or productive experience . . . in many cases it has been perceived as an exploitative, superficial attempt to comply with legislation rather than an attempt to genuinely engage with Maori and co-produce solutions." Especially if you work for a multinational behemoth and are conducting consultations in poor, rural communities, be aware of the power differential and unequal resources in your relationship and work extra hard to communicate respect for your interlocutors and ensure that they have an equal voice in your conversations.

By engaging in two-way dialogue from the outset, you can gain the kinds of insights into local communities that made Lian's strategy a success. You can also head off potential conflict and opposition. For example, Mago (2012, p. 17) reports that, in Nigeria's Niger Delta where multinational corporations extract oil, companies "work with the government to deploy heavily armed soldiers to quell community protests that could have been handled through simple explanations, respect, dialogue and relationship building."

One valuable thing that you will learn through engaging in such two-way communication is local social expectations of your business. These vary significantly in different communities around the world. For example, as I will discuss in Chapter 11, in Latin America, members of local communities will not hesitate to ask corporations to build roads or schools for them—activities that in other nations would be seen as strictly within the government's purview. It is therefore critical for you to learn about local customs and demands *before* you enter a new community so that you can set yourself up to meet—and hopefully exceed—local expectations.

Just as you will need to learn about your new neighbors, they will also be eager to appraise you. Local reactions to your presence may be influenced by both stereotypes of your home country as well as by (often well-founded) fears that you will remove valuable resources from the country. Rodrigo Soares, General Manager of Communications at Vale, the Brazilian mining company, recalls that after Vale purchased Canada's largest mining company, "a local newspaper published a picture of a Brazilian woman in Carnival, exposing the stereotype they had about us." Soares says that the firm tried to combat this impression by stressing that they would be working in collaboration with locals instead of trying to impose a Brazilian way of doing business in Canada. Be sure to emphasize from the outset that you are committed to working with your new community to find locally appropriate and responsible ways of doing business.

Of course, you will need to allow plenty of time to find local partners and engage in such processes of consultation and two-way communication with local communities before your organization begins operating in a new environment. This will often require patience, flexibility, stepping outside your comfort zone, and departures from your typical ways of engaging stakeholders. For example, as Motion, Haar, and Leitch (2012, p. 62) note,

> within Maori culture, a *hui* or meeting adopts a consensus-based approach to decision making: differences of opinion are aired and discussed until a consensus is reached. . . . Engagement may thus be a lengthy process. However, such an engagement process would be viewed as culturally acceptable to Maori, who are thus more likely to perceive the engagement process (and those undertaking it) in a favorable light, irrespective of the actual outcome.

In other words, building respectful, productive relationships in the local communities in which you work will require significant investments at the outset of your entry into each new market. However, doing so effectively will pay invaluable dividends over the long term, in the form of strong community relations and insights to guide your local public relations strategies.

Performing Local Audits

Copyright: Bacho

When entering a new market, you should also conduct a local audit to inform your local public relations strategy. I recommend that you start by answering the following questions:

- What local regulations do we need to follow? For example, Appelbaum, Belmuth, and Schroeder (2011, p. 245) note that

  U.S. regulatory guidelines allow pharmaceutical companies to cre-ate messages raising awareness about a medical condition and advis-ing consumers to see their doctors and to ask about a drug by name, whereas British regulatory guidelines cannot direct the consumer to ask for a drug explicitly by name.

- How will our work in this new market benefit the local community or country? For example, are we making significant local investments and/or creating jobs? Bringing valuable new products or services to the market? How can we tell this story?
- What fears or concerns will members of the community have about our operations in this location? How can I proactively address them?
- How are businesses from my country and in my industry perceived in the local community? As every public relations practitioner knows, "percep-tions are facts because people believe them" (Hayes, 1989, p. 432). How can I disabuse the community of any false or negative stereotypes and harness positive views of my company's industry and country of origin as part of our public relations strategy?
- What pre-existing relationships, if any, do we have with local govern-ment officials who will be critical to our ability to operate in this com-munity? How can we build and strengthen them?
- What geopolitical and local developments stand to impact our ability to do business here? For example, could exchange rate fluctuations, proposals such as new trade agreements, or regulations such as tariffs and restrictions on foreign businesses impact our company? If so, how can we craft a public relations strategy to influence the debate about such issues in our favor?
- What pre-existing relationships, if any, do we have with influencers in the community? How can we build and strengthen them?
- What pre-existing relationships, if any, do we have with members of the media in the community? How can we build and strengthen them?
- What pre-existing relationships, if any, do we have with civil society groups in the community? How can we build and strengthen them?
- Will our work attract the attention of local activist groups? How can we build positive relationships with them?
- Is bribery a common problem here? (Check Transparency International's Global Corruption Barometer at www.transparency.org to find out.) What can we do to ensure that the legitimate purposes of any payments we make are clearly documented so that we are not accused of paying bribes?
- How are other organizations conducting public relations campaigns in this market? What can we learn from their successes and failures?

- What types of public relations strategies, tactics, and messages are our competitors implementing in this market? What can we do to stand apart?
- What do I understand about the local culture from this book and from my company's research and local partners? (See Chapter 2 as well as the regional and national profiles in Chapters 8–12). How should we adapt our public relations practices and workplace behavior accordingly?
- Is my organization facing criticism in other parts of the world that we will need to address in this new market?

Of course, you will also want to ask a lot of questions about your company's practices to ensure that you are having a positive social and environmental impact on your host community. This will be discussed in the next section and will be a critical component of your public relations efforts. For now, however, the above questions can begin to guide your initial communication and relationship-building strategy in each new market.

While you should primarily be focused on assessing the local environment, you should also be prepared for any issues that your organization is facing in other markets to pop up in your new location. For example, Molleda (2010, p. 683) notes that when U.S. mega-retailer Walmart opened a discount store called Bodega Aurrera less than two miles from the historic pyramids of Teotihuacán in Mexico, "in general, Mexican consumers and government officials were supportive of the new supermarket because it brought competitive prices, quality products and services, a convenient location, and sponsored social and cultural programs." However, activists in the U.S. criticized the opening of the store so close to an important heritage site as a way of building support for their fight against the expansion of Walmart into communities in their own country. With rapid responses from spokespeople at both the local and global levels, Wal-Mart was able to successfully diffuse the opposition. However, the story goes to show that you should be prepared for your opponents to follow you around the world. This is one reason why it is so important for your international public relations team to have strong internal communications, so that colleagues apprise one another of local issues that could go global. (It is also why every member of your communication team, everywhere in the world, must be stellar, because a poorly handled issue in one location can quickly become a problem for everyone else.) The following chapter, which will explain the strategies and tactics used by modern global activists, is also a must-read for corporate practitioners, so that you can anticipate and be prepared to respond to any such campaigns. However, the best line of defense against criticism is reputable business practices communicated effectively.

To be sure, the answers to the above questions will always be changing. Therefore, your work as a public relations practitioner will never be done. In every community in which you work, you should use the above questions to guide your ongoing "environmental scanning"—which Dozier and Ehling (1992, p. 176) define as "remaining sensitive to 'what's going on out there.'" By doing so, you can capitalize on opportunities to improve your communications and relationships and identify and address issues before they become full-fledged crises. A critical part of doing so will also be practicing corporate social responsibility—the subject to which I will now turn.

Practicing Corporate Social Responsibility

Copyright: ClawsAndPaws

As previously discussed, communities have different social expectations of businesses, and you will need to learn about them before you begin working in a new location. However, people around the globe all expect modern companies to be good neighbors—or, in other words, to practice corporate social responsibility (colloquially called "CSR"). A 2015 study found that nine out of ten consumers around the world expect businesses to not just make a profit, but also "operate responsibly to address social and environmental issues" (Cone Communications, 2015). Practicing corporate social responsibility entails not just ensuring that your business does not harm local communities, but also proactively making your community—and the world—a better place.

Corporate social responsibility is good for a company's bottom line because it grants the company a "license to operate" from the community. As Burke (1999, p. xiv) explains, companies "that are positioned favorably in the community are treated differently and respectfully. Time and expense needed to obtain permits are shorter and cheaper. Mistakes that happen are given the benefit of the doubt." Ultimately, corporate social responsibility fosters trust within the communities in which you operate. As Burke (1999, p. 24) notes,

> when there is trust, there is respect, a willingness to take someone's expressions and actions at their face value. There are no suspicions, no hidden agendas. Problems and difficulties can be worked out. People who trust each other understand that mistakes can happen, that people will work to correct the mistakes.

Corporate social responsibility also drives sales. A study of 30,000 consumers in 60 countries recently found that citizens around the world are willing to pay more to purchase products and services from businesses that are committed to having a positive environmental and social impact. "Consumers around the world are saying loud and clear that a brand's social purpose is among the factors that influence purchase decisions," says Amy Fenton, Global Leader of Public Development and Sustainability at Nielsen. "This behavior is on the rise and it provides opportunities for meaningful impact in our communities, in addition to helping to grow share for brands" (Nielsen, 2014). Consumers in emerging markets such as India, China, and Brazil are especially likely to seek out products that are made responsibly and to switch to brands that support social causes (Cone Communications, 2015).

Practicing corporate social responsibility will also help you attract top talent. Sixty-two percent of global consumers report that they would work for a business that is socially and environmentally responsible even if it required accepting a lower salary (Cone Communications, 2015).

However, corporate social responsibility requires thinking about more than just dollars and cents. While businesses in the past focused on the "bottom line"—that is, profits—today, Elkington (1998) argues that corporations must focus on the "triple bottom line," which includes their profits as well as their environmental and social impacts. Focusing on your organization's "environmental bottom line" requires evaluating your effects on the planet. Some questions you should ask for every market in which you operate are:

- Are we in compliance with all local environmental regulations? If not, how can we immediately come into compliance? Can we improve upon these minimum standards?
- Are we receiving public complaints about our environmental practices? What do the complaints allege? Are they true? How can we improve our practices?
- Do our operations create hazards to the environment and/or the health of human and animal life, such as harmful pollutants, waste, litter, and noise? How can we eliminate these hazards?
- Are we consuming large quantities of critical natural resources, such as water and energy? How can we reduce our consumption?
- How do our practices compare with best practices and standards advocated by environmental experts and civil society and practiced by industry leaders? How can we meet and exceed these standards?

Focusing on your "social bottom line" requires assessing the impact of your business on society. Some questions you should ask for every community in which you operate are:

- What impact does our organization have on local employees, organizations, and people? Do we hire members of the communities in which we operate and support local businesses? How can we have a more positive social impact?

- Is our business trusted by members of the community? If not, what can we do to earn the community's trust? How can we improve our relationships with members of the community?
- Do we contribute in any way to government regimes which oppress their people or politicians whose practices are ethically questionable? How can we rectify this immediately?
- Are all products that we produce safe for human use? Can we make them safer? Are they tested without harming humans, animals, or the environment? If not, how can we fix this immediately?
- Are all of our marketing claims and other communications completely and fully accurate? Do we proactively, clearly, and fully inform our customers/clients of any possible risks associated with our products and services? How can we improve?
- Where do the raw materials that we use come from? Are they obtained ethically—by our company or by the corporation(s) from which we procure them?
- Are employee wages fair? Are working conditions safe, fair, and conducive to work-life balance? How can we improve them?
- Are our hiring practices fair? Do we employ a diverse workforce, including women and minorities? How can we improve our practices to ensure inclusivity? How can we create more opportunities for our current employees to grow?
- What is the current level of "human capital" in the communities in which we operate? How can we help to improve the education, skills, and health of local peoples—which, in addition to supporting our community, will also ensure that we are able to hire the skilled workforce we need over the long term?
- How do we help improve our community through corporate social responsibility initiatives such as charitable donations and volunteerism? Can we do more? How?
- Is our organization prepared for any type of natural disaster or emergency that might strike our local community? Will we be able to protect our employees and avoid harming our neighbors in such an event? Are there ways in which we can be better prepared to help others who will be in need during such a situation?

The answers to these questions will likely help you identify needed changes. A good place to start your corporate social responsibility practice is by establishing a code of conduct that your entire organization will follow. As Ewing (2011, p. 343) notes, "a code of conduct communicates minimum standards for employees, suppliers, or business partners. Codes also convey messages to corporate stakeholders generally." Another way to signal that your company behaves ethically is to seek certification from an external validator. For example, your organization can join the United Nations Global Compact. Members of the Compact are required to abide by ten principles that focus on human rights, labor, the environment, and fighting corruption. They are als, required to advocate publicly for the Compact and its principles and to submit an annual report on their progress, which is public. You can likewise have your company certified as fair trade by the organization FLOCERT or by Fair Trade USA, if you meet standards such as paying fair wages to workers and ensuring worker safety and the protection of the environment.

As previously discussed, corporate social responsibility entails much more than simply avoiding harm. It also requires proactively undertaking initiatives that have a positive social impact. For example, Unilever—the global corporation that sells consumer goods in more than 190 countries—reports reaching 183 million people around the world with its programs that promote handwashing. Proper handwashing is the most cost-effective way to prevent diarrhea, which kills 2.1 million children around the world annually. In the village of Thesgora in Madhya Pradesh, India, for example, Unilever reports that its handwashing campaign—which included a film shown locally in the community—resulted in a drop in the incidence of diarrhea from 36 percent to 5 percent. The company has now launched this campaign in Bangladesh, Brazil, Egypt, Ghana, India, Indonesia, Kenya, Malaysia, Nigeria, Pakistan, South Africa, Sudan, Uganda, and Vietnam—and credits it with saving lives. Of course, the campaign has also boosted sales of Unilever's health soap, Lifebuoy. The company reports that "Lifebuoy's handwashing programmes are not only helping to change habits to combat disease. . . . They are also driving volume growth in key markets. Lifebuoy has achieved three years of double-digit growth to become the world's number one anti-bacterial brand" (Unilever, 2014).

A scene from the film Gondappa, which Lifebuoy used to promote handwashing with soap as part of the brand's campaign called "Help A Child Reach 5." Photo courtesy of Unilever

host of global issues that you can choose to tackle as part of
rate social responsibility initiatives—including global poverty,
nt, diseases, education, global conflict, or the empowerment of
ls. As the Unilever campaign shows, the causes your organiza-
hould tie in with your identity in some way. Any time that you
attempt to communicate brand values, however, you need to be sure that they
will feel authentic to your audiences. If your organization is owned by a larger
parent company, you should also ensure that your messages do not conflict
with those of the parent company's other brands.

For example, one of Unilever's other soap brands, Dove, implemented a widely
acclaimed global "Campaign for Real Beauty" to send the message that women
of all shapes and sizes are beautiful and to help women and girls overcome their
insecurities about their bodies. While the campaign garnered a lot of praise for
its message, many critics noted that it blatantly contradicted the messages being
sent by another Unilever brand: Axe. As Austen-Smith, Galinsky, Chung, and
LaVanway (2012) note, "in stark contrast, Unilever's Axe brand of men's toilet-
ries upheld . . . stereotypes, with slick, often sexually explicit ads featuring young,
scantily clad, conventionally attractive women and promising that the deodor-
ants and body sprays would 'give men the edge in the mating game.'"

Critics argued that Dove's parent company relied on the same stereotypes that the
Campaign for Real Beauty sought to combat in order to sell Axe deodorant to men.
Copyright: Robcartorres

The Unilever campaigns for Lifebuoy and Dove also illustrate the diverse
forms that corporate social responsibility initiatives can take. Such initiatives
can include donating money to charities, donating products to poor communities, engaging your employees in volunteer efforts, or undertaking prosocial

public relations campaigns to influence behaviors or attitudes. Another option is to partner with non-profit organizations. For example, the U.N. Millennium Campaign, which promoted the world's plan for ending poverty at the time, partnered with U.S. ice cream maker Ben & Jerry's, which printed messages about combatting global poverty on select ice cream cartons. When I worked for the Campaign, we also partnered with the global fashion brand G-Star RAW, which included messaging about global poverty in their fashion show during New York Fashion Week in 2008. Be creative: the possibilities are endless!

Of course, before you formalize any partnership, you will need to carefully vet your potential partner in order to ensure that your company fully agrees with the organization's philosophy and mode of operation and that your potential partner does not have donors or positions with which you would not want to be associated. Your potential partner will be doing the same type of assessment of your company: proactively provide the information they need. The trick to making such partnerships work is to be clear about expectations on both sides from the beginning. It will help to draft a Memorandum of Understanding that both you and a representative of your partner organization sign, clearly laying out each party's rights and responsibilities under your agreement.

As always, be sure that your corporate social responsibility initiatives are culturally appropriate. As previously discussed, social expectations of businesses differ dramatically in different parts of the world. For example, Mago (2012, pp. 115–116) argues that one reason for the poor relationship between oil companies and the local peoples of the Niger Delta is that "the [multinational corporations] failed to ask what was important to the communities they were operating in, which was a critical error because what motivates CSR in a developing country such as Nigeria is quite different from in Europe and North America." Start by understanding the culture and the needs and expectations of local peoples so that you can tailor your local corporate social responsibility initiatives accordingly.

Once you do undertake corporate social responsibility initiatives, make sure that you communicate your positive impact effectively. More than half of global consumers report that they will assume that a business is not acting responsibly unless they hear information to the contrary (Cone Communications, 2015). Furthermore, these days, citizens expect greater transparency from organizations (Elkington, 1998, p. 7). This is why, today, the vast majority of the world's biggest companies publish non-financial reports about their triple bottom lines. The Global Reporting Initiative (GRI) provides a framework—used by companies such as Nike and Starbucks—which you can use to report on your corporate social responsibility practices (Ewing, 2011, pp. 345–346). Be vocal about how you protect and contribute to your community and the world. This should be a key component of any public relations strategy.

Now that you are prepared to engage responsibly with stakeholders in your new market, we can begin to think more broadly about how you will position your brand within it.

Crafting Your Identity

Another thing you will need to think about when you work in a new country or culture is how you will present your company to local consumers. In order to answer this question, you should begin by considering what type of brand you are. According to Research International, consumers place global brands into three categories: "Prestige brands" have large price tags and are strongly associated with their nations of origin. For example, BMW automobiles are valued because they are made in Germany. "Master brands," such as Nike and Coca-Cola, are the best known and most successful in their categories, but they are not necessarily valued for their country of origin. "GloCal brands" are global brands that are positioned as local wherever they are sold (Clegg, 2005, p. 43).

BMW is a "prestige brand" valued for its German engineering. Copyright: servickuz

If you are working for a prestige brand, you will want to communicate your country of origin as part of your brand identity. Numerous studies find that consumers view a product's country of origin as an indicator of its quality or attributes, particularly when they have little other knowledge about the product—a phenomenon known as "country equity" (Kotler & Gertner, 2002, p. 252; Shimp, Samiee, & Madden, 1993, p. 327). Consumers use country images "as shortcuts for information processing"—assuming, for example, that wines from Italy or electronics from Japan will be of high quality—and will often pay more for products from industrialized countries (Kotler & Gertner, 2002, pp. 250–251). Leclerc, Schmitt, and Dubé (1994) report that when products are perceived as hedonic, consumers prefer those with French names and evaluate them more positively than those with English names. On the other hand, consumers may assume that products from countries with low country equity—such as Suriname and Myanmar—will be of low quality (Kotler & Gertner, 2002, p. 250).

Caption: Nike is a "master brand" known around the world. Copyright: andersphoto

If you are a true master brand, you should be hesitant to present your product differently in different local markets, because "that could leave consumers feeling less certain about what the product stands for" (Clegg, 2005, p. 43). As Holt, Quelch, and Taylor (2004) explain,

> consumers look to global brands as symbols of cultural ideas. They use brands to create an imagined global identity that they share with like-minded people. Transnational companies therefore compete not only to offer the highest value products but also to deliver cultural myths with global appeal.

One study of more than 3,000 consumers in 41 countries found that most people select brands based upon differences in their global qualities (Holt, Quelch, & Taylor, 2004). However, even with master brands, there is still *some* room for local adaptation. For example, Coca-Cola launched its wildly popular "Share a Coke" campaign in Australia in 2012 by printing popular Australian names on the outside of their cans—a practice they went on to replicate in many individualistic countries, such as the United Kingdom and United States of America. By contrast, in Japan—a collectivist and nationalistic society—instead of printing individual names on cans, the company printed codes that consumers could use to download music and share it with their friends, through a partnership with the Japanese company Sony (Liang,

2014). In China—another collectivist society—Coca-Cola customized bottles with nicknames that are popular online, song lyrics, and movie quotes (Doland, 2015). Still, the campaign had a consistent global theme around the concept of sharing beverages.

Although its campaign was adapted for local markets, Coca Cola used a common theme of sharing a Coke. Copyright: photobyphotoboy

If you are working for a company that is "on the next rung down" from the master brands, meaning that is "universally recognised, but not iconic"—for example, American Express, Pepsi, or Shell—Research International reports that you can afford to make greater modifications in local markets (Clegg, 2005, p. 43).

According to Research International, brands such as Shell can afford to make greater adaptations in local markets. Copyright: kreatorex

Finally, of course, if your brand is perceived by consumers to be a local product—even if, like Nestle's products, it really is not—you should absolutely tailor your branding strategy to your local market and de-emphasize global elements in your communications.

Another factor that you should consider when crafting your local messages is how locals perceive your product category. Rapaille (2006) argues that people of different cultures perceive products differently, based upon their earliest experiences with them. For example,

> in France, people drink champagne, as they do all wine, for its taste, not its alcohol content. The purpose of drinking wine in France is almost never to get drunk, but to enjoy the flavor of the wine and the way it enhances food. French children get their first taste of champagne at a very early age. They dip sugar cubes or cookies into it and in doing so learn its flavor and distinctive qualities. . . . Most American teenagers receive their first real imprint of alcohol when they are teenagers. This is a very different window in time from the one in which the French learn about alcohol, and therefore the connection made is different. For most Americans, alcohol serves a function: it makes you drunk. Few American teens ponder the bouquet of the beer as they guzzle (Rapaille, 2006, p. 23).

In addition to understanding how people view different types of products, Rapaille argues that it is also important to ascertain how different cultures view ideals and experiences which may be communicated in your public relations campaigns—such as love, beauty, work, money, quality, perfection, shopping, and luxury. For example, he (2006, p. 61) notes that

> Arab nations . . . see a woman's appearance as a reflection of her man's success. If a woman is skinny, this suggests that her husband doesn't have the means to feed her properly. . . . In Norway, beauty is a reflection of one's connection with the natural world. Norwegian men consider slim women with athletic builds the most beautiful, because they see them as active and capable of running and skiing long distances.

You therefore need to discover how local peoples view both your product or service category and different ideals with which your product or service is associated before you can begin to determine how to position your product for them.

Additionally, Holt (2004) argues that, if you want your brand to become iconic within a country, your communications must be attuned to the current mood of the culture. He (2004, p. 4) distinguishes between brands that are valued for their quality and reliability—such as Clorox and Southwest Airlines, a U.S. carrier—and those that are valued because their perceived attributes help consumers signal their identities—such as Levi's jeans and the luxury fashion brand Chanel. Holt (2004, p. 6) argues that the latter "identity brands" must engage in cultural branding by understanding "the collective anxieties and desires of a nation"—which often result from contradictions between the official ideology of a country and the reality people are actually experiencing on the ground (for example, the U.S. is known to be a prosperous nation, but American citizens may be unemployed or disillusioned with the country's rampant consumerism). Once you understand the mood and feelings of your target groups, you can craft your brand's identity to reflect and speak to them. For example, Budweiser beer's "Whassup" campaign appealed to men who felt alienated from the U.S. corporate culture of the time by making fun of uptight professionals (Holt, 2004, p. 118).

Chanel is an "identity brand." Copyright: Martin Good

Engaging in such cultural branding means that your brand identity will not remain static over time; it requires keeping your finger on the pulse of the moods of local peoples and adapting your branding strategy accordingly. Holt (2004, p. 37) reports that every brand he has studied has

> had to make significant shifts to stay iconic. These revisions of the brand's myth are necessary because, for a myth to generate identity value, it must directly engage the challenging social issues of the day. Coke celebrated America's triumphs against Nazi Germany in World War II, shifted to dramatize ways to heal internal strife around war in the early 1970s, and then shifted again to attend to racial divisions in the early 1980s.

Therefore, even once you have crafted a brand identity that is successful, you will need to keep scanning the environments in which you operate in order to stay on top of local cultural changes and consider adjusting your messaging accordingly.

Snapshot of Two Tactics

Although these tactics should be considered as part of any global public relations campaign, they are often particularly effective for corporations:

Coca-Cola's sponsorship of the 2014 World Cup was "ambushed" by Pepsi. Copyright: urbanbuzz

Global Events: Particularly if you work for a master brand, you should consider crafting campaigns around global events that capture the world's attention, such as the Olympics and the World Cup. There are two ways to do this: the first is to actually sponsor the event. Globally, corporations were expected to spend $57.5 billion on sponsorships in 2015 (IEG, 2015). The second option is "ambush marketing," which Chadwick, Liu, and Thwaites (2014, p. 63) explain "occurs when companies who are not official sponsors try to affiliate themselves with an event in order to gain the benefits of being official sponsors." Such campaigns allow companies to be associated with high-profile, beloved events without the costs of actual sponsorships. They also may weaken your competitors; studies show that consumers do confuse official sponsors with ambush marketers (Chadwick, Liu, & Thwaites, 2014, p. 73). For example, in 2014, Coca-Cola sponsored the World Cup, but this did not stop Pepsi from launching a campaign celebrating football called "Now Is What You Make It" (Fera, 2014). Two weeks after the World Cup began, a study found that Pepsi's brand awareness had grown by four percent, while Coca-Cola's grew by five percent

(Perlberg, 2014). Some efforts have been made to outlaw ambush marketing; for example, prior to hosting the 2010 World Cup, South Africa passed anti-ambush marketing legislation. Under this legislation, models wearing dresses promoting the Dutch beer company Bavaria were arrested at the games (the official World Cup sponsor in this product category was Budweiser). However, Chadwick, Liu, and Thwaites (2014, p. 79) conclude that the publicity surrounding the arrests and subsequent deal to release the women only generated more publicity for Bavaria. Ultimately, they say, most ambush marketing doesn't fall afoul of the law, and so the best way for official sponsors to handle it is simply to make the most they can out of their own sponsorships. Of course, with any sponsorship, do your due diligence on potential partners first. In 2015, for example, the Fédération Internationale de Football Association (FIFA), which organizes the World Cup, became embroiled in a major corruption scandal.

Another event that happens on a daily basis is the opening and closing of stock exchanges. When your company has an important announcement to make, consider asking if you can ring the opening or closing bell of the stock exchange, which is a great (and free!) way to garner attention.

Issuing global reports is a way to position your company as a thought leader and generate global and local media coverage. Copyright: Dragon Images

Global Reports: Another effective tactic at the global level can be releasing reports on global topics. For example, the professional services firm Deloitte releases global reports on topics such as Millennials (the generation born after 1983) and the luxury goods market. Such reports can position your company as a thought leader and generate a great deal of media coverage at both the global and national levels. You can issue a press release to the global media from your headquarters with the top-level findings, and then issue different releases at the regional or country levels emphasizing region- or country-specific findings.

References

Appelbaum, L., Belmuth, G. S., & Schroeder, K. (2011). Global corporate communication. In J. Doorley & H. F. Garcia (Eds.), *Reputation management: The key to successful public relations and corporate communication* (2nd ed.) (pp. 228–257). New York, NY: Routledge.

Austen-Smith, D., Galinsky, A. D., Chung, K. H., & LaVanway, C. (2012, December 1). The Axe and the Dove: Managing across brands at Unilever. Kellogg School of Management at Northwestern University. Retrieved from http://insight.kellogg.north western.edu/article/the_axe_and_the_dove_managing_across_brands_at_unilever

Burke, E. M. (1999). *Corporate community relations: The principle of the neighbor of choice.* Westport, CT: Quorum Books.

Chadwick, S., Liu, R., & Thwaites, D. (2014). Ambush marketing and the football world cup. In S. Frawley & D. Adair (Eds.), *Managing the football world cup* (pp. 63–81). New York, NY: Palgrave Macmillan.

Clegg, A. (2005, October 20). A word to the worldly-wise. *Marketing Week*, 43–48.

Cone Communications (2015, May 27). Cone releases the 2015 Cone Communications/Ebiquity global CSR study. Retrieved from http://www.conecomm.com/2015-global-csr-study-press-release

Doland, A. (2015, June 5). Coca-Cola tries new twist on 'Share a Coke' in China. *Advertising Age*. Retrieved from http://adage.com/article/cmo-strategy/coca-cola-a-twist-share-a-coke-china/298884/

Dozier, D. M., & Ehling, W. P. (1992). Evaluation of public relations programs: What the literature tells us about their effects. In J. E. Grunig (Ed.), *Excellence in public relations and communication management* (pp. 159–184). Hillsdale, NJ: Lawrence Erlbaum Associates.

Elkington, J. (1998). *Cannibals with forks: The triple bottom line of 21st century business.* Gabriola Island, Canada: New Society Publishers.

Ewing, A. P. (2011). Corporate responsibility. In J. Doorley & H. F. Garcia (Eds.), *Reputation management: The key to successful public relations and corporate communication* (2nd ed.) (pp. 334–357). New York, NY: Routledge.

Fera, R. A. (2014, April 10). Pepsi celebrates the art of football in global campaign. *Fast Company*. Retrieved from http://www.fastcocreate.com/3028797/the-walk-through/pepsi-celebrates-the-art-of-football-in-global-campaign

Hayes, R. (1989). Public relations in the world marketplace. In B. Canton (Ed.), *Experts in action: Inside public relations* (2nd ed.) (pp. 423–433). White Plains, NY: Longman.

Holt, D. B. (2004). *How brands become icons: The principles of cultural branding.* Boston, MA: Harvard Business Press.

Holt, D. B., Quelch, J. A., & Taylor, E. L. (2004). How global brands compete. *Harvard Business Review, 82*(9), 68–75.

IEG (2015, January 6). New year to be one of growth and challenges for sponsorship industry. Retrieved from http://www.sponsorship.com/IEGSR/2015/01/06/New-Year-To-Be-One-Of-Growth-And-Challenges-for-Sp.aspx

Kotler, P., & Gertner, D. (2002). Country as brand, product and beyond: A place marketing and brand management perspective. *Brand Management, 9*(4–5), 249–261.

Leclerc, F., Schmitt, B. H., & Dubé, L. (1994). Foreign branding and its effects on product perceptions and attitudes. *Journal of Marketing Research, 31,* 263–270.

Liang, C. (2014, August 3). "Share a Coke"—Coca-Cola global campaign analysis. *Public Relations 2.0.* Retrieved from https://cl2639.wordpress.com/2014/08/03/share-a-coke-coca-cola-global-campaign-analysis/

Mago, M. (2012). Nigeria, petroleum and a history of mismanaged community relations. In K. Sriramesh & D. Verčič (Eds.), *Culture and public relations: Links and implications* (pp. 105–123). New York, NY: Taylor & Francis.

Molleda, J. C. (2010). Cross-national conflict shifting: A transnational crisis perspective in global public relations. In R. L. Heath (Ed.), *The SAGE handbook of public relations* (2nd ed.) (pp. 679–690). Thousand Oaks, CA: Sage.

Motion, J., Haar, J., & Leitch, S. (2012). A public relations framework for indigenous engagement. In K. Sriramesh & D. Verčič (Eds.), *Culture and public relations: Links and implications* (pp. 54–66). New York, NY: Taylor & Francis.

Nielsen (2014, June 17). Global consumers are willing to put their money where their heart is when it comes to goods and services from companies committed to social responsibility. Retrieved from http://www.nielsen.com/us/en/press-room/2014/global-consumers-are-willing-to-put-their-money-where-their-heart-is.html

Perlberg, S. (2014, June 27). Coke and Pepsi score in World Cup marketing battle while McDonald's misses. *The Wall Street Journal.* Retrieved from http://blogs.wsj.com/cmo/2014/06/27/world-cup-brand-perception/

Rapaille, C. (2006). *The culture code: An ingenious way to understand why people around the world live and buy as they do.* New York, NY: Broadway Books.

Shimp, T. A., Samiee, S., & Madden, T. J. (1993). Countries and their products: A cognitive structure perspective. *Journal of the Academy of Marketing Science, 21*(4), 323–330.

Unilever (2014, April 4). Unilever Lifebuoy campaign reduces diarrhoea from 36% to 5%. Retrieved from http://www.csrwire.com/press_releases/36887-Unilever-Lifebuoy-Campaign-Reduces-Diarrhoea-from-36-to-5-

5 Public Relations on Global Issues

Do you know what kills more children than malaria, HIV/AIDS, and tuberculosis combined? Diarrhea. So why have we all heard so much more about the former diseases? Likely because diarrhea is disgusting and no one wants to talk about it—though the U.N. recently launched a campaign against open defecation, which contributes to the water contamination that causes diarrhea. As this example shows, the problems that get solved in our world today are not necessarily those that are most pressing. Rather, they are the issues that public relations practitioners like you and me take up and fight to get on the social and political agenda.

Too often, the role of public relations practitioners is seen to be one of countering attacks by activists on behalf of corporate or political clients (Demetrious, 2013, p. 24). However, a different facet of public relations that is deeply rewarding and critical to modern society is working on behalf of non-profit organizations (also known as non-governmental organizations, or NGOs) to champion social or environmental causes. Such global public relations campaigns can truly change the world. For example, between 1992 and 2010, the International Campaign to Ban Landmines convinced 150 countries to ratify a treaty forbidding the use, production, stockpiling, and transfer of land mines. Similarly, the Make Poverty History campaign, run by activists in the United Kingdom, built support for billions of dollars in aid and debt relief for poor countries (Cox, 2011).

Such global public relations campaigns are run by activists, whom Grunig (1992, p. 504) defines as "a group of two or more individuals who organize in order to influence another public or publics through action that may include education, compromise, persuasion, pressure tactics, or force." The target of such campaigns may be corporations, governments, and/or citizens.

As Demetrious (2013, p. 42) notes,

> compared to other contemporary business and state organizations, these groups have limited resources, such as time and money, to mount their campaigns. As a result, they tend to have bold and inventive approaches to communication and a willingness to adopt and experiment with new technologies to coordinate action and promote their cause.

The International Campaign to Ban Landmines helped convince governments to ban the use, production, stockpiling, and transfer of land mines. Copyright: Vadim Ivanov

In particular, social media platforms have revolutionized the practice of non-profit global public relations. Wakefield (2011, p. 175) notes that

> social media have empowered individuals and groups in ways never thought possible just a decade ago. . . . These social media offer the means to monitor behaviors of transnational organizations and a forum for rallying together to exert direct pressure on what these groups see as wrong. As a result, transnationals can be held accountable and be made to prove legitimacy to society.

If you are considering working for a non-profit organization on international issues, this chapter will teach you how to craft and implement strategic global public relations campaigns. (If you are looking for such a job, I highly recommend the website www.ReliefWeb.org, which posts media and communication job openings in non-profits around the globe.) As the previous chapter indicated, even if you work for a corporation, you will be expected to implement corporate social responsibility campaigns, so the techniques described in this chapter will still be of use. And if you plan to work for a government or a corporation, you are likely to be targeted by activists at some stage, so this chapter will give you a sense of the types of campaigns you may be up against.

This chapter will begin by explaining how to come up to speed on the issues for which you advocate, before discussing questions you need to answer before embarking upon a global non-profit public relations campaign, how to frame your issues in order to build support, how to collaborate with like-minded groups, and the four key strategies that transnational activists (activists working across national boundaries) use. Finally, I will spotlight two tactics that can be particularly effective for global non-profits: influencer engagement and local events organized by citizens around the globe.

Read on to learn how to change the world.

Researching Your Issues and Countries

Copyright: Voronin76

Before you can begin to even think about developing a public relations campaign on a global issue, you will need to make yourself an expert on the topic. You should carefully identify both the technical and political causes of your problem. For example, a famine in a particular country may ostensibly be caused by a drought, but it is likely that a lack of political will to stop it (by both the government of the country in which the famine is occurring and by other governments and actors) is also perpetuating the problem. You will need to learn the history of your problem or issue in detail. Who is affected by the problem, what needs to happen to resolve it, who (if anyone) benefits from the status quo, who are the key players involved, why hasn't more progress been made to date, what other organizations are advocating on this issue, and what are their positions? Without a detailed understanding of your issue and the political environment that perpetuates it, you will not be able to craft strategic messages or rebut the arguments of your critics and opponents.

Here are some resources you can use to educate yourself on your issue:

- **The media**. Read coverage of your issue going back several years, to get a sense of how reporters frame the issue and how the issue has evolved over time. Is the issue covered differently in different countries and different types of media outlets? What perspectives and voices are included in media coverage? What is left out? Which media outlets and reporters are regularly covering the topic?

- **Blogs.** There are groups of bloggers who cover most global issues in great detail. Often, they have strong personal positions and opinions, which will be obvious from their posts.
- **Websites and social media platforms** of any and all organizations involved in the issue. What are the positions of other groups? What initiatives do they have underway?
- **Policy briefs and reports** explaining your issue. Chances are that your organization has written many; other groups almost certainly will have, as well.
- **Statements by government officials and international organizations such as the United Nations, World Bank, and International Monetary Fund on your issue.** You will usually be able to find such statements on their websites.
- **Public opinion research.** Ideally you will be able to conduct primary research before beginning your campaign. However, even if you do not have a budget for this, extant research may be able to give you indications of global public awareness and opinion on your issue.
- **Academic journal articles and books** written by scholars on your issue. You can search Google Scholar to find journal articles and Amazon.com or your library's database for books.

Only once you are fully up to speed on your issue will you be prepared to influence the debate. Of course, you will need to continually monitor these resources in order to identify how the landscape is changing over time.

As with any public relations campaign, you will also need to learn about the cultures and countries in which you will implement your public relations strategy. Chapters 2 and 8–12 will help. However, when working on global issues, there is an additional question you need to ask: How does change actually happen in the countries or cultures in which I am working? For example, in the United States of America, Kingdon (1995) argues that change never occurs unless policy entrepreneurs first invest in "softening up" the public over an extended period of time, by educating citizens about their cause and gradually bringing them around to support their position, so that when a short-term opportunity in the environment—or triggering event—occurs, the country will be prepared for change. Kingdon (1995, p. 128) argues that "without the preliminary work, a proposal sprung even at a propitious time is likely to fall on deaf ears." You can get a sense of how change happens in other countries by studying past campaigns that have succeeded or failed and, as always, working with communicators who have local expertise.

Laying the Ground Rules

Before you can begin crafting your public relations strategy, you and your colleagues will need to answer some important questions. As with any strategy, you will need to first define your goals and objectives. A key question you will need to answer is to what degree your objective is to promote your organization and to what degree your objective is to promote your cause. Will your boss be happy, for example, if you place numerous stories in the global media raising awareness of the problem of human trafficking but the name of your organization is not mentioned in any of them? It is not vain or shameful to have an objective to promote both your cause *and* your organization; indeed, the only way that many organizations can continue to operate is by raising enough awareness and support to command donations. On the other hand, if you work for an organization such as the United Nations or the World Bank, which has a steady stream of funding from governments, perhaps you will feel less need to promote your name and prefer that the issue for which you are advocating gets all of the exposure. You should have a candid discussion with your colleagues on this subject, since the answer you arrive at will significantly influence your public relations strategy. And, of course, your objectives and tactics may be different for different countries or audiences; you may choose, for example, to run local campaigns in poor communities educating parents about how to protect their children from malaria, while in richer countries you may promote your organization in order to raise money to fund such initiatives.

Secondly, you need to determine what types of tactics you will use. As Gass and Seiter (2009, p. 161) note, "a balancing act may be involved: an organization that is seen as too controversial may scare away potential donors or volunteers, but an organization with too low a profile may not attract enough donors or volunteers." Some organizations are comfortable with radical tactics: Greenpeace, for example, relies upon dramatic, headline-grabbing stunts to build support for its environmental agenda. In 2013, the organization's activists were arrested after attempting to illegally board an oil rig to protest drilling in the Arctic; in 2014, Greenpeace activists faced criminal charges after accidentally damaging a sacred archeological site in Peru (Associated Press, 2014; Vidal, 2014). However, if you will be going after major corporate donors or government grants, such controversial tactics will be ill advised. Define your organization's comfort zone.

Greenpeace activists are known for their bold tactics. Copyright: Stefano Tinti

Third and finally, you will need to decide how you will approach the target(s) of your campaign. For example, if you seek to change a government policy, will you be more successful if you try to partner with or aid the government in order to help reach your goals? Or will you never associate with the organization you are criticizing, because you view it as diabolical?

Once you have become an expert on your issue and come to internal agreement on these preliminary questions, you will be ready to start crafting your messages and strategies.

Typifying Your Issue and Crafting Your Messages

Copyright: Konstantin Chagin

One of the most important factors that will determine your level of success in advocating for your issue is how you discuss it. As Salmon, Post, and Christensen (2003, p. 11) note, "the meaning of an issue is not inherent, but rather intentionally defined and redefined by groups seeking to make their issue more 'marketable.'" This process starts with "typification," or naming and defining your problem or cause (Salmon, Post, & Christensen, 2003, p. 9). For example, Keck and Sikkink (1998, p. 20) note that

> before 1976 the widespread practice of female circumcision in many African and a few Asian and Middle Eastern countries was known outside these regions mainly among medical experts and anthropologists. A controversial campaign, initiated in 1974 by a network of women's and human rights organizations, began to draw wider attention to the issues by renaming the problem. Previously the practice was referred

to by technically "neutral" terms such as female circumcision, clitori-dectomy, or infibulation. The campaign around female genital "mutila-tion" raised its salience, literally creating the issue as a matter of public international concern. By renaming the practice the network broke the linkage with male circumcision (seen as a personal medical or cultural decision), implied a linkage with the more feared procedure of castration, and reframed the issue as one of violence against women.

As you strategically craft the name of your cause, a key question that you should ask yourself is whether you can define your problem in such a way as to predetermine your desired solution. Salmon, Post, and Christensen (2003, pp. 10–11) note that

> defining a social problem of violence in society in terms of violent con-tent in films and TV programs automatically defines its solution: regula-tion of media content. Through typifying a problem in a particular way, a claims making group often does not have to reveal its agenda explicitly, so it can let the media and policy makers draw the conclusion regarding the most appropriate policy outcome. Related to this, typification of a problem can also be used to imply the sector of society that is optimally suited to address it. For example, defining alcoholism as a disease auto-matically medicalizes it and empowers the medical community to pro-scribe its favored solution to this problem.

Of course, some types of problems will generate more attention and out-rage than others, and so it helps if you frame your issue accordingly. As Tar-row (2005, p. 147) explains, campaigns for labor or indigenous rights around the globe are often presented as campaigns for human rights, because human rights issues generate greater international attention. Bob (2005, p. 31) simi-larly notes that "on the world stage, local land disputes may appear as envi-ronmental issues and ethnic clashes as battles for rights and democracy." Keck and Sikkink (1998, p. 27) report that the most successful advocacy campaigns have focused on "issues involving legal equality of opportunity" and bodily harm to individuals, "especially when there is a short and clear causal chain (or story) assigning responsibility."

No matter what your issue, chances are that its causes and solutions are highly complex. However, in order to communicate effectively, you will need to find a way of talking about it in clear, accessible terms. Salmon, Post, and Christensen (2003, p. 13) note that "in general, issues defined in highly technical terms will get bogged down in debate and jargon . . . the more technical a policy debate becomes, the less accessible it is to the gen-eral population." Keck and Sikkink (1998, p. 19) likewise advise that you should frame your issue "simply, in terms of right and wrong." Furthermore, "an effective frame must show that a given state of affairs is neither natural nor accidental, identify the responsible party or parties, and propose credible solutions. These aims require clear, powerful messages that appeal to shared principles."

In addition to identifying causes and solutions, in all of your messaging about your issue, you need to be very direct about what you want the audiences you reach to do. This is called providing a "call to action." Do you want people to donate money? Sign a pledge to boycott a corporation? Write to their elected officials? (Although writing to elected officials is a common practice in the U.S., in the past, when I made this proposal to my colleagues in other countries, it was often met with derision. If you are living under a dictatorship, the idea of writing a letter to ask the president, for example, to end corruption, is often laughable. As always, you need to do what makes sense in local environments).

If you are not extremely explicit about what you want the targets of your campaign to do, they may take nominal actions and attempt to pass them off as solutions. For example, Cox (2011) argues that the reason why a campaign by the Save Darfur Coalition was not more effective in building support to end the genocide in Sudan was because the campaign lacked a clear call to action, which enabled the U.S. government to "respond with rhetoric rather than policy initiatives."

Remember that your demands need not always be realistic. For example, a 2013 study of divestment movements—which ask people not to invest in companies or countries in order to protest their policies—found that even if all university endowments and public pension funds joined a movement, for example, not to invest in stocks of fossil fuel companies, the actual monetary damage to the companies would be small. However, the reputational damage to the companies could be very significant. Ben Caldecott, one of the study's authors, notes that "it becomes much harder for stigmatized businesses to recruit good people, to influence policy, and, occasionally, to raise capital." Bill McKibbon, founder of 350.org, which has led the divestment movement, explains that while divestment alone cannot destroy the fossil fuel industry, "we can help politically bankrupt them. We can impair their ability to dominate our political life" (Gelles, 2015).

Devi Thomas, Director of the Shot@Life campaign at the United Nations Foundation, which raises support and funds in the U.S. to vaccinate children around the world, also recommends offering audiences "a menu of options" for how they can support your cause. "Our data shows that people like choices," Thomas says. For example, the Shot@Life website gives visitors a range of options for getting involved, including donating money, promoting the cause on personal blogs, writing to local newspapers, and contacting representatives in the U.S. Congress.

Once someone does take action, Thomas says that it is important to reassure your supporter that his or her actions have had an impact, so that hopefully (s)he will become more engaged in the future. Cognitive scientists have

The Shot@Life website gives users a "menu of options" for getting involved in the cause.

found that people are more likely to support a cause when they believe that their behavior will make an appreciable difference (Small, Loewenstein, & Slovic, 2007, p. 144). Thomas explains,

> not everyone is going to be your most engaged volunteer, but they still want to know they can make a difference. Your job as a cause communicator is to assure them that they have made a difference no matter how small the lift. For example, someone who just triggered a donation by clicking on a share icon helps to save a child just as much as someone who opened their wallet with the same donation—the impact is the same.

Also, work hard to explain how the issue you are championing is relevant to the people with whom you are communicating. For example, when the United Nations discusses the world's plan for ending poverty and its root causes, I believe that it is especially effective to emphasize how it will help both people and the planet—since extreme poverty may seem like a distant phenomenon to some citizens of rich countries, but most people can recognize that they stand to be impacted by the destruction of the environment (Alaimo, 2014a).

Just as important as your actual messages is who delivers them. For example, one type of non-profit public relations practice is development communication (practiced by governments and non-profit organizations alike). This often consists of communication campaigns that provide poor people with information that is vital to their health and well-being, such as how to prevent diseases, engage in family planning, and improve agricultural outputs (Taylor, 2000, p. 182). If you are crafting such a campaign, you will want to find local people who have the credibility to deliver your messages. In 2014, for example, when an outside group traveled to an isolated village in Guinea to warn local people about the country's deadly outbreak of the Ebola virus, the visitors were stoned and killed by villagers who feared that the officials had brought the virus with them. Across Guinea, other officials were likewise "threatened with knives, stones and machetes" (Callimachi, 2014). It is critical to understand how local people view problems and, in such situations, to use surrogates who they trust.

In summary, when crafting your messages, think carefully about how you can best frame your issue to provoke the reactions you favor. Simplify your issue so that it is understandable. Make it clear that the status quo is not inevitable or normal and explain who is to blame. Tell your audiences what you want them to do. Ideally, give them several options for getting involved and stress that the actions they take will make a difference and that the issue is relevant to their own lives. Finally, ensure that your messages are communicated by people whom your audiences view as credible and trustworthy.

Building Advocacy Networks and Boomerangs

Copyright: karenfoleyphotography

These days, chances are that your organization is not the only group attempting to build support for your cause. Countless organizations around the world advocate for the same major issues, from human rights to the environment. The organizations work as part of transnational advocacy networks, which Keck and Sikkink (1998, p. 8) define as "forms of organization characterized by voluntary, reciprocal, and horizontal patterns of communication and exchange" that "are organized to promote causes, principled ideas, and norms." It will be important for you to coordinate with your counterparts at other organizations in order to share information and perhaps collaborate on initiatives, but at the very least to ensure that you are not working at cross-purposes. Ideally, you will find ways to work together to become more than the sum of your parts. Cox (2011, p. 4) argues that "coalition is king. The most successful campaigns are all coalitions—and generally big ones."

Cox (2011, pp. 37–40) reports that there are three different ways that advocacy groups can work together. A Secretariat-led campaign creates a central office, called a Secretariat, which is responsible for leading the campaign. The benefits of a Secretariat are that you create a "single brand" with coherent messaging on your issue and allow for strong leadership and faster decision-making. However, many organizations may not be willing to join such a coalition because it requires giving up a degree of their own power. Also, because a Secretariat has so much authority to make decisions, it may not adequately consult its member organizations.

A second option is a collaborative campaign, in which member groups work together more closely to craft and manage a campaign. The benefits of this approach are that it creates a sense of joint ownership and all of the members of an organization (hopefully) realize that they must stay engaged, since they cannot outsource the work to a Secretariat. However, such a structure may not have clear leadership, may suffer from competition among members, and may lack the consensus needed to move forward on initiatives.

Your third option would be a "flotilla" approach. This entails a looser degree of coordination among organizations, which work independently but all try to move in the same direction. The advantages of this structure are that it is easy to join, there are not a lot of costs involved in coordination, it promotes a diversity of ideas, and organizations retain the freedom to control their own initiatives. However, with such limited organization, it may be difficult to execute coordinated campaigns.

Another reason why you may need to partner with other organizations is if yours is not powerful enough on its own to successfully advocate for the change it believes in. One such approach is called the "boomerang" strategy. This strategy is often used by activists in countries with authoritarian regimes that are not answerable to their people. Since the activists cannot successfully pressure their own government, they ask citizens in other (usually democratic) countries to pressure their governments to hold the offending government accountable. Keck and Sikkink (1998, pp. 12–13) explain,

> when channels between the state and its domestic actors are blocked, the boomerang pattern of influence . . . may occur: domestic NGOs bypass their state and directly search out international allies to try to bring pressure on their states from outside. This is most obviously the case in human rights campaigns. Similarly, indigenous rights campaigns and environmental campaigns that support the demands of local peoples for participation in development projects that would affect them

frequently involve this kind of triangulation. Linkages are important for both sides: for the less powerful third world actors, networks provide access, leverage, and information (and often money) they could not expect to have on their own; for northern groups, they make credible the assertion that they are struggling with, and not only for, their southern partners.

Tarrow (2005, p. 151) notes that another option is for activists to appeal to regional or international organizations for help.

Information, Symbols, Leverage, and Accountability

Once your objectives, messages, and partners are in place, it is time to determine your strategies. Keck and Sikkink (1998, pp. 18–25) explain that there are four key political approaches that transnational activists use:

1 **Information:** This strategy involves uncovering and sharing information—such as exposing human rights abuses by a government, documenting corporate malfeasance, or issuing a report with new facts about the impact of a policy on people and/or the planet. For example, the organization Human Rights Watch sent researchers into Syria to document the killings of innocent civilians. As *The New York Times* notes, "their findings from missions like this, disseminated in the news media and at conferences, illuminate oppressive regimes and can influence national policies" (Catsoulis, 2014).
    Keck and Sikkink (1998, p. 19) explain that,

> to be credible, the information . . . must be reliable and well documented. To gain attention, the information must be timely and dramatic. Sometimes these multiple goals of information politics conflict, but both credibility and drama seem to be essential components of a strategy aimed at persuading publics and policymakers to change their minds.

Of course, modern technology such as smartphone cameras and social media platforms has made it easier than ever to document and share events that take place in nearly every corner of the world. However, this also means that diabolical actors are taking greater care than ever before to conceal the evidence of their misdeeds. For example, Rejali (2007) argues that modern countries continue to practice torture, but they have now switched to methods of "clean torture," which leave fewer scars and less evidence behind, making it harder for their practices to be exposed. Rejali (2007, p. 3) explains,

> a democratic public may be outraged by violence it can see, but how likely is it that we will get outraged about violence . . . that . . . may not leave traces, violence that we can hardly be sure took place at all? A victim

with scars to show to the media will get sympathy or at least attention, but victims without scars do not have much to authorize their complaints to a skeptical public.

This means that you will need more sophisticated forms of monitoring than ever before. Often, you will rely on local partners to help you gather evidence. Be sure that you can trust them to produce accurate information, given the ease with which photographs and other evidence can be doctored.

Once you have gathered information and are absolutely certain that you have your facts straight, the traditional media and social media are often the best ways to disseminate it. Expect intense scrutiny and even counter-campaigns to follow. Demetrious (2013, p. 76) notes, for example, that some corporations have aggressively countered activist campaigns with deeply unethical practices, including lying, spying, concealing information, producing "counter-science," and even threatening and harassing activists. Be forewarned!

Tarrow (2005, p. 158) argues that the strategy of exposing information is likely to be successful when the subject is bodily harm and when it occurs in nations that have constitutional traditions. "When it is employed where there are no such traditions or where divisible goods, but not human lives, are at stake—as in industrial relations—it is less likely to succeed."

Furthermore, exposing information works best when you are trying to shed light on the practices of organizations. If you are advocating for individuals to change their behavior, simply providing information will often not be enough. As Coffman (2003, p. 4) notes, these days, most people who smoke cigarettes are already aware that smoking can cause lung cancer, so simply reminding smokers of this fact is unlikely to be an effective strategy. Rather, researchers in the U.S. report that campaigns are more effective when they focus on convincing people that they are capable of doing what is being asked of them (a concept called self-efficacy) and when campaigns attempt to change their perceptions of what others, such as their friends and family, are doing or want them to do. For example, if someone perceives that all of his or her friends and family members believe that smoking is disgusting, the person might be more likely to quit!

2 **Symbols:** This strategy involves using "symbols, actions, and stories to make sense of a situation for those far away" (Keck and Sikkink, 1998, p. 16). For example, during the pro-democracy protests in Hong Kong in 2014, demonstrators used umbrellas as a symbol of their movement, creating umbrella-themed "enormous outdoor art exhibitions." *The New York Times* noted that "the art, pointedly political and often witty, has become as much an expression of the protest as the megaphone speeches and the metal street barricades" (Lau, 2014).

Another very effective strategy is to humanize a problem by sharing dramatic stories of how your issue is impacting people. *New York Times* columnist Nicholas Kristof (2009) discussed the importance of this strategy when he bemoaned the fact that his reporting on the humanitarian crisis in the Darfur region of Sudan did not provoke greater global outrage. Kristof "interviewed people who

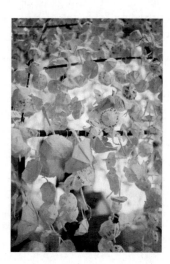

Umbrellas were used as the theme of pro-democracy protests in Hong Kong in 2014. Copyright: Gary Yim

had seen men pulled off buses and killed because of their tribe and skin color, and . . . spoke to teenage girls who had been taunted with racial epithets against blacks while being gang-raped by the Sudanese-sponsored Arab militia, the janjaweed." Around the same time, Kristof reports,

> Manhattan erupted in a controversy showing that even cynical New Yorkers can brim with empathy for a hawk. A red-tailed hawk dubbed Pale Male, one of the best-known residents of the Central Park area, had become embroiled in a housing dispute with the Upper East Side co-op on which he had a nest. The co-op removed Pale Male's nest, outraging New Yorkers and generating considerable news coverage. Now, don't get me wrong: I was on Pale Male's side, but I also dreamed that the plight of people driven from their villages in Darfur or Congo could get the same sympathy as a homeless bird.

Why did this bird seemingly garner greater concern than the human beings being slaughtered in Darfur? Part of the reason, Kristof explains, is that it is easier to connect with the story of another living being than it is to process and react emotionally to the more abstract idea of large-scale problems impacting huge numbers of far-away people.

Slovic (2010, p. 38) explains that the reason why people do not intervene during a genocide lies partly in the framing of messages. "The statistics of mass-murder or genocide, no matter how large the numbers, fail to convey the true meaning of such atrocities. The numbers fail to spark emotion or feeling." Slovic argues that our brains may be designed to detect small changes in our environment, making it difficult for us to conceptualize large-scale problems such as mass genocide. This principle—which he calls "psychophysi- cal numbing"—explains why human beings will go to extraordinary lengths to save a single human life, but stand by while millions are killed. He (2010, p. 45) reports that

> psychologically, the importance of saving one life is diminished against the background of a larger threat—we will likely not 'feel' much different, nor value the difference, between saving 87 lives and saving 88, if these prospects are presented to us separately.

As a result, "all too often the numbers represent dry statistics, 'human beings with the tears dried off,' that lack feeling and fail to motivate action" (Slovic, 2010, p. 47).

One of the best public relations strategies for communicating on global issues is therefore to humanize problems. Slovic (2010, pp. 48–50) explains that cognitive scientists have found that "when it comes to eliciting compas- sion, the identified individual victim, with a face and a name, has no peer." For example, one study found that people would donate significantly more money when told about Rokia, a seven-year old girl in Mali who was described as "des- perately poor" and facing the possibility of starvation, than when they were given statistical information about hunger in Africa (Small, Loewenstein, & Slovic, 2007, p. 152). Another study found that the benefits of personal iden- tification may diminish when we are asked to consider a group as small as two. The 2009 study found that when people were asked to donate money that would help both Rokia and Moussa—a seven-year old boy from Mali also in need of food—they were willing to give less money than people asked to help either Rokia or Moussa individually (Slovic, 2010, p. 53). (Interestingly, they gave mean donations of $25.20 to Rokia and $25.30 to Moussa. However, Kristof (2009) says that he believes that "readers cared above all about girls, so when I came across a young man with a compelling story, I would apologize and ask him if he knew any girls with similar problems.")[1]

Therefore, when you are communicating on global issues, find and tell powerful stories of actual human beings. For example, to promote global vol- unteerism, Jennifer Stapper, Chief of Communications for United Nations Volunteers, often shares stories of people who have made a difference in com- munities around the world. Stapper says that it can be particularly powerful to include people with compelling stories on the same platforms as global policy- makers and dignitaries. For example, in the lead-up to Rio + 20, a huge confer- ence on sustainable development organized by the United Nations in 2012, United Nations Volunteers ran a contest asking volunteers to create videos showing how they are contributing to sustainable development. The winners of the contest—individuals who volunteered on community projects in Jamaica and the Philippines—shared the stage at the conference with Helen Clark, head of the United Nations Development Programme. "If you can bring real people on the ground into the conversation, it really makes a big difference, because people stop and listen if they can identify with a person," Stapper says.

U.N. Volunteer Michelle Curling-Ludford (right) shared the stage with United Nations Development Programme Administrator Helen Clark (left) at the Rio + 20 summit. Photo courtesy of United Nations Volunteers

Another way to use symbols as part of your campaign is to seek awards and/or celebrity endorsements. Bob (2005, p. 44) notes that

> humanitarian awards such as the Nobel Peace Prize, the Goldman Environmental Prize, the Robert F. Kennedy Memorial Human Rights Prize, and the Right Livelihood Prize confer name recognition, as well as money. Similarly, attracting a celebrity to one's cause—a Princess Diana or a Richard Gere—builds stature through reflected glory.

Influencer engagement is described in greater detail in the "two tactics" section at the end of this chapter.

3 **Leverage:** This strategy entails calling upon powerful people to take action. There are two types of leverage strategies. The first involves material leverage. For example, you can call on consumers to boycott a company or countries to implement economic sanctions against a government until the regime changes its behavior.

The second type involves exerting moral leverage, which is sometimes called the "mobilization of shame." This strategy relies upon the assumption that most modern corporations and countries care about their reputations, and therefore if they are embarrassed or shamed for certain practices, they are likely to change them. With a few notable exceptions, such as the governments of North Korea and Syria, whose leaders do not seem at all bothered by the fact that the whole world knows that they are committing vicious atrocities against their own people, I believe that this assumption is generally true (Alaimo, 2014b). In an increasingly complex and interdependent world, countries have greater needs and incentives to cooperate with one another for a host of reasons—from coordinating air traffic and postal services to fighting terrorism and global pandemics, which know no boundaries. There is one key ticket to realizing the benefits of international cooperation: remaining a member of the international community in good standing. In order to do this, countries must adhere to the underlying rules of international society. As Franck (1998, p. 758) argues,

> it is . . . circumstantially demonstrable that there are obligations that states acknowledge to be necessary incidents of community membership. These are not perceived to obligate because they have been accepted by the individual state but, rather, are rules in which states acquiesce as part of their own validation; that is, as an inseparable aspect of 'joining' a community of states. . . . They acknowledge this because they must, so as to obtain and retain the advantages of belonging to an organized, sophisticated community.

Similarly, as was discussed in the previous chapter, today consumers around the world expect businesses to be responsible global citizens and make purchase decisions accordingly. According to the global public relations firm Weber Shandwick, a company's reputation is responsible for 63 percent of its market value (Gaines-Ross, 2008, p. 7).

If modern countries and corporations must protect their reputations in order to operate effectively, then shaming them for poor practices is a great way to catalyze behavior change. This requires not just sharing information about their behavior but also emphasizing that their conduct is reprehensible. The more barbarous you can present the practices of your target to be, the more likely it is that this strategy will be effective.

4 Accountability: One of my favorite strategies, this involves targeting a government or corporation with its own words. As Keck and Sikkink (1998, p. 24) explain,

> once a government has publicly committed itself to a principle—for example, in favor of human rights or democracy—networks can use those positions, and their command of information, to expose the distance between discourse and practice. This is embarrassing to many governments, which may try to save face by closing that distance.

Risse and Sikkink (1999) report that activists have successfully used this tactic to pressure governments to end human rights violations in countries as diverse as Kenya, Uganda, South Africa, Tunisia, Morocco, Indonesia, the Philippines, Chile, and Guatemala. They outline a five-step process through which this change occurs. In the first phase, the government represses its citizens and activists begin to gather information about the human rights violation(s). In the second stage, the activists begin to disseminate information about the violation(s), raise public awareness, and lobby international human rights organizations and other countries to act. In this stage, the regime almost always denies the accusations and rejects international human rights norms, arguing that they represent illegitimate infringements on their national sovereignty.

In stage three, sufficient pressure builds on the government and it decides to make tactical concessions, implementing what it considers to be merely cosmetic reforms in order to pacify the criticism. For example, the head of state may pledge to uphold human rights, even if the government actually has no intention of doing so. "Leaders of authoritarian states . . . tend to believe that 'talk is cheap' and do not understand the degree to which they can become 'entrapped' in their own rhetoric" (Risse & Sikkink, 1999, p. 27). However, once the regime makes a verbal concession, domestic and international activists mobilize and demand that it lives up to its promises. Eventually, the pressure becomes too much to bear and the regime is forced to change its practices. By stage four, the regime no longer contests the principles of the activists, and in stage five, the regime actually ceases the violations.

This is why it can be a good public relations strategy to simply ask a corporation or government whose practices you wish to change to make a commitment on your issue. Corporate executives, for example, may believe that making a pledge, especially if it is vague—for example, to avoid harm to the environment in production processes—will be a good way to pacify critics, even if they have no intention of radically overhauling their practices. However, once a company representative makes the verbal commitment, you can use those words as part of a larger campaign demanding more substantive change. When your target is an authoritarian government, this approach can be especially useful, because once the government makes a pledge, you can claim that you are *supporting the government's own efforts* to achieve the goal it has set, rather than criticizing the government (which, in too many countries, comes with significant risks, including imprisonment and torture).

This was the approach that we used when I worked for the United Nations Millennium Campaign. In the year 2000, 189 world leaders signed the Millennium Declaration at the United Nations, pledging to eradicate extreme poverty and its root causes by the year 2015. Of course, the heads of state did not fully follow through on their commitments, but the fact that they had signed the document gave us cover to help citizens around the world run campaigns claiming that they were supporting their governments. As the United Nations, we ourselves could likewise never have run and supported such communications campaigns if they were seen as adversarial towards country policies.

Perhaps the most dramatic example of the successful use of this strategy is the case of the former Soviet Union. In an astonishing book, Thomas (2001) argues that the use of this strategy by transnational activists led to the collapse of the Soviet Union. As Thomas (2001) notes, in 1969, members of the Warsaw Pact (the former Soviet Union and neighboring Eastern European communist states with which it was aligned) convened for a summit in Budapest with members of the European Community. Suffering from a stagnant economy and emerging dissent, the Soviet Union and its allies sought to attain legitimization as members of the European Community and to access markets in the West. Members of the European Community insisted that the issue of human rights be on the agenda as a precondition for their participation in the conference. While the Soviet Union criticized the inclusion of human rights as an improper intervention in their internal affairs and an inappropriate subject matter for international relations, they ultimately agreed to this condition because they saw improving their relations with the European Community as critical to solving their political and economic problems. The Warsaw Pact's decision to participate in the conference thus

> reflected a widely recognized irony of Soviet and Eastern European rule: despite its absolute monopoly on domestic political space and its effective military parity with the West, the Kremlin and its allies remained deeply concerned about its image abroad . . . This sensitivity to international public opinion . . . was driven by the [desire for] access to the political, economic, and strategic benefits accorded to 'normal' members of the European and international community (Thomas, 2001, pp. 189–190).

All thirty-five countries that participated in the conference ultimately signed the Helsinki Final Act of 1975, in which they agreed not only to respect but also to promote and encourage the individual exercise of human rights, to protect the rights of minorities, and to uphold the Universal Declaration of Human Rights and the United Nations Charter, which include broader and more specific rights and obligations. Thomas (2001, p. 267) notes that the Warsaw Pact agreed to such strong language on human rights in the final agreement in exchange for vague references to issues of primary concern to the Soviet Union, a prime example of "the value that states place on recognition and legitimation by international society."

Once the agreement was made by Warsaw Pact states, their citizens began mobilizing to demand that their governments live up to their commitments. Helsinki Watch Groups soon emerged in Moscow as well as in Armenia, Georgia, Lithuania, and Ukraine to advocate for their governments to implement the Final Act, while the group Charter 77 emerged in Czechoslovakia and Solidarity emerged in Poland. Thomas (2001) notes that the Helsinki Act provided opposition groups with a common platform to advocate for reform and decreased their risk of repression because they simply claimed to support their governments' own commitments. As Czech activist Jan Kavan argued, his government "cannot declare that the demands in the Charter [of Charter 77] are illegitimate or counter-revolutionary, because that would mean renouncing its signature on the Helsinki agreement and the UN covenants" (Thomas, 2001, p. 179).

Thomas argues that the use of such discourse by these groups helped prevent more severe human rights violations against dissidents. In Czechoslovakia, for example,

> the regime's decision to respond to such a serious challenge first with harassment and intimidation and then with reasoned arguments, rather than with the far harsher measures at its disposal, must be attributed, at

least in part, to the international legitimacy and profile that Chartarists gained through their identification with human rights norms (Thomas, 2001, p. 183).

A "boomerang" effect also kicked in at the international level. Soviet and Eastern European dissidents asked for help from citizens in the U.S. and Europe. While the U.S. government had initially disagreed with the decision to press for human rights at all in negotiations with the War-saw Pact, the newly formed U.S. Helsinki Commission as well as Helsinki network activists in Europe "flooded" their governments with "massive documentation of human rights violations submitted by nongovernmen-tal organizations in the new 'Helsinki network'" (Thomas, 2001, p. 130). They ultimately succeeded in persuading members of the U.S. Congress and the initially skeptical administration of U.S. President Jimmy Carter to secure

> the elevation of human rights in U.S. foreign policy from a low-priority issue that the White House and State Department preferred to ignore, to an inescapable high-priority in U.S. relations with the East bloc, includ-ing unprecedented rhetorical confrontations and issue-linkage diplomacy (Thomas, 2001, p. 155).

The pressures of social mobilization and international criticism became so strong that Soviet leader Gorbachev came to believe that "the continued denial of basic human rights was both morally unacceptable and politically unsustainable," even if it meant the collapse of the Soviet empire (Thomas, 2001, p. 233). Not too shabby an impact for the Helsinki Final Act—a written agreement lacking any formal enforcement mechanisms!

Snapshot of Two Tactics

Although these tactics should be considered as part of any global public relations campaign, they are often particularly effective for non-profits:

Influencer Engagement: You may seek support for your campaign from celebrities or luminaries in your field. Their participation can range from providing quotes for a press release to sharing your social media posts with their followers to participating in your events. For example, when I worked for the United Nations, we often reached out to mem-bers of The Elders—a group of global luminaries including former U.N. Secretary-General Kofi Annan, former Irish President Mary Robinson,

Hollywood actress Angelina Jolie, who serves as a Goodwill Ambassador for the U.N. Refugee Agency, speaks with victims of a flood in Pakistan. Copyright: Asianet-Pakistan

and former Archbishop of Cape Town, South Africa Desmond Tutu— who can speak with authority on global issues. Celebrities can draw a lot of attention too, but don't just consider Hollywood celebrities—find out who is popular regionally and locally. For example, when I worked at the U.N., we booked the famous African singers Angelique Kidjo and Femi Kuti to participate in our events. Bollywood stars are hugely popular in India and in other parts of the world.

Angelique Kidjo is a famous singer from Benin. Copyright: Aija Lehtonen

However, remember that today's influencers are not necessarily celeb-rities: They may be ordinary people who are influential within their local communities—from a village chief in Africa, to an independent journalist in China who has a huge following on social media because citizens do not trust the government-censored press, to a teenager in the U.S. whose YouTube videos set trends. Can you get these people to share your messages and/or publicly support you?

Of course, be sure to thoroughly vet any potential influencers before partnering with them to make sure that they are unlikely to become an embarrassment to you.

Event in A Box: You can organize press conferences, speeches, and other launch events with an eye towards generating media coverage. However, to engage ordinary people around the world, another option is to encourage citizens to host their own local events. For example, when I worked for the U.N. Millennium Campaign, each year we organized "Stand Up and Take Action"—a three-day event in which we invited people around the world to organize events in their communities to demand that world leaders end extreme poverty. The event shattered the Guinness World Record for the largest mobilization of human beings in recorded history. We asked people to organize events within their communities and provided an "Event in a Box" on our website with tips and resources to help, such as templates for press releases and promotional materials.

Remember that your events can also be "virtual," as well. For exam-ple, you can organize an online contest. Or, you can use a platform such as a TweetChat on Twitter in order to have an online conversation with core or new audiences.

Note

1   Adapted from Alaimo, K. (2015). What new developments in cognitive science teach public relations professionals about how to persuade. *World Communication Review*. Retrieved from http://www.forumdavos.com/WCFA

References

Alaimo, K. (2014a). *How the United Nations should promote the post-2015 development agenda*. Boston, MA: Center for Governance and Sustainability. Retrieved from http://www.umb.edu/cgs/publications/issue_brief_series

Alaimo, K. (2014b, June 21). Words more powerful than weapons in modern global governance. Paper presented at the Annual Meeting of the Academic Council on the United Nations System, Istanbul, Turkey.

Alaimo, K. (2015). What new developments in cognitive science teach public rela-tions professionals about how to persuade. *World Communication Review*. Retrieved from http://www.forumdavos.com/WCFA

Associated Press (2014, December 10). Peru to take legal action over Greenpeace stunt at ancient Nazca lines. *The Guardian*. Retrieved from http://www.theguardian.com/world/2014/dec/10/peru-legal-action-greenpeace-stunt-nazca-lines

Bob, C. (2005). *The marketing of rebellion: Insurgents, media, and international activism.* New York, NY: Cambridge University Press.

Callimachi, R. (2014, September 18). Fear of Ebola drives mob to kill officials in Guinea. *The New York Times*. Retrieved from http://www.nytimes.com/2014/09/19/world/africa/fear-of-ebola-drives-mob-to-kill-officials-in-guinea.html?_r=0

Catsoulis, J. (2014, October 21). Gallantry and glamour in a war zone. *The New York Times*. Retrieved from http://www.nytimes.com/2014/10/22/movies/e-team-examines-human-rights-watch-investigators.html?_r=0

Coffman, J. (2003, June). *Lessons in evaluating communications campaigns: Five case studies.* Washington, DC: Communications Consortium Media Center. Retrieved from http://www.hfrp.org/publications-resources/browse-our-publications/lessons-in-evaluating-communications-campaigns-five-case-studies

Cox, B. (2011, May). *Campaigning for international justice.* Bond UK. Retrieved from http://www.bond.org.uk/data/files/Campaigning_for_International_Justice_Brendan_Cox_May_2011.pdf

Demetrious, K. (2013). *Public relations, activism, and social change: Speaking up.* New York, NY: Routledge.

Franck, T. (1998). Legitimacy in the international system. *The American Journal of International Law, 82*(4), 705–759.

Gaines-Ross, L. (2008). *Corporate reputation: 12 steps to safeguarding and recovering reputation.* Hoboken, NJ: John Wiley & Sons.

Gass, R. H., & Seiter, J. S. (2009). Credibility and public diplomacy. In N. Snow & P. M. Taylor (Eds.), *Routledge handbook of public diplomacy* (pp. 154–165). New York, NY: Routledge.

Gelles, D. (2015, June 13). Fossil fuel divestment movement harnesses the power of shame. *The New York Times*. Retrieved from http://www.nytimes.com/2015/06/14/business/energy-environment/fossil-fuel-divestment-movement-harnesses-the-power-of-shame.html

Grunig, J. E. (1992). Activism: How it limits the effectiveness of organizations and how excellent public relations departments respond. In J. E. Grunig (Ed.), *Excellence in public relations and communication management* (pp. 503–530). Hillsdale, NJ: Lawrence Erlbaum Associates.

Keck, M. E., & Sikkink, K. (1998). *Activists beyond borders.* Ithaca, NY: Cornell University Press.

Kingdon, J. (1995). *Agendas, alternatives, and public policies.* New York, NY: Harper Collins.

Kristof, N. (2009). Nicholas Kristof's advice for saving the world. *Outside*. Retrieved from http://www.outsideonline.com/outdoor-adventure/Nicholas-Kristof-s-Advice-for-Saving-the-World.html

Lau, J. (2014, November 14). Art spawned by Hong Kong protest: Now to make it live on. *The New York Times*. Retrieved from http://www.nytimes.com/2014/11/15/world/asia/rescuing-protest-artwork-from-hong-kongs-streets.html?_r=1

Rejali, D. (2007). *Torture and democracy.* Princeton, NJ: Princeton University Press.

Risse, T., & Sikkink, K. (1999). The socialization of international human rights norms into domestic practices: Introduction. In T. Risse, S. C. Ropp, & K. Sikkink (Eds.), *The power of human rights: International norms and domestic change* (pp. 1–38). New York, NY: Cambridge University Press.

Salmon, C. T., Post, L. A., & Christensen, R. E. (2003, June). *Mobilizing public will for social change*. Washington, DC: Communications Consortium Media Center. Retrieved from http://www.ncdsv.org/images/MobilizingPublicWillSocialChange.pdf

Slovic, P. (2010). If I look at the mass I will never act: Psychic numbing and genocide. In S. Roeser (Ed.), *Emotions and risky technologies* (pp. 37–59). New York, NY: Springer.

Small, D. A., Loewenstein, G., & Slovic, P. (2007). Sympathy and callousness: The impact of deliberative thought on donations to identifiable and statistical victims. *Organizational Behavior and Human Decision Processes, 102*(2), 143–153.

Tarrow, S. (2005). *The new transnational activism*. New York, NY: Cambridge University Press.

Taylor, M. (2000). Toward a public relations approach to nation building. *Journal of Public Relations Research, 12*(2), 179–210.

Thomas, D. C. (2001). *The Helsinki effect: International norms, human rights, and the demise of communism*. Princeton, NJ: Princeton University Press.

Vidal, J. (2014, June 6.) Arctic 30: Russia releases Greenpeace ship. *The Guardian*. Retrieved from http://www.theguardian.com/environment/2014/jun/06/arctic-30-sunrise-russia-to-release-greenpeace-ship

Wakefield, R. (2011). Critiquing the generic/specific public relations theory: The need to close the transnational knowledge gap. In N. Bardhan & C. K. Weaver (Eds.), *Public relations in global cultural contexts: Multi-paradigmatic perspectives* (pp. 167–194). New York, NY: Routledge.

6   Global Public Relations for Governments

Why did Czechoslovakia declare independence on October 19, 1918? Because Edward Bernays, who is considered to be the father of modern public relations, advised the nationalist leader Tomáš Garrigue Masaryk that Sundays are generally slow news days, so the new nation would have a better chance of getting high profile coverage in the following day's global newspapers if he waited until a Sunday to make the big announcement (Tye, 2002, pp. 87–88).

As this story shows, not all public relations clients (or employers) are corporations or non-profit organizations. Today, there is significant demand for professionals to manage global public relations on behalf of governments—a practice also known as **public diplomacy**. Seib (2013, p. 5) defines public diplomacy as "reaching out to global publics directly, rather than through their governments." Generally, public diplomacy involves attempting to win the "hearts and minds" of foreign peoples. Governments now attempt to influence the thinking of people in foreign countries "based on the assumption that in a more democratic world, people do have an increasing influence on the positions, policies, and attitudes of their elected governments" (Signitzer & Wamser, 2006, p. 438). In addition to influencing foreign policy, public diplomacy also helps governments attract needed aid, business investment, and tourist dollars.

Practitioners of public diplomacy wield **soft power**. Nye (2004, p. x), who coined the term, describes soft power as

> the ability to get what you want through attraction rather than coercion or payments. It arises from the attractiveness of a country's culture, political ideals, and policies. When our policies are seen as legitimate in the eyes of others, our soft power is enhanced.

Snow (2009a, p. 4) argues that three dimensions give a country a soft power advantage: "when culture and ideas match prevailing global norms," "when a nation has greater access to multiple communication channels that can influence how issues are framed in global news media," and "when a country's credibility is enhanced by domestic and international behavior."

Of course, soft power is often used in conjunction with hard power—as when, for example, the government of the United States of America embedded journalists with soldiers during its 2003 invasion of Iraq, which the former head of media relations for the U.S. Marine Corps admitted was an "attempt to dominate the information environment" (Kahn, 2004). Yet soft power also stems from the behavior of actors outside the government. For example, the Hollywood film industry, which is beloved by people around the world, gives the U.S. soft power across the globe. Citizens of other countries will often draw a distinction indicating, for example, that they like the American people, but dislike U.S. foreign policy (Wyne, 2009, p. 42). Similarly, the Bollywood movie industry has "provided a popular definition of India and helped to make it an attractive, not to say, exotic and colorful, tourist and investment destination" (Thussu, 2013, p. 131).

Traditionally, public diplomacy was pursued by governments through persuasion and propaganda—tactics still advocated today by some in the "tough-minded school" of public diplomacy. In fact, traditional public diplomacy initiatives were so widely considered to be propagandistic that in 1972 the U.S. Congress passed the Foreign Relations Act banning the promulgation within the U.S. of "information about the U.S., its people and its policies" that had been prepared for foreign audiences (Heller & Persson, 2009, p. 226).

Such "tough-minded" tactics continue to be practiced today; for example, the U.S. government broadcasts the news from a U.S. perspective through its international broadcasters Voice of America; Radio Free Europe/Radio Liberty in Central Europe and the former Soviet Union; Radio Sawa and Television Alhurra in the Middle East; Radio Free Asia; and Radio and TV Marti in Cuba (Signitzer & Wamser, 2006, p. 459). Major international broadcasters funded by governments including China, France, Germany, Japan, and Russia are discussed in Chapter 7. However, it is unclear that this approach is always successful. For example, one study of university students in five Arab countries found that, as they listened to Radio Sawa and viewed Television Alhurra more, their views of U.S. policy became *less* favorable (El-Nawawy, 2006). "If you try to manipulate people's perceptions, it can be counterproductive," the author of the study told *The New York Times*. "The very knowledge of being manipulated, of knowing you are being manipulated, can really back-fire" (Knowlton, 2014).

The modern practice of public diplomacy is shifting to efforts to foster mutual understanding between peoples, practiced by those in the so-called "tender-minded school" of public diplomacy (Snow, 2009a, p. 9). Signitzer and Wamser (2006, p. 438) explain that

> the tough-minded want to exert influence . . . conveying hard politi-
> cal information through *fast media* such as radio, television, newspapers,
> and news magazines to attain fairly short-term policy ends. The tender-
> minded school sees public diplomacy as a predominantly cultural function
> that—in the long-range—should create a climate of mutual understand-
> ing through *slow media* such as academic and artistic exchanges, films,
> exhibitions, and language instruction.

Another major distinction between the two schools is that the "tough-minded" school tends to favor one-way communication, while the "tender-minded" school fosters mutual, two-way dialogue among peoples. Snow (2009a, p. 10) notes that

> our public diplomacy philosophies, strategies and tactics are shifting from
> one-way informational diplomatic objectives to two-way interactive
> public exchanges; exchange and reciprocity are becoming trust-building
> measures and we are adding a personal and social dimension . . . to other
> variables of influence and persuasion.

Of course, many such exchanges are now happening via social media plat-forms, which give people around the world an opportunity to talk back to governments. As Wyne (2009, pp. 41–42) notes, the spread of the Internet has given ordinary people around the globe the power to influence global debates, and as a result "the number of players in the court of global public opinion has risen dramatically, and their demographics and characteristics are much more diverse."

This chapter will discuss how to practice public diplomacy on behalf of governments. First, I will briefly reiterate the importance of understanding your issues and audiences. Second, I will discuss how to craft and maintain a positive global reputation, or "competitive identity," on behalf of a nation. Third, I will outline a range of diplomacy initiatives that you can consider. Fourth, I will explain how to craft your public diplomacy messages. Fifth, I will describe how to work with communication officers in embassies and consulates around the world in order to craft and implement strategies that will be effective at the local level. Sixth, I will discuss new techniques that governments are using in an attempt to fight terrorism on social media. Finally, I will provide a snap-shot of two tactics that work particularly well in this space: interpersonal communication and "twiplomacy."

Researching and Monitoring Your Issues and Audiences

Copyright: Jirsak

As in all aspects of public relations, the first step in practicing public diplomacy is learning about your issues and audiences. The previous chapter opened with an overview of how to come up to speed on your issues when you work for a non-profit organization. This section will be a helpful resource for you as a government public relations practitioner, as well. The difference is that politics takes on heightened importance when you work for a government. While you will be able to glean a lot about politics from the press, you will also need to rely on briefings from your colleagues about the nuances of your government's relationship with other nations before beginning any public diplomacy campaign. Remember that you need to be aware of all major issues between your government and the country or countries in which you seek to communicate—even ones that are seemingly unrelated to the topic on which you are messaging. For example, when I worked for the U.S. Treasury, just days before we were scheduled to participate in our annual Strategic and Economic Dialogue with government officials in Beijing, a Chinese human rights activist who was being held by Chinese authorities under house arrest escaped and fled to the U.S. embassy, seeking protection. When the news broke that he was being harbored in our embassy, it threatened to derail our upcoming meeting (which, in this instance, did take place).

You will also need to monitor public opinion towards your country, which is often reported in polls conducted by organizations such as the World Values Survey, Pew Research Center, and Gallup. As the *Free China Review* once memorably observed, "in diplomacy, you can't buy friends, you only rent them." Carefully stay on top of how opinion towards your country is evolving (Rawnsley, 2009, p. 284).

Finally, of course, you will need to research your target audiences carefully before crafting your strategies and messages. Remember that concepts that are understood and/or valued within your own culture may be viewed entirely differently in other nations. Vlahos (2009, p. 26), for example, argues that during the early years of the war on global terror after the September 11, 2001, terror attacks, U.S. messages in the Arab world were often "no more than a reseller of core domestic messages: hawking 'transformation' and 'freedom' and 'democracy,' *as Americans embraced them*, to Muslims." Instead, you should craft your messages to appeal to *local* values.

You will also need to be aware of local social dynamics and how they will impact the way your strategies are received. For example, another tactic employed by the U.S. government after it invaded Iraq in 2003 was giving soccer balls to local children in an effort to foster better relationships with local communities. However, Armstrong (2009, p. 69) notes that

> the real impact was the emasculation of the fathers with whom the U.S. was trying to build trust and ultimately influence. More effective was giving the soccer balls to the Iraqi police, who were members of the community. This tactic is based on Arab tribal and community culture.

As always, research and help from local experts are the keys to crafting culturally appropriate strategies. In the next section, I will discuss how to improve your own country's reputation abroad, before discussing a range of tactics that can be used to target foreign audiences.

Crafting Your Competitive Identity

Copyright: Shamleen

As a practitioner working for a government, one of the most critical things that you will be called upon to do is help manage your country's global reputation. This process is often referred to as nation branding, although Anholt (2007, p. xi) now calls it crafting a "competitive identity."

A country's reputation has an enormous influence on whether it is able to meet critical goals such as boosting trade, exerting influence in international affairs and organizations such as the United Nations, and attracting foreign direct investment, foreign aid, tourism, skilled immigrants, and global events. Even business investment decisions that are ostensibly made based upon dollars (or yuan) and cents are affected by perceptions and prejudices about a country. As Anholt (2007, p. 11) notes, when a business chooses a new location for its operations,

> the management may choose a country on the basis of its infrastructure, climate, location, security, transport links, quality and location of supplier firms, business-friendly government, skilled workforce, tax breaks and incentive packages, but it's still the wrong decision if the managers who actually have to relocate there don't fancy the sound of that particular country. And even if they can be persuaded, can their families?

Similarly, in the foreign policy arena, Anholt (2007, pp. 13–14) notes that if a country with a poor reputation proposes a policy, "almost no amount of promotional skill or expenditure can cause the policy to be received with enthusiasm, and it will either be ignored or taken as further proof of whatever evil is currently ascribed to the country."

A country's reputation also affects purchasing decisions by global consumers. As discussed in Chapter 4, in a phenomenon known as the "country of origin effect," consumers assume that products made in countries with high "country equity"—such as Italian clothing or Japanese electronics—will be of high quality and will often pay a premium for them (Kotler & Gertner, 2002, p. 252; Shimp, Samiee, & Madden, 1993, p. 327).

Yet, even if foreign perceptions of a nation become outdated, it can be decades before a country's reputation catches up with the reality on the ground (Anholt, 2007, p. 28). It is therefore essential for countries to manage their reputations deftly. Anholt (2007, p. 25) argues that a country's reputation is comprised of six elements:

1   The country's promotion as a tourist destination, along with the first-hand experiences of people who visit the country for business or for pleasure.
2   The brands the country exports.
3   The government's policies.
4   The business climate.
5   The country's cultural products, from cinema to sports.
6   The people of the country, including both celebrities and ordinary people. This is impacted by how individual citizens behave towards the foreigners they encounter both at home and abroad.

The difficulty in managing a country's reputation, of course, lies in the fact that so many different, independent actors—ranging from the government to the business community to ordinary citizens—are responsible for perceptions of the nation abroad (Anholt, 2007, p. 27). However, Anholt (2007, p. 31) argues that the *only* way to successfully change a country's global reputation is to induce these actors to work together. This is because a country's reputation cannot be fundamentally altered with a snazzy new logo or savvy advertising campaign—although Anholt (2007, p. 87) says that such campaigns can be useful for building the feeling of common purpose within a domestic population that is necessary in order to implement a strategy to improve a country's reputation. However, on the global stage, Anholt (2007, p. 29) says, "people only change their minds about places if the people and organizations in those places start to change the things they make and do, or the way they behave."

The first step in managing a country's reputation—or competitive identity—is, of course, to conduct research in order to identify how the nation is currently perceived by key stakeholders. Next, you should determine how people would need to perceive the country in order for it to achieve its goals. Finally, Anholt (2007, p. 30) advises, you must "work out a democratic, effective, and accountable process for getting from the current brand to the future one." Since this will require a range of actors to actually change their behavior as well as to "speak with one voice," it must be implemented internally within a country (Anholt, 2007, p. 31). Anholt (2007, pp. 33, 74) argues that the strategy should be a component of the country's national policy, and must have the personal backing of the head of state so that others within the government will view it as a priority. He (2007, pp. 36–37) recommends creating "innovation groups" within a government to circulate creative ideas. Governments must also convince others—from public officials to members of the business community to private citizens—to reflect the country's intended identity through both their words and their actions.

Since Anholt (2007, p. 34) argues that behavioral change forms the real basis for reputational change, he advises governments, "*don't talk unless you have something to say.*" This is because "consumers and the media aren't interested in countries talking about why they think they should be more famous, but they are usually interested in real events that are striking, relevant, and part of a bigger, compelling story."

What are the types of ideas that innovation groups should recommend, which will capture the world's attention? Anholt (2007, pp. 76–78) says that a competitive identity strategy should have as many of the following characteristics as possible:

1   *Creative*: Anholt (2007, p. 76) defines creative as "the opposite of boring"—something "surprising, arresting, [and/or] memorable."
2   *Ownable*: Something "ownable" is "uniquely and unarguably about the place and not anywhere else." (Anholt, 2007, p. 76).

3   *Sharp*: Something sharp is focused rather than bland or generic and tells a story about the country that is very specific. This often means being "daring or striking" enough to capture attention (Anholt, 2007, p. 77).
4   *Motivating*: The strategy should change the way people behave inside your country.
5   *Relevant*: The strategy should be relevant to the people who you are trying to reach abroad, giving them a reason to do what you desire.
6   *Elemental*: Because it will represent an entire country, your strategy must not be too specific. Rather, it should be broad and flexible enough to apply to "many people in many situations" (Anholt, 2007, p. 78).

The local culture should be highlighted as part of any strategy to improve a country's reputation. Anholt (2007, p. 100) notes that messages about a culture stand to be effective because people are less suspicious of them than they are about commercial messages. Culture also adds richness and depth to a country's reputation, helping, for example, people to view a Caribbean country as more than just a destination for beach vacations (Anholt, 2007, p. 101). Anholt (2007, p. 102) argues that "the raw materials for a rich, varied and attractive cultural life are often lying around, just waiting to be assembled in a new way."

This is an important point because we cannot create national brands from scratch, in the same way as we could for a new product, for example, since countries always already have pre-existing identities. In Aronczyk's (2008, p. 49) interviews with nation branding professionals in London, she found that

> branders see their work as skillful manipulation rather than creation or invention . . . [they] offer their expertise not as makers or producers of a nation brand, but merely as facilitators who apply the tools and techniques of their trade to help nations meet the requirements of the contemporary context. It is a process of uncovering, not generating, value.

The nation branders whom she interviewed reported that, when consulting for a country, they work to help the government identify a "brand essence" or "core idea" about the nation. A country's brand essence should differentiate it from other nations, yet at the same time cannot be so unique that it is "outside the calculus of exchange." The brand essence must inspire emotional attachment, or loyalty, yet also have a rational appeal, in order to generate political and economic investment (Aronczyk, 2008, pp. 52–53). Of course, any such "core idea" about a country will ultimately be simplistic, since "branding cannot account for the plurality of voices, legacies and competing visions of the nation-state" (Aronczyk, 2008, p. 58). Unsurprisingly, two characteristics that countries commonly attempt to convey through their "brand essences" are normalcy and peacefulness, in order to reassure the outside world that their nations are stable (Aronczyk, 2008, p. 53).

Another element of a successful strategy is education. Children can be educated in schools to be proud ambassadors for their country (Anholt, 2007, p. 107). Ultimately, for a nation branding strategy to work, citizens must be willing to "live the brand"—or, in other words, to behave and believe in ways that are compatible with the competitive identity strategy (Aronczyk, 2008, p. 54).

Since so many different groups will need to be on board in order for a strategy to work, it is critical to consult "well and widely enough to build a sense of shared ownership" before deciding upon any strategy (Anholt, 2007, pp. 83–84). Consultants who specialize in nation branding advise governments that it is essential to include the business community in the process of deciding upon a strategy; one such initiative in New Zealand was actually initiated and funded by the private sector (Aronczyk, 2008, p. 51). Another challenge will be that politicians often demand demonstrable results within a single electoral cycle so that they have accomplishments to run on in their next election, yet strategies for building competitive identity often must be implemented over the longer term (Anholt, 2007, p. 83). One practitioner described the process as having "a 15- to 20-year timeline" (Aronczyk, 2008, p. 52). Because building a nation's competitive identity often requires a great deal of internal change, it is one of the hardest processes to undertake as a global public relations practitioner. However, it is worth the investment.

Of course, practicing global public relations on behalf of governments also involves engaging foreign publics. The next section explains how to do so.

Types of Public Diplomacy Initiatives

This section will introduce you to different types of public diplomacy initiatives that you should consider when targeting foreign audiences in order to build relationships or communicate specific messages. Zaharna (2009, pp. 93–96) notes that there are eight key tactics that governments can use to build relationships with publics in different nations:

1 **Cultural and educational exchange programs.** For example, the U.S. State Department's Fulbright program and the Japan Foundation operate exchange programs for foreign students to study abroad in their nations (Zaharna, 2009, p. 93). Similarly, the Chinese tradition of "panda diplomacy"—gifting or loaning panda bears to other nations as a goodwill gesture—dates back to the seventh century (Rawnsley, 2009, p. 285). This tactic is described in greater detail in the "two tactics" section below. Another tactic is "arts diplomacy," which brings artists and/or their work to foreign countries for performances or exhibition. Brown (2009, p. 57) notes that "art creates powerful impressions that are often remembered forever. At the very least, arts diplomacy can make people abroad associate [a country] with the kind of unique moments that make our lives worth living."

"Panda diplomacy" has been practiced as a form of cultural exchange by China for centuries. Copyright: Hung Chung Chih

2 Visits by heads of state to other countries. Zaharna (2009, pp. 93–94) notes that an official visit by a head of state to another nation—a strategy that has been used since ancient times—is "more than 'pomp and ceremony,'" because, on such trips,

> heads of states can engage directly in public diplomacy by holding joint press conferences, speaking at official ceremonies, addressing the national

U.S. President Barack Obama arrives in Thailand. Copyright: 1000 Words

parliament, or granting media interviews. Direct interaction with the public can speak volumes in terms of public diplomacy. The former Soviet leader Mikhail Gorbachev was particularly adept at public diplomacy. He shattered U.S. images of Russian rigidity when he spontaneously stepped out of his official motorcade to shake hands with pedestrians on a busy Washington street; a scene that was broadcast over and over on U.S. national television.

3 **Cultural and language institutes,** such as France's Alliance Française, the United Kingdom's British Council, Germany's Goethe-Institut, and China's Confucius Institutes, which teach their native languages and share their cultures with foreigners. Zaharna (2009, p. 94) notes that "they accord channels for direct interaction with publics, allow for coordination between respective counterparts, represent relationship access and commitment, and provide a platform for relationship-building and networking beyond the individual level."

The Goethe-Institut in Prague, Czech Republic. Copyright: DeepGreen

4 **Development aid projects.** Zaharna (2009, p. 94) notes that

in such initiatives, relationship-building operates on two dimensions. One is the symbolic dimension that the aid or project represents an expression of the ties between two entities. Another dimension is the actual relationship that develops between the personnel of the sponsor and their counterparts as they work together on the project.

For example, Japan has built "friendship bridges" in countries including Cambodia, Egypt, Palau, Thailand, Sri Lanka, and Vietnam (Zaharna, 2009, pp. 94–95). Similarly, China has provided billions of dollars in debt cancellation and preferential loans and credits to Africa in recent years and invested in infrastructure such as clinics, roads, and schools across the continent (Pratt & Adamolekun, 2008). Of course, such programs often come with conditions that benefit the donor nation beyond the relationships that accrue from them. For example, Rawnsley (2009, p. 284) notes that "the diplomatic 'de-recognition' of Taiwan [which China considers to be part of its country and not an independent nation] is a fundamental precondition for those areas of the developing world which wish to receive Chinese aid. The strategy has worked: only 24 countries maintain full and formal diplomatic relations with Taiwan."

Canada and Scandinavian countries also provide significant foreign aid, assistance with humanitarian issues, and crisis mediation in other parts of the world, as a way of bolstering their global reputations and gravitas in world affairs (Thussu, 2013, pp. 29–30).

5 "Twinning" arrangements that partner cities or towns as "sister cities." Zaharna (2009, p. 95) notes that

> these agreements help promote cooperation and exchanges in a variety of areas such as economics, trade, and tourism, as well as education, technology, and sports. However, the major significance in pairing, beyond fostering cross-cultural contact and understanding, is that it serves to institutionalize the relationship-building process.

For example, New York City recently re-vamped its sister cities program, which is now called "New York City Global Partners" and includes more than 100 cities around the globe that have partnered with New York on programs such as online youth exchanges and international summits (City of New York, 2013).

6 Campaigns that seek to build relationships between publics in other countries. Zaharna (2009, p. 95) notes that "the primary goal is to build relationships with publics, rather than disseminate information to publics." For example, the United Kingdom's GREAT Britain campaign is designed to showcase "the best of what the UK has to offer to inspire the world and encourage people to visit, do business, invest and study in the UK." The campaign organizes about 100 events around the world each month. GREAT British Week in Singapore in March 2015 featured an exhibition of British design at Singapore's National Design Centre, while in February 2015 the country promoted its "automotive excellence" by unveiling a handmade Aston Martin car in Japan. The first passenger was Prince William, the Duke of Cambridge (GREAT Britain, 2015).

Prince William was the first passenger in an Aston Martin, promoting the U.K.'s "automotive excellence" as part of the GREAT Britain campaign. Photo courtesy of British Embassy Tokyo/ Alfie Goodrich

Countries such as India often try to enlist their own diaspora populations to help with such initiatives (Thussu, 2013, p. 73).

7 **"Non-political networking schemes."** These are initiatives that "build relationships between like-minded individuals or institutions working on a variety of areas such as science, health, environment, or literacy promotion." For example, the U.K. government created a Science and Innovation Network to promote collaboration among scientists on major research and projects (Zaharna, 2009, pp. 95–96).

8 **Building coalitions with other nations and non-state actors to achieve policy goals.** For example, Canadian foreign minister Lloyd Axworthy partnered with the International Campaign to Ban Landmines, which was discussed in the previous chapter, to launch a process that led to an historic treaty banning landmines (Zaharna, 2009, p. 96).

Of course, another tactic not discussed by Zaharna is **"media diplomacy,"** which "utilizes news media channels to conduct open diplomacy" (Van Dyke & Verčič, 2009, p. 825). This can be as simple as booking media interviews with foreign news outlets. As Kunczik (2009, p. 780) notes, "mass media reporting of foreign affairs often governs what kind of image . . . a country or culture has in another country." Therefore, governments have a major incentive to shape the narrative. The next section explains how to do so.

A government-NGO partnership helped broker a historic treaty banning landmines.
Copyright: Alexey Stiop

Finally, "social media diplomacy," or **"twiplomacy,"** involves using social media to reach foreign audiences (Burson-Marsteller, 2015). This is discussed in the "two tactics" section at the end of this chapter.

Crafting Your Public Diplomacy Messages

Copyright: style-photography

Now that you have selected your public diplomacy tactics, it is time to start crafting your messages. As an official spokesperson for a government, your words will carry enormous weight. When I served as Spokesperson for International Affairs in the U.S. Treasury, I knew that with just one poorly calibrated statement—expressing just how concerned we were, for example, that Europe's sovereign debt crisis could negatively impact the U.S. economy—I could have single-handedly tanked global markets. Likewise, a single slip of the tongue could have caused a diplomatic incident; I was always particularly afraid that I would accidentally call the members of the Asia-Pacific Economic Cooperation (APEC) forum "countries," which would have enraged China, since Taiwan is a member of APEC but not recognized by China as an independent nation. It therefore goes without saying that you will want to carefully vet your messages with subject matter experts before finalizing them.

Several other strategies will help you craft effective messages. First, you should eliminate jargon. Public diplomacy requires taking complicated policies and positions and making them intelligible to the ordinary person. Remember that your audiences are not primarily policy or political professionals, and therefore you should not be speaking in the language of policy and politics. Rather, you will need to work hard to find colloquial ways of explaining the (complicated) issues on which you communicate. James Thomas Snyder (2013, pp. 27–28), who formerly worked in the public diplomacy division of the North Atlantic Treaty Organization (NATO), explains that, when speaking to ordinary citizens,

> I stripped my visual presentations of all text, especially the dreaded Power-Point bullets, and left powerful images, mostly photographs, to illustrate what I was talking about. I worked in sharp one-liners, emphasizing what I wanted audiences to remember. I purged jargon. I stripped my talks to 20 minutes—still too long—to leave 30 to 40 minutes for questions and discussion. My presentations verged on the meta only because I had to let the audience know I would not allow the acronym-thick environment I normally inhabited contaminate theirs.

Can you do the same?

Second, all of your messages should promote confidence in your government. In fact, the level of confidence that investors have in a country is often a more important factor than the state of the country's actual finances in determining its level of foreign investment and access to loans and aid. As Kunczik (2009, p. 783) notes,

> in 1926 French economist Albert Aftalion published his theory (Théorie psychologique du change) based on the hypothesis that the exchange rate of a country's currency is determined mainly by trust in the future of that country. A deficit of the balance of payments will not cause a devaluation of the currency as long as the belief in the future of the currency attracts foreign capital thus balancing the deficit.

For this reason, it is critical to reinforce your country's stability, strong economic prospects, and intentions to live up to commitments in order to build and maintain this confidence in your nation's future—even, and in fact especially, when times are tough. For example, when I worked in the U.S. Treasury during Europe's economic crisis, my colleagues would often say that the Europeans would have to "fake it until they make it." Of course, you should never under any circumstances distort actual facts. However, the tone of your rhetoric makes a big difference, so you will need to calibrate it carefully and back it up with facts that do support your claims. Optimistic rhetoric can lead to improved confidence in your economy, which can drive the investments that make your messages a self-fulfilling prophecy.

To maintain confidence, you should also try to avoid negative media coverage that takes people (and markets) by surprise. One way to do this is by calibrating expectations in advance of major events and announcements. For example, in the U.S. Treasury Department, prior to traveling to a major global summit, such as a meeting of G-7 finance ministers, we typically held a background briefing for reporters to give them a sense of what to expect from the upcoming trip. By letting reporters know what types of outcomes could reasonably be expected from such meetings in advance, we helped prevent later media coverage expressing shock that the meetings had not resulted in agreements fully resolving the world's problems. Similarly, when I worked for a group of heads of state and other eminent thinkers convened by the U.N. Secretary General to write a recommended plan for ending global poverty, I issued a communique to the media following each of the group's major meetings, explaining what had been agreed. This likewise helped to calibrate expectations for what their final report would—and would not—contain.

Another way to guard against negative media coverage is to consult with important stakeholders and partners (such as foreign governments, international organizations, and domestic constituencies who have a stake in your decisions) prior to making major decisions and announcements, since they will likely be called upon by the press for reactions. Often, the very fact of being consulted makes people feel that their opinions are respected and can help dampen the tenor of their criticism if they disagree with you. There are typically a small, predictable group of government officials and outside experts who are quoted over and over in the press on particular issues (read past media coverage and make a list of names). You should share "talking points" (literally, fact sheets with suggested messages that they can share with the press) on major policies and initiatives with your allies, since third-party validators can lend significant credibility to your claims. As for prominent voices who disagree with you, it is worth reaching out to them directly—perhaps immediately prior to making official announcements—to give them a heads up and explain the reasons for your decisions. Such overtures can help reinforce the notion that, even though you have a policy disagreement, your decision was not made hastily or irresponsibly—hopefully helping to at least tone down the bitterness of their reactions.

Finally, in the world of public diplomacy, practitioners face a particular challenge: the messages we wish to send domestically on a particular issue are often very different from those that work best internationally. For example, it can be very effective to build domestic support for a war by framing a conflict in terms of "us" vs. "them"—but doing so risks alienating citizens of the state you are fighting, who you will also want to win over (Vlahos, 2009, p. 30). Similarly, when the U.S. invaded Iraq in 2003, the U.S. government developed a plan that it called "shock and awe" to overwhelm the Iraqi government's efforts to fight back (Chan, 2003). While this term may have been effective in convincing the U.S. public that its government was prosecuting the war strategically, retired U.S. General Anthony Zinni explains,

> that was a way to say [to the Iraqi people]: "Your fate is inevitable. We're going to crush you. The might of America will defeat you. Just surrender and throw down your arms." You don't speak to Arab pride and Arab manhood in this way. That whole psychological business gave them another cause to fight for, more than they would have fought just for [then-Iraqi President] Saddam [Hussein] (Rhoads, 2009, p. 174).

In the past, governments often got away with promulgating different messages to domestic and international publics. But in the era of the Internet, this is no longer realistic. You should think carefully about how any message you craft will be interpreted by audiences both domestic and foreign—and, in cases where optimal messages for such groups are contradictory, you will need to conduct a careful cost-benefit analysis before deciding upon your final messages.

Working with Local Embassies and Consulates

Copyright: koya979

Of course, before you decide on any tactics and messages, you will want to receive input from local experts. Your best allies in such an endeavor will usually be embassy communication officers. Most governments station communication officers in their embassies (an embassy is a diplomatic office that is typically located in the capital of a foreign country and is headed by an ambassador) and consulates (diplomatic offices not located in foreign capitals). The primary responsibility of such professionals is to communicate with local people in the countries in which they are stationed. If you work in public relations for a government, these communication officers will be valuable resources who can advise you of local public opinion about your country and recommend the public relations strategies, tactics, and messages that will be most (and least) effective in the countries in which they are stationed.

For example, when I worked for the U.S. Treasury Department, the first thing I did when our senior officials planned to travel abroad was to contact our embassies for help developing local public relations plans. Typically, I would ask the embassy or consulate's communication officer to recommend one or two journalists whom they knew well and trusted, and we offered media interviews to those reporters. The embassy communication officers provided tactical support to facilitate these interviews—often setting them up for me and later tracking down copies of the stories and translating them into English. The communication officers were also very helpful in preparing for interviews. I always asked them for insight into what topics were being covered in the local press and what types of questions our officials were likely to get from local reporters.

The author (seated, center) types notes on her Blackberry while the U.S. Deputy Treasury Secretary is interviewed in the U.S. Embassy in Kinshasa, Democratic Republic of the Congo.

Embassy communication officers also helped me prepare for any other types of media encounters that our officials experienced on their foreign trips. For example, when government officials travel abroad, they typically meet with their foreign counterparts. The offices of foreign heads of state and government ministries have different conventions regarding media access to such meetings. Often, they will allow a "photo spray at the top," meaning that photographers are allowed to enter the room for the first minute or two of the meeting (before it officially commences) in order to obtain photos of the officials together. In addition, it is commonplace to have a "press avail" at the conclusion of such meetings, in which reporters have an opportunity to ask questions of both the local and visiting government officials. Therefore, before our officials went to any meetings abroad, I asked our embassy communication officers to be in touch with the local government for details on any access that they planned to allow to the media, so that I could brief my principals in advance on what to expect. (Of course, if they were going to be questioned by the press, I provided them with likely questions and suggested answers).

In addition to preparing your principals, another reason why it is important to know what types of press opportunities there will be on government officials' overseas trips is so that you can advise your own press corps of such opportunities in advance, and journalists who report on your government can decide whether to travel abroad to cover them. It is terrible form not to provide the same level of access to reporters in your own country as foreign reporters are accorded. Therefore, even when I knew that U.S.-based journalists would not travel to cover particular media opportunities (for example, when the Deputy Secretary of the U.S. Treasury traveled to Botswana to meet with local government officials) I always issued a media advisory in advance, indicating exactly where and when there would be photo sprays or media avails on each day of the trip.

Finally, embassy communication officers can provide you with the most reliable information on local news coverage. They typically provide a daily summary of local media coverage to embassy or consulate staff; I asked communication officers in key countries to add me to their distribution lists so that I could monitor local news in critical countries, from France to Japan.

In sum, embassy and consulate communication officers will be invaluable sources of advice, intelligence, and tactical support in executing local public relations strategies. Consult them before you begin planning initiatives for guidance on best practices and what to expect in the countries in which they are stationed.

Combatting Global Terrorism

A new, modern challenge for governments is that, today, terrorist groups are also using savvy public relations strategies in an effort to bolster support for their causes. Taylor (2009, p. 14) notes that "terrorists . . . know that their activity is 10% violence and 90% publicity." They use publicity to attract recruits and support for their causes and also to instill fear in their enemies that attacks are imminent.

In particular, Knowlton (2014) notes that the terrorist group the Islamic State of Iraq and al-Sham (ISIS) "has demonstrated a skill and sophistication with social media previously unseen in extremist groups." ISIS members and supporters produce up to 90,000 messages on social media every day (Schmitt, 2015). According to *The New York Times*,

> the group has started new Twitter and YouTube accounts as soon as old ones are suspended, and it has used parts of the hit video game Grand Theft Auto to radicalize and recruit young Muslims. The militants also latch on to trending hashtags, like one used for the Scottish independence referendum, to get wide distribution of their material (De Freytas-Tamura, 2014).

ISIS members recently spent thousands of hours communicating with one young woman in the state of Washington in the U.S. in an effort to convert her, even plying her with money and gifts. One man who recruited people for extremist groups for years told *The New York Times* that "we look for people who are isolated. . . . And if they are not isolated already, then we isolated them." A recruitment guide published by the terrorist group Al Qaeda in Iraq, which became ISIS, instructs recruiters to stay in close communication with a potential recruit, "share his joys and sadness," and next educate the recruit about Islam without initially mentioning jihad (Callimachi, 2015). Vlahos (2009, p. 36) argues that "it is the task of [American] public diplomacy to send the message that we offer a better deal."

Of course, ISIS is not the first terrorist group to use social media in an effort to build support for its cause. As Anzalone (2013) has reported, the Somali terrorist group al-Shabab has long used social media to attempt to promulgate counter-narratives to official government and press reports. When the group began executing civilians at the Westgate shopping mall in Nairobi, Kenya, on September 21, 2013, it posted live updates on Twitter in order to gain the attention of the global media and discredit the Kenyan government's claims that the situation was under control.

In 2010, the U.S. State Department set up an office called the Center for Strategic Counterterrorism Communication to counter terrorist messaging on the Internet (Knowlton, 2014). Posting in Arabic, English, Punjabi, Somali, and Urdu using the hashtag #ThinkAgainTurnAway, the Center works to "counter terrorist propaganda and misinformation, offering a competing narrative that seeks to strike an emotional chord. The analysts also post messages on English-language websites that jihadists use to recruit, raise money and promote their cause" (Knowlton, 2014; Mazzetti & Gordon, 2015). The Center's communicators also share content produced by others in order to amplify it. As Knowlton (2014) reports,

> recent Twitter posts quoted Muslim scholars as saying "#ISIS murder of aid worker a violation of Islamic law" and described a Turkish nurse as "tired of treating #ISIS fighters so they can go behead people."

When a Twitter user called Islam4Libya on Tuesday posted this: "Video emerging of #Children being killed in #Syria BY #US airstrikes, as if #Assad wasn't killing them fast enough," the "Think Again" feed quickly replied: "@ISLAM4L LIES: They say in the video that these children were wounded in Assad airstrikes. Stop recycling footage as anti-U.S. propaganda."

The United Arab Emirates also recently created a center to respond to ISIS propaganda. In addition, *The New York Times* reports that "a crucial part of the public diplomacy [by the U.S.] has involved encouraging Arab religious leaders, Muslim scholars, and Arab news media organizations to denounce the Islamic State as a distortion of Islam." However, a 2015 internal U.S. State Department memo obtained by *The New York Times* concludes that efforts to combat ISIS online have largely been unsuccessful, in part due to lack of sufficient coordination among countries (Mazzetti & Gordon, 2015).

Another challenge governments face in combatting terrorism is that their views generally do not hold weight with potential terrorists. The director of the U.S. National Counterterrorism Center has acknowledged that "unfortunately, as we all know, the government is probably not the best platform to try to communicate with the set of actors who are potentially vulnerable to this kind of propaganda and this kind of recruitment." He reports that the U.S. government attempts "to find ways to stimulate this kind of counternarrative, this kind of countermessaging, without having a U.S. government hand in it" (Schmitt, 2015).

As of now, diplomacy efforts to fight terrorism via social media appear to have been largely unsuccessful, because government communicators on social media are vastly outnumbered by ISIS posters, countries are poorly coordinating their efforts in this space, and official postings by the likes of the U.S. government are not very credible to potential recruits. However, this is an area where demand for creative strategies by practitioners of public diplomacy is likely to grow.

Snapshot of Two Tactics

Although these tactics should be considered as part of any global public relations campaign, they are often particularly effective for governments:

Interpersonal Communication: A hallmark of modern public diplomacy strategies has been fostering interpersonal communication between citizens. For example, in 1940, the U.S. State Department created the International Visitor Leadership Program (IVLP), which brings 5,000 professionals from around the world to the U.S. each year for short visits (typically for three weeks). Participants generally visit four different communities in the U.S., where they meet with their counterparts in the public and private sectors. The U.S. Department of State Bureau of Educational and Cultural Affairs (2015) says the program's alumni— which include 335 current or former heads of state and government— "cultivate lasting relationships . . . with their American counterparts." As previously discussed, student exchanges are another common form of interpersonal diplomacy. For example, after World War II, more than five million French and German high school students participated in exchanges between the two countries, helping to repair their relations (Scott-Smith, 2009, p. 50).

Copyright: hxdbzxy

Aloy Gowne, a public affairs and stakeholder relations practitioner who previously served as a Public Affairs Specialist for the U.S. consulate in Cape Town, South Africa, says that an added benefit of such exchanges is that participants typically chronicle their experiences on social media. He explains that

> everyone has a perception about imperialism, about the West, but when they get there they see things differently. They take pictures, they tweet, and when it's a young person from a rural community going to the U.S., that's a different, very credible story. Or they go through the visa process, which South Africans think is very difficult but is really seamless, and they share that. And then the embassy or consulate can use and share those posts.

Of course, this is a tactic that comes with some risk, because the reactions by individuals to such experiences are unpredictable and will not always be positive. As Scott-Smith (2009, pp. 52–55) notes,

> the most notorious case . . . is the visit of Seyyed Qutb to the United States in 1948. Qutb, an Egyptian civil servant, went to study the education system in Colorado for the benefit of implementing reforms in his home country. Instead, his disgust at American society and its immoral materialism only furthered his own path towards a pure form of Islamic radicalism, and he subsequently became a major influence within anti-Western fundamentalism. This case highlights how things can seriously go awry, but while the chance of a culture-clash is ever-present, it would be a mistake to use Qutb as a reason to limit exchanges in general. . . . Research into the post-war German programs and other investigations into psychological warfare techniques highlighted the fact that critics will rarely be swayed, but doubters may become believers and supporters will feel empowered.

However, such exchanges are generally positive; as Scott-Smith (2009, p. 50) notes, "not for nothing have U.S. ambassadors around the world referred to the IVLP . . . as the most valuable tool of public diplomacy at their disposal." Snow's (2009b, p. 242) review of the extant literature on educational exchanges likewise found that "such contacts do generally translate into greater tolerance in general and such tolerance can serve as a reservoir of goodwill from which one can draw in times of international crisis." Snyder (2013, p. 69) notes that studies consistently find that "the more likely people are to know counterparts from other cultures—or to know people, perhaps family members, who have friends in other cultures—the more likely they are to view people from other cultures with equanimity and respect."

When undertaking such initiatives, it is critical to select participants who are open-minded. Such exchanges will be most impactful if they occur before a person is familiar with his or her host nation and if they offer opportunities that the participant can later use for personal or professional benefit (Scott-Smith, 2009, pp. 53–54).

Although exchange programs are often funded by governments, independent organizations are often hired to administer them. Mueller (2009, p. 103) argues that this is a good strategy because "it preserves the credibility of the program by keeping the government at arm's length. It signals that exchange programs are authentic two-way educational experiences rather than purveyors of brainwashing propaganda."

As with any public diplomacy strategy, you will want to make sure that you set the expectations of participants from the outset. For example, Scott-Smith (2009, p. 52) notes that

> during the early years of the IVLP, it was discovered that the most complaints about the Program were coming from participants in India. The reason was that the U.S. embassy was selecting mainly individuals from the higher castes who expected far more of a VIP treatment than they received, and they did not understand how the U.S. government could run such a Program with so little official protocol (when that was in fact the whole point).

The case study in Chapter 8 discusses how interpersonal communication can also be a valuable strategy for corporations.

"Twiplomacy:" Today, 86 percent of U.N. member states, 172 heads of state and government, and more than 4,100 ambassadors and embassies are tweeting (Burson-Marsteller, 2015). One benefit of using social media is that it allows you "to pre-empt journalists from being the first to get their interpretation of events before a wider audience," ultimately giving you greater control over your messages (Sengupta, 2013). Peter Susko (2015), Director of the Slovac Republic Foreign Ministry's Press Department, says the most common way that diplomats use Twitter is to share official statements. He notes that "these may not be sexy or glamorous, but they expose policy statements to casual users not likely to seek out or come across official communications." Susko says Twitter

is also a good tool for "sort-of balloons to test the wind and the public opinion, tokens of appreciation for one another, especially after visits to another country, and/or invitations to a forum or a meeting."

Burson-Marsteller's annual (2015) Twiplomacy study reports that, with a few significant exceptions, most senior government officials rely on their staff to tweet for them, and the offices that invest the most resources in their online presences really are the most effective. As always, think twice before you tweet. In 2015, Argentine President Cristina Kirchner was forced to apologize after seemingly mocking Chinese accents in a tweet during an official visit to China (Kantchev, 2015).

Chapter 7 contains much more information on how to use social media as part of global public relations campaigns.

References

Anholt, S. (2007). *Competitive identity: The new brand management for nations, cities and regions*. New York, NY: Palgrave Macmillan.

Anzalone, C. (2013). The Nairobi attack and al-Shabab's media strategy. *CTC Sentinel*, 6(10), 1–6.

Armstrong, M. C. (2009). Operationalizing public diplomacy. In N. Snow & P. M. Taylor (Eds.), *Routledge handbook of public diplomacy* (pp. 63–71). New York, NY: Routledge.

Aronczyk, M. (2008). "Living the brand": Nationality, globality, and the identity strategies of nation branding consultants. *International Journal of Communication*, 2, 41–65.

Brown, J. (2009). Arts diplomacy. In N. Snow & P. M. Taylor (Eds.), *Routledge handbook of public diplomacy* (pp. 57–59). New York, NY: Routledge.

Burson-Marsteller (2015). Twiplomacy. Retrieved from http://twiplomacy.com/blog/twiplomacy-study-2015/

Callimachi, R. (2015, June 27). ISIS and the lonely young American. *The New York Times*. Retrieved from http://www.nytimes.com/2015/06/28/world/americas/isis-online-recruiting-american.html?hpw&rref=world&action=click&pgtype=Homepage&module=well-region&region=bottom-well&WT.nav=bottom-well

Chan, S. (2003, January 24). Iraq faces massive U.S. missile barrage. *CBS News*. Retrieved from http://www.cbsnews.com/news/iraq-faces-massive-us-missile-barrage/

City of New York (2013). NYC's partner cities. Retrieved from http://www.nyc.gov/html/ia/gp/html/partner/partner.shtml

De Freytas-Tamura, K. (2014, September 17). For Muslims, social media debate on extremism is reflected in dueling hashtags. *The New York Times*. Retrieved from http://www.nytimes.com/2014/09/28/world/for-muslims-social-media-debate-on-extremism-is-reflected-in-dueling-hashtags.html?_r=1

El-Nawawy, M. (2006). US public diplomacy in the Arab world: The news credibility of Radio Sawa and Television Alhurra in five countries. *Global Media and Communication*, 2(2), 185–205.

GREAT Britain (2015). GREAT Britain campaign: Bringing the best of Britain to the world. Retrieved from http://www.greatbritaincampaign.com/#!/about

Heller, K. S., & Persson, L. M. (2009). The distinction between public affairs and public diplomacy. In N. Snow & P. M. Taylor (Eds.), *Routledge handbook of public diplomacy* (pp. 225–247). New York, NY: Routledge.

Kahn, J. (2004, March 18). Postmortem: Iraq war media coverage dazzled but it also obscured. *UC Berkeley News Center*. Retrieved from http://www.berkeley.edu/news/media/releases/2004/03/18_iraqmedia.shtml

Kantchev, G. (2015, February 24). Diplomats on Twitter: The good, the bad, and the ugly. *The Wall Street Journal*. Retrieved from http://blogs.wsj.com/digits/2015/02/24/diplomats-on-twitter-the-good-the-bad-and-the-ugly/

Knowlton, B. (2014, September 26). Digital war takes shape on websites over ISIS. *The New York Times*. Retrieved from http://www.nytimes.com/2014/09/27/world/middleeast/us-vividly-rebuts-isis-propaganda-on-arab-social-media.html?_r=0

Kotler, P., & Gertner, D. (2002). Country as brand, product and beyond: A place marketing and brand management perspective. *Brand Management, 9*(4–5), 249–261.

Kunczik, M. (2009). Transnational public relations by foreign governments. In K. Sriramesh & D. Verčič (Eds.), *The global public relations handbook: Theory, research, and practice* (2nd ed.) (pp. 769–794). New York, NY: Routledge.

Mazzetti, M., & Gordon, M. R. (2015, June 12). ISIS is winning the social media war, U.S. concludes. *The New York Times*. Retrieved from http://www.nytimes.com/2015/06/13/world/middleeast/isis-is-winning-message-war-us-concludes.html

Mueller, S. (2009). The nexus of U.S. public diplomacy and citizen diplomacy. In N. Snow & P. M. Taylor (Eds.), *Routledge handbook of public diplomacy* (pp. 101–107). New York, NY: Routledge.

Nye, J. S. (2004). *Soft power: The means to success in world politics*. New York, NY: PublicAffairs.

Pratt, C. B., & Adamolekun, W. (2008). The People's Republic of China and FAPRA: Catalysts for theory building in Africa's public relations. *Journal of Public Relations Research, 20*(1), 20–48.

Rawnsley, G. D. (2009). China talks back. In N. Snow & P. M. Taylor (Eds.), *Routledge handbook of public diplomacy* (pp. 282–291). New York, NY: Routledge.

Rhoads, K. (2009). The culture variable in the influence equation. In N. Snow & P. M. Taylor (Eds.), *Routledge handbook of public diplomacy* (pp. 166–186). New York, NY: Routledge.

Schmitt, E. (2015, February 16). U.S. intensifies effort to blunt ISIS' message. *The New York Times*. Retrieved from http://www.nytimes.com/2015/02/17/world/middleeast/us-intensifies-effort-to-blunt-isis-message.html

Scott-Smith, G. (2009). Exchange programs and public diplomacy. In N. Snow & P. M. Taylor (Eds.), *Routledge handbook of public diplomacy* (pp. 50–56). New York, NY: Routledge.

Seib, P. (2013). Public diplomacy and the media in the Middle East. *CPD Perspectives on Public Policy, Paper 6*. Retrieved from http://uscpublicdiplomacy.org/sites/uscpublicdiplomacy.org/files/legacy/publications/perspectives/CPDPerspectivesPDand%20MediaandMiddle%20East%20-%20Linked.pdf

Sengupta, S. (2013, October 3). New diplomatic avenue emerges, in 140-character bursts. *The New York Times*. Retrieved from http://www.nytimes.com/2013/10/04/world/new-diplomatic-avenue-emerges-in-140-character-bursts.html?smid=tw-share&_r=5&

Shimp, T. A., Samiee, S., & Madden, T. J. (1993). Countries and their products: A cognitive structure perspective. *Journal of the Academy of Marketing Science, 21*(4), 323–330.

Signitzer, B., & Wamser, C. (2006). Public diplomacy: A specific governmental public relations function. In C. H. Botan & V. Hazleton (Eds.), *Public relations theory II* (pp. 435–464). Mahwah, NJ: Lawrence Erlbaum Associates, Inc.

Snow, N. (2009a). Rethinking public diplomacy. In N. Snow & P. M. Taylor (Eds.), *Routledge handbook of public diplomacy* (pp. 1–11). New York, NY: Routledge.

Snow, N. (2009b). Valuing exchange of persons in public diplomacy. In N. Snow & P. M. Taylor (Eds.), *Routledge handbook of public diplomacy* (pp. 233–247). New York, NY: Routledge.

Snyder, J. T. (2013). *The United States and the challenge of public diplomacy*. New York, NY: Palgrave Macmillan.

Susko, P. (2015). Twiplomacy 2.015. *World Communication Review*. Retrieved from http://www.forumdavos.com/WCFA

Taylor, P. M. (2009). Public diplomacy and strategic communications. In N. Snow & P. M. Taylor (Eds.), *Routledge handbook of public diplomacy* (pp. 12–16). New York, NY: Routledge.

Thussu, D. K. (2013). *Communicating India's soft power: Buddha to Bollywood*. New York, NY: Palgrave Macmillan.

Tye, L. (2002). *The father of spin: Edward L. Bernays and the birth of public relations*. New York, NY: Henry Holt and Company.

United States Department of State Bureau of Educational and Cultural Affairs (2015). About IVLP. Retrieved from http://eca.state.gov/ivlp/about-ivlp

Van Dyke, M. A., & Verčič, D. (2009). Public relations, public diplomacy, and strategic communication: An international model of conceptual convergence. In K. Sriramesh & D. Verčič (Eds.), *The global public relations handbook: Theory, research, and practice* (2nd ed.) (pp. 822–842). New York, NY: Routledge.

Vlahos, M. (2009). Public diplomacy as loss of world authority. In N. Snow & P. M. Taylor (Eds.), *Routledge handbook of public diplomacy* (pp. 24–38). New York, NY: Routledge.

Wyne, A. S. (2009). Public opinion and power. In N. Snow & P. M. Taylor (Eds.), *Routledge handbook of public diplomacy* (pp. 39–49). New York, NY: Routledge.

Zaharna, R. S. (2009). Mapping out a spectrum of public diplomacy initiatives. In N. Snow & P. M. Taylor (Eds.), *Routledge handbook of public diplomacy* (pp. 86–100). New York, NY: Routledge.

7 The Global Media and Social Networks

One of your most important responsibilities as a global public relations professional is harnessing both the traditional media and social media in order to tell your story and communicate with key stakeholders. Although many people now believe that social media is the future of public relations, *do not underestimate the power of the traditional press*. This is because, in many countries, such as the United States of America, a lot of people may now receive their news via social media, but the stories they share on such platforms are still written by traditional media outlets such as *The New York Times* (Asur, Yu, & Huberman, 2011). Of course, this is not universally the case. As I will later discuss in greater detail, in China, for example, citizens are so skeptical of the government-censored press that they have come to rely upon a new generation of independent influencers on social media for credible information. However, it will be impossible for you to practice global public relations successfully without a strong understanding of media relations and key global and regional outlets. The following section will therefore focus on the traditional global media. I will then turn to key social networks that likewise have global reach.

The Traditional Global Media

There are three key types of traditional media outlets today: global outlets that reach massive international audiences, regional media players that reach important regional audiences, and domestic media outlets that primarily reach audiences or readers within a particular country or community. Modern global media outlets have come to enjoy such a massive penetration that it is now possible for you to reach a significant percentage of the people on earth by pitching just a few key outlets, such as Al Jazeera, the BBC, CNN International, the Associated Press, and Reuters. In fact, in my first job at the United Nations, I was responsible for pitching these top global media outlets nearly exclusively (I then coordinated with communicators around the world, who pitched regional and domestic media). However, it is exceedingly difficult to place stories with these outlets, because the competition is so fierce.

Copyright: eldar nurkovic

First and foremost, you need to thoroughly understand media outlets before you can pitch them. Because it is likely that you don't naturally read and view all of the key global media players in the course of your everyday life, it is especially important for you to make the extra effort to become deeply familiar with them. Watch and read their coverage religiously to learn about their programs, personalities, and styles of coverage so that you can craft successful story ideas for them. For example, while Al Jazeera and the BBC World Service cover global social issues—from the plight of migrant workers to the realities of living in poverty—in great detail, I have always found it to be significantly harder to successfully pitch a story about global poverty to CNN International.

Although it is terribly frustrating and unjust, the reality is that media outlets tend to cover certain types of stories. For example, countries with greater political, economic, and military power garner a disproportionate amount of global media coverage (Golan, 2010, p. 128). One study, for example, found that Nigerian newspapers devoted more coverage to the Presidential election in the U.S. than to the election in nearby Ghana (Akinfeleye, Amobi, Okoye, & Sunday, 2009)! However, studies have also found that media outlets are generally more likely to cover international news stories when they occur in countries that are geographically close to the media outlet's country of origin and when the countries are culturally similar (Golan, 2010, p. 127). You will get a sense of what types of stories individual media outlets typically cover by consuming them regularly.

Just as important, you need to ascertain *how* stories are covered by these organizations and by individual reporters and presenters. For example, if you went to the BBC World News website, saw that they have an interview program called HARDtalk, wrote to a producer, and booked one of your senior executives for the show without doing further research or preparation, you would essentially be sending your boss to be eaten alive. As the name implies, HARDtalk is one of the toughest interview programs in the world. You would only want to allow a remarkably intelligent, well-spoken, and composed representative to be interviewed by Stephen Sackur (a journalist whom I greatly admire as a citizen, but slightly fear as a public relations practitioner)—and even then, you would book such an interview only after allowing plenty of time for preparation and practice sessions.

To be sure, all modern journalists are inundated with pitches for more stories than they can possibly cover. However, reporters and producers at the media outlets with the biggest global reach are truly deluged. Therefore, never pitch a story without first doing your homework, understanding the outlet, and ensuring that your idea is right for it. It goes without saying that you will want to deliver a tightly crafted pitch and make it as enticing as possible. Many of the same elements that are appealing to reporters at the domestic level are applicable at the global level. Is your story timely? Is it interesting or unusual in some way? Is there an element of human interest or conflict? Does the topic stand to impact the media outlet's core readership or viewership in some way (Rich, 2013)?

Also make sure that you thoroughly understand a media outlet before pitching it. It will be rather embarrassing, to say the least, if you pitch a story to a broadcaster, a producer says that a famous presenter can do the interview, and you do not know who the presenter is. Once you ruin a relationship with a reporter, either through ignorance or by wasting his or her time with ill-suited pitches, it is unlikely that your future ideas will be given serious consideration. Of course, you, savvy reader, have this book, so you won't be making such mistakes!

Another trick to pitching the global media is to make it as easy as possible for an outlet to cover a story. For example, as discussed in Chapter 5, when I worked at the United Nations, one of the biggest stories I pitched each year was "Stand Up and Take Action." As part of the three-day annual initiative, millions of citizens organized local events in their communities to demand that world leaders end extreme poverty. In my first year of pitching "Stand Up," I learned that CNN International would not send reporters to local events. Therefore, in my second year on the job, we hired local videographers to shoot and upload background footage (known in the biz as "b-roll") of a few key events in Africa, Asia, and Europe. I provided the footage to CNN I and brought a spokesperson to their studio in New York for a short interview—and, sure enough, this time they ran the story, using the footage we provided! Although this involved a lot of extra expense and work on my part, CNN I's massive global reach made it more than worth the investment.

If you want a global media outlet to cover an event or conduct an interview in person, figure out where its global bureaus are located and try to schedule the event for as close as possible to one of them. It is a lot more likely, for example, that a producer will book an interview in Bangkok, Thailand, if his or her outlet already has a reporter there than if a journalist needs to fly in from an Asia desk in New Delhi, India! Also, think through all of the elements that a reporter will need to cover the story (likely photos for a print publication and footage for a broadcaster, plus interview subjects and facts and figures) and try to supply as many of them as possible.

Once you do successfully pitch a story, or when you are approached by a reporter who is working on a story, make sure that you come to an explicit agreement with the journalist about the ground rules. For example, the term "off the record" means different things to different people. If you speak to a reporter off the record, does it mean that (s)he cannot use the information at all, or can the journalist use his or her new knowledge to go find someone else who will go on the record and state the facts you have provided? If you speak "on background" to a reporter, how exactly can (s)he identify you? As a "company spokesperson," or perhaps as "a source close to the negotiations?" What will be the specific topic and scope of the interview? Because reporters and media outlets from different countries (and often within the same country!) will have different traditions, expectations, and assumptions, it is critical that you and the journalist with whom you are working come to an explicit agreement before you provide information or an interview.

One concept with which you will be expected to be familiar when working with the global media is that of the "Chatham House Rule." You will often hear people refer to "Chatham House Rules," but there is actually only one rule, which originated at Chatham House, the Royal Institute of International Affairs in London. It states that "when a meeting, or part thereof, is held under the Chatham House Rule, participants are free to use the information received, but neither the identity nor the affiliation of the speaker(s), nor that of any other participant, may be revealed" (Chatham House, 2015). Of course, as with any other agreement, make sure that you define the term to ensure that everyone understands it if you decide to host an event under the Chatham House Rule.

It goes without saying that, in each of your interactions with a reporter, you should be thinking not just about the present story on which (s)he is working, but also about your long-term relationship. When you work with a reporter for the first time, try to use your interactions as an opportunity to learn more about the types of stories that (s)he is interested in covering in the future and make notes for yourself so that you don't forget. (After well over a decade of working with the global media, my own personal spreadsheet contains my notes on the interests of more than 1,000 reporters around the globe!)

As discussed in Chapter 1, you will likely want to issue global press releases that can be adapted and translated by your team for release at the regional, national, and sub-national levels. When writing press releases about global topics, I recommend communicating your top-line messages in the body of the press release and then adding local facts in a "Note to Editors" at the end of the release, in order to make it easier to digest. The example below is a global press release I wrote on "Stand Up and Take Action" using this approach.

FOR IMMEDIATE RELEASE

CITIZENS' VOICES AGAINST POVERTY WILL CRESCENDO IN NOISES HEARD AROUND THE WORLD AS HEADS OF STATE TRAVEL TO UN SUMMIT

Citizens Will Make Their Expectations that Governments Achieve the Millennium Development Goals Too Loud to Ignore at Events Across the Globe on September 17–19

September 9, 2010 — On September 17–19, people across the globe will turn up the volume on their call for heads of state gathering at the United Nations on September 20–22 to demonstrate leadership in order to achieve the Millennium Development Goals (MDGs).

Citizens will gather at events across continents to amplify their support for the eight MDGs, a set of targets to eradicate extreme poverty and its root causes by 2015 that marks its tenth anniversary this week. They will be singing, chanting, blowing whistles, playing drums, blowing vuvuzelas, banging pots and pans and setting off alarm clocks. The sounds of these noises emanating from villages, towns and cities around the world as part of the three day mobilization "Stand Up, Take Action, Make Noise for the MDGs" will make citizens' commitments to track and support their countries' achievement of the Goals visible, vocal, and impossible to ignore.

"The Secretary General's recent report on the Millennium Development Goals has made it clear that with only five years until the deadline by which world leaders have promised to eradicate extreme poverty and its root causes, the active partnership of citizens and governments is more important than ever," said Corinne Woods, Director of the UN Millennium Campaign. "The citizens participating in 'Stand Up and Take Action' on September 17–19 will make it clear to heads of state gathering at the United Nations the following week that they support and want to be a part of the realization of the Goals."

The mobilization will serve as a launching point for a new initiative of real-time monitoring by citizens of basic service delivery in their communities. The availability of and access to quality, reliable, and consistent basic services are essential for the MDGs to be realized at the country level. The Millennium Campaign will work with governments, civil society, technology partners, and the media to launch pilot citizen tracking programs in India and Kenya in 2011.

Note to editors:

"Stand Up" events being organized across the globe include:

- Concerts across Bangladesh, Cambodia, Columbia, Ghana, India, Indonesia, Korea, Nepal, Papua New Guinea, the Philippines, Rwanda, Senegal, and Zimbabwe, where local artists will sing their support of the MDGs.
- In Jordan, 40,000 children are expected to simultaneously blow whistles in support of the MDGs, in an attempt to set a new world record.
- In India, "Stand Up" will kick off with a film festival on September 17.
- In New York City, Lincoln Plaza will be the hub of Stand Up activity on September 19, with exhibitions on promises and progress to end poverty as well as speakers and performers.
- In Paris, French citizens and civil society organizations are organizing a flash mob and Stand Up moment in front of the Eiffel Tower on September 18.
- In Washington, D.C., citizens will come together with local musicians, drummers, and bands just two blocks from the White House to amplify their voices in support of the MDGs.
- In the Philippines, various fiestas in towns and cities nationwide will be dedicated to the call for the achievement of the MDGs, including events from September 17–19 where citizens will play indigenous materials including coconuts and bamboo guitars.
- In Colombia, the United Nations, in partnership with the National Soccer League, will invite 30,000 spectators at one of the most important soccer matches of the season to Stand Up on September 19.
- In Egypt, religious leaders will give sermons calling for an end to poverty in more than 50,000 mosques and at Sunday masses in churches across the country. A national youth rally will take place on September 17 at the historic site of the Giza pyramids, entitled "The Sphinx Stands Against Poverty."

The "Stand Up and Take Action" mobilization comes amidst an ongoing process of citizen engagement with their leaders in support of the MDGs. Upcoming activities include the launch of an alternate report on MDG progress in India and the Philippines on September 15; a dedicated MDG Week in the Philippines House of Representatives, where citizens will launch a roadmap for poverty reduction; and a collective appeal in support of the MDGs to be presented to the government of Nepal on September 15.

Last year, more than 173 million people participated in "Stand Up," setting a new Guinness World Record. "Stand Up and Take Action" is organized globally by the United Nations Millennium Campaign, in collaboration with a wide range of partners, including the Global Call to Action against Poverty (GCAP).

For event listings, photos, sounds from Stand Up events, and more information, visit www.standagainstpoverty.org.

Media Contact for b-roll, interviews and further information:

Kara Alaimo
+1 212–906–6399
kara.alaimo@undp.org

About the UN Millennium Campaign

The UN Millennium Campaign was established by the UN Secretary General in 2002. The Campaign supports citizens' efforts to hold their governments to account for the achievement of the Millennium Development Goals. The Millennium Development Goals were adopted by 189 world leaders from rich and poor countries as part of the Millennium Declaration which was signed in 2000. These leaders agreed to achieve the Goals by 2015. Our premise is simple: we are the first generation that can end poverty, and we refuse to miss this opportunity. For more information, visit www.endpoverty2015.org.

Finally, when working with the global media, which operates across so many different time zones, a particular challenge will be timing. You should, of course, avoid calling a reporter when (s)he is about to go on the air or is on a tight deadline on a different story. Working with the global media often means working early mornings and late nights in order to reach and communicate with journalists in different time zones.

Another timing challenge, of course, will be ensuring that you do not make an announcement when you will be competing for attention with other major news stories. This will require careful monitoring of media coverage. If you are focused specifically on the U.S., U.K., and Western Europe, you can also subscribe to the international package of the AP Planner, which regularly updates its calendar of more than 100,000 upcoming events in those regions, to ensure that you do not schedule major news announcements during other significant events.

However, the bigger challenge is finding the right time of day to roll out campaigns that you wish to be covered by reporters globally. For example, when I worked at the United Nations, I often issued global press releases from New York. However, if I were to make an announcement at 9:00 a.m. in New York, it would be, for example, 3:00 p.m. in Cape Town, South Africa, 6:30 p.m. in New Delhi, India, and 10:00 p.m. in Tokyo, Japan—much too late for many reporters! One option is therefore for you to provide the information "under embargo" to journalists, which means that they can digest it and prepare their stories, but they cannot publish or air their stories until the time you specify that the embargo will lift.

Often a good time to lift an embargo is midnight EDT (midnight in New York, which is 5:00 a.m. in London, United Kingdom, 6:00 a.m. in Cape Town, South Africa, and 9:30 a.m. in New Delhi, India—allowing the story to run in the world's morning news cycles). The other benefit of embargoing information— particularly when it is complex—is that it gives reporters an opportunity to take their time, get their stories right, and perhaps approach you with any questions, without the pressure of trying to file their stories immediately in order to beat out the competition from other news outlets. It also gives you time to call and confirm that your priority reporters received your announce-ment and encourage them to cover it.

If you are going to embargo a press release, you need to make sure that you make this fact impossible for reporters to miss so that no one publishes or airs their story ahead of the time you have designated. I recommend a sentence at the top of your press release in red, bold, and a larger size than the rest of your text, stating **"Embargoed until 12:00 midnight EDT on 1 January 2017,"** for example. (Note that, while in the U.S. it is common to write the month before the day—January 1, for example—in the United Kingdom and many other parts of the world, it is customary to write the day before the month. When communicating globally, be sure to always write out the name of the month you are referring to, since 1/2/2017 could mean January 2 or Febru-ary 1!) Also definitely consider streaming press conferences live online and taking questions via social media so that reporters in other parts of the world can participate.

The following section describes the key media organizations with truly global audiences. If you can craft an enticing story, placing stories in these outlets will give you the biggest possible reach. Of course, bigger audiences are not always better, so, as always in public relations, you'll need to start by thinking carefully about whom you wish to reach and where you can find them. Either way, be sure to also consider regional and domestic media. In the Middle East, for example, a number of major regional media outlets can deliver audiences that are truly pan-Arab. (Major regional and national media outlets will be described in the chapters that follow.)

You should also consider pitching global bloggers with the biggest reach. Your targets will vary depending upon your industry. For example, when the

Ford Motor Company launched its Fiesta car, it gave the model on loan for six months to 100 bloggers, who were simply required to post monthly videos and encouraged to write about the vehicle (McMahon, 2011, p. 263). (Another cool strategy that Ford used for the Fiesta will be described in the social media section below.)

However, let's start with the global media.

Broadcasters

Al Jazeera

Copyright: 360b

Funded by the government of Qatar, Al Jazeera broadcasts in English, Arabic, Bosnian-Croatian-Serbian, and Turkish, reaching over 220 million households in more than 100 countries. The network has nearly 60 global newsrooms, from Afghanistan to Zimbabwe (Al Jazeera, 2015). Key programs on Al Jazeera English include the discussion-based programs Inside Story, The Stream, Empire, Head to Head, and Talk to Al Jazeera, along with newsmagazine programs such as The Listening Post. Zayani (2005, p. 2) argues that

> Al Jazeera enjoys an unprecedented margin of freedom which makes it a haven for free speech in the Arab world. In fact, it is popular precisely because it openly discusses sensitive topics and tackles controversial issues. . . . Its talk shows unabashedly tackle such unmentionables as government corruption, the human rights record of Arab regimes, the persecution of political dissenters, Islamic law (or Sharia), the (in)compatibility of Islam and democracy, and Islamic fundamentalism.

Teljami (2013, p. 51) argues that "because Al Jazeera is well funded and doesn't need to make a profit, it can provide extensive coverage where others have failed," such as in Gaza. He also (2013, p. 51) notes that

> even though Al Jazeera is often accused of bias or of an ideological bent, it has been bold in ensuring presentation of multiple views, including presenting Israeli views dating back to the 1990s, when few other Arab stations dared do so, as well as airing Bin Laden tapes, Iranian views, and hosting or covering speeches and news conferences of American officials—including then-secretary of defense Donald Rumsfeld, American military commanders and spokesmen, and White House and State Department officials—during the Iraq war. So while Al Jazeera officials understood and catered to their audience, they also made sure they always aired views that challenged, sometimes even offended their audience. There was also a price to be paid for Al Jazeera's extensive coverage. Almost every government in the region was offended by Al Jazeera at some point. . . . The United States accused Al Jazeera of incitement, and even China in 2012 was angered by Al Jazeera coverage.

Yet despite this history, Al Jazeera is today a respectable mainstream global media outlet that is a "must" to pitch if you are targeting citizens in the Arab world, and a valuable outlet for reaching audiences in other parts of the world, as well. To connect with a producer, email aji-doha-planning@aljazeera.net or call the assignment desk at their headquarters in Doha, Qatar, on +974 489 2266.

BBC World News and BBC World Service

Copyright: chrisdorney

The British Broadcasting Corporation (BBC) operates "the biggest broadcast newsgathering operation in the world" (Shuster, 2015). The BBC began as the United Kingdom's national broadcaster and gave the world the concept of public service broadcasting (Küng-Shankleman, 2000, p. 68). Under a public model, a media outlet is owned by the state rather than private interests. Proponents of this model believe that it better allows the media to fulfill its role as a watchdog in a democracy, because news coverage is not influenced by commercial considerations, such as the need to turn a profit or promulgate views that favor the interests of the owner (Stokes, 1999). Unlike many other public broadcasters, which are funded directly by the state, the BBC in the U.K. is funded by a license fee that is paid by television owners.

BBC World News is the commercial, global arm of the BBC. It provides television news programming that is available in about 300 million households and 1.8 million hotel rooms in more than 200 countries and territories around the world. Additionally, BBC World Service radio has a weekly audience of 166 million and broadcasts in 28 languages (BBC, 2015, 2012). Its most popular language services are English, Hausa, Arabic, Swahili, and French for Africa, making World Service radio one of the very best ways to reach audiences in Africa— especially those who are illiterate (BBC, 2012). Key television programs include BBC World News, World News Today, Newsday, Focus on Africa, Dateline London, World Business Report, Africa Business Report, Asia Business Report, India Business Report, Middle East Business Report, and the previously discussed interview program HARDtalk, which has genuinely earned its name! Some of its most important presenters are HARDtalk host Stephen Sackur, World News Today host Zeinab Badawi, World News presenter Adnan Nawaz, and Business Editor Kamal Ahmed, who contributes to multiple programs. Key radio programs include The Newsroom, Newsday, Newshour, and World Update.

To connect with a BBC producer, call the main switch in London on +44 (0)20 8743 8000 and ask to be transferred to the program you are interested in pitching. (For all London phone numbers, drop the zero in parentheses when dialing from outside the country.)

Stephen Sackur is famous for his hard-hitting questions. Photo courtesy of the BBC

Bloomberg

Copyright: Gil C

The business-focused Bloomberg TV reaches more than 330 million households worldwide. Bloomberg describes its audiences as affluent and influential, including entrepreneurs and "leaders of the new economy." Bloomberg also operates a wire service providing breaking business, financial, and economic news to more than 325,000 professionals who subscribe to its professional service; its magazine *BusinessWeek* has a circulation of 980,000 in 150 countries; and its radio programming has a reach of 27 million (Bloomberg, 2015a, 2015c). Key programs include the interview program Charlie Rose, whose presenter is famous for interviewing top players in global affairs; First Up with Angie Lau (which opens the business day and is produced out of Asia); and Countdown, which broadcasts breaking news before European markets open. The company has 150 news bureaus worldwide; visit http://www.bloomberg.com/company/news-bureaus/?utm_source=bloomberg-menu for phone numbers of bureaus around the globe (Bloomberg, 2015b).

CCTV News

The international arm of China's state-run broadcaster, CCTV News (formerly known as CCTV-9 or CCTV International) is an English-language news channel. According to CCTV (2015), "free-to-air satellite signals can be received by more than 85 million viewers, in over 100 countries and regions. Access is also carried by Cable, DTH, IPTV, and even Terrestrial TV platforms or systems in many nations." Key news programs include News Hour and News Update. Asia Today and China 24 focus on the latest developments in the region and country. Other programs include Dialogue and World Insight (which offer perspectives on global affairs), Biz Asia, and Biz Talk.

Although CCTV has hired experienced journalists who previously worked at outlets such as CNN, the BBC, and Bloomberg, experts still see the hand of the Chinese government in its coverage. One professor argues that

> what's missing conspicuously from these programmings are actually any real political news about China itself. CCTV America unfortunately can't really reveal anything that's beyond [the] scripted version of what happened in China. CCTV America is very much on the [Chinese Communist] party's short leash (Folkenflik, 2013).

Rawnsley (2009, p. 286) reports that "without a doubt . . . it receives instructions from the [Chinese] Ministry of Foreign Affairs about what to include in its programming, based on guidance provided by embassies in the target areas." If you would like to pitch CCTV, call its Beijing, China office on + 86–10–68507207 to connect with the right producer.

China Xinhua News Network Corporation (CNC)

In 2010, China's state news agency, Xinhua, launched an English television service called CNC (Xinhua, 2010). The news organization's website indicates that it is accessible "on cable & wireless digital TV networks in more than 60 countries and regions, including the United States, Canada, the United Kingdom, the Netherlands, New Zealand, Sub-Saharan Africa, Thailand, Hong Kong and Macao," although no viewership figures are reported (CNC, 2015).

The network professes to "present an international vision with a China perspective," but *The Guardian* reports that it is "inevitably shadowed by China's extensive censorship" (to be discussed in greater detail in Chapter 8). One Chinese professor predicts that the channel will be short-lived (Branigan, 2010).

To pitch the network, contact its editorial office in Beijing, China on +8610–63076688 or email cnc@cncnews.cn (CNC, 2015).

CNN en Español

CNN en Español's cable news broadcasts in Spanish, reaching 31.5 million households in Latin America and 4 million households in the U.S. CNN en Español radio also reaches households in both Latin America and the U.S. (Turner Broadcasting System, Inc., 2015). Key programs include the morning show Cafe CNN; the international news program Panorama Mundial; Nuestro Mundo, which focuses on news from the Americas; the evening news program Conclusiones; the women's-focused show NotiMujer; the entertainment program Showbiz; and Aristegui, a program focused on current affairs in Mexico, presented by the influential and hard-hitting Mexican journalist Carmen Aristegui. Other key presenters include the powerhouse reporter Patricia Janiot, who likewise conducts interviews with top players in global affairs and

Carmen Aristegui is one of CNN en Español's most influential presenters. Photo courtesy of CNN en Español

Patricia Janiot is one of the journalists most followed by world leaders on Twitter. Photo courtesy of CNN en Español

is one of the journalists most followed by world leaders on Twitter; Fernando del Rincon, Janiot's co-host on Panorama Mundial; Conclusiones host Fernando del Rincon; and Ismael Cala, who hosts an interview-based program called Cala (Castrejon, 2015). CNN en Español radio also broadcasts in the U.S. and Latin America. To pitch a story, contact its news desk in Atlanta, Georgia in the U.S. on +1 404–878–8555.

CNN International

CNN International's Chief International Correspondent Christiane Amanpour is one of the most influential and hard-hitting reporters in the world. Copyright: Northfoto.

Colloquially known among public relations practitioners as "CNN I," the international version of the domestic U.S. broadcaster CNN reaches more than 250 million households in over 200 countries and territories (CNN, 2015). Key news programs include the CNN Newsroom, Connect the World with Becky Anderson, Amanpour (featuring CNN I's famously hard-hitting Chief International Correspondent, Christiane Amanpour), and the more intellectual Fareed Zakaria GPS (which stands for Global Public Square)— a primarily interview-based program with very high-level players in global affairs. You can also pitch regional stories to the business and economy-focused programs Marketplace Middle East or Marketplace Africa; the current affairs programs Inside Africa or Inside the Middle East; as well as to Talk Asia or African Voices, which profile opinion leaders in areas ranging from fashion to technology. If you work for a non-profit organization, you may also wish to connect with CNN I's Impact Your World unit—a team that works across CNN platforms to help share information on important causes. Call the International Desk in Atlanta, Georgia, in the U.S. on +1 404–827–1519 for help connecting to the right producer.

Deutsche Welle

Germany's international public broadcaster reaches a global audience of 100 million weekly, with television news in German, English, Spanish, and Arabic and radio programming in 30 languages (Deutsche Welle, 2015). English-language television news programs include DW News and Business. The media organization's headquarters in Bonn, Germany can be reached on +49 228 429 4000.

Deutsche Welle's headquarters in Bonn, Germany. Copyright: Christian Mueller

France 24

France's publicly owned France 24 broadcasts television news in French, English, and Arabic, reaching 255 million households in 177 countries (France 24, 2015). Key programs include Focus, Business Daily, The World This Week, The Debate, and The Interview. You can submit a message to be forwarded to a France 24 journalist at http://www.france24.com/en/contact-us.

NHK World

NHK World is the international arm of Japan's public broadcaster. NHK World TV provides English language news available in 273 million households in over 140 countries and territories. NHK World Radio Japan broadcasts the news in Arabic, Bengali, Burmese, Chinese, English, French, Hindi, Indonesian, Japanese, Korean, Persian, Portuguese, Russian, Spanish, Swahili, Thai, Urdu, and Vietnamese (NHK World, 2015). Key news programs are Newsline and News Room Tokyo.

NHK's headquarters in Tokyo can be reached on +81-(0)3-3465-1111.

RT

Formerly known as Russia Today, the broadcaster publicly funded by Russia's government reports reaching 700 million people in over 100 countries (RT, 2015a). RT broadcasts in English, while its Arabic language channel is called Rusiya Al-Yaum and its Spanish channel is called RT Actualidad.

RT is widely seen as a propaganda arm of the Russian President. Copyright: KOZYREV OLEG

Shuster (2015) describes the outlet as "the Kremlin's most sophisticated propaganda machine," which produces "marathon(s) of spin." By way of example, following the 2015 death of Boris Nemtsov, a key critic of Russian President Vladimir Putin,

> RT anchors and pundits cast the killing variously as a "huge gift to Putin haters"; possibly the work of "foreign assassins" to provide a "beautiful propaganda shot" for Western officials and media. . . . The coverage did not mention the fears Nemtsov, 55, had expressed in an interview less than three weeks before his murder that Putin could have him killed. It ignored the fact that Nemtsov was preparing to publish an investigation into Russia's support for separatist rebels waging war in eastern Ukraine. It sidestepped the pattern of more than a dozen murders and violent attacks against Kremlin critics in the 15 years since Putin came to power.

Ioffe (2010) likewise notes that the station has "featured fringe-dwelling 'experts,' like the Russian historian who predicted the imminent dissolution of the United States."

Key news programs include In the Now, hosted by Senior Political Correspondent Anissa Naouai out of Moscow, and the discussion-based program Worlds Apart, hosted by Oksana Boyko.

RT's producers can be reached at producersgroup@rttv.ru or on +7 499 750–03–01 (RT, 2015b).

Sky News International

The homepage of Sky News. Copyright: chrisdorney

British subscription television broadcaster Sky reaches an audience of 21 million across the United Kingdom, Ireland, Italy, Germany, and Austria (Sky, 2015). The broadcaster's international arm, Sky News International, is available on cable stations across Europe, Africa, Asia, and the Middle East. Key programs include Sky News on the Hour; News, Sport & Weather; Sky World News; Sky News at Ten; Sunrise; and Sky News Tonight. Based in Abu Dhabi in the United Arab Emirates, Sky News Arabia broadcasts in Arabic throughout the Middle East and North Africa. Sky News Australia broadcasts news 24 hours per day to subscribers in Australia and New Zealand.

Sky was founded by Rupert Murdoch, the Australian media mogul who owns numerous media outlets around the world, including the conservative media outlets FOX News and *The Wall Street Journal* in the U.S.

To pitch a story, call the U.K. switchboard on +44 (0) 333 100 0333.

Wire Services

Another great way to reach large global audiences is by pitching major wire services. As you will likely know, a wire service produces and distributes content for subscriber media outlets, which are free to publish them. In this way, a single article written by Agence France-Presse, for example, can be printed in hundreds or even thousands of media outlets around the globe. Below are the largest global wire services.

Agence France-Presse

Known as "AFP," the wire service Agence France-Presse covers 150 countries from 200 bureaus, providing news in French, English, Spanish, Arabic,

Portuguese, and German, as well as photos and videos to more than 4,000 media outlets around the globe (AFP, 2015). Visit its website at http://www. afp.com/en/agency/afp-in-world to obtain contact information for its offices around the world.

Associated Press

Copyright: 360b

"The AP," as it is colloquially known, claims that its content reaches more than half of the people on earth every day (Associated Press, 2014). The agency operates in more than 280 locations around the world, supplying text stories in English, Spanish, and Arabic to 15,000 media outlets around the globe, along with photos and audio and video footage (Associated Press, 2014, 2015).

The AP also, of course, publishes its famous *Stylebook* used by many media organizations around the world, with detailed rules on everything from when to write out numbers to how to abbreviate words. You may consider adopting this as your organization's global style guide so that your communications are written consistently.

You can find contact information for each of its bureaus on its website at www.ap.org/contact-us/bureaus.

EFE

The Spanish news agency promotes itself as covering "the world from a Latin perspective." The fourth-largest news agency in the world, EFE reports from 180 cities in 120 countries and has editorial desks in Miami, Florida in the U.S.; San Juan, Puerto Rico; Madrid, Spain; New Delhi, India; and Cairo,

Egypt, providing wire stories, photos, and videos to more than 2,000 media outlets (EFE, 2015). The agency's head office in Madrid can be reached on +34913467100.

Reuters

Copyright: PhotoStock10

Another of the world's largest news wire services, Reuters has 200 news bureaus around the world that place a particular emphasis on business coverage, providing photos as well as wire stories and videos in languages including English, Arabic, French, Spanish, German, Italian, and Russian to media outlets around the world (Reuters, 2015a, 2015b). The phone number for the main switch in London is + 44 (0)207 250 1122.

Newspapers

The Guardian

The progressive and influential London-based English-language newspaper *The Guardian* enjoys a wide readership outside of the U.K. *The Guardian* (2013) reports having a global monthly web reach of 36 million users (10.2 million of whom are in the U.K. and 10.9 million of whom are in the U.S.), which it says gives it "the largest global audience of any UK quality newspaper website." Its website features an International edition, U.K. edition, U.S. edition, and Australia edition.

To pitch *The Guardian*, ring its main switch in London on +44 (0)20 3 353 2000.

Copyright: Radu Bercan

Financial Times

Copyright: Radu Bercan

Famous for being printed on salmon-colored paper, the London-based English-language business and economics-focused publication the *Financial Times* reports having 720,000 print and digital subscribers and reaching an audience of nearly 2 million in 100 countries, including "business leaders, government ministers, international entrepreneurs, bankers, investors, educators and students" (Financial Times, 2015a, 2015b). The paper has English-language editions for the U.S., U.K., Europe, Asia, and the Mid East, as well as a Chinese edition.

Key commentators include Chief Economics Commentator Martin Wolf, Chief Foreign Affairs Columnist Gideon Rachman, and U.S. Managing Editor Gillian Tett, who writes columns on economics, finance, politics, and social issues.

To pitch a story to a reporter or columnist, call its office in London on +44 (0)20 7873 4920.

International New York Times

Copyright: Gil C

The international edition of the newspaper of record in the U.S. reports a worldwide readership of 423,306 in 130 countries, including 228,654 readers in the Atlantic region and 194,652 readers in Asia and the Pacific. Such readers are well-educated and affluent (*International New York Times*, 2014). The newspaper posts an editorial calendar on its website at http://www.nyt mediakit-intl.com/editorial-calendar.aspx?publications=7, which you can use to pitch relevant stories for upcoming issues.

The paper shares content with *The New York Times*. Key reporters include David Leonhardt, who covers economics, and Andrew Ross Sorkin, who covers the financial world. Key columnists include Thomas Friedman, who covers globalization, technology, and foreign affairs; Nicholas Kristof, who covers global affairs, including development and human rights; Paul Krugman, who focuses on economics and trade; the more conservative David Brooks, who covers culture, politics, and the social sciences; and Maureen Dowd, who writes about popular culture, American politics, and international affairs.

The *Times* also publishes a Chinese edition in Mandarin, featuring both material from its U.S. edition and content written specifically for its Chinese audience (Taylor, 2012).

To pitch the *Times*, call the foreign desk in New York on +1 212–556–7415.

The Wall Street Journal

Copyright: Gil C

The Wall Street Journal is a New York-based English-language business and economics-focused publication whose main competitor is the *Financial Times*. The U.S. edition has the largest paid circulation in the country, with 2.2 million subscribers (*The Wall Street Journal*, 2015b). The paper also publishes an Asia edition, which has 338,982 readers, and a Europe edition, with 183,389 readers. Its Latin America edition is published in the business sections of 16 top newspapers across the region and is reportedly read by "six million business decision makers, opinion leaders and affluent consumers." The paper has different English-language website editions for the U.S., Asia, India, Europe, and Latin America, as well as websites in Chinese, Japanese, Korean, Bahasa Indonesia, and a Portuguese site focused on Brazil (*The Wall Street Journal*, 2015a).

The Wall Street Journal is known for combining its conservative editorial pages with more balanced overall news coverage.

To pitch the *Journal*, call the news desk in New York on +1 212–416–2500.

Social Networks

More than two billion of the people on earth are now on social media, and it goes without saying that the use of social media is now a core component of

Copyright: Bloomua

most public relations strategies (Kemp, 2015). Unsurprisingly, studies show that companies that engage more on social media are more financially successful (Paine, 2011, p. 77).

Pam Didner (2015), a global content marketing strategist based in the U.S., says that the "holy grail" of developing content for social media platforms is striking a delicate balance between global headquarters and local offices in order to decide upon responsibilities and a plan. In particular, Didner says that headquarters and local teams need to agree upon seven elements in order to craft a strategy for global social media content.

First, before you start thinking about content, you should be clear about your business and communication objectives. What are you trying to accomplish? Do you seek to increase sales or donations? Build brand equity? One objective that you should definitely consider is recruiting and retaining employees. Michael Marinello (2015), Head of Global Communications for Technology, Innovation, and Sustainability at Bloomberg, says that this is one of his primary goals on social media. In their outstanding book on visual storytelling, Walter and Gioglio (2014, p. 127) say that common goals of leading companies are: awareness and education, branding, competitive differentiation, consumer engagement, corporate social responsibility, customer retention, fan and community growth, lead generation, loyalty, positive press, product launches, promotions, referral traffic, sales, and thought leadership.

Second, who are your "personas?" A persona is a semi-fictional representation of your ideal audience member based upon research and real data about your existing customers or supporters. Be specific about your persona. For example, simply thinking of Millennials is not specific enough; your persona might be a four-year college student in the U.S. named Kelly. You will need to conduct extensive research in order to gain as much insight as possible into your personas. What are their needs, likes, and dislikes? How do they get their information? If your product is homogeneous around the world, Didner says that you will be able to conceptualize a single global persona. If it is not, you will often need to have numerous local personas. It is not uncommon for a global organization to have 10 or more personas!

To decide whether you can have a single global persona, Didner recommends thinking about the commonalities between your audiences in different countries and cultures. "Consumers all value their families, cherish holidays, care about their careers and bodies, and want financial stability and safety," Didner says. "Is it possible that you can focus the conversation or your messages and positioning on something that they have in common? Sometimes you can; sometimes you can't."

Third, you need to consider your company's country priorities based upon your objectives. The country priorities will also dictate how you plan your social media content.

Fourth, fifth, and sixth, you will need to agree upon high-level editorial topics, a high-level editorial timeline, and a list of content. Start by listing your organization's major initiatives over the coming year and then fill in additional editorial topics based upon your product offerings and your persona's interests, pain points, and challenges. For social media content planning, you will need a mix of original content that you create and content produced by third parties that you curate.

Finally, you will need to agree upon a budget. If your budget is dispersed from your headquarters, solicit the local team's input and work closely with them to allocate the budget to support your communication objectives.

Sheri Herrmann, Communication Coordinator in the U.S. for the global tire manufacturer Continental, recommends creating different social media pages for different countries—both because products often differ by country and because the types of content that are most popular in different countries can differ dramatically. "Our German counterparts will post lengthy content with more generic photographs on Facebook, and they also have a very different sense of humor," she says. "To get shares and likes in the United States, I need short and snappy posts and dramatic, flashy pictures, such as ones I posted recently of a Lamborghini and the Guinness World Record for the world's largest burnout." Hermann also says that the platforms that are most popular in the countries where Continental has a presence vary greatly.

Different social media platforms allow for different levels of local adaptation. For example, Jack Lundie, Director of Communications for the anti-poverty organization Oxfam (who is profiled in Chapter 9), says that "every tweet is a tweet to the world. That's the power of the platform, but it also presents risk. You can't change it, but you have to take it into account if you're a global organization." However, Oxfam's global headquarters in the U.K. and

17 affiliate offices around the world have separate Facebook pages with cultur-ally specific messaging. Lundie says that Oxfam is currently looking into geo-targeted Facebook pages so that audiences in different locations see posts that are relevant to them.

Ekaterina Walter, Global Evangelist at Sprinklr, a social media manage-ment platform, recommends that if you use different pages or platforms in dif-ferent markets, you create a central repository for all content created for social media platforms both at global headquarters and in different regions so that your teams in different countries can borrow from and adapt content created elsewhere. She explains that

> visuals especially can often be re-used. The messages that come with them might be slightly different, but if you have a content library then your team in different countries can cherry pick the pieces that will work for them and do their own translations. Right now, organizations are creat-ing a lot of content that could be reused because people work in silos and don't know it exists.

Many of the same rules of working with social media at the domestic level also apply at the global level. In an important article, Kent and Taylor (1998) argued that five principles apply to public relations online (they originally discussed websites, but their principles are clearly applicable to social media interactions, as well). First is the principle of "dialogic loops." In other words, customers talk back to you online and expect you to respond. Therefore, you must carefully track comments and "respond to public concerns, questions, and requests" in a timely fashion (Kent & Taylor, 1998, p. 327). You will want to set up a system for monitoring what is being said about you in real time, around the clock, so that you can respond rapidly to correct any false rumors, address complaints, and put out any fires (more on this later). Second, you should provide information that is useful and has value. Third, you want to spark return visits, so you need to feature content that keeps people coming back for more. Fourth, the information you provide should be "easy to figure out and understand" (Kent & Taylor, 1998, p. 329). Finally, you want to con-serve visitors by not leading them to platforms other than your own.

In a study of how Fortune 500 companies use Twitter, Rybalko and Seltzer (2010, p. 339) found that companies are most guilty of violating the principle of providing useful information. They also recommend that companies pro-vide information about who is tweeting on their behalf, because this

> demonstrates the company's commitment to . . . using social networking to facilitate interpersonal communication between an individual repre-sentative and stakeholders; in other words, it is no longer some faceless public relations department or corporate entity communicating with the publics but an actual person.

Of course, with any content you craft for social media, you'll want to think twice before posting—and ideally get a second set of eyes on your content before doing so—to make sure that your posts cannot be misconstrued and that you won't regret them later. And you will need a steady stream of content. One study of non-profit organizations fighting breast cancer found that those groups that tweeted more not only had more followers, but were perceived to be more transparent and more credible simply by virtue of their level of activity. The researchers concluded that "public relations practitioners must keep their Twitter and Facebook pages active in order to be perceived as transparent and credible. . . . Having a social media presence is not enough; the organization must ensure high quality interactions to keep individuals engaged" (Fussell Sisco & McCorkindale, 2013, p. 298). In a study of U.S. university students, Sung and Kim (2014) likewise found that evaluations of a company become significantly more positive when a company interacts more by responding to consumer comments.

You will also want to create an authentic online brand identity. This should be informed by data but not overtaken by it. For example, as Marinello (2015) explains, you need to take into account the fact that 60 percent of Twitter users are female, but if you are working for the motorcycle maker Harley Davidson, whose customers are primarily male, you are not going to change your identity as a result. Your online identity should be fairly consistent over time. For example, Instagram's (2015a) official advice for how businesses can use their platform suggests, "choose story lines that are authentic to your brand and are best conveyed through captivating imagery. Create posts that follow these themes for a diversity of content that also remains consistent over time."

To attract and keep followers, provide content that is entertaining, interesting, and valuable—not strictly promotional. Copyright: Gustavo Frazao

This diversity of content should not all be promotional. People follow brands and other organizations in order to be entertained and to obtain information that is interesting and valuable, not to receive a slew of sales pitches. As one report explains,

> consumers expect and want brands to promote their products and services, but these messages must be balanced with information that benefits the consumer. Hard sell tactics can work in person, but they fail online because you lack the personal interaction to counter the hard-sell message. No matter how personal they are, Email, Facebook, and Twitter don't allow you to replicate a face-to-face conversation (ExactTarget, 2011).

Often, social media is an opportunity to show a lighter side of your organization and to further develop your personality. One way to get noticed is to be part of conversations that are trending at the moment. This requires an ability to think and come up with creative ideas on your feet. (In order for this to work, you'll also need to have the authority to post without cumbersome approval processes.) Also, share content from other sources that your followers will appreciate. As Didner explains, curating such content "shows that you care for your target audience, not just [about] sharing your own point of view" (Alaimo, 2015).

Above all, create content that encourages users to engage with you. As DeLisle (2015) explains, "social is about online engagement and conversation. You could have the best video, you could have the best blog, but if you're not in a dialogue with me, you're not getting me to come back. I have to be in a relationship with you." A recent study of consumers in the U.S., United Kingdom, France, Germany, and Australia found that they expect brands today to craft messages that are "personalized and relevant" (Bulldog Reporter, 2015). When you create original and compelling content, your followers will share it, allowing you to reach new audiences, who, with any luck, will go on to engage with you.

Don't just post content: ask your followers questions and respond to their content. Kerpen (2011, p. 120) explains that asking questions helps you "guide the social media conversation without appearing forceful," allows you to focus on your audience rather than your organization, and demonstrates that you are open and care about what your followers have to say. He (2011, p. 121) notes that "you can ask your community questions about your products and services, their perceptions and attitudes, their opinions, their knowledge of competitors, and an infinite number of other topics." As Sabrina Lynch, a global public relations consultant based in the U.S., puts it, "P.R. is not just an abbreviation for Public Relations anymore; it's about People's Reaction."

Michael Leis (2015), Senior Vice President of Social Strategy at Digitas Health Lifebrands, concurs that the first step in using social media is listening to your audiences to understand how they make decisions and represent themselves. He recommends getting to know subcultures on social media "through the kind of artifacts they leave behind," such as their profile photos, how users are connected to one another, what they are talking about beyond your subject matter, and how they are using technology.

Once you understand your audience, you can find appropriate ways to engage with them personally. One great way to do so (and to end up with great content, to boot) is to encourage your audiences to create content for you. So, Leis says the second step is to invite your audiences to engage in your preferred behavior and create content—for example, by posting photographs of themselves eating at your restaurant. Next, reward your followers in some way for following through. Fourth and last, celebrate this content by amplifying it on your own platforms, such as by sharing and re-tweeting it.

For example, the Ford Motor Company promoted its new Fiesta car in Europe by asking people to upload photos on Instagram with the hashtag #Fiestagram and other hashtags promoting the features of the vehicle. Some of the company's favorite photos were shown on online galleries and on billboards across the continent. The winner of the contest received a free car.

Ford's social media campaign promoting the new Fiesta in Europe generated engagement with thousands of followers. Copyright: GoBOb

Walter and Gioglio (2014, p. 98) note that,

> the campaign particularly focused on the car's state-of-the-art features to raise awareness of the high-tech aspects of the car—something that would appeal to a new, younger, fashion-conscious audience—and to change perceptions of the traditional views of the Fiesta, which was already one of the most popular and recognized cars in Europe. Instagram's users (young, stylish, tech aware) were the ideal target audience. . . . More than 16,000

photos were submitted to the contest, and Ford's Facebook community gained 120,000 new fans during the six-week campaign, with hundreds of thousands of visitors coming to the galleries to view the submissions.

Research suggests that participating in or even just viewing content from such contests can promote purchases. One study that analyzed Air Miles, a program that rewards Canadian shoppers with airline miles, found that people who participated in a contest on a social media platform increased their spending over both the short and long term. Even social media users who merely viewed posts made by others as part of a contest increased their spending (Malthouse, Vandenbosch, & Kim, 2014).

Another great way to engage audiences is by posting visual content. Content with compelling images generates 94 percent more views than content without visuals (Cohen, 2013). It also generates more shares. One study of 739,000 tweets found that 76 percent of those that were shared contained a photo and 18 percent contained a video (Walter & Gioglio, 2014, p. 20). As Walter and Gioglio (2014, p.15) explain,

> research indicates that consumer interest in visual content isn't necessarily just a preference; it's actually easier and faster for humans to process. The right picture can go further than just telling your story visually; it can make you feel emotions, evoke memories, and even make you act differently.

Of course, images are often interpreted by people of different cultures in different ways, so just as with your written and verbal messages, you should tailor your images to your audiences. As Walter and Gioglio (2014, p. 17) explain,

> whereas images such as star-spangled flags and eagles can appeal to an American sense of patriotism, the same effect may be achieved by a maple leaf, a lion, or a kangaroo in other countries. And what appears strong and decisive to one audience could seem aggressive to another.

Visual content also, of course, includes video. As Murdico (2011) notes, "if social media is the rocket launcher, video is the rocket." Funny, entertaining, and/or edgy videos can quickly go viral online, which can also even generate traditional news stories. Signore (2013) explains that "on social channels, posting videos increases engagement by 100 percent or more, depending on which survey you read. So, if 50 people click on your text-based post, on average, then you can expect 100 clicks if you include video." After watching a product video, consumers are 85 percent more likely to buy the product (Walter and Gioglio, 2014, p. 21). Murdico (2011) also suggests posting videos of your events on social media to give them wider reach. And, post videos of your top leaders. As Murdico (2011) also explains, videos help build trust and credibility because "instead of reading a text quote from a company spokesperson, viewers are able to actually see that spokesperson speaking." Pete Borum, the New York-based Co-founder and Chief Executive Officer of Reelio, which matches brands with YouTube content producers around the world, explains that "now, platforms like Facebook and Twitter are most effective because they don't require high speed Internet, but as mobile phones become more sophisticated in both developed and developing countries, video's importance will continue to grow."

You will also want to think about how you can convey complex ideas visually. A great way to do this is through infographics—also often called data visualizations, or "data viz" for short—which convey facts and ideas in picture form. One study found that publishers using infographics saw 12 percent more traffic than those who did not use them (Walter & Gioglio, 2014, p. 21). Websites that can help you create infographics include Infogr.am, InfoActive, Easel.ly, Piktochart, Visual.ly, and iCharts (Walter & Gioglio, 2014, p. 165).

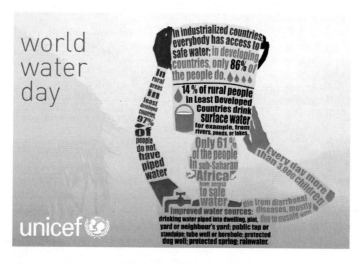

Infographics convey facts and ideas in picture form. Courtesy of UNICEF/Designed by Olivier Marie

As you experiment with all of these tactics, keep careful track of what types of messages and mediums generate the most engagement from your followers, so that you can adapt your strategies accordingly—but also remember that you should use a diverse range of content to keep folks interested. Cassandra Olivos, Senior Social Media Account Analyst at Driven Local, a New York-based firm that develops social media campaigns, says,

> at the end of the day, you can't make everyone happy. While some people may love watching videos on social media, others are strongly against them. The key is finding a balance that is unique to that particular

audience, and to remember what might be working in one country will not always translate across other markets.

Social media is also a great way to engage with reporters. A 2014 study of journalists around the world found that half of them now rely on social media as their main source of information (ING, 2014). Social media is a great place to start building your relationships with reporters and learning more about their interests. Like everyone else, journalists want their content to be shared and liked, so that is a great way to start. Also, try engaging in conversations with reporters about the subject matter they cover, so that they come to see you as a knowledgeable, valuable source of information when you go on to pitch them—online or off.

With all this engaging that you will be doing on social media, it is inevitable that, sometimes, you won't be thrilled with what people have to say about your organization online. However, deleting negative comments is generally bad form—unless, of course, they are completely inappropriate. As Kerpen (2011, p. 77) explains, "the do-not-delete (DND) rule states that *unless a comment is obscene, profane, bigoted, or contains someone's personal and private information, never delete it from a social network.*" Instead, monitor your platforms religiously and do your best to get any individual complaints offline to resolve them. Olivos warns that "if bad reviews go unanswered, users can and will voice their opinions elsewhere, not only by posting reviews on other sites, but also by turning to competitors." Ideally, if you handle them well, you'll have those users posting positive comments before long! Olivos says that you should also "show your audiences how you've made attempts to rectify the situation." Ultimately, however, Leis (2015) says the best way to handle a few negative posts on your platforms is to surround them with overwhelmingly positive content.

Of course, if your organization experiences a larger crisis, be prepared for it to spread like wildfire on social media. One recent study found that 28 percent of corporate crises spread internationally within an hour and 69 percent spread internationally within one day, reaching on average 11 countries. Yet it takes an average company 21 hours to issue a meaningful response, leaving them vulnerable to "trial by Twitter" (Freshfields Bruckhaus Deringer, 2013). Don't let this happen to you. Be prepared for any crises that your organization could face and have pre-approved messages and crisis responses at the ready. Crisis expert Helio Fred Garcia (2012, p. 83) explains that the concept of the "Golden Hour of Crisis Response," a term borrowed from emergency medicine, reminds us that "incremental delays in fielding an appropriate response have a greater than incremental effect on the outcome." This is because, while you are staying silent,

> more and more people are reaching conclusions about the situation, making judgments, and believing and acting on what they hear. What would have been sufficient in the early phases of a situation becoming

public would be woefully inadequate hours or days or weeks later (Garcia, 2012, p. 116).

Garcia (2012, pp. 116–117) explains that, according to the "rule of 45 minutes, six hours, three days, two weeks," if you can control the message within 45 minutes of a crisis going public, "relatively few stakeholders will have heard of the issue from others, and things are likely to settle down with minimal impact." If you miss this window of opportunity,

> it is still possible to take control of the communication back, but it will be harder: You'll need to reach more people, and overcome more competition for attention. And some people may have already formed opinions that will be very hard to change. But if it can be done within the first six hours of the issue becoming public, then things should settle down relatively quickly.

Garcia (2012, p. 118) says that if it takes you more than several hours to "define the situation, motives, and actions," you should expect about three days of negative coverage. Still, if you react effectively within three days, you should be able to resolve a situation. However, "if it takes more than two weeks to define your issue, motives, and actions, then there's a very good chance of significant damage, sometimes irreparable."

If your organization is vulnerable to serious crises, such as, for example, oil spills, you might consider preparing a "dark site"—a website that discusses your organization's record on the issue and response plan and does not go live unless and until the crisis actually occurs. When you need to share responses on social media that are too complex to convey in 140 characters or less, you can always include links to your (by then, live) site for further information.

Also, take care not to tweet trivialities while your organization, your community, or even a competitor is experiencing a major crisis or tragedy. (This is a danger of using tools such as HootSuite that allow you to set up tweets to be posted at specified later times. You may forget to cancel them if such a situation develops.)

Finally, ensure that your passwords are protected, so that you don't fall victim to hackers or disgruntled employees. For example, in 2013, Burger King's Twitter handle was overtaken by a hacker who changed the name of its account to McDonalds, tweeted McDonalds offers, re-tweeted complaints about Burger King, and made racist and other offensive comments (Langley, 2013; Ward, 2013). As one person tweeted, "Somebody needs to tell Burger-king that 'whopper123' isn't a secure password" (Ward, 2013). However, as Langley (2013) notes, Burger King did go on to pick up 30,000 new followers that month, so it is unclear who had the last laugh. Similarly, after being fired by the British retailer HMV, one employee took over the company's Twitter handle, posting messages including, "There are over 60 of us being fired at once! Mass execution, of loyal employees who love the brand. #hmvXFac-torFiring" (Jones, 2013).

Ready? The next section will explore some of the largest social media plat-forms in the world, excluding those used primarily in China (Kemp, 2015). Since almost none of the typical platforms can be accessed in China, that country gets its own section, which will follow.

Facebook

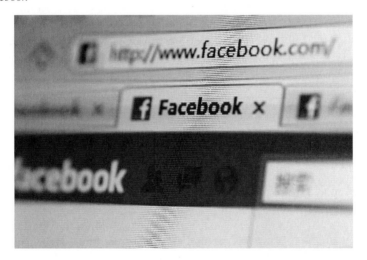

Copyright: Pan Xunbin

How It Works: Individual users create profiles allowing them to post text, links, images, and videos. Users also comment on and "like" the postings of others. Users have the option of making their posts open to the public or view-able only by those with whom they are friends. Organizations and prominent individuals create Facebook pages, which users can "like" in order to follow their posts.

User Base: The world's largest social media platform has a staggering 1.415 billion active users (Statista, 2015a). It can be used in more than 90 languages. This platform is truly global: it is one of the top two websites everywhere except China (Walter & Gioglio, 2014, p. 79). The countries with the largest number of Facebook users are the U.S., India, Brazil, Indo-nesia, Mexico, the United Kingdom, Japan, France, Germany, and Italy (Statista, 2014a). Facebook also has the oldest users among the eight larg-est non-Chinese social networks; almost 25 percent are over age forty-five (Mander, 2014).

How to Use It for PR: Build a Facebook page, which people will be able to "like" in order to receive your updates. Share content regularly. Olivos suggests building a different Facebook page for each market. "It is important to account for the varying cultural nuances and psychographics per region," she says. "Messaging and imagery that may attract customers in the United States may be viewed as abrasive in other cultures. Additionally, if content is not translated properly, consumers in other regions can be dissuaded."

Olivos says that "with the Facebook algorithm constantly changing, it's also critical for brands to experiment with multiple posting styles (text only posts, images, video posts, etc.)."

Walter and Gioglio (2014, p. 81) advise being visual, because people on Facebook are more likely to comment on, like, and share photos. Videos work well on Facebook, too. Olivos says that

> links to videos can be shared, but Facebook will always favor native videos (meaning those that are uploaded directly to their site, rather than links to videos you post on other sites). If you share a YouTube link, Facebook will automatically shrink the post to a small thumbnail preview. If a video is uploaded natively to a Facebook page, the reach and views will skyrocket. This isn't to say YouTube videos should not be shared, since YouTube is still the second largest search engine in the world, but brands should work to utilize both options.

In August 2015, Facebook confirmed that, in the future, verified profiles will be able to broadcast live on their platform (Constine, 2015).

However, be careful not to overwhelm your followers with content. Consumers who follow brands on Facebook expect them "to keep their Facebook pages fresh and interesting, and to limit their posts to avoid drowning out social interactions" (ExactTarget, 2011).

Olivos also recommends considering Facebook ads. She explains that

> Facebook's organic reach is declining rapidly. With all the algorithm changes, brands are finding it more difficult to receive the same reach and engagement as they did once upon a time. Facebook ads are helping to boost that content and information to the masses.

Porter (2010) also notes that

> Facebook Groups are an excellent way to manage membership relationships for a group or organization. If you're just starting a group, or looking for a more cost-effective tool for managing communications to your members, posting an events calendar, or providing additional networking benefits for your members, Facebook Groups is an excellent option.

Finally, if you have a physical location, a Facebook "place" page will allow people to virtually "check in," alerting their friends when they visit your location.

YouTube

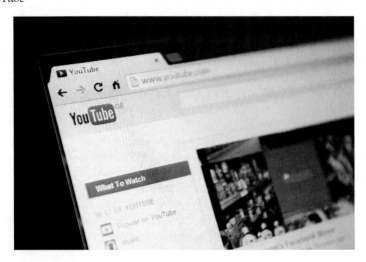

Copyright: JuliusKielaitis

How It Works: Anyone can set up a channel and upload videos.

User Base: YouTube has an astonishing one billion monthly active users (Billboard, 2015). Owned by Google, it is banned in some countries but is still the world's most popular video-sharing site, available in 61 languages (Amir, 2014). The 100 most-viewed YouTube channels get the most views in the United Kingdom, India, Germany, Canada, France, South Korea, Russia, Japan, Brazil, and Mexico. A fifth of YouTube traffic is generated in the U.S. (Amir, 2014). About 75 percent of YouTube traffic comes from countries whose primary language is not English. Saudi Arabians have been described as "the world's most avid YouTube viewers." Gutelle (2014) explains that "since Facebook and Twitter are monitored by the government, Saudis flock to the unregulated YouTube. The average Saudi contributes three views each day."

How to Use It for PR: Post videos! Olivos recommends using many different types of videos, including animated videos, slideshows, and people on camera in how-to videos about your organization. "Having a nice selection of different types of videos is a good way to keep viewers interested," she says. Kerpen (2011, pp. 240–241) advises that you "think about why you search online. It's usually because you want to know something—how to do something or where to find something. Consider creating videos that answer those questions relating to your products or customer experiences."

You can make videos yourself or partner with people who already enjoy large YouTube followings to promote your organization. Companies such as

Reelio, FameBit, and Grapevine match brands with individuals who create videos that have huge audiences on YouTube for product placement. Borum, of Reelio, explains that

> most brands, especially in the developing world, but also in countries like the United States, don't have experience with video creation. So rather than learning how to create videos and make them popular, working with people who are already popular among your audience becomes a really viable alternative.

Borum also finds that a lot of the viewers of videos on YouTube come from outside of the countries where the videos are produced. For example, he says that videos produced in the U.S., Canada, and United Kingdom enjoy huge followings in the Middle East. Therefore, your best partners will not necessarily be in your home country. The U.S.-based women's magazine *Cosmopolitan*, for example, used Reelio to strike a partnership with YouTube content creator Joanna Soh to promote their subscription-based video workout service called CosmoBody. Borum says that

> Joanna lives in Malaysia, and CosmoBody is only available in the United States. However, because such a large percentage of her audience is in the U.S., Joanna's video was a smash success with Cosmo, driving more traffic and purchases than any of their other partners. Just goes to show how truly global YouTube is, and how its celebrities have influence far beyond the countries where they live.

Platforms such as Tubular and Reelio can provide you with audience breakdowns by country for different YouTube content creators.

Your videos should generally be short. Walter and Gioglio (2014, p. 72) note that

> the average video duration is 2 minutes 46 seconds, so if it is much more than that, there is a chance you could lose viewers' interest. Avoid putting too much information in one video; if it is too long, you could consider breaking it into several videos covering separate topics.

Also, although Google+ is undergoing major changes at the time of writing, remember that you can host Google hangouts with up to 150 participants, which Google will record and give you the option to share on YouTube (Kerpen, 2011, p. 242). For example, Breakenridge (2012, p. 96) notes that Daria Musk, the indie music artist, achieved popularity by hosting 24-hour concerts using Google hangouts:

> She had approximately 9,000 fans join her in a hangout, with more than 100 countries represented . . . there was no mistaking the results of her efforts. She's been booked as a guest speaker/performer at various music

and tech conferences, and she's also solidified a worldwide music following post Google+ concert hangout.

LinkedIn

Copyright: JuliusKielaitis

How It Works: LinkedIn calls itself the "world's largest professional network." Users create profiles of their professional experience and invite other users to connect with them. Users can also post content which is seen by their connections.

User Base: LinkedIn has 347 million active users (Statista, 2015a). According to its website, the platform "shows content . . . in English, Arabic, Chinese (Simplified), Chinese (Traditional), Czech, Danish, Dutch, French, German, Indonesian, Italian, Japanese, Korean, Malay, Norwegian, Polish, Portuguese, Romanian, Russian, Spanish, Swedish, Tagalog, Thai, and Turkish. Other languages are being considered for the future" (LinkedIn, 2015). The countries with the most users are the U.S., India, Brazil, the United Kingdom, and Canada (Tetchner, 2014). Ahna Hendrix, Chief Executive Officer and Lead Social Media Specialist of the New York-based ARCH Digital Agency, says she finds that while people in the U.S. are generally comfortable posting their profiles, the platform still has a stigma to overcome in Asia and Europe, where some employees feel that using the site signals to their employers that they are hunting for new jobs.

How to Use It for PR: Craft long-form posts on behalf of your senior executives. This allows members who are not personally connected with the executive to choose to follow their posts. Posts on LinkedIn tend to be industry and/

or career-related, and are a nice way to position your executives as thought leaders in your industry and your organization as an attractive place to work.

Olivos recommends that you share this content as an "update" to the executive's LinkedIn page as well as post it on LinkedIn Pulse, because

> Pulse is a great tool for sharing content and information with the masses. Anyone is able to post their blogs there. It can be a good way to network and reach new connections, showing an executive as the true expert in his or her field. Being active in groups is another way to get your company and its employees noticed.

Twitter

Copyright: Bloomua

How It Works: Users create a Twitter handle, which begins with the symbol @, and post (i.e., "tweet") content of 140 characters or less, which is shared in the feeds of everyone who follows their handle. (My Twitter handle is @karaalaimo. Follow me!) Tweets can be posted in any language; a recent study of Twitter users who indicated that they have a preferred language found that roughly half tweeted in English and half in other languages, especially Japanese, Spanish, and Portuguese (Seshagiri, 2014). Hashtags (the symbol #) are used to tag tweets that are part of a larger conversation, so that the hashtag can be searched. For example, the official hashtag of the Olympics is #Olympics. Kerpen (2011, p. 236) notes that

> one of the main distinctions of Twitter versus Facebook is that Twitter's conversations are typically much more public. While people on Facebook mostly share with friends they know, less than 5 percent of all Twitter

users keep their updates private since most of them opt for all-inclusive, completely open conversations.

User Base: Twitter has more than 300 million monthly active users (Kim, 2015). The countries with the most users are the U.S., United Kingdom, Canada, Australia, Brazil, Germany, the Netherlands, France, India, and South Africa (Lipman, 2014).

How to Use It for PR: Limits of 140 characters make brevity the key challenge on Twitter. Olivos advises that "tweets should be a mix of text posts and images. Twitter allows for multiple images to be posted. Take advantage of this when possible."

Since most people will view your tweets from their own stream rather than from your Twitter page, you should not assume that people have seen past tweets for context on what you are taking about. Walter and Gioglio (2014, p. 89) explain that "each tweet should therefore be able to be understood on its own."

Peter Susko (2015), Director of the Slovac Republic Foreign Ministry's Press Department, advises that you should "avoid publishing lots of tweets one after the other, as people are likely to get bored and scroll past you. How many tweets a day? 1–2 a day is fine, just to keep your followers interested."

Walter and Gioglio (2014, p. 89) also advise that you "consider the location of the people in your audience. . . . If you have a worldwide audience, maybe it makes sense to repeat some of your tweets during different times of the day when your followers will be most likely able to see them."

Much of the content that gets re-tweeted and goes on to "trend" on Twitter is generated by the traditional U.S. media, such as *The New York Times*, CNN, and ESPN, which covers sports (Asur et al., 2011). So, ironically, one of the best ways to influence the conversation on Twitter is actually to influence the traditional press!

A good way to pick up followers on Twitter is to join popular conversations online by using hashtags that are "trending" at the moment. However, Susko (2015) warns that you need to make sure that the hashtag you use means what you think it does, so you don't inadvertently associate yourself with something "unsavory or embarrassing." He recommends using the website hashtagify.me to research hashtags. And, be sure to craft and communicate an official hashtag for each of your events and initiatives, to encourage "tweeps" (people on Twitter) to join your conversations.

Be aware that consumers tend to take to Twitter to address customer service issues. Be prepared to respond rapidly. Kerpen (2011, p. 237) notes that, unlike on Facebook, brands can send private direct messages to followers. So while you should make clear publicly that you are addressing a problem, direct messages allow you to follow up privately—for example, to ask for an order number.

Olivos also recommends organizing Twitter Chats, in which a group of tweeps go online at a predetermined time to discuss a designated topic using a specific hashtag. She also suggests participating in Twitter Chats hosted by other users. For example, Olivos recently logged into Twitter as one of her clients—a transportation company—to participate in a Twitter Chat hosted by travel influencers, both tweeting questions to them and answering questions posted by other tweeps.

Finally, Olivos says that you should make sure that your website and/or blog are set up to generate Twitter Cards. With Twitter Cards, you can attach rich photos, videos, and media to your tweets to drive traffic to your website or blog. If you include a few lines of code to your site, whenever you or others Tweet a link to your content, a "card" will be visible with additional information, acting as a preview of your content. This is helpful since you can write only 140 characters before sharing your link.

Instagram

Copyright: OlegDoroshin

How It Works: Users take pictures and record videos to share with their followers, applying filters to create artistic shots and clips. Walter and Gioglio (2014, p. 91) note that

> Instagram relies on users' posting hashtags with their images, which allows people to discover related images or search for something very specific. But the hashtags also work through other supporting sites like Twitter to make it a social network that stands alone or that integrates seamlessly into other platforms.

User Base: Instagram has 300 million active users and supports twenty-three languages, from Afrikaans to Turkish (Statista, 2015a; Instagram, 2015b). Countries with the most traffic on Instagram are the U.S., Russia, Brazil, the

United Kingdom, and Turkey (Statista, 2015c). Along with Tumblr, it has the youngest users among the eight largest non-Chinese social networks; more than 75 percent are under age thirty-five (Mander, 2014).

How to Use It for PR: Upload creative photos and videos that will grab attention. Olivos says that Instagram "requires unique, real-time content: visually appealing photos (avoid stock images), micro videos (such as 'how-tos,' announcements, sneak peeks, etc.), and re-posting quality photos from followers using the 're-post' app." Think about images and videos that will offer a unique glimpse into your organization—for example, a picture of the President's office or a video of the inside of your production plant. Walter and Gioglio (2014, p. 92) note that videos shared by brands on Instagram get twice as much engagement as photos.

Give users incentives to upload photos of themselves interacting with your brand or promoting your cause in some way and tag your account on the photos. For example, you can offer rewards for the best pictures or randomly give prizes to people who enter a contest by uploading and tagging photos following your instructions. Share some of the best photos uploaded by other people interacting with your products or promoting your cause (be sure to give photo credit where it's due).

Use hashtags so that your posts are easily found by others interested in the same topic (who will hopefully go on to follow your organization). Instagram.com launched a search feature in July 2015 making it much easier for users to find content based upon your account, location, and the hashtags you use (Bell, 2015). Walter and Gioglio (2014, p. 97) recommend that you "build a community by putting your official hashtag in your banner heading for fans to know how to tag you." They also suggest creating hashtags for different campaigns or promotions that you run—but not too many, because you don't want to splinter your community.

Finally, consider cross-promotion with other organizations whose followers are likely to be interested in your organization. On Instagram, it's not unheard of to see brands sharing the photos of their competitors! If they will do the same for you, it can be an interesting way for you both to pick up new followers.

Walter and Gioglio (2014, p. 93) report that "the best-suited brands for Instagram are obviously the ones that lend themselves easily to images: luxury brands, retail, lifestyle, and fashion and design companies are natural fits for this platform." Luxury brands such as Tiffany and Gucci are among those with the highest numbers of followers on the platform.

Snapchat

How It Works: Users post pictures and videos called "stories" that are viewable for the next 24 hours by those friends who they have approved. They also send pictures or videos with a short line of text to friends, called "Snaps,"

Copyright: focal point

which disappear within a few seconds of being sent (the sender is notified if the recipient screenshots the message).

User Base: Snapchat has 200 million active users and is available in English, Arabic, Bokmål, Norwegian, Danish, Dutch, French, German, Indonesian, Italian, Japanese, Korean, Polish, Portuguese, Romanian, Russian, Simplified Chinese, Spanish, Swedish, Traditional Chinese, and Turkish (Statista, 2015a; iTunes, 2015). About 55 percent of Snapchat's users are in North America, with 32 percent in Europe, 5 percent in Oceania, and 4 percent in South America (Statista, 2014b).

How to Use It for PR: Olivos says that "this is where the youth demographic is: think early teens to about age 25. If this isn't your target audience, your presence may not be necessary here."

If this is an audience you are trying to reach, create an account for your organization and post content to your stories section. Olivos says that

> Snapchat requires commitment in the form of regular updates. It is more about building honest relationships with followers—really entertaining and engaging with "friends"—while still holding true to your brand. This isn't a traditional marketing or public relations platform. Content can't be repeated over and over in exhaustion. All content here must be created specifically for this platform, and must be creative and authentic. Is your brand casual and playful? This is the most common tone here.

Olivos points to Amazon's "Snaps" showing "crazy reviews" people posted and asking users to guess the product they were talking about as an example of what works well on this platform. She explains that

> Snapchat is good for brands looking to generate some type of hype. You can promote new product launches, offer sneak peeks, and provide a behind-the-scenes look at things. It's also good for contests: you can have users go on scavenger hunts, ask them to submit their photos for chances to win prizes, or ask trivia questions.

Olivos says that a key benefit of Snapchat over platforms such as Twitter is that it is harder for users to miss your messages on Snapchat:

> When a user goes into his or her stories section, at the top he or she will see a list of all the recent updates. Once the user views them, they go to the end of the user's list. So it's harder to miss a story. Whereas if you were just Tweeting about topics, if a user isn't on Twitter at the moment, that update will get bogged down in their feed. They may miss it entirely.

However, Conlin (2014) notes that, because posts on this site are so ephemeral, "the challenge with Snapchat is time . . . so brands have to think about how to capitalize on urgency and demand." He recommends posting teasers for upcoming events and using strong calls to action, because "the urgency of a 10-second photo or video shared with a 'friend' means that you have a captive audience." For example, one organization that sells sports tickets gave users a chance to win tickets to a game if they had five friends add the organization on Snapchat. Each of the five friends had to send a snap to the organization with the name of the person who wanted to win.

Finally, during major global events, such as the Olympics and the World Cup, Snapchat curates some of the best content that users have uploaded in real time and shares it in a section called "Live." To be considered for this section, send your content to @Snapchat.

Tumblr

How It Works: Sign up to create a blog and post text, photos, videos, and links. Other users can follow your blog and re-blog and comment on your posts. Walter and Gioglio (2014, p. 101) note that "one of the great features about Tumblr is that users can add comments only if they reblog your post," which cuts down on comments from trolls.

User Base: Tumblr has 230 million active users and supports English, French, German, Italian, Japanese, Polish, Russian, Spanish, and Turkish (Statista, 2015a; Tumblr, 2012). Countries with the most traffic on Tumblr are the U.S.,

Copyright: dolphfyn

United Kingdom, Canada, Brazil, and Germany (Statista, 2015d). Tumblr users tend to be young; more than 70 percent are under the age of thirty-five (Mander, 2014).

How to Use It for PR: Walter and Gioglio (2014, p. 101) report that "the key to Tumblr is its simplicity. Tumblr isn't about long blog posts and information-loaded content. Instead, it's for quick visual inspiration and consumer lust. Photos, videos, charts, quotes, and Q&As fill Tumblr streams." They (2014, p. 105) also advise you to "use relevant tags so that your images show up in searches" and "reblog plenty of content from other users." Furthermore, "relationships on Tumblr are important. Follow other users and comment on posts."

Walter describes Tumblr as an "underused resource for connecting with your customers' passion points, because it uses visuals, which are the best form to connect emotionally with people." She recommends using pictures in the Graphics Interchange Format, known as "GIFs," which are especially popular on the platform. As Walter and Gioglio (2014, p. 163) explain,

> GIFs can help bring a static image to life by fusing images together to create animation-like motion. Companies can use GIFs to create bite-sized stories about products, events, and funny one-liners and actions, whether it's a model strutting down a runway, a cake being decorated, or a motivational quote.

They (2014, p. 164) recommend Photoshop as the program that "still reigns supreme" for creating GIFs. Walters recommends checking out brands such as Nike and GE on Tumblr for examples of creative GIFs.

Social Media in China

When it comes to social media platforms, there is the rest of the world, and then there is China. China is the largest social media market in the world; Forty-seven percent of Chinese people have active social media accounts (Chiu, Ip, & Silverman, 2012; Kemp, 2015). However, because the Chinese government has blocked access to major non-Chinese social media sites such as Facebook, Twitter, Instagram, and YouTube, Chinese social media users utilize primarily Chinese platforms in Mandarin, which are little understood by non-Chinese public relations practitioners.

The first thing to know when using social media in China is to be careful. Under Chinese law, social media users must register with their real names, government censors delete posts "as they see fit," and the government can punish users with prison sentences if they post content which the government deems to be inaccurate and the content goes on to garner more than 500 shares (Simcott, 2014). Another challenge is that many companies actively spread false rumors about their competitors online, so you will need to be hyper-vigilant to immediately correct any inaccurate information (Chiu et al., 2012). Furthermore, Chiu et al. (2012) note that Chinese social media users "expect responses to each and every post."

However, there is also huge opportunity in engaging social media users and influencers in China. Simcott (2014) reports that 91 percent of China's online population has a social media account (the corresponding number in the U.S. is 67 percent) and Chinese social media users are more likely to purchase items that are recommended by other users. Furthermore, as I discuss in greater detail in Chapter 8, social media influencers in China are particularly influential because the Chinese people, skeptical of the government-censored press, turn to independent online sources that they view as more reliable sources of information. Chiu et al. (2012), of the global management consulting firm McKinsey, offer the following advice for using social media platforms in China:

Make content authentic and user oriented. Estée Lauder's Clinique brand launched a drama series, *Sufei's Diary*, with 40 episodes broadcast daily on a dedicated Web site. (Viewers also could watch segments on monitors located on buses, trains, and airplanes.) While skin care was part of the story line and products were prominently featured, *Sufei's Diary* was seen as entertainment—not a Clinique advertisement—and has been viewed online more than 21 million times. Clinique's online brand awareness is now 27 percent higher than that of its competitors, although social-media content costs significantly less than a traditional advertising campaign.

Adopt a test-and-learn approach. When Dove China first imported the Real Beauty social-media campaign to promote beauty among women of all looks and body types, Chinese consumers viewed the real women as overweight and unattractive. Dove switched tack and partnered with

Ugly Wudi, the Chinese adaptation of the US television show *Ugly Betty*, to weave the Real Beauty message into story lines and mount a number of initiatives, including a blog by Wudi and live online chats. The effort generated millions of searches and blog entries, increased uptake of Dove body wash by 21 percent year over year after the show's first season, and increased unaided awareness of Dove's Real Beauty by 44 percent among target consumers. The estimated return on investment from this social-media campaign was four times that of a traditional TV media investment.

Support overarching brand goals with sustained social-media efforts. Starbucks China promotes the same message of quality, social responsibility, and community building across all of its social-media efforts, as well as in its stores. And Durex didn't just establish a corporate account on . . . Weibo: it built a marketing team that both monitors online comments around the clock and collaborates closely with agency partners to create original, funny content. The company's approach is designed to interact meaningfully with fans, generate buzz, and deepen customer engagement with the brand.

Unless you are fluent in Mandarin, you will need to hire locals to manage your social media presence in China. Nevertheless, it will be important for you to be generally familiar with the key social media platforms in China if you oversee a global team or campaign. Maggie Chan, Director for Greater China of Newell Public Relations China, says that the two most important social media platforms for public relations purposes in China are Weibo and WeChat.

Weibo

Copyright: Gil C

How It Works: Weibo is often referred to as the "Chinese version of Twitter" (Liu, 2015). Users on this popular microblogging network create either an unverified account or a verified account. Verified accounts confirm the identities of companies, government entities, and celebrities. As on Twitter, you can post messages containing up to 140 characters, along with links, images, and videos. Chen Liang, Account Executive for the global public relations firm Ruder Finn, notes, however, that "one Chinese character can carry much more meaning than one English character." User profiles show a user's name, a short description, the number of followers the user has, the number of accounts the user follows, the number of tweets the user has posted, and the user's recent tweets and re-tweets (Asur et al., 2011). Asur et al. (2011) explain that

> the equivalent of a retweet [on Twitter] on . . . Weibo is instead shown as two . . . amalgamated entries: the original entry and the current user's actual entry which is a commentary on the original entry . . . Weibo also has a functionality absent from Twitter: the comment. When a Weibo user makes a comment, it is not rebroadcasted to the user's followers. Instead, it can only be accessed under the original message.

They also report that "the number of retweets that authors get on . . . Weibo are several orders of magnitude greater than the retweets for the trending topics on Twitter."

User Base: In the third quarter of 2014, Weibo had 167 million monthly active users (China Internet Watch, 2014).

How to Use It for PR: Asur et al. (2011) found that the most popular content on Weibo consists of jokes, images, and videos—in contrast to Twitter, where people tend to share traditional media content. The most popular accounts "seem to have a strong focus on collecting user-contributed jokes, movie trivia, quizzes, stories and so on." A large percentage of the most popular tweets contain images, and many also include videos or links. So, to be popular on this network, you'll need to be visual, entertaining, and informal. Steimle (2015) argues that Weibo is actually a "far friendlier" platform than Twitter for companies, "as brands can promote their events and online stores through video, live broadcast, and celebrity interviews." For example, in 2013, the American fashion company Coach ran a "New York Style" campaign on Weibo, including a video featuring five Chinese fashion bloggers. Fans were invited to vote on their favorite styles in order to be eligible to win Coach products.

WeChat

How It Works: WeChat has a "seemingly endless suite of features including voice and group chat, video call, walkie-talkie, and people nearby" (Steimle, 2015).

Copyright: dolphfyn

User Base: China's most popular social platform has 549 million monthly active users (Liu, 2015; Statista, 2015b).

How to Use It for PR: Despite the fact that WeChat is "more of an instant messenger app" than a social network, you can still set up an official account for your organization and post photos and videos (Simcott, 2014). As on Weibo, there are 140 character limits. Steimle (2015) explains that

> brands can set up a WeChat service account, which allows them to engage with customers by sending targeted material and use affiliate sales channel Weidian to analyze their users' shopping habits and preferences. Businesses can also place QR codes in high- trafficked places for users to follow their brand, use the location-based service function to target offers, and ads to nearby users, and use the "throw a bottle" feature to raise awareness about charities or discounts.

Liang notes that a new feature of WeChat called "Shake Shake" allows users to access special information—such as information about museum exhibits or store promotions—when they are within five meters of a specified location and activate the function. "'Shake Shake' can also be linked with time, so, for example, if a television show partners with WeChat, the show can send users who 'Shake Shake' during their program an interactive quiz or pop up," she says.

References

AFP (2015). AFP in numbers. Retrieved from http://www.afp.com/en/agency/afp-in-numbers/

Akinfeleye, R., Amobi, I. T., Okoye, I. E., & Sunday, O. (2009). The continued dominance of international news agencies in Nigerian newspapers: Comparing news coverage of the 2008 elections in America and in Ghana. *African Communication Research*, 2(3), 449–472.

Al Jazeera (2015). About us. Retrieved from http://www.aljazeera.com/aboutus/

Alaimo, K. (2015, July 20). Build compelling brand identities: A memo from the Social Media Strategies Summit. *The Public Relations Strategist*. Retrieved from https:// www.prsa.org/Intelligence/TheStrategist/Articles/view/11129/1113/Build_Compel ling_Brand_Identities_A_Memo_From_the#.Vb0qR_mAH6A

Amir (2014, October 20). Top 10 YouTube viewing countries in the world. *Country Ranker*. Retrieved from http://www.countryranker.com/top-10-youtube-viewing-coun tries-in-the-world/

Associated Press (2014). AP by the numbers. Retrieved from http://www.ap.org/an nual-report/2014/ap-by-the-numbers.html

Associated Press (2015). Text. Retrieved from http://www.ap.org/products-services/text

Asur, S., Yu, L., & Huberman, B. A. (2011, August 21). What trends in Chinese social media. Paper presented at the SNAKDD Workshop, San Francisco, CA.

BBC (2012). *BBC World Service 80th anniversary 1932–2012 media pack.* Retrieved from http://downloads.bbc.co.uk/mediacentre/World-Service-Media-Pack.pdf

BBC (2015). Around the world. Retrieved from http://www.bbc.co.uk/aboutthebbc/ insidethebbc/whatwedo/aroundtheworld#heading-bbc-world-news

Bell, K. (2015, July 20). Instagram's powerful new search is now on the web. *Mashable*. Retrieved from http://mashable.com/2015/07/20/instagram-new-web-search/?utm_ cid=mash-com-fb-socmed-link

Billboard (2015, February 26). YouTube reportedly still unprofitable, even with 1 billion monthly users. Retrieved from http://www.billboard.com/articles/business/6487324/ youtube-profit-1-billion-monthly-users-4-billion-revenue

Bloomberg (2015a). History and facts. Retrieved from http://www.bloomberg.com/ company/bloomberg-facts/

Bloomberg (2015b). News bureaus. Retrieved from http://www.bloomberg.com/ company/news-bureaus/?utm_source=bloomberg-menu

Bloomberg (2015c). TV. Retrieved from http://www.bloombergmedia.com/platforms/tv

Branigan, T. (2010, July 1). China funds English TV news channel CNC World in push for soft power. *The Guardian*. Retrieved from http://www.theguardian.com/ world/2010/jul/02/china-english-tv-news-channel-cnc-world

Breakenridge, D. K. (2012). *Social media and public relations: Eight new practices for the PR professional.* Upper Saddle River, NJ: Pearson Education.

Bulldog Reporter (2015, June 23). Messaging manifesto: Consumers are tuning out the old-fashioned brand strategy of blasting the same message over and over. *Bulldog Reporter*. Retrieved from https://www.bulldogreporter.com/dailydog/article/pr-biz-update/messaging-manifesto-consumers-are-tuning-out-the-old-fashioned-brand-

Castrejon, R. (2015, January 7). Los periodistas más seguidos en Twitter. *América Latina Business Review*. Retrieved from http://www.businessreviewamericalatina.com/lead ership/1232/Los-periodistas-m%C3%A1s-seguidos-en-Twitter

CCTV (2015). CCTV news, your link to Asia. Retrieved from http://english.cntv. cn/20100426/104481.shtml

Chatham House (2015). Chatham House rule. Retrieved from http://www.chatham house.org/about/chatham-house-rule

China Internet Watch (2014, November 14). Weibo had 167m monthly active users in Q3 2014. Retrieved from http://www.chinainternetwatch.com/10735/weibo-q3-2014/

Chiu, C., Ip, C., & Silverman, A. (2012, April). Understanding social media in China. *McKinsey Quarterly*. Retrieved from http://www.mckinsey.com/insights/marketing_sales/understanding_social_media_in_china

CNC (2015). About CNC. Retrieved from http://en.cncnews.cn/e_about_cnc/about.html

CNN (2015). Contact us/CNN International. Retrieved from http://www.cnn.com/feedback/cnni/.

Cohen, H. (2013, March 12). 5 facts prove visual content is a guaranteed winner! Retrieved from http://heidicohen.com/5-facts-prove-visual-content-is-a-guaranteed-winner/

Conlin (2014, May 27). Cheat sheet: Snapchat for marketing and PR. *Cision*. Retrieved from http://www.cision.com/us/2014/05/cheat-sheet-snapchat-for-marketing-and-pr/

Constine, J. (2015, August 12). Facebook confirms live broadcasting will soon open to journalists and verified profiles. *Techcrunch*. Retrieved from http://techcrunch.com/2015/08/12/facebook-live-livestreaming/

DeLisle, D. (2015, June 9). *Relationship marketing 101: Social media, content, mobile and more*. Presented at the Social Media Strategies Summit, New York, NY.

Deutsche Welle (2015). Deutsche Welle at a glance. Retrieved from http://www.dw.de/about-dw/profile/s-30688

Didner, P. (2015, June 9). *Global content marketing: Create a scalable content marketing strategy*. Presented at the Social Media Strategies Summit, New York, NY.

EFE (2015). International news service in English. Retrieved from http://www.efe.com/efe/productos/english/text/news/4/3000/3001

ExactTarget (2011). *The social breakup*. Retrieved from http://www.exacttarget.com/resources/SFF8.pdf

Financial Times (2015a). About the Financial Times. Retrieved from http://aboutus.ft.com/#axzz3e6zjkmFy

Financial Times (2015b). Products: FT weekday. Retrieved from http://fttoolkit.co.uk/d/products/weekday.php

Folkenflik, D. (2013, April 25). China seeks soft power influence in U.S. through CCTV. *NPR*. Retrieved from http://www.npr.org/2013/04/25/179020185/chinas-cctv-america-walks-the-line-between-2-media-traditions

France 24. (2015). France 24, the company. Retrieved from http://www.france24.com/en/company

Freshfields Bruckhaus Deringer (2013). *Containing a crisis: Dealing with corporate disasters in the digital age*. Retrieved from http://www.freshfields.com/uploadedFiles/SiteWide/News_Room/Insight/Campaigns/Crisis_management/Containing%20a%20crisis.pdf

Fussell Sisco, H., & McCorkindale, T. (2013). Communicating "pink": An analysis of the communication strategies, transparency, and credibility of breast cancer social media sites. *International Journal of Nonprofit and Voluntary Sector Marketing, 18*(4), 287–301.

Garcia, H. F. (2012). *The power of communication: Skills to build trust, inspire loyalty, and lead effectively*. Upper Saddle River, NJ: Pearson Education.

Golan, G. J. (2010). Determinants of international news coverage. In G. J. Golan, T. J. Johnson, & W. Wanta (Eds.), *International media communication in a global age* (pp. 125–144). New York, NY: Routledge.

The Guardian (2013). *Our audience story*. Retrieved from http://image.guardian.co.uk/sys-files/Guardian/documents/2013/01/25/GuardianKeyAudienceStats.pdf

Gutelle, S. (2014, May 22). Guess which country has the most avid YouTube viewers [INFOGRAPHIC]. *Tubefilter.* Retrieved from http://www.tubefilter.com/2014/05/22/youtube-viewers-around-the-world-downloader-infographic/

ING (2014). 2014 study impact of social media on news: More crowd-checking, less fact-checking. Retrieved from http://www.ing.com/Newsroom/All-news/NW/2014-Study-impact-of-Social-Media-on-News-more-crowdchecking-less-factchecking.htm

Instagram (2015a). Content strategy tips. Retrieved from https://business.instagram.com/gettingstarted/

Instagram (2015b). How do I change my language settings? Retrieved from https://help.instagram.com/111923612310997

International New York Times (2014). Audience & circulation. Retrieved from http://www.nytmediakit-intl.com/newspapers/international-new-york-times/audience-circulation.aspx

Ioffe, J. (2010). What is Russia today? *Columbia Journalism Review.* September/October. Retrieved from http://www.cjr.org/feature/what_is_russia_today.php

iTunes (2015). Snapchat. Retrieved from https://itunes.apple.com/us/app/snapchat/id447188370?mt=8

Jones, S. (2013, January 31). HMV workers take over official Twitter feed to vent fury over sacking. *The Guardian.* Retrieved from http://www.theguardian.com/business/2013/jan/31/hmv-workers-twitter-feed-sacking

Kemp, S. (2015, January 21). Digital, social & mobile worldwide in 2015. *We Are Social.* Retrieved from http://wearesocial.net/blog/2015/01/digital-social-mobile-worldwide-2015/

Kent, M. L., & Taylor, M. (1998). Building dialogic relationships through the World Wide Web. *Public Relations Review, 24*(3), 321–334.

Kerpen, D. (2011). *Likeable social media: How to delight your customers, create an irresistible brand, and be generally amazing on Facebook (and other social networks).* New York, NY: McGraw Hill.

Kim, E. (2015, April 30). This chart shows one major reason why investors are so worried about Twitter. *Business Insider.* Retrieved from http://www.businessinsider.com/twitters-monthly-active-user-growth-is-slowing-2015-4

Küng-Shankleman, L. (2000). *Inside the BBC and CNN: Managing media organisations.* New York, NY: Routledge.

Langley, H. (2013, March 21). Getting hacked—the best thing for your brand? *TechRadar.* Retrieved from http://www.techradar.com/us/news/internet/getting-hacked-the-best-thing-for-your-brand-1139696

Leis, M. (2015, June 10). *Listen, invite, reward, celebrate: Behavioral storytelling method.* Presented at the Social Media Strategies Summit, New York, NY.

LinkedIn (2015, April 8). Supported languages. Retrieved from https://help.linkedin.com/app/answers/detail/a_id/999/~/supported-languages

Lipman, V. (2014, May 24). Top Twitter trends: What countries are most active? Who's most popular? *Forbes.* Retrieved from http://www.forbes.com/sites/victorlipman/2014/05/24/top-twitter-trends-what-countries-are-most-active-whos-most-popular/

Liu, H. (2015, August 17). China's social media explosion has shattered the official silence. *The Financial Times.* Retrieved from http://www.ft.com/cms/s/0/637a0e0e-44cb-11e5-af2f-4d6e0e5eda22.html#axzz3jUE9DRhS

Malthouse, E. C., Vandenbosch, M., & Kim, S. J. (2014). The effects of social media engagement on purchase behaviors: Co-creating benefits in social media contests and its effects on purchase behaviors. *Medill IMC Spiegel Digital & Database Research Center*. Retrieved from http://spiegel.medill.northwestern.edu/_pdf/Speigel%201.0-Social-Engagement.pdf

Mander, J. (2014, December 1). Tumblr and Instagram have the youngest audiences. *GlobalWebIndex*. Retrieved from http://www.globalwebindex.net/blog/tumblr-instagram-audiences

Marinello, M. (2015, June 10). *Coffee talk: Using brand to drive performance*. Presented at the Social Media Strategies Summit, New York, NY.

McMahon, T. P. (2011). Integrated communication. In J. Doorley & H. F. Garcia (Eds.), *Reputation management: The key to successful public relations and corporate communication* (2nd ed.) (pp. 258–277). New York, NY: Routledge.

Murdico, D. (2011, June 27). 10 reasons PR pros should use video. *Ragan's PR Daily*. Retrieved from http://www.prdaily.com/Main/Articles/10_reasons_PR_pros_should_use_video__8710.aspx

NHK World (2015). About NHK World. Retrieved from http://www3.nhk.or.jp/nhkworld/english/info/aboutnhkworld.html

Paine, K. D. (2011). *Measure what matters: Online tools for understanding customers, social media, engagement, and key relationships*. Hoboken, NJ: John Wiley & Sons.

Porter, J. (2010, January 21). Facebook for public relations. Retrieved from http://blog.journalistics.com/2010/facebook-for-public-relations/

Rawnsley, G. D. (2009). China talks back. In N. Snow & P. M. Taylor (Eds.), *Routledge handbook of public diplomacy* (pp. 282–291). New York, NY: Routledge.

Reuters (2015a). International news services. Retrieved from http://thomsonreuters.com/en/products-services/reuters-news-agency/international-news-services.html

Reuters (2015b). Reuters world service. Retrieved from http://thomsonreuters.com/en/products-services/reuters-news-agency/international-news-services/reuters-world-service.html

Rich, C. (2013). *Writing and reporting news: A coaching method* (7th ed.). Belmont, CA: Wadsworth.

RT (2015a). About RT. Retrieved from http://rt.com/about-us/

RT (2015b). Contact info. Retrieved from http://rt.com/about-us/contact-info/

Rybalko, S., & Seltzer, T. (2010). Dialogic communication in 140 characters or less: How *Fortune* 500 companies engage stakeholders using Twitter. *Public Relations Review*, 36(4), 336–341.

Seshagiri, A. (2014, March 9). The languages of Twitter users. *The New York Times*. Retrieved from http://bits.blogs.nytimes.com/2014/03/09/the-languages-of-twitter-users/?_r=0

Shuster, S. (2015, March 5). Inside Putin's on-air machine. *Time*. Retrieved from http://time.com/rt-putin/

Signore, S. (2013, June 5). 3 ways video helps with PR. *Ragan's PR Daily*. Retrieved from http://www.prdaily.com/Main/Articles/3_ways_video_helps_with_PR_14600.aspx

Simcott, R. (2014, February 27). Social media fast facts: China. *Social Media Today*. Retrieved from http://www.socialmediatoday.com/content/social-media-fast-facts-china.

Sky (2015). Sky plc. Retrieved from https://corporate.sky.com/about-sky/ataglance/sky-plc

Statista (2014a). Leading countries based on number of Facebook users as of May 2014 (in millions). Retrieved from http://www.statista.com/statistics/268136/top-15-countries-based-on-number-of-facebook-users/

Statista (2014b). Regional distribution of Snapchat users worldwide as of July 2014. Retrieved from http://www.statista.com/statistics/315405/snapchat-user-region-distribution/

Statista (2015a). Leading social networks worldwide as of March 2015, ranked by number of active users (in millions). Retrieved from http://www.statista.com/statistics/272014/global-social-networks-ranked-by-number-of-users/

Statista (2015b). Number of monthly active WeChat users from 2nd quarter 2010 to 1st quarter 2015 (in millions). Retrieved from http://www.statista.com/statistics/255778/number-of-active-wechat-messenger-accounts/

Statista (2015c). Regional distribution of Instagram traffic in the last three months as of April 2015, by country. Retrieved from http://www.statista.com/statistics/272933/distribution-of-instagram-traffic-by-country/

Statista (2015d). Regional distribution of Tumblr traffic in the last three months as of April 2015, by country. Retrieved from http://www.statista.com/statistics/261413/distribution-of-tumblr-traffic-by-country/

Steimle, J. J. (2015, January 4). The state of social media in China. *ClickZ*. Retrieved from http://www.clickz.com/clickz/column/2383850/the-state-of-social-media-in-china

Stokes, J. (1999). The structure of British media industries. In J. Stokes, & A. Reading (Eds.), *The media in Britain: Current debates and developments* (pp. 1–24). London, UK: Palgrave.

Sung, K. H., & Kim, S. (2014). I want to be your friend: The effects of organizations' interpersonal approaches on social networking sites. *Journal of Public Relations Research, 26*(3), 235–255.

Susko, P. (2015). Twiplomacy 2.015. *World Communication Review*. Retrieved from http://www.forumdavos.com/WCFA

Taylor, A. (2012, June 27). The New York Times' Chinese edition just went live. *Business Insider*. Retrieved from http://www.businessinsider.com/new-york-times-chinese-edition-2012-6

Teljami, S. (2013). *The world through Arab eyes: Arab public opinion and the reshaping of the Middle East*. New York, NY: Basic Books.

Tetchner, I. (2014, July). Which countries have the most LinkedIn users? *Link Humans*. Retrieved from http://linkhumans.com/blog/linkedin-usage-2014

Tumblr (2012). Hello, guten tag, bonjour, Привет! Retrieved from http://support.tumblr.com/post/21397501618/hello-guten-tag-bonjour

Turner Broadcasting System, Inc. (2015). CNN in Latin America. Retrieved from http://www.turner.com/brands/cnn-latin-america

Wall Street Journal (2015a). Global. Retrieved from http://www.wsjmediakit.com/products/global#latin-america

Wall Street Journal (2015b). Newspaper. Retrieved from http://www.wsjmediakit.com/products/newspaper

Walter, E., & Gioglio, J. (2014). *The power of visual storytelling: How to use visuals, videos, and social media to market your brand*. New York, NY: McGraw Hill Education.

Ward, A. (2013, February 18). "The Whopper flopped": Burger King Twitter feed is hacked . . . and starts sending out messages about McDonald's. *Daily Mail*. Retrieved from http://www.dailymail.co.uk/news/article-2280625/Burger-King-Twitter-feed-hacked-McDonalds-fan.html#ixzz3cffQOV4V

Xinhua (2010, July 1). Xinhua launches CNC World English channel. Retrieved from http://news.xinhuanet.com/english2010/china/2010-07/01/c_13378575.htm

Zayani, M. (2005). Introduction—Al Jazeera and the vicissitudes of the new Arab media landscape. In M. Zayani (Ed.), *The Al Jazeera phenomenon: Critical perspectives on new Arab media* (pp. 1–46). London, UK: Pluto Press.

8   Public Relations in Asia and the Pacific

Welcome to Asia and the Pacific! Asia is the world's largest continent by both size and population. A region of enormous diversity, Asia and the Pacific has been influenced by traditions as varied as Buddhism, Hinduism, Confucianism, Islam, and Christianity, with economic structures ranging from capitalism to communism and governments ranging from democracies to dictatorships. Asia is home to some of the most densely populated countries on earth, such as China, Singapore, and Bangladesh. On the other hand, Central Asia—a region including Western China, Mongolia, Kazakhstan, Kyrgyzstan, Tajikistan, Turkmenistan, and Uzbekistan—has an average population density of just 24 people per square mile, who largely herd livestock (Haque, 2004, p. 349). Japan has one of the world's highest standards of living; the physical growth of many North Koreans has been stunted as a result of starvation by their dictator.

The region has a storied history, of which its people are generally very proud. Haque (2004, p. 247) notes that "Asia is known to be the cradle of human civilization. Asians founded the first cities, started agriculture and trading, set up the first systems of law, invented writing, paper and moveable type, and created the earliest literatures." However, between the sixteenth and the nineteenth centuries, large parts of the continent were conquered by Western European countries, widening the economic gap between Asia and the West.

Over the past several decades, many economies in the region have grown rapidly. Devereux and Peirson-Smith (2009, p. 214) note that, as countries in the region have become richer, public relations practice has shifted from government-led nation building campaigns to significantly greater corporate practice. However, the government is still the focus of a particularly large share of the efforts of public relations practitioners in the region. Sriramesh (2004, p. 330) reports that "there can be no doubt that establishing robust government relations is crucial to the strategic management of public relations in Asia, unlike the popular concept of public relations where the government is but one relevant public."

David Brain, President and CEO of Edelman's Asia Pacific, Middle East, and Africa business, notes that as the region's astonishing rate of economic growth has slowed in recent years—from an annual range of 2–10 percent to 0–6 percent—governments are under pressure to prove that they are performing and to protect domestic businesses. "This can make them unpredictable towards businesses and brands, especially 'foreign' ones," Brain says. "So it's more important than ever to show your wider economic, social, and environmental contribution in this region."

The region's overall economic growth has fueled demand for top global brands. Devereux and Peirson-Smith (2009, p. 91) observe that, "across Asia Pacific, the desire for brands appears to be insatiable. . . . Consumers in developing economies across Asia, such as China, India, and Korea, . . . tend to display this need to buy into premier brands as a badge of personal achievement and social standing."

Another characteristic of public relations practice across the majority of this diverse region is the personal influence model. As discussed in Chapter 2, under this model, "practitioners try to establish personal relationships—friendships, if possible—with key individuals in the media, government, or political and activist groups" (Grunig et al., 1995, p. 180). Relationships are critical in this part of the world, and practitioners who attempt to work in the region without firmly establishing them are likely to be thwarted at every turn.

Brain emphasizes that because the average daily commute in Asia and the Pacific is one hour and many people spend this time on their phones, mobile strategies are a must for this region. However, the traditional press is still critical. Brain notes that 41 percent of tweets in Singapore, 40 percent of tweets in Korea, and 35 percent of tweets in India link to content. The top sources of linked content are national newspapers.

Sadly, as in many regions of the world, the public relations profession has not garnered a positive reputation for itself in Asia and the Pacific. Sriramesh (2004, p. 328) notes that "although the term 'public relations' itself is widely used in Asian countries, it is often indicative of 'spin doctoring', or mere self-serving publicity by the source of a message." Here's hoping that we will change that! Read on for best (and worst) public relations practices in the region's three cultural clusters: Confucian Asia, South Asia, and the Anglo cluster.

Confucian Asia

This cultural cluster includes the parts of Asia that have been influenced by Confucianism, including China, Hong Kong, Japan, Singapore, South Korea, and Taiwan (Gupta & Hanges, 2004, p. 191). Confucianism is a social tradition derived from the teachings of Confucius, a philosopher who lived in China from 551–479 BC. Incredibly influential across this region, Confucianism places supreme importance on *social harmony* and avoiding conflict. For this reason, Confucianism encourages indirect rather than direct communication (or, in the terminology of Chapter 2, high-context rather than low-context communication) in order to avoid conflict and allow individuals to save "face" (Samovar, Porter, McDaniel, & Roy, 2013, p. 169). This often prevents individuals from openly criticizing others, questioning authority, and revealing mistakes (Yu & Wen, 2003).

Newsom (2004, p. 373) explains that "the Asian tradition of preserving 'face,' . . . includes not only personal self-respect but also respect for the entire group to which one belongs." This is the case because this culture is extremely collectivist. In contrast to the Western focus on the individual, Confucianism emphasizes the responsibilities that people have as part of their *relationships* in society; people are thought of not as individuals, but as members of a family unit (Rhee, 2002, p. 162). Such relationships are hierarchical and reciprocal; for example, children are expected to be respectful to their parents, just as the governed are expected to be loyal to their rulers. As discussed in Chapter 2, whereas the United States of America worships youth, in Confucian societies, elders are revered; deference is always given to the more senior person in any situation. However, in return for such respect and obedience, the senior member in each relationship owes the more junior member consideration and protection (Hofstede, Hofstede, & Minkov, 2010, p. 237). Because of the importance of relationships in this culture, it is critical to spend time building familiarity and trust with people before conducting business.

The Confucian tradition also emphasizes *humility*, *virtue*, and *benevolence* and places great importance on conformance to social rituals and conventions. One of the key concepts in Confucianism is *li*, which means "to arrange in order." As Livermore (2013, p. 58) explains, "*li* means etiquette, customs, and manners; it's ceremony, courtesy, civility, and behaving with propriety." This is yet another reason why members of this culture tend to be high-context communicators. Livermore (2013, p. 62) notes that

> people give as much attention to where individuals are seated, how they dress, and how they carry themselves as to what is actually said. Given the

importance of *li*, the way you communicate verbally and nonverbally is more prescribed than it is in other places.

Another important characteristic of this culture is its long-term orientation. In sharp contrast with the emphasis on the near term in countries such as the U.S., members of this cultural cluster focus on the longer term. Livermore (2013, p. 62) notes that, as a result, "people in Confucian cultures are . . . less likely to spend money they don't have than people in short-term oriented cultures might do. Governments and businesses in this region tend to be cash-rich." Rhee (2002, p. 163) explains that

> virtue with regard to one's tasks in life consists of trying to acquire skills and education, working hard, not spending more than necessary, being patient, and persevering. Conspicuous consumption is taboo, as well as losing one's temper. Moderation is enjoyed in all things.

In sum, this cultural group is characterized by high in-group collectivism, institutional collectivism, and performance orientation as well as moderate assertiveness, future orientation, gender egalitarianism, humane orientation, power distance, and uncertainty avoidance (Gupta & Hanges, 2004, p. 193).

The next sections profile public relations practice in three of the largest markets in this cultural group: China, Japan, and South Korea.

People's Republic of China

Time zone: Coordinated Universal Time (UTC) + 8:00
International dialing code: +86

When you practice public relations in China, be prepared to build *guanxi*.

More than one in six people on the planet live in China, the most populous nation on earth and the world's second-largest economy (CIA, 2014; World Bank, 2014). Yet the communist country remains enigmatic for many global public relations professionals.

China has a long and proud history as one of the world's oldest civilizations. The twentieth century was characterized by massive upheaval in China. The collapse of the Qing Dynasty in 1911 was followed by a civil war between China's ruling Nationalist party and Communists beginning in 1927, as well as by Japan's invasion and partial occupation of China from 1937–1945. In 1949, Mao Zedong established the Communist People's Republic of China (PRC). A period of isolation followed. After Mao's death in 1979, the country's new leader, Deng Xiaoping, began opening the country to the West.

Since then, the country's economy has grown at an astonishing pace; according to Goldman Sachs (2006, p. 47), China has "surpassed all records and created a new standard in the history of economic development," although

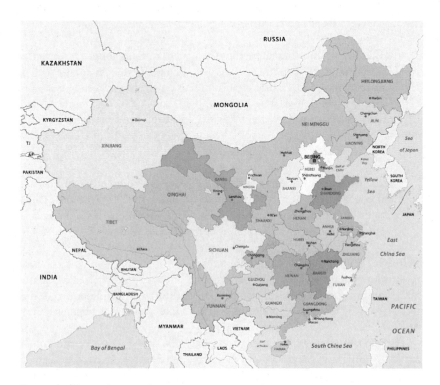

its growth has more recently slowed (Yao & Qing, 2015). This growth has made China an increasingly important market for global corporations. The wealth of Chinese adults tripled between 2000–2012 (Credit Suisse, 2012, p. 48). While the net worth of the Chinese elite remains shrouded in secrecy, it is clear that their wealth has skyrocketed, making China a particularly important country for the luxury goods market. For example, *Forbes* reports that China had no billionaires ten years ago; in 2014, China was home to 152 billionaires—the world's second-highest number, after the U.S. (Sharma, 2013; Flannery, 2014). Today, China has the fourth highest number of high net worth individuals in the world (Capgemini & RBC Wealth Management, 2014, p. 7). China's currency is the renminbi, also popularly referred to by the name of its basic unit, the yuan.

Despite the ostensible partial privatization of China's economy, how much of Chinese businesses remain owned by the government and controlled by the country's only political party, the Chinese Communist Party (CCP), is also a mystery to the outside world. The country's political leaders are selected in ultra-secret Party conclaves. The Party's Central Organization Department also selects the heads of other institutions under state control—including the country's political institutions, media, major businesses, universities, and think tanks. *Financial Times* reporter Richard McGregor (2012, p. 72) notes that

> a similar department in the [United States of America] would oversee the appointment of the entire US cabinet, state governors and their deputies, the mayors of major cities, the heads of all federal regulatory agencies, the chief executives of GE, ExxonMobil, Wal-Mart and about fifty of the remaining largest US companies, the justices on the Supreme Court, the editors of the *New York Times*, the *Wall Street Journal* and the *Washington Post*, the bosses of the TV networks and cable stations, the presidents of Yale and Harvard and other big universities, and the heads of think-tanks like the Brookings Institution and the Heritage Foundation. Not only that, the vetting process would take place behind closed doors, and the appointments announced without any accompanying explanation why they had been made.

Since the leaders of all of the country's institutions are members of the Party, "even if [the Party] were disbanded or fell apart, it would have to be put back together again, because its members alone have the skills, experience and networks to run the country" (McGregor, 2012, p. xxii).

While the Chinese government recognizes 56 different ethnic groups, more than 90 percent of the population is Han Chinese (CIA, 2014). Although the government promotes the official language, Mandarin, in an effort to unite the country, numerous languages and dialects are spoken, and more than 400 million Chinese people cannot speak the national language (Blanchard, 2013).

The Chinese government cracks down on a movement for independence in the region of Tibet; the leader of this movement, the Dalai Lama, fled Tibet in 1959 and established a government in exile in Dharamsala, India. A movement for independence by the Uyghur people, a Muslim, ethnic Turkish group who live in China's Xinjiang Uyghur Autonomous Region, results in sporadic episodes of violence. In 2014, the people of Hong Kong—a Special Autonomous Region of China—protested in the streets for democracy. There is also an independence movement in Taiwan, which China claims to be under its sovereignty. China has threatened to respond with military force if Taiwan asserts independence.

China is also notorious for its system of censorship, which significantly hinders the practice of public relations in the country. As Brady (2007) explains in her fascinating book *Marketing Dictatorship: Propaganda and Thought Work in Contemporary China*, the Communist Party licenses journalists and issues guidance for what can be reported in the Chinese press and how it should be reported. Some subjects are completely off limits, such as corruption by Party leaders, the growing income gap, and even the names of certain critics. Limited exposés are allowed when they serve to root out local abuses that the Party cannot control or to diffuse social pressure, but critiques of the system itself are never permitted. Members of the press are required to consult with propaganda officials before reporting on sensitive topics, and officials also dictate the terminology the media may use, with terms such as "Party-State," for example, completely banned (Brady, 2007, p. 101). Government officials direct the media to actively promote other subjects.

A complex system of laws and regulations governs the country's communications; for example, officials may not accept telephone calls from Taiwanese journalists, foreign investment in media is limited, and it is illegal for ordinary Chinese citizens to install satellites to view international television. Outside Internet sites are blocked; emails are filtered and may never reach their intended recipients; cartoon characters on websites remind citizens that they are being watched online; foreign radio stations are jammed. When media disobey the rules, Chinese journalists are harassed and jailed, foreign reporters are banished from the country, and media outlets and websites are shut down. Journalists are also occasionally subject to physical attacks (Freedom House, 2014a).

Yet while outsiders often view such blatant censorship as crude, Brady (2007) argues that the Chinese government actually practices a *sophisticated* form of public relations. Brady (2007, p. 191) reports that, in 1989, when student protestors in Tiananmen Square in China's capital city of Beijing were met with tanks and massacred, the Party learned a lesson that "force is only a limited and short-term means of social control in modern society; the most sustainable means of social control is persuasion." Today, the Party uses the Internet to guide discussions, organizes demonstrations, and sponsors pop music, game shows, and computer games (such as one inviting Chinese people to shoot the Taiwanese president). Freedom House (2014a) notes that

> since 2004, CCP and government officials at all levels have recruited and trained an army of paid web commentators, known informally as the Fifty Cent Party. Their tasks include posting progovernment remarks, tracking public opinion, disrupting or diverting criticism, and participating in public online chats with officials to provide the appearance of state-citizen interaction.

In order to reach nomadic communities with its messaging, the government has provided them with satellite televisions. The Party carefully crafts its messaging to cultivate nationalistic feelings, generating a degree of anti-foreign sentiment useful for uniting the Chinese people and preventing the admiration of the West that could threaten the Party's hold on power. Additionally, the Party employs fear by inculcating the notion that chaos would ensue without its control.

Though the government does control the media, Hung and Chen (2004, p. 52) note that the Chinese press is also dependent upon advertising revenues, which gives organizations such as corporations access to the media.

However, paying for media coverage is also commonplace in China (Hung & Chen, 2004, p. 37). Farey-Jones (2013) reports that

> journalists often expect clients to pay a "transport allowance" to get to an event. Payment for coverage can creep into the equation, while media have been known to blackmail companies, especially outside the biggest cities, with the threat of negative coverage.

Holly Zheng, President of the international division of the Chinese communication group BlueFocus, says that an important factor to be aware of is regional nuances of the media in this vast nation. She says,

> for example, Beijing has been the historical center of culture and politics, so media there is relatively more interested in political news; Shanghai, on the other hand, as China's iconic metropolitan city and financial center, keeps a close eye on finance related topics; and the press in Shenzhen, which is recognized as China's Silicon Valley, tends to report more on business, high-tech, and innovation related news.

However, given the difficulties of influencing the mainstream media, many practitioners focus on trying to influence individuals with major followings on China's social media platforms (Farey-Jones, 2013). Indeed, social media strategies are a must in this market. More than 300 million Chinese people use social media, which is equivalent to the populations of the United Kingdom, France, Germany, Italy, and Spain combined (Chiu, Ip, & Silverman, 2012). Chiu et al. (2012) note that "China's social-media users not only are more active than those of any other country but also, in more than 80 percent of all cases, have multiple social-media accounts, primarily with local players (compared with just 39 percent in Japan)."

Chen Liang, a public relations practitioner from China who is profiled below, explains that because of censorship, many Chinese people do not view the traditional media as a reliable source of news, and therefore turn to public figures such as actors, independent journalists, professors, and writers who have garnered reputations for sharing reliable information on social media. Chiu et al. (2012) likewise report that "because many Chinese are somewhat skeptical of formal institutions and authority, users disproportionately value the advice of opinion leaders in social networks."

You also must be prepared for negative attacks on Chinese social media platforms. Chiu et al. (2012) report that

> many companies regularly employ "artificial writers" to seed positive content about themselves online and attack competitors with negative news they hope will go viral. In several instances, negative publicity about companies—such as allegations of product contamination—has

prompted waves of microblog posts from competitors and disguised users. Businesses trying to manage social-media crises should carefully identify the source of negative posts and base countermeasures on whether they came from competitors or real consumers. Companies must also factor in the impact of artificial writers when mining for social-media consumer insights and comparing the performance of their brands against that of competitors. Otherwise, they risk drawing the wrong conclusions about consumer behavior and brand preferences.

As is the case elsewhere in Asia, the practice of public relations in China is extremely relationship based (Huang, 2000). Hung and Chen (2004, p. 35) note that

> in China the major function of public relations is viewed as a form of building and cultivating *guanxi*, the Chinese version of the personal influence model. Public relations professionals make efforts to cultivate interorganizational and interpersonal relationships by exchanging gifts, favors, and hospitality.

Hackley and Dong (2001, p. 16) explain that

> *guanxi* is a combination of two Chinese characters: *Guan* and *Xi*. *Guan* means door, gate, or pass . . . while *Xi* means department, group or organization. These two Chinese characters form the term that refers to access to a group or organization. When the Chinese say that "we have to find *Guanxi*," that is to say we have to find the entree to the group or organization. To find the door, personal connections or ties must be developed.

Thus, while Westerners are "sometimes . . . inclined to fly in, get down to substantive business right away, and then leave," this will not work in China, where it is important to first invest in building relationships with your partners (Chen & Culbertson, 2009, p. 179). In this relationship-based culture, friends and relatives are often given priority for hiring and promotion, which partners from other cultures may view as unethical (Chen & Culbertson, 2009, p. 179). While *guanxi* is often thought of in a negative light and associated with nepotism and manipulation, Hung and Chen (2004, p. 35) note that "because of competition from international public relations agencies, Chinese practitioners have started to think about how to manage *guanxi* ethically."

Because Chinese culture is so relationship based and distinctions are drawn between members of a group and outsiders, who are viewed with suspicion, newcomers must work especially hard to be accepted in China. Hung and Chen (2004, p. 55) report that the best way to do so is to demonstrate a long-term commitment to the country, such as through donations and financial investments. For example, the multinational corporation Unilever gained acceptance in the Chinese market by making community donations, sending senior managers to visit China, and making a major announcement that it would move its Asia headquarters from Singapore to Shanghai (Hung & Chen, 2004, p. 57).

Because Chinese society is very hierarchical, it is important to ensure that communicators have equal rank with those whom they approach. Individuals trying to reach high-level officials in China

> usually encounter the reply that if they intend to reach the party secretary, they would need someone holding an equivalent position to meet the party secretary. In resolving the difficulty, multinational companies usually have the chief executive officer (CEO) from headquarters to visit China to talk with the high-ranking officers (Hung & Chen, 2004, p. 51).

Another critical element of practicing public relations in China is the concept of face. Chinese people value protecting both their own "face" and that of others in each of their interactions. Chen and Culbertson (2009, p. 181) note that "in China, loss of face is often considered to be worse than loss of a limb." Therefore, "when working in China, public relations professionals must plan their activities so that they do not create a situation in which a native might encounter a loss of face." This concern with face and relationships may lead practitioners in China to tell "white lies" that practitioners from other cultures find to be unethical (Chen & Culbertson, 2009, p. 182). Furthermore, the Chinese tend to avoid what Yu and Wen (2003, p. 54) call "risky communication." This is because "Chinese people believe that talking about their problems may bring them even more problems in the future, so they are socialized to 'keep their mouths shut.'"

This avoidance of risky communication, combined with the culture's concern with face, often leads organizations to deny or attempt to cover up problems. For example, when the Sanlu Dairy Corp. learned just before China hosted the 2008 Olympic games that its infant formula had been contaminated with an industrial chemical and "hundreds of thousands of babies . . . were slowly being poisoned," the company decided to cover up the problem instead of warning parents not to feed the formula to their babies (McGregor, 2012, p. 171). Additionally, because of China's authoritarian history, "communication has often been one-way—with little careful listening or attention to dissenting viewpoints" (Chen & Culbertson, 2009, p. 176). A major challenge for public relations practitioners working in China is therefore convincing organizations to be transparent with the public and to engage in two-way communication.

Public relations practitioners in China must also be prepared to engage with the government. Chen (2007, p. 499) notes that, because of the practice of *guanxi*, "*people—not laws—play a crucial role in government affairs.*"

Organizations must have strong relationships with government officials so that laws are interpreted in their favor. For this reason, multinational organizations often find the government to be their most important public in China (Hung & Chen, 2004, p. 36).

Obtaining third-party endorsements is a particularly successful public relations strategy in China because authority figures are accorded such strong respect (Chen & Culbertson, 2009, p. 178). "Guest relations," such as translating and guiding tours, are also a major part of public relations practice in China (Chen & Culbertson, 2009, p. 182).

Outside of mainland China, practitioners have greater freedom. For example, Taiwan is now a democracy and capitalist economy with a press that is relatively free and open to influence (Sha & Huang, 2004, p. 164). The press is also considerably freer in Hong Kong—a global center of business and finance, where investor relations is a major component of public relations practice (Chen, 2004, p. 110).

Media

The Chinese press is heavily censored by the government. Copyright: Mario Savoia

Reporting by the country's state-run news agency, Xinhua, is widely picked up in the Chinese press.

Major newspapers include the state-run *People's Daily* and English-language *China Daily* (BBC, 2014a).

Although there are several hundred regional and local television channels, the only national television channel is the state-owned China Central Television (Farey-Jones, 2013).

Major social media platforms in China were profiled in the previous chapter.

Practitioner Profile: Chen Liang, Account Executive, Rudder Finn, Hong Kong

Chen Liang

Chen Liang is a Hong Kong-based Account Executive for the global public relations firm Ruder Finn, where she works on accounts in the fashion and luxury industry for clients including Kering, Headline Seoul, and PERNELLE. Originally from Dalian, China, Chen started her career working in internal communications for Hai Nan Airlines, China's largest privately owned airline, in Shanghai. She then moved to Hong Kong to work as a public relations officer for the airline from 2011–2013. Chen says that the difference between practicing public relations in China and in Hong Kong is like night and day.

In China, Chen says, Hai Nan Airlines has very little ability to influence the media because the airline is privately owned, while the media is state owned. "If we had been publicly owned, we would have had huge influence," Chen explains. "That's the huge difference between China and Hong Kong." For example, in June 2012, six people attempted to hijack a flight en route from Hotan to Ürümqi, China. Airline officials apprehended the terrorists in mid-air, successfully averting a disaster. Chen saw this story as an opportunity to build the airline's reputation, and began sharing details of the episode on the Chinese social media platform Weibo. However, she was reprimanded for doing so by her employer and instructed to take her posts down because "you can't communicate to external audiences without permission from very high ranking people." In particular, senior airline officials feared being punished by the Chinese government, since government officials had not been consulted on what the "official story" about the incident would be.

Chen says that the government typically releases only partial information about such episodes out of a concern to maintain social stability.

Chen says that "it's considered very risky to reach out to the press in Shanghai. Normally, the press comes to us." When Chen did work with the Chinese press in her role at Hai Nan Airlines, she was given a list by her boss outlining what the company would pay for stories. "In mainland China, all companies pay journalists to write stories," she reports. "In Hong Kong, you can't do that."

When she worked for the airline in Hong Kong, Chen was regularly able to reach out to reporters proactively. She says that Hong Kong practitioners also focus heavily on corporate social responsibility initiatives and networking events. For example, airline staffers volunteered weekly to teach children in a poor district of Hong Kong how to play musical instruments, and she helped organize a major day-long summit in 2012 to introduce airline executives to "important people" in Hong Kong.

Chen recently completed her master's degree in public relations and corporate communication at New York University. After graduating, instead of returning to her native China, she decided to go to Hong Kong, where she says that a more open press and society give public relations professionals greater freedom to practice their craft.

Case Study: Promoting the Wines of Bordeaux, France in China[1]

Between the years 2000–2012, exports of Bordeaux wine to China increased by a staggering 26,900 percent. Photo courtesy of the Conseil Interprofessionnel du Vin de Bordeaux

For hundreds of years, the region of Bordeaux, France, has been renowned for producing some of the world's finest wines. In 1855, an official classification system was developed for French wines at the behest of the Emperor Napoleon III. The so-called premier crus, or "first growths," are officially classified as the region's best wines. These include red wines from five chateaus in Medoc and Graves and sweet white wines from twelve chateaus in Sauternes and Barsac.

Because the first growths typically sell for at least hundreds—and often thousands—of dollars per bottle, they are generally purchased by individuals of high net worth. By the year 2000, it was evident that China was becoming home to an increasing number of such consumers. As China's elite began to amass record wealth and consume luxury goods, the country became an important potential market for the Bordelais. However, the Chinese lacked a tradition of drinking wine. In the year 2000, China imported a tiny volume of Bordeaux wines and, to the horror of top executives of the first growths, Chinese drinkers often mixed their wines with soft drinks. If the Bordelais were to effectively promote their wines in China, they would need to craft and execute a sophisticated, culturally appropriate public relations strategy that would educate wealthy individuals in China about the first growths.

Such a communication campaign would, of course, need to be adapted to the Chinese context, where traditions differ significantly from those of the French. As this chapter has discussed, Chinese culture has been heavily influenced by Confucianism, which places major importance on relationships. Accordingly, the Bordelais decided to eschew traditional approaches such as media relations and advertising, and to instead focus on in-person relationship building with wealthy Chinese citizens who could afford to purchase their wines.

One of the major ways in which the chateaus have promoted their wines in China has been through participating in private dinners with the Chinese elite. Thibault Pontallier of Chateau Margaux, whose father is the chateau's Managing Director, moved to Hong Kong in 2010 specifically to court the Asian market. Instead of traditional public relations tools, he explained, "it's only special dinners. . . . It's a bit more subtle and relationship based, doing these dinners." Pontallier has partnered with banks who he explained "entertain their top clients with a few special things that money can't buy" in order to participate in private dinners in China, introducing top clients of the banks to Chateau Marguaux wine. Pontallier explained that the banks pay for the dinners; he estimated that one recent dinner with a French chef in Macau cost at least $5,000 per head. Pontallier said that he has participated in dinners for clients of Credit Swisse Bank in Taiwan, UBS in mainland China, and a Swiss bank in Hong Kong, and is currently in talks with Goldman Sachs to participate in an annual dinner for their top twenty clients. He explained that such dinners typically involve 20 to 30 people and offer an important opportunity to promote his wine to prospective customers.

Pierre Lurton, Managing Director of Chateau d'Yquem, explained that such dinners typically consist of 15 to 20 people and are organized by partners such as major chefs and a Hong Kong yacht club. Like Pontallier, Lurton described such meals as opportunities for cultivating relationships and emphasized that this was therefore his preferred public relations strategy for the Chinese market. He explained that he began each dinner with a short speech because "the Chinese people don't love long speeches with long tastings; they prefer an exchange." He indicated that, at first, "the people are just a little shy with Y'quem, but, dinner by dinner, Y'quem has more success in China." As a result of such meals, Lurton indicated, "I have a lot of good friends in China."

Virginie Achou-Lepage, Head of Business Development and Communication for Chateau Climens, described a similar process of relationship building through such dinners. She explained that "we speak together; that's how we try to build our network in China." She indicated,

> people who are wine lovers, we organize a dinner at their home, we pour the wine, [and] they become influencers for us because they are going to do the same, to show the wine to their friends and do dinners together. It's very important for us to work with those people.

Achou-Lepage indicated that she had met many dinner hosts at public tastings and at dinners that they attended in other homes. "They say, 'next time it will be in my home.' It's small networking, but . . . we really think it's worth it because this is a wine for wine lovers and that is unique and needs to be appreciated as a masterpiece, so we really need to explain by showing the wine. . . . Now people are becoming very good fans."

What distinguishes these modern private dinners from marketing is the fact that the chateau representatives do not sell their wine at the events in which they participate in China. All sales are conducted through their importers. According to Broom and Sha (2013, p. 5), marketing is "the management function that . . . causes transactions that deliver products and services to users in exchange for something of value to the provider."

In addition to private dinners, the chateaus all also organize and participate in larger events to court the Chinese. Chateau representatives often participate in "master classes" in China, in which they explain how their wine is made and how to pair it with food. For example, Xavier Planty, Joint Owner and General Manager of Chateau Guiraud, noted that, in 2011, Chateau Guiraud partnered with a famous Asian wine connoisseur, Jeannie Cho Lee, to host a master class which taught the Chinese how to pair vintages with food by breaking up Chinese cuisine into eight groups.

Many of the chateaus indicated that they also participated in trips to China organized at least once per year by the Union des Grand Crus de Bordeaux, a trade organization dedicated to promoting their wine, in which they traveled to different cities across the country for major tastings and other events for both consumers and members of the trade. Chinese wine distributors also often organize such events, which are attended by chateau representatives.

Like the private dinners, such events are typically not described by the Bordelais as efforts to promote their wines, but rather as opportunities for cultural exchange and education, using language and tactics more resonant of the diplomacy practiced by governments than of the public relations practices of other luxury brands. Didier Frechinet, Sales Manager for Chateau La Tour Blanche, explained that, in discussing La Tour Blanche wine, "we try to make a parallel between wine and tea. . . . It's easier to understand when we compare with tea. There are different varieties, they depend on region and soil, and tea ceremonies are important for the Chinese."

Even the titles of the chateau representatives are borrowed from the world of diplomacy. Pontallier's title is "Ambassador in Asia," while Chateau Guiraud employs a staff member known not as a public relations manager but rather as "Brand Ambassador America (North and South) and Asia."

While the Bordelais actively participate in events in China, they rarely engage in traditional media relations activities such as pitching stories. Hervé Gouin, Commercial Director of Chateau Mouton Rothschild, explained, it "may [sound] a little self-centered but we have 'enough' requests all year long coming from all over the world. We're not especially looking for more articles about us [and] most of

[the] first growths are acting with the same discrete culture." Achou-Lepage, of Chateau Climens, indicated, "We do not ask journalists to speak about Climens. They come by themselves, attracted by pleasure and love for the wine."

Christophe Salin, President and CEO of Chateau Lafite Rothschild, said Lafite did not pitch stories "thank God" or issue press releases, citing a French saying *pour vivre heureux vivons cachés*, which means "in order to live happily, live hidden." He explained, "then they discover you and they're happy. They're coming to you instead of you going to them." Salin explained, "We don't have a developed marketing strategy, like selling toothpaste or cars. It's very different . . . we are wine farmers. What do we do? We try to make, every year, a good wine."

The approach of the Bordelais to the Chinese market has been remarkably successful. Between the years 2000–2012, exports of Bordeaux wine to China increased by a staggering 26,900 percent. Exports skyrocketed from 200,000 liters in the year 2000 to a record 53.8 million liters in the year 2012, before dipping to 45.2 million liters in 2013 amidst weather conditions which resulted in a smaller harvest in Bordeaux and a Chinese government crackdown on corruption which reduced spending by the elite (Bordeaux Wine Trade Council, 2014, p. 22; Anson, 2014). By 2011, the Chinese—who had barely purchased Bordeaux wines just a few years earlier—had become their largest importer (Bordeaux Wine Trade Council, 2014, p. 22). Chinese demand fueled a remarkable increase in the prices of the first growths. Since 2003, the London International Vinters Exchange (Liv-ex) Fine Wine 50 index, which tracks the prices of the first growths, has increased by 166 percent (Liv-ex, 2014).

Of course, the Bordeaux first growths occupy a privileged position because they have been renowned as among the world's finest vintners for hundreds of years, making many of the public relations strategies utilized by other brands largely unnecessary. It is unsurprising that, as the Chinese have become wealthier, they have used the finest Bordeaux wines to signal their success and sophistication. Nevertheless, this case study makes clear that, while the Bordelais have eschewed outward signs of promotion, they have in fact employed a sophisticated public relations strategy in order to build relationships that have contributed to their success in China. Two features of their approach are especially remarkable.

First, the chateaus have largely focused on building personal relationships with China's elite through private dinners and other events.

The relationship management approach is a relatively recent development in Western public relations, though it of course has a long tradition in China and other Confucian cultures. This case study demonstrates the value of using local approaches to public relations in local markets.

Second, the success of the Bordelais approach suggests that, in a field increasingly focused on the latest communications technologies, public relations practitioners should not forget interpersonal communication strategies. To be sure, this face-to-face approach to public relations is only possible because there is a relatively small group of people who are wealthy enough to purchase the first growths. However, there is also a small global elite who can afford to purchase other luxury products, such as high-end cars, jewelry, and fashion brands. Such an approach could be particularly effective for other luxury brands whose potential customer base is limited and would appreciate the opportunity to hobnob with the progenitors of their status symbols.

Other Western brands would also benefit from emulating the Bordelais approach to educating clients and potential customers about their products, as a growing group of wealthy elite across Asia, Sub-Saharan Africa, and Latin America are expected to drive much of the future growth in the luxury market (Euromonitor International, 2013). The diplomatic approach of the first growths to building relationships based upon mutual cultural exchange is also a model example of the two-way symmetrical approach to communication discussed in Chapter 1, which "consists more of a dialogue than a monologue" (Grunig & Hunt, 1984, p. 23).

Finally, the public relations approach of the first growths is notable for the insistence of the chateau representatives that they do not practice public relations. The estimated value of Chateau Lafite Rothschild is more than $5 billion (Liv-ex, 2011)—more than that of Air France-KLM and roughly equivalent to the values of Konica Minolta and Sears Holdings (Forbes, 2014). It would be difficult to imagine the CEO of Konica or Sears insisting that he knows nothing about promotion and wishes to "stay hidden," as Salin professed.

As Hall and Mitchell have argued (2008, p. 296),

one of the great myths of the wine industry is that 'a great wine will sell itself'. Unfortunately, while this is a wonderful sound bite that is often heard . . . it is just not true. In order to be sold . . . the consumer has to know about the wine and then decide to purchase it, often in the face of competition from many other options, many of which will not even be wine.

In fact, the Bordelais are evidently purposefully seeking to cultivate the impression that public relations activities are unnecessary because the reputation, history, and quality of their wines speak for themselves. However, perhaps in the future, as the global reputation of the public relations profession improves, the Bordelais will come to embrace the term to describe one of the things they do best.

Japan

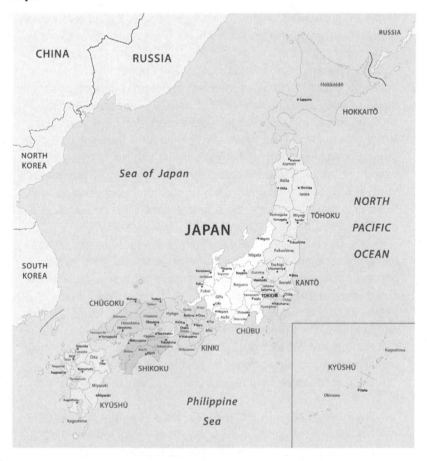

Copyright: Rainer Lesniewski

Time zone: Coordinated Universal Time (UTC) + 9:00
International dialing code: +81

When you practice public relations in Japan, give the Japanese people permission to try new things.

A lot has changed since Japan went to war with China in the 1930s and the United States of America in the 1940s. Today, the nation of islands is an ally of the U.S. and the world's third largest economy (CIA, 2014; World Bank, 2014). Unlike many modern states, the country is extremely homogeneous; nearly 99 percent of the population is Japanese, and the national language is Japanese (CIA, 2014). As a collectivist society, the Japanese government places great emphasis on achieving social goals through its economic policy. Accordingly, the government intervenes in the economy more than other capitalist countries, in order to provide important sectors such as automobiles and technology with special protections that are controversial among Japan's global trade partners, along with state subsidies, low-cost financing, and other forms of assistance. Duhé and Sriramesh (2009, pp. 37–38) note that "redundant staffs and lifetime employment, designed to promote social harmony, reflect the Japanese resistance to the downsizing, rightsizing, and outsourcing tactics so frequently utilized in the U.S." The country's currency is the yen and its capital is Tokyo.

Ross Rowbury, President of Edelman in Japan, says that the practice of public relations in Japan differs significantly from other countries. He explains that

in countries such as the United States, public relations is about seeding the debate so that people can make better informed decisions. However, Japan is one of the least diverse countries on earth. Everyone has the same cultural, educational, and basically religious background, so there is really no need for debate and discussion because everyone understands everyone. In Japan, what goes unsaid is almost as important as what is said. And people talk about behavior that is or isn't "Japanese." So public relations is more about creating permission for people to do something that hasn't previously been seen as Japanese behavior—to try something new or take a different point of view.

For example, Rowbury says that Japanese mothers do not typically like to feed their children Western sweets, because they are perceived as unhealthy. However, Nestlé has successfully promoted its Kit Kat chocolate bars in Japan through an innovative campaign playing off of the fact that the name "Kit Kat" sounds similar to a Japanese phrase meaning that a person will surely win or be successful. The campaign presented Japanese mothers as giving Kit Kat bars as a midnight snack to their children who were studying for the country's notoriously difficult college entrance exams. Later, the campaign showed friends giving Kit Kats as gifts to one another. "They created permission for people to eat and give Kit Kats to their kids, by turning it into something intrinsically Japanese," Rowbury says.

Japan might at first glance appear to be a public relations practitioner's dream, in the sense that the culture's emphasis on social harmony discourages activism in protest of organizations (Wakefield, 2011, p. 179.) However, "the dark side of harmony means that executives prefer either cover-ups or doing nothing to going public with bad news" (Cooper-Chen, 1996, p. 225). Inoue (2009, p. 132) explains that

> the Japanese cultural concepts of *haji* (or embarrassment—when one refrains from notifying outsiders of facts when a mistake is made), *amae* (over-dependency), and *wa* (harmony) . . . militate against the openness and speediness that is part of the preferred environment of the public relations world.

There is simply not a tradition in Japan of offering up excuses and explanations when something goes wrong.

> This [has] led to an inability to take responsibility and an inability to explain one's actions or express oneself to others clearly. As a result, misunderstandings and friction often occur when the Japanese interact with people from other countries and cultures (Inoue, 2009, p. 131).

This custom has also caused problems within Japanese society. Culbertson (1996, p. 7), for example, notes that Japanese officials often "give up and resign" (or even commit suicide) when they face accusations of wrongdoing, rather than "defend themselves in a way that might insure a full airing of issues so as to enhance long-term public understanding." Therefore, as in China, a major challenge for practitioners in Japan is to convince their organizations to practice transparent, two-way communication.

Another challenge for practitioners in Japan is that the culture's consensus-based approach often means that it takes longer for organizations to arrive at decisions (Cooper-Chen, 1996, p. 225). Furthermore, Japanese companies typically use a rotation system, moving employees into different departments every few years (Inoue, 2009, p. 128). This means that individuals practicing public relations may not have specialized public relations skills and training—though Haque (2004, p. 359) notes that it also means that, by the time senior managers get to the top of an organization, they are likely to have prior public relations experience.

The country enjoys a very free press; the Japanese media extensively cover both domestic and foreign news, and media consumption in Japan is very high (Inoue, 2009, pp. 123, 133). Rowbury says that trust in the traditional media is high in Japan, making media outreach an essential component of any public relations strategy. However, he says, because the Japanese press is mostly national as opposed to regional, competition to place stories is fierce. "The Japanese papers mostly write about Japanese companies, and then you have the foreign companies all toughing it out for the five percent that is devoted to them," Rowbury says. "So you need research, context, and compelling stories."

A notable feature of Japanese public relations is the existence of "press clubs," particularly within government and industry organizations. These are groups of reporters who cover and typically work on site at an organization. Inoue (2009, p. 134) notes that this system is convenient for organizations because it allows them to easily and rapidly disseminate information to the media (though it also provides fewer opportunities to offer exclusives to reporters). In the past, such press clubs were notorious for refusing to admit all journalists, including foreign correspondents, though they began to become more open in the 1990s.

Rowbury says that, unlike other countries where social media grew out of the concept of sharing, in Japan people originally used social media to anonymously "release complaints that were inappropriate in society"—such as, for example, gripes about their bosses. He says that, since the country's 2011 earthquake, the Japanese people have felt a need to be more connected and are now "getting better about being private in public." Still, he emphasizes, "there is an undercurrent of feeling that social media can't quite be trusted" because such platforms were historically used anonymously.

In general, Rowbury says, "the unfamiliar is treated with suspicion in Japan" and the Japanese people have not heard of many major global brands because of language differences, so foreign companies need strong public relations operations in order to build trust and familiarity. He also says that influencers are especially respected in Japanese society, so using people who are perceived as credentialed or celebrities as ambassadors is a particularly effective strategy in the country.

Japan's Confucian tradition means that public relations agencies in Japan often have long-standing relationships with their clients; given such loyalty, "on the agency side, not doing one's utmost for a client would be unthinkable" (Cooper-Chen, 1996, p. 225). Japan is the headquarters of four of the 250 largest public relations firms in the world: Vector, Dentsu, PRAP Japan, and Kyodo PR (The Holmes Report, 2015).

Finally, Rowbury says that views of corporate social responsibility are changing in Japan. He says that

> Japanese people and Japanese companies have traditionally shied away from large scale philanthropic donations when compared to their Western peers. This may be the result of mistaken pride that Japan is a wealthy country and does not need donations. However, in the aftermath of the 2011 earthquake and tsunami disaster, Japanese companies and corporate leaders were at the forefront in making donations to assist the survivors. And, the sheer scale of that disaster and the scars left on society seem to have triggered a longer term interest in CSR, community, and social purpose, with many more individuals and companies now engaging in volunteer or philanthropic activities.

However, Rowbury notes that many corporate social responsibility initiatives in Japan today are "disjointed and lack an overall strategy," leaving a real opening for practitioners who can implement such projects more strategically.

Media

Kyodo News is a Japanese news agency.

Japan has the highest circulation of newspapers and magazines in the world (Inoue, 2009, p. 133). Major daily newspapers include the conservative *Yomiuri Shimbun*, its "liberal archrival" the *Asahi Shimbun*, as well as the *Manichi Shimbun*, *Nihon Keizai Shimbun*, and *Sankei Shimbun*. (Soble, 2014; BBC, 2014d.) *Nikkei* is the major business daily (Sudhaman, 2010b).

Japan's public broadcaster, NHK, is the "most trusted" national broadcaster (Sudhaman, 2010b). Other national networks are TV Asahi, Fuji TV, Nippon TV (NTV), and the Tokyo Broadcasting System (TBS) (BBC, 2014d).

Nineteen percent of Japanese people have active social media accounts. The most popular social networks are Twitter, Facebook, and the Japanese social network Mixi (Kemp, 2015).

Republic of Korea (South Korea)

Time zone: Coordinated Universal Time (UTC) + 9:00
International dialing code: +82

When you practice public relations in South Korea, whatever you do, do not offer exclusives to reporters.

South Korea was occupied by Japan beginning in 1905 and gained independence after Japan lost World War II in 1945. Following this war, a democratic government was established in the south of Korea, which became known as the Republic of Korea, while a communist government took hold in the north, calling itself the Democratic People's Republic of Korea (DPRK). Between 1950 and 1953, the DPRK invaded the south, with support from the former Soviet Union and China. The United States of America and United Nations aided the south. In 1953, an armistice divided the country between the Republic of Korea in the south and the DPRK in the north, with a demilitarized zone in between—a division that remains to this day. While South Korea has become a modern, industrialized nation and the world's fourteenth-largest economy, North Korea is ruled by a mercurial dictator, Kim Jong-un, who continues to starve his people and seclude them from the outside world, with ongoing support from China (World Bank, 2014). According to the United Nations Food and Agriculture Organization (2014, p. 42), 37.5 percent of North Koreans are malnourished. The DPRK has admitted to developing nuclear weapons and has threatened to attack both South Korea and the U.S. (Kwon, 2013; BBC, 2014f). South Korea, meanwhile, held its first free election for the presidency under an updated democratic constitution in 1987.

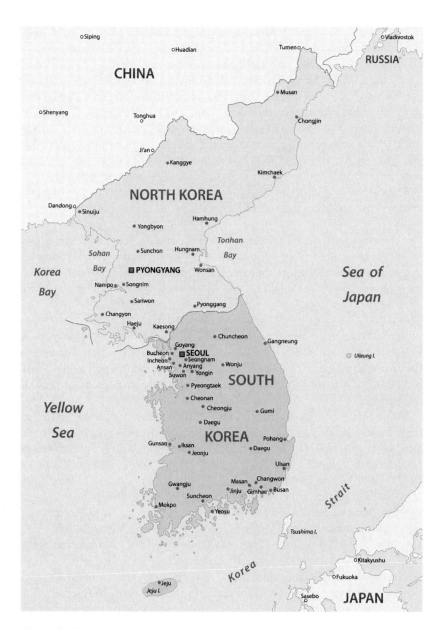

The country's capital is Seoul, its currency is the won, and its official language is Korean, though English is also taught widely (CIA, 2014).

Rhee (2002) notes that, beginning in the 1980s, political democratization and the expansion of foreign firms in the South Korean market and South

Korean businesses abroad resulted in increased demand for public relations. Today, social and digital media are driving the demand for public relations. The vast majority of South Koreans are online, and they are rapid adopters of technology including smart phones, creating a demand for digital strategies (Hay, 2010b). However, the profession continues to suffer from a poor reputation in Korea. Kim (2009, p. 140) notes that the term *hong-bo* is often used instead of public relations. The term, which "often refers to publicity activities aimed at evading negative media coverage of organizations"—dates back to the collaboration in the 1970s between the country's authoritarian government and *chaebols*—or conglomerations of businesses owned by families.

The culture's collectivism exerts a strong influence on the practice of public relations in South Korea. Jo and Kim (2004, pp. 243, 252) note that

> the power of primary affiliations such as school, region, and blood take precedence over everything in Korea. . . . Family and regional affinity has thus made factionalism an inseparable part of Korean life, and Koreans cannot exist without associating themselves with the groups to which they belong.

Jim Morris, senior consultant for the Seoul, Korea, affiliate of global public relations agency MSLGROUP, says that these ties are so strong that "if you let an employee go and he has a relationship from his school days with a reporter of a third-tier media outlet, the reporter may create a crusade against you."

This emphasis on group identity may initially make it difficult for foreign organizations seeking to operate in Korea, because "Korean people often separate 'we' from 'others' and foreign businesses or multinational corporations are considered as 'others'" (Cho & Cameron, 2010, p. 348). Choi and Cameron (2005, p. 185) report that leaders of multinational corporations (MNCs) often fear the local media, which exerts enormous influence over public opinion, because "how media interpret MNCs' business issues . . . is often based on nationalism, anti-American sentiment, patriotism, and emotion." Morris concurs that "if there is an issue between a Korean firm and a multinational, the local firm is going to get the favorable coverage."

The personal influence model is also predominant in public relations practice. Shin and Cameron (2003) found that this takes many forms, including unofficial calls and private meetings between practitioners and journalists; regional, alumni, and blood relations; press tours; travel for press clubs; bargaining through advertising; exercising power through managers and editors; perks such as dinners and drinks; activities such as golf; free tickets and other presents; and bribes. Journalists themselves must be members of a *kijadan*, or press club, in order to gain access to cover the government (Jo & Kim, 2004, p. 255). Organizational crises tend to be handled by reaching out to members of one's network (Kim, 2009, p. 144). Jo and Kim (2004, p. 243) report that the practice of giving Korean journalists *chonji*, or *ddukgab*—money during festivals for purchasing cakes—is "used to evade the seriousness of giving bribes."

Morris says that, in the country's tough economic environment, a trend has appeared where media are turning more and more to advertorial and paid sponsorship types of articles, making it harder to obtain earned coverage. He says that the most influential media is terrestrial television, which will expect payment for product placement in entertainment programming. The next most influential media are the country's top three daily newspapers, *Chosun Ilbo*, *JoongAng Ilbo*, and *Dong-a Ilbo*, which Morris says are now favoring advertorials and sponsored stories. Morris says that many of the country's "power bloggers" likewise expect fees, which are about U.S. $200 per post. However, it is still possible to obtain earned media coverage in general daily and business publications in South Korea, as well as in the trade press.

Morris says that it is easier to place photographs than stories in the mainstream press, especially for companies that advertise in the media regularly. Account executives will often arrange interesting photo opportunities to promote products and newspapers will send photojournalists to take pictures at such events, publishing the images with captions.

Morris says that it is easier to place photographs than stories in the mainstream press in South Korea. The MSLGROUP organized this photo opportunity to promote California pomegranates.

When working with the media in Korea, Morris advises against offering exclusives on major news stories at all costs. He says that, if you give information to just a single reporter, "you will make one friend and may make a hundred enemies."

While Morris recommends inviting all reporters to press conferences, he advises that, depending upon the client and its purpose, it is better to bring journalists to other events—such as tours of a company's headquarters—in different groups, bringing all of the top-tier mainstream press in one group, the trade press on a different tour, and bloggers in a third group, due to perceived "class differences" among the media. Morris says that one-on-one visits with reporters are not only an opportunity to educate them about a client's business or product, but also to engage informally with them and gain intelligence about an industry and the competition.

Another practice that helps public relations professionals in Korea is that journalists will typically give businesses and influential individuals a heads-up before publishing negative stories about them. Kent and Taylor (2011, p. 59) note that "Korean editors allow organizations a chance to provide a response *before* a damning story is published."

Although the press in South Korea is generally free, in practice, powerful political and business interests exercise influence over editorial coverage. Kim (2009, p. 150) reports that "*chaebols* are one of the primary groups that are able to wield such influence. Some *chaebols* own media companies and participate in management decision-making. Most media companies depend on advertising revenue provided by *chaebols*."

Another challenge is that public relations practitioners in Korea still have an uphill battle to fight in convincing organizations to be transparent. Kim (2009, p. 143) reports that "conveying factual information, or being a neutral disseminator, is a tough task in South Korea because Korean organizations prefer to withhold information. Some practitioners were also found to consider information manipulation as a major public relations activity."

Practitioners may generally struggle to influence top leaders in Korea because, in this hierarchical culture, managers often make decisions with little input from their staff (Kim, 2009, pp. 147–148). In fact, in all professional and social interactions, Jo and Kim (2004, p. 251) explain that

> those who meet for the first time traditionally engage in a conversation to determine quickly who is the elder. The parties then assume their culturally prescribed roles as the senior who merits respect, loyalty, and obedience and the junior who complies. Koreans typically address each other formally by professional title or social position, such as company president or supervisor, rather than informally by name.

Furthermore, the importance of face means that "saving anothers' face as well as that of oneself should be a prime consideration in public relations practices" (Kim, 2009, p. 148). Kim reports that

> South Korean public relations practitioners seldom take advantage of competitors' vulnerabilities. Most of the time, a company that criticizes

other companies would be an outcast in that business circle. Yet, organizations have attacked their competitors by releasing unfavorable information about them to the media.

However, in recent years, another group has also been gaining the attention of the media: non-governmental organizations (NGOs). The country's democracy movement spawned a new era of civil activism. Kim (2009, p. 145) reports that "NGOs are taking an active role in policy making and often oversee and object to the wrongdoings of the government and chaebols." This is forcing organizations to respond. Accordingly, Kim and Kim (2010, p. 497) report that, today, "social responsibility overcoming profit orientation is becoming a norm among Korean public relations practitioners." Morris concurs that corporate social responsibility is recommended in this market. "Some companies don't do it, and that's okay until some issue arises and people start pointing a finger and saying that they are making too much profit in Korea and not returning anything to society," he explains.

Morris also recommends offering promotions and contests to encourage Koreans to engage with consumer brands on their social media platforms. "Consumers expect something in return," he explains. "You don't get a lot of loyalty out of people unless you are offering something." Morris says that in-person, consumer-focused events are another great way to learn more about your Korean customers and, as an added bonus, customers often post a great deal of content from such events on social media.

Another strategy that practitioners in South Korea should consider is interpersonal communication. Kim (2009, p. 147) reports that "South Korean publics tend to mistrust information announced officially by organizations, thereby requiring public relations practitioners to communicate indirectly through interpersonal channels."

Media

The Yonhap News Agency is publicly funded.

Major daily newspapers are the *Chosun Ilbo*, *JoongAng Ilbo*, and *Dong-a Ilbo* (BBC, 2014e). *The Korea Herald* and *Korea Times* are published in English (Kim, 2009, p. 149).

As previously discussed, South Koreans view television as more credible than newspapers (Kim, 2009, p. 149). The state-owned Korean Broadcasting System (KBS) operates numerous stations; the other market leader is the Munhwa Broadcasting Corporation (MBC), which focuses on current affairs (BBC, 2014e; Hay, 2010b).

KBS and MBC also operate radio stations (BBC, 2014e).

Thirty percent of Koreans have active social media accounts. The most popular social networks are Facebook and Twitter (Kemp, 2015).

South Asia

The South Asian cultural cluster encompasses countries including Cambodia, India, Indonesia, Iran, Laos, Malaysia, Pakistan, the Philippines, and Thailand (Gupta & Hanges, 2004, p. 191; Livermore, 2013, p. 65). The culture is characterized by high humane orientation and in-group collectivism, as well as a moderate degree of assertiveness, future orientation, gender egalitarianism, institutional collectivism, performance orientation, power distance, and uncertainty avoidance (Gupta & Hanges, 2004, p. 193).

Gupta and Hanges (2004, p. 188) note that a distinctive feature of this cultural group is the peaceful coexistence of many diverse communities. "In this region, one frequently finds Islamic mosques next to Hindu temples with families of gods and goddesses, and Buddhist pagodas or Christian churches or Skih Gurudwaras with images of their teachers." To be sure, however, this tolerance is not universal, as is evidenced by the ongoing conflict between India and Pakistan (Livermore, 2013, p. 66).

Another key feature of this region is its unique form of collectivism. Livermore (2013, p. 66) notes that

> South Asia is very Collectivist, but in a way that's different from Confucian Asia. Family is an important source of one's collective identity, just as is true in Confucian Asia, but there's a greater ease with individualism here than there is in Confucian Asia. There's less pressure to conform to your in-group's expectations, and more freedom to pursue individual dreams.

This collectivism also translates into the practice of the personal influence model of public relations. One country where this is a particular challenge is the Philippines, because "the mutual back-scratching has brought about a Filipino brand of PR that is vulnerable to unethical breaches of professional conduct" (Sarabia-Panol & Lorenzo-Molo, 2004, p. 146). Sarabia-Panol and Lorenzo-Molo (2004, p. 148) note that "envelopmental journalism"—a practice you will also read about in Chapter 12, in which reporters are paid for coverage—is an issue in the Philippines, as is a phenomenon known as "AC-DC" or "Attack-Collect/ Defend-Collect," in which organizations are bribed by reporters in order to keep negative stories out of the press or to defend them when they are under attack.

Despite the GLOBE study's ranking, Livermore (2013, p. 69) notes that the South Asian cultural cluster, like Confucian Asia, has relatively high power distance, and "you can clearly see a stratification of people according to their status and roles. There are prescribed roles for people according to their caste, or status, and overlooking these norms is met with great resistance."

As in Confucian Asia, face is very important, and South Asians are high-context communicators (Livermore, 2013, p. 69). In the Philippines, for example, Sarabia-Panol & Lorenzo-Molo (2004, p. 145) note that

> because Filipinos value relationships and maintaining 'face,' they avoid even slight expressions of explicitness and criticism. Filipinos find it

difficult to say 'no' as a result of which it is not uncommon to get a positive or tentative answer to a question when what is meant is a negative response.

Livermore (2013, p. 70) also notes that South Asia's moderate level of uncertainty avoidance means that many countries in this group have more relaxed attitudes towards life and the law.

A frequent Thai expression is 'Ma pen rai,' which means 'No worries' or 'Never mind about that.' This captures the very laid back, moderate level of Uncertainty Avoidance that exists among many of the cultures in this cluster. Most of the countries . . . have worked hard to minimize the number of rules and laws that infringe upon people's diverse perspectives in order to promote the curried, peaceful co-existence of so many different faiths and backgrounds.

Organizing fun events can also be a particularly effective strategy in Thailand. Thai people are famous for *sanuk*, or their "fun-pleasure orientation." Ekachai and Komolsevin (2004, p. 305) describe sanuk as "adopting a joyful and pleasant perspective toward life and work in order to maintain smooth interpersonal relationships." For this reason, public relations strategies focused on fun are likely to be successful in this country. Ekachai and Komolsevin (2004, pp. 306–307) note, for example, that

United Broadcasting Corporation (UBC) is known for its 'fun' activities held regularly throughout the year. Recently, UBC attracted the attention of the public by proposing the 'World's Biggest Painting' project, in which more than 4,000 children and their families participated in painting on a 100 x 100 meter canvas, to commemorate the King's 52nd royal wedding anniversary. It has set a record as the world's largest painting in the Guinness Book of Records, . . . in the bargain getting much positive publicity for UBC.

The following sections profile public relations practice in two of this cultural group's most important markets: India and Indonesia.

India

Time zone: Coordinated Universal Time (UTC) + 5:30
International dialing code: +91

When you practice public relations in India, segment your audiences.

The world's second most populous country, India's recent rapid economic growth has made it an increasingly important market for public relations practitioners. McKinsey (2007) has called Indians "the next big spenders," predicting that by 2027 the country will edge out Germany to become the

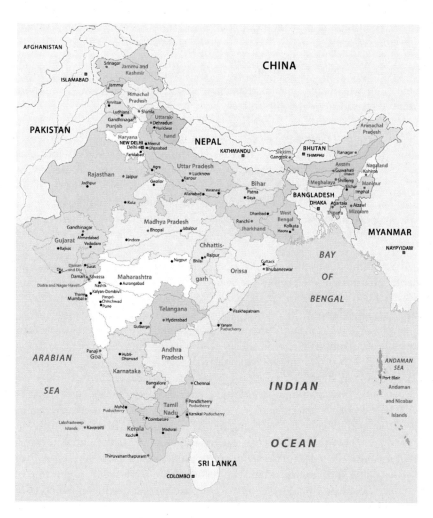

fifth-largest consumer market in the world. In 2015, India outpaced China as the fastest-growing large economy on earth (Bellman, 2015). Yet despite sharp strides in reducing poverty, the country continues to be plagued by hunger, corruption, and overpopulation (CIA, 2014).

India won independence from Great Britain in 1947, following a non-violent campaign led by Mohandas Gandhi and Jawaharlal Nehru (CIA, 2014). Amidst widespread violence, the country was partitioned into two different nations— India and Pakistan—and in 1971 East Pakistan became the separate country of Bangladesh. Today, India and Pakistan remain in a territorial dispute over land in Kashmir. Although over 80 percent of Indians are Hindu, while Pakistan is largely Muslim, India remains a diverse society: 13.4 percent of Indians are Muslim, 2.3 percent are Christian, and 1.9 percent are Sikh. Modern India is a federal republic. While 41 percent of the population is fluent in Hindi, the most widely spoken language, English is widely used in politics and business (CIA, 2014). The country's currency is the rupee and its capital is New Delhi. The post-independence Indian economy was "a mixed economy with socialist leanings." (Bardhan & Sriramesh, 2006, p. 41). However, in the early 1990s, India began transitioning to a market economy and opened to foreign investment, which "provided a fillip to the public relations industry" (Bardhan & Sriramesh, 2004, p. 67). Bardhan (2003, pp. 238–239) notes that, in addition to increasing the demand for public relations, economic deregulation and privatization also helped drive the professionalization of the industry. Practitioners became more specialized in areas beyond traditional media relations, in fields such as investor relations and crisis management. However,

> for the public relations industry the most significant impact of this shift in philosophy was the growth in recognition and acceptance of public relations as a key management function. In general, top management began to pay more attention to the ability of public relations to contribute to managing the reputation of an organization (Bardhan & Sriramesh, 2006, p. 42).

Over the past several decades, the growth in non-governmental organizations and consumer activism has made organizations realize the importance of being responsive to public opinion. "Private as well as public sector companies are increasingly feeling the pressure to be more accountable to internal as well as external publics" (Bardhan & Sriramesh, 2004, p. 77).

Most major news organizations have bureaus in India and Sudhaman (2010a) notes that "a diverse and vibrant news environment contributes to a famously free media." The country is also home to the major Mumbai-based Hindi language film industry known as "Bollywood," which produces about 1,000 films per year and sells about a billion more tickets per year than Hollywood (Thussu, 2013, p. 131). Still, today, Sudhaman (2010a) characterizes the practice of public relations in India as, like the country itself, paradoxical, reporting that "pockets of dazzling sophistication co-exist with the most time-honoured of media relations techniques." A recent study found that the number one challenge for public relations leaders in India is staff recruitment and retention—something that Patwardhan and Bardhan (2014, p. 417) characterize as "a major and somewhat unique challenge" for the industry in India.

Sujit Patil, Vice President of Corporate Communications for Godrej, a Mumbai-based Indian conglomerate that sells everything from consumer goods to real estate, says that "in a country like India, the biggest factor is the sheer diversity in terms of the number of languages spoken, the number of races we have, the number of states and, most importantly, the population." Accordingly, he says that "public relations in India is all about segmentation and customization. There are different consumption points for different segments of the population. For students, its social media. In villages, its radio."

While a few major newspapers reach an educated, urban elite, Patil says that local media in vernacular languages also remain important for reaching different communities. To reach rural Indians, where poverty and illiteracy remain widespread, he says that companies such as Godrej and Unilever will often host village fairs to promote fast-moving consumer goods such as soap and mosquito repellent. Such events often include exhibits, promotions, games, and entertainment. Other forms of folk media, such as dances and plays, can also be very effective (Sriramesh & Verčič, 2009, p. 17).

Patil says that internal employee communication is likewise a particular challenge in India because, within a single firm, often

> you have highly skilled workers such as Ph.D.s and doctors, a midrange, and then people who are not very educated because labor in India is still manual rather than automated—so an intranet or newsletters are not going to work for these employees.

In his former role as Head of Corporate Communications for Tata Chemicals from 2005 to 2013, Patil therefore used the medium of theatre to bring his employees together. Each year, employees would be invited to work together in teams to create skits on a different theme, such as organizational values, safety, and sustainability. Every year, more than 500 employees voluntarily participated. Patil says that the widespread participation of employees from across different areas of the company helped institutionalize the themes within the organization.

For organizations operating in India, the government is also a critical stakeholder. Because economic policy is very centralized and India has a high degree of regulation, a study of German multinational organizations operating in the country found that they view the government as their most important stakeholder and that they are particularly challenged by India's large bureaucracy, "widespread corruption," and "different time orientation" (Berg & Holtbrügge, 2001, p. 110).

Public relations practice in India also remains characterized by use of the personal influence model (Gupta & Bartlett, 2009; Bardhan & Sriramesh, 2006, p. 49; Bardan, 2003, pp. 245–246; Sriramesh, 1996, p. 186). Bardhan and Sriramesh (2004, p. 82) note that

> practitioners engage in various techniques aimed at establishing personal friendships with strategically placed individuals whom they call "contacts." These individuals include members of the media, officers, and secretaries of key government departments, airline and railway employees, and workers in municipal and tax offices. Public relations professionals humor these individuals by taking them out to lunches or dinners, and by giving gifts. One senior executive used the term *quid pro quo* to describe the public relations practiced by his organization. He stated that by giving gifts and hosting dinners, a good public relations officer "fans the egos" of

the recipients, thus laying the foundation for seeking return favors when needed by the organization.

Traditionally, in Indian society, power was determined by the caste into which a person was born. The caste system segregated Indians into groups ranging from the venerated Brahmins to the Dalits, or "untouchables." Sriramesh (1996, p. 188) notes that modern India remains characterized by social distinctions, though today they are class-based, rather than caste-based. He reports that

> with the dawn of independence and the adoption of a new constitution that has instituted and enforced affirmative action programs (including quotas), the focus has shifted from caste to class. Especially in urban areas, people are able to garner wealth and political power regardless of their caste. Wealth and power in turn have brought social status to them. The shift has not wiped out social distinctions. It has only shifted the focus of power and wealth to a different group of people.

Other traditions in India are also changing. While Bardhan and Sriramesh (2004, pp. 79–80) note that, traditionally, India has been characterized by high uncertainty avoidance, high power distance, and collectivism, "the newer generation of professionals are taking more risks and being innovative," and in some sectors, they are more willing to disagree with their managers and to switch employers in order to advance.

Media

India's national news agencies are the Press Trust of India and United News of India (Bardhan & Sriramesh, 2006, p. 55).

Although India is home to thousands of English-language newspapers, Hindi-language papers have the highest circulation (Bardhan & Sriramesh, 2004, pp. 84–85). Major Hindi-language newspapers include *Dainik Jagran* and *Dainik Bhaskar* (Sudhaman, 2010a). Major English-language newspapers include *The Times of India, The Hindustan Times,* and *The Indian Express* (BBC, 2013). Bardhan and Sriramesh (2006, p. 53) note that "newspapers are not directly aligned with, or controlled by, political parties although observers do discern the political leanings of many newspapers." The country also has a robust trade and business press, with publications including the *Economic Times, Financial Express,* and *Business Standard* (Bardhan & Sriramesh, 2006, pp. 53, 85).

India's public broadcaster, Doordarshan, operates the flagship television station DD1, along with numerous other services. The country's many private broadcasters include CNN-IBN, which airs news 24 hours per day in English, New Delhi TV (NDTV), Star TV (owned by the News Corporation), and Zee TV (BBC, 2013). Because private satellite and cable television are solely advertising-based, Bardhan and Sriramesh (2004, p. 88) note that they "target the urban affluent almost exclusively."

The public All India Radio Network operates both domestic and external radio stations; other major radio networks include Radio One and Radio City (BBC, 2013).

Nine percent of Indians have active social media accounts. The most popular networks include Facebook, Twitter, and LinkedIn (Kemp, 2015).

Indonesia

Time zone: Spans 3 time zones, ranging from Coordinated Universal Time (UTC) + 7:00 to UTC + 9:00
International dialing code: +62

When you practice public relations in Indonesia, be prepared to be social and visual.

An archipelago of more than 17,000 islands along the Equator between the Indian and Pacific Oceans, Indonesia is home to the largest Muslim population on earth and a fast-growing economy that could surpass the United Kingdom and Germany to become the world's seventh-largest by 2030 (CIA, 2014; Pew Research Center, 2009; McKinsey, 2012). Indonesia was historically part of Hindu, Buddhist, and Muslim kingdoms before coming under the control of, at various times, the Portuguese, Dutch, British, and French, and even being invaded by Japan during World War II. In 1945, the country achieved independence. The national language is Bahasa Indonesia, a form of Malay, but hundreds of languages are spoken in this polyglot nation. More than 87 percent of Indonesians are Muslim, while 7 percent are Christian, nearly 3 percent are Roman Catholic, and 1.7 percent are Hindu (CIA, 2014). The country's currency is the rupiah and its capital is Jakarta, on the island of Java.

Despite a history of significant governmental control and regulation of the media, in recent years, as a result of a political reform process begun in the 1990s, media outlets in Indonesia have proliferated and enjoyed only minimal regulation (Thomas, 2004, pp. 387–389). The privatization policy also begun by the Indonesian government in the 1990s boosted demand for the practice of public relations considerably (Ananto, 2004, p. 268). Thomas (2004, p. 399) notes that, as a result of these reforms,

> there is greater editorial independence for each medium and journalists and public relations executives are motivated toward greater professionalism. No longer is it taboo for journalists to criticize the activities of conglomerates, their major shareholders, or their powerful allies in government. Consequently, no longer can public relations executives take for granted that a positive spin will be given automatically to those firms,

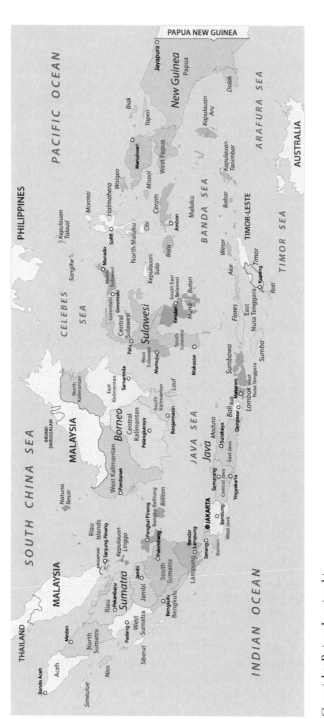

Copyright: Rainer Lesniewski

shareholders, and political leaders in these media, or that their press releases, annual reports, and corporate events will be taken at face value.

Thus, while the greater number of media outlets has resulted in more opportunities for practitioners to disseminate their messages, Thomas (2004, p. 400) also warns that increased competition among outlets for readership and audiences has created "the risk to firms of negative publicity being fueled by journalists as a consequence of the push for greater sales or ratings in the short term." The reforms have also made it more critical for organizations in Indonesia to engage with their stakeholders. Thomas (2004, p. 401) notes that

> an outcome of the reformation struggle in the late 1990s has been greater political awareness and activism among the general public. Therefore, corporations and organizations in Indonesia need to realize that there is greater accountability for its decisions, policies, and actions.

This has increased the need for organizations to practice two-way communication (Ananto, 2004, pp. 276–277).

Indira Abidin, who runs the Jakarta-based firm Fortune PR and has the official title of Chief Happiness Officer, says that corporate social responsibility initiatives are also especially important in the Indonesian market and that a particularly successful strategy is to involve employees and customers in pro-social initiatives, because "we connect through doing good things together." She says that another reason why corporate social responsibility is so important is because

> Indonesians are bombarded by so many brands, so engagement is key to success in the marketplace. Brands need to connect on an emotional level, and also you have to educate Indonesians about *why* they should use particular brands. You also need to be really creative because people are so bombarded by messages.

Social media strategies are also a must for this market, which one BBC reporter describes as having a "love affair with social media" (Vaswani, 2012). Demand for digital strategies is driving much of the industry's growth (Shearman, 2013). Abidin says that because Indonesians "are busy communicating on social media" and actively discuss the products they use on social media, using such platforms is a great way for organizations to turn their customers into advocates. She also advises that multimedia, including images and video, is much more effective than text-based messages in the country.

Today, Freedom House (2014b) notes that Indonesians generally have access to a range of perspectives through the media and the country officially guarantees freedom of speech and the press, but

> there is ongoing concern about the ability of political parties, large corporations, and powerful individuals to control media content, either

indirectly through the threat of lawsuits or directly through ownership, with many major media outlets openly reflecting the political or business interests of their proprietors.

A study of Indonesian journalists indeed found that, while news value was the number one influence on whether they used public relations materials, the reporters "tended to accommodate or compromise with the business interests of their media organizations. Like other employees in the country, journalists live in a rough-and-tumble economic situation" in a country that still faces significant poverty and unemployment, and "therefore, journalists may simply have to adapt to the difficult economic reality" (Sinaga & Wu, 2007, p. 85).

The study also confirmed the prevalence of the personal influence model of public relations, finding that networking was a "significant factor" predicting reporters' use of public relations materials (Sinaga & Wu, 2007, p. 86).

Another problem is "envelope journalism," or bribery of reporters. Freedom House (2014b) reports that "media companies do not pay competitive salaries to their employees, which leads many journalists to take second jobs with corporate sponsors or accept bribes for coverage."

Media

Indonesia's national news agency is Antara (BBC, 2014c).

Major local language newspapers include *Media Indonesia, Bisnis Indonesia, Kompas*, and *Harian Tempo*, along with the business publications *Harian Investor* and *Suara Pembaruan*. *The Jakarta Post* and *The Jakarta Globe* are published daily in English (Sinaga & Wu, 2007, p. 76; BBC, 2014c).

The country's "dominant medium" is television. In addition to the public Televisi Republik Indonesia (TVRI), private outlets include Surya Citra Televisi Indonesia (SCTV) and Rajawali Citra TV Indonesia (RCTI) (BBC, 2014c).

Radio stations also proliferate in Indonesia, including the public Radio Republik Indonesia (RRI), which operates the external Voice of Indonesia (BBC, 2014c).

Twenty-eight percent of Indonesians have active social media accounts. The most popular networks include Facebook, Twitter, LinkedIn, and Instagram (Kemp, 2015).

Anglo Cluster

The GLOBE study found that Australia and New Zealand, which lie in the southwest Pacific Ocean, fall under the Anglo cultural group (Gupta & Hanges, 2004, p. 183). Hofstede found that both countries are individualistic and masculine with low power distance and low uncertainty avoidance. People in these countries prize achievement, assertiveness, self-actualization, and self-interest (Motion, Leitch, & Cliffe, 2009, p. 116). A more detailed discussion of the Anglo cultural cluster can be found in Chapter 11.

Commonwealth of Australia

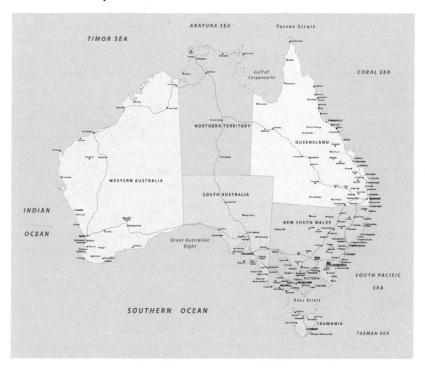

Copyright: Rainer Lesniewski

Time zone: The mainland spans time zones ranging from Coordinated Universal Time (UTC) + 8:00 to UTC + 11:00 during daylight savings time International dialing code: +61

When you practice public relations in Australia, be prepared for tough questions from reporters.

Originally settled by ex-convicts from Great Britain, Australia today is a modern, technologically advanced nation and the world's twelfth-largest economy (World Bank, 2014). The country is a federal parliamentary democracy but remains part of the Commonwealth and continues to recognize the Queen of England as its ceremonial leader. Ninety-two percent of Australians are white, while 7 percent are Asian. The country's indigenous aboriginal people today comprise less than one percent of the population, and racism against aboriginal Australians remains a contentious issue. The country's capital is Canberra, its currency is the Australian dollar, and although it has no official language, English is widely spoken (CIA, 2014).

Public relations is practiced with sophistication in Australia. A recent study of Australian practitioners found that they have a wide range of responsibilities—

from media relations to internal, marketing, and crisis communication. Senior practitioners are often "close and trusted" advisers to the chief executive officers of Australian organizations. The study found that practitioners tend to be well educated and well paid, though the profession still suffers from a poor overall reputation in Australia (de Bussy and Wolf, 2009). In addition, Hay (2010a) reports that the industry struggles with a shortage of talent because many top practitioners leave the country. While major global agencies have a strong presence in Australia, boutique firms also play a significant role in the market, often specializing in particular niches and executing unexpected and forward-thinking campaigns (Hay, 2010a).

Louise Nealon, Joint Managing Director of the Sydney-based firm Callidus PR, says that it is essential to re-tool global campaigns for the Australian market. Nealon says that in contrast to her native Ireland, where much media coverage focuses on developments abroad, the Australian media and people focus predominantly on local developments. Nealon says that

it may be a result of our geographical distance from the rest of the world, but while Australians are very interested in what's happening globally, and we are also affected by global economic events, the community and the media focus heavily on local events. Therefore, the public relations tactics that are successful here—whether that be media or social media relations, community engagement or experiential marketing— are the ones that are highly relevant to the local market and take into account the local environment from a business, political, or consumer perspective.

Accordingly, when Nealon is hired to implement global strategies in Australia, she practically starts from scratch by conducting research to find local stories and statistics to support the message of the campaign. She says that

you'll also usually need local spokespeople, or local supporters to engage media and social media, unless the campaign has a very high-profile and in-demand international spokesperson, but it's much better to be locally-focused and to have relevance to get cut through.

Nealon also reports that, while social media engagement and self-publishing are becoming a larger part of the focus of practitioners, traditional media still remain very influential, and most clients value top-tier media placements. However, it is important to set clients' expectations. Nealon describes Australian journalists as "tough and investigative." They expect hard news and will not cover softer stories, such as a company's anniversary. Additionally, the media market is relatively small in Australia. Nealon explains that

in the Asia-Pacific market, you can get 60 journalists to a media conference. In Australia, we may have 60 journalists in a business beat in the entire country and that number is reducing all the time as the traditional media outlets reduce staff numbers. If you have a media conference and six journalists leave their desks to attend, that would be a success.

For this reason, Nealon focuses on the quality, rather than quantity, of media placements. Furthermore, because so many public relations practitioners target a relatively small number of Australian journalists, it is critical to ensure that your pitches are well tailored to the reporters you approach and to invest in long-term relationships with members of the media.

Social media is also important in the Australian market. However, just as Australian reporters are tough, Nealon warns that the Australian people are "very informed consumers" and will be unforgiving if, for example, a company attempts to run a social media campaign that ignores another issue it is currently facing. "People will jump on that, and there's not a huge amount of tolerance," Nealon says. "We're a very small market, so if you get it wrong, it will be known very quickly. There's a lot less room for error."

There is also a robust environmental movement in Australia (Motion et al., 2009, p. 110). The country accounts for 10 percent of the biodiversity on earth and, because it is the world's driest continent, is particularly susceptible to the effects of climate change (CIA, 2014). Australians are also particularly fond of sports, which "are considered the national religion," so public relations strategies tied to sports stand to be particularly effective (Motion et al., 2009, p. 115).

Finally, if you are practicing public affairs in Australia, it is important to note that proposed legislation is written in government departments and then sent to Parliament for review. To influence the process, be in touch with the relevant government ministry and also with opposition Parliamentarians, who can support or block legislation in Parliament (Devereux & Peirson-Smith, 2009, p. 100).

Media

The Australian Associated Press (AAP) is a privately owned national news agency (BBC, 2014b).

Major daily newspapers include *The Australian, The Sydney Morning Herald,* and the Melbourne-based *Herald Sun.* The major business daily is the *Australian Financial Review.* The vast majority of the country's newspapers are owned by the News Corporation or Fairfax Media (BBC, 2014b).

The Australian Broadcasting Corporation (ABC) is the country's public broadcaster, with national and local television stations (BBC, 2014b). Another public broadcaster, the Special Broadcasting Service (SBS), broadcasts in numerous languages. Major national commercial television networks are the Seven Network, Nine Network, and Ten Network (BBC, 2014b; PR Week, 2012).

The ABC and SBS also operate numerous radio stations (BBC, 2014b).

Fifty-seven percent of Australians have active social media accounts. The most popular social networks include Facebook, Twitter, Instagram, and LinkedIn (Kemp, 2015).

Note

1   Adapted from Alaimo, K. (2015). Public relations as personal relationships: How top Bordeaux wines are promoted in China. *Case Studies in Strategic Communication*, 4(3). Retrieved from http://cssc.uscannenberg.org/cases/v4/

References

Ananto, E. G. (2004). The development of public relations in Indonesia. In K. Sriramesh (Ed.), *Public relations in Asia: An anthology* (pp. 261–282). Singapore: Thomson Learning.

Anson, J. (2014, March 18). China slowdown knocks Bordeaux wine exports in 2013. *Decanter*. Retrieved from http://www.decanter.com/news/wine-news/586702/china-slowdown-knocks-bordeaux-wine-exports-in-2013#wAH1e0k0bZHoF0wt.99

Bardhan, N. (2003). Rupturing public relations metanarratives: The example of India. *Journal of Public Relations Research*, 15(3), 225–248.

Bardhan, N., & Sriramesh, K. (2004). Public relations in India: A profession in transition. In K. Sriramesh (Ed.), *Public relations in Asia: An anthology* (pp. 63–96). Singapore: Thomson Learning.

Bardhan, N., & Sriramesh, K. (2006). Public relations in India review of a programme of research. *Journal of Creative Communications*, 1(1), 39–60.

BBC News Asia. (2013, September 11). India profile. Retrieved from http://www.bbc.com/news/world-south-asia-12557390

BBC News Asia. (2014a, March 21). China profile. Retrieved from http://www.bbc.com/news/world-asia-pacific-13017881

BBC News Asia. (2014b, December 1). Australia profile. Retrieved from http://www.bbc.com/news/world-asia-15675260

BBC News Asia-Pacific. (2014c, December 1). Indonesia profile. Retrieved from http://www.bbc.com/news/world-asia-pacific-15105923

BBC News Asia. (2014d, December 1). Japan profile. Retrieved from http://www.bbc.com/news/world-asia-pacific-15217593

BBC News Asia-Pacific. (2014e, December 1). South Korea profile. Retrieved from http://www.bbc.com/news/world-asia-pacific-15291415

BBC News Asia. (2014f, December 22). Sony hack: North Korea threatens US as row deepens. Retrieved from http://www.bbc.com/news/world-asia-30573040

Bellman, E. (2015, February 11). India passes China to become fastest-growing economy. *The Wall Street Journal*. Retrieved from http://blogs.wsj.com/indiarealtime/2015/02/11/its-official-india-has-passed-china-to-become-the-worlds-fastest-growing-economy/

Berg, N., & Holtbrügge, D. (2001). Public affairs management activities of German multinational corporations in India. *Journal of Business Ethics*, 30(1), 105–119.

Blanchard, B. (2013, September 5). Say what? China says 400 million can't speak national language. *Reuters*. Retrieved from http://www.reuters.com/article/2013/09/05/us-china-language-idUSBRE9840E220130905

Bordeaux Wine Trade Council. (2014). *Bordeaux wines press kit 2014*. Bordeaux: France, Bordeaux Wine Trade Council.

Brady, A. M. (2007). *Marketing dictatorship: Propaganda and thought work in contemporary China.* Lanham, MD: Rowman & Littlefield.

Broom, G. M., & Sha, B. L. (2013). *Cutlip and Center's effective public relations* (11th ed.). New York, NY: Pearson.

Capgemini and RBC Wealth Management. (2014). *World wealth report 2014.* Retrieved from https://www.worldwealthreport.com/.

Central Intelligence Agency (CIA). (2014). World factbook. Retrieved from https://www.cia.gov/library/publications/the-world-factbook/

Chen, N. (2004). Public relations in Hong Kong: An evolving field in a fast-changing city. In K. Sriramesh (Ed.), *Public relations in Asia: An anthology* (pp. 97–125). Singapore: Thomson Learning.

Chen, Y. R. (2007). Effective government affairs in China: Antecedents, strategies, and outcomes of government affairs. In E. L. Toth (Ed.), *The future of excellence in public relations and communication management: Challenges for the next generation* (pp. 477–505). Mahwah, NJ: Lawrence Erlbaum Associates.

Chen, N., & Culbertson, H. M. (2009). Public relations in mainland China: An adolescent with growing pains. In K. Sriramesh & D. Verčič (Eds.), *The global public relations handbook: Theory, research, and practice* (2nd ed.) (pp. 175–197). New York, NY: Routledge.

Chiu, C., Ip, C., & Silverman, A. (2012, April). Understanding social media in China. *McKinsey Quarterly.* Retrieved from http://www.mckinsey.com/insights/marketing_sales/understan ding_social_media_in_china

Cho, S., & Cameron, G. T. (2010). Netizens unite! Strategic escalation of conflict to manage a cultural crisis. In G. J. Golan, T. J. Johnson, & W. Wanta (Eds.), *International media communication in a global age* (pp. 345–365). New York, NY: Routledge.

Choi, Y., & Cameron, G. T. (2005). Overcoming ethnocentrism: The role of identity in contingent practice of international public relations. *Journal of Public Relations Research, 17*(2), 171–189.

Cooper-Chen, A. (1996). Public relations practice in Japan: Beginning again for the first time. In H. M. Culbertson & N. Chen (Eds.), *International public relations: A comparative analysis* (pp. 223–237). Mahwah, NJ: Lawrence Erlbaum Associates.

Credit Suisse. (2012, October). *Global wealth report 2012.* Retrieved from https://www.thefinancialist.com/wp-content/uploads/2012/10/2012-GlobalWealthReport-.pdf

Culbertson, H. M. (1996). Introduction. In H. M. Culbertson & N. Chen (Eds.), *International public relations: A comparative analysis* (pp. 1–13). Mahwah, NJ: Lawrence Erlbaum Associates.

de Bussy, N. M., & Wolf, K. (2009). The state of Australian public relations: Professionalisation and paradox. *Public Relations Review, 35*(4), 376–381.

Devereux, M. M., & Peirson-Smith, A. (2009). *Public relations in Asia Pacific: Communicating effectively across cultures.* Singapore: John Wiley & Sons.

Duhé, S. C., & Sriramesh, K. (2009). Political economy and public relations. In K. Sriramesh & D. Verčič (Eds.), *The global public relations handbook: Theory, research, and practice* (2nd ed.) (pp. 22–46). New York, NY: Routledge.

Ekachai, D., & Komolsevin, R. (2004). From propaganda to strategic communication: The continuing evolution of the public relations profession in Thailand. In K. Sriramesh (Ed.), *Public relations in Asia: An anthology* (pp. 283–320). Singapore: Thomson Learning.

Euromonitor International. (2013, October 8). Global luxury goods sales exceed US $318 billion. Retrieved from http://www.marketwired.com/press-release/global-luxury-goods-sales-exceed-us318-billion-1838681.htm

Farey-Jones, D. (2013, November 25). Postcard from China. *PR Week.* Retrieved from http://www.prweek.com/article/1220471/postcard-china

Flannery, R. (2014, March 3). 2014 Forbes billionaires list: Growing China's 10 richest. *Forbes*. Retrieved from http://www.forbes.com/sites/russellflannery/2014/03/03/2014-forbes-billionaires-list-growing-chinas-10-richest/

Forbes. (2014, May). The world's biggest public companies. Retrieved from http://www.forbes.com/global2000/list/#page:4_sort:6_direction:asc_search:_filter:All%20industries_filter:All%20countries_filter:All%20states

Freedom House. (2014a). Freedom of the press: China. Retrieved from https://freedom-house.org/report/freedom-press/2014/china#.VKRm5Huy5QI

Freedom House. (2014b). Freedom of the press: Indonesia. Retrieved from https://www.freedomhouse.org/report/freedom-press/2014/Indonesia

Goldman Sachs. (2006). *Will China grow old before getting rich?* Retrieved from http://www.goldmansachs.com/our-thinking/archive/archive-pdfs/brics-book/brics-chap-3.pdf

Grunig, J. E., Grunig, L. A., Sriramesh, K., Huang, Y. H., & Lyra, A. (1995). Models of public relations in an international setting. *Journal of Public Relations Research*, 7(3), 163–186.

Grunig, J. E., & Hunt, T. (1984). *Managing public relations*. New York, NY: Holt, Rinehart and Winston.

Gupta, C., & Bartlett, J. (2009). Recruiting local public relations professionals for global public relations practice: A comparative analysis between Australian and Indian public relations recruitment advertisements. *PRism*, 6(2), 1–13.

Gupta, V., & Hanges, P. J. (2004). Regional and climate clustering of societal clusters. In R. J. House, P. J. Hanges, M. Javidan, P. W. Dorfman, & V. Gupta (Eds.), *Culture, leadership, and organizations: The GLOBE study of 62 societies* (pp. 178–218). Thousand Oaks, CA: Sage.

Hackley, C. A., & Dong, Q. (2001). American public relations networking encounters China's guanxi. *Public Relations Quarterly*, 46(2), 16–19.

Hall, C. M., & Mitchell, R. (2008). *Wine marketing*. New York, NY: Elsevier Ltd.

Hay, P. (2010a, June 21). Focus on . . . Australia. *PR Week*. Retrieved from http://www.prweek.com/article/1010931/focus-on-australia

Hay, P. (2010b, August 2). Focus on . . . South Korea. *PR Week*. Retrieved from http://www.prweek.com/article/1019923/focus-on-south-korea

Haque, M. (2004). Overview of public relations in Asia. In D. J. Tilson & E. C. Alozie (Eds.), *Toward the common good: Perspectives in international public relations* (pp. 346–362). Boston, MA: Pearson.

The Holmes Report. (2015). Global top 250 PR firms 2015. Retrieved from http://www.holmesreport.com/ranking-and-data/world-pr-report/agency-rankings-2015/top-250

Hofstede, G., Hofstede, G. J., & Minkov, M. (2010). *Cultures and organizations: Software of the mind*. (3rd ed.) New York, NY: McGraw Hill.

Huang, Y. H. (2000). The personal influence model and Gao Guanxi in Taiwan Chinese public relations. *Public Relations Review*, 26(2), 219–236.

Hung, C. J. F., & Chen, Y. R. R. (2004). Glocalization: Public relations in China in the era of change. In K. Sriramesh (Ed.), *Public relations in Asia: An anthology* (pp. 29–62). Singapore: Thomson Learning.

Inoue, T. (2009). An overview of public relations in Japan and the self-correction concept. In K. Sriramesh & D. Verčič (Eds.), *The global public relations handbook: Theory, research, and practice* (2nd ed.) (pp. 122–139). New York, NY: Routledge.

Jo, S., & Kim, J. (2004). In search of professional public relations: *Hong bo* and public relations in South Korea. In K. Sriramesh (Ed.), *Public relations in Asia: An anthology* (pp. 239–259). Singapore: Thomson Learning.

Kemp, S. (2015, January 21). Digital, social & mobile worldwide in 2015. *We Are Social*. Retrieved from http://wearesocial.net/blog/2015/01/digital-social-mobile-worldwide-2015/

Kent, M., and Taylor, M. (2011). How intercultural communication theory informs public relations practice in global settings. In N. Bardhan & C. K. Weaver (Eds.), *Public relations in global cultural contexts: Multi-paradigmatic perspectives* (pp. 50–76). New York, NY: Routledge.

Kim, Y. (2009). Professionalism and diversification: The evolution of public relations in South Korea. In K. Sriramesh & D. Verčič (Eds.), *The global public relations handbook: Theory, research, and practice* (2nd ed.) (pp. 140–154). New York, NY: Routledge.

Kim, Y., & Kim, S. Y. (2010). The influence of cultural values on perceptions of corporate social responsibility: Application of Hofstede's dimensions to Korean public relations practitioners. *Journal of Business Ethics, 91*(4), 485–500.

Kwon, K. J. (2013, December 20). North Korea threatens to 'strike South Korea mercilessly.' *CNN*. Retrieved from http://www.cnn.com/2013/12/20/world/asia/north-korea-threats/

Liv-ex. (2011, June 24). Valuing the great estates of Bordeaux—who is in the €50m club? Retrieved from http://www.blog.liv-ex.com/2011/06/valuing-the-great-estates-of-bordeaux-who-is-in-the-50-m-club.html.

Liv-ex. (2014). Liv-ex fine wine indices. Retrieved from https://www.livex.com/static PageContent.do?pageKey=Indices

Livermore, D. (2013). *Expand your borders: Discover ten cultural clusters*. East Lansing, MI: Cultural Intelligence Center.

McGregor, R. (2012). *The Party: The secret world of China's communist rulers*. New York, NY: HarperCollins.

McKinsey Global Institute. (2007, May 19). Next big spenders: India's middle class. Retrieved from http://www.mckinsey.com/Insights/MGI/In_the_news/Next_big_spenders_Indian_middle_class

McKinsey Global Institute. (2012, September). The archipelago economy: Unleashing Indonesia's potential. Retrieved from http://www.mckinsey.com/insights/asia-pacific/the_archipelago_economy

Motion, J., Leitch, S., & Cliffe, S. (2009). Public relations in Australasia: Friendly rivalry, cultural diversity, and global focus. In K. Sriramesh & D. Verčič (Eds.), *The global public relations handbook: Theory, research, and practice* (2nd ed.) (pp. 101–121). New York, NY: Routledge.

Newsom, D. (2004). Singapore poised for prominence in public relations among emerging democracies. In D. J. Tilson, & E. C. Alozie (Eds.), *Toward the common good: Perspectives in international public relations* (pp. 363–386). Boston, MA: Pearson.

Patwardhan, P., & Bardhan, N. (2014). Worlds apart or a part of the world? Public relations issues and challenges in India. *Public Relations Review, 40*(3), 408–419.

Pew Research Center. (2009, October 7). Mapping the global Muslim population. Retrieved from http://www.pewforum.org/2009/10/07/mapping-the-global-muslim-population/.

PR Week. (2012, August 24). Global: Focus on . . . Australia. Retrieved from http://www.prweek.com/article/1146581/global-focus-australia

Rhee, Y. (2002). Global public relations: A cross-cultural study of the excellence theory in South Korea. *Journal of Public Relations Research, 14*(3), 159–184.

Samovar, L. A., Porter, R. E., McDaniel, E. R., & Roy, C. S. (2013). *Communication between cultures* (8th ed.). Boston, MA: Cengage Learning.

Sarabia-Panol, Z., & Lorenzo-Molo, C. (2004). Public relations in the Philippines: A cultural, historical, political, and socio-economic perspective. In K. Sriramesh

(Ed.), *Public relations in Asia: An anthology* (pp. 127–159). Singapore: Thomson Learning.

Sha, B. L., & Huang, Y. H. (2004). Public relations on Taiwan: Evolving with the infrastructure. In K. Sriramesh (Ed.), *Public relations in Asia: An anthology* (pp. 161–185). Singapore: Thomson Learning.

Sharma, R. (2013, March 13). What the billionaires list tells us about Asian emerging markets. *Forbes.* Retrieved from http://www.forbes.com/sites/forbesasia/2013/03/13/what-the-billionaires-list-tells-us-about-asian-emerging-markets/

Shearman, S. (2013, July 1). Spotlight: Jakarta. *PR Week.* Retrieved from http://www.prweek.com/article/1275324/spotlight-jakarta

Shin, J. H., & Cameron, G. T. (2003). Informal relations: A look at personal influence in media relations. *Journal of Communication Management, 7*(3), 239–253.

Sinaga, S. T., & Wu, H. D. (2007). Predicting Indonesian journalists' use of public relations-generated news material. *Journal of Public Relations Research, 19*(1), 69–90.

Soble, J. (2014, November 28). Japanese newspaper prints apology for using the term 'sex slaves'. *The New York Times.* Retrieved from http://mobile.nytimes.com/2014/11/29/worl d/asia/japan-yomiuri-shimbun-apology-sex-slaves.html?_r=0

Sriramesh, K. (1996). Power distance and public relations: An ethnographic study of southern Indian Organizations. In H. M. Culbertson & N. Chen (Eds.), *International public relations: A comparative analysis* (pp. 171–190). Mahwah, NJ: Lawrence Erlbaum Associates.

Sriramesh, K. (2004). Epilogue. In K. Sriramesh (Ed.), *Public relations in Asia: An anthology* (pp. 321–341). Singapore: Thomson Learning.

Sriramesh, K., & Verčič, D. (2009). A theoretical framework for global public relations research and practice. In K. Sriramesh & D. Verčič (Eds.), *The global public relations handbook: Theory, research, and practice* (2nd ed.) (pp. 3–21). New York, NY: Routledge.

Sudhaman, A. (2010a, February 8). Focus on . . . India. *PR Week.* Retrieved from http://www.prweek.com/article/981890/focus-on-india

Sudhaman, A. (2010b, April 23). Focus on . . . Japan. *PR Week.* Retrieved from http://www.prweek.com/article/998996/focus-on-japan

Thomas, A. O. (2004). The media and *Reformasi* in Indonesia: Public relations revisited. In D. J. Tilson & E. C. Alozie (Eds.), *Toward the common good: Perspectives in international public relations* (pp. 387–404). Boston, MA: Pearson.

Thussu, D. K. (2013). *Communicating India's soft power: Buddha to Bollywood.* New York, NY: Palgrave Macmillan.

United Nations Food and Agriculture Organization. (2014). *The state of food insecurity in the world.* Retrieved from http://www.fao.org/3/a-i4030e.pdf

Vaswani, K. (2012, February 16). Indonesia's love affair with social media. *BBC News Asia.* Retrieved from http://www.bbc.co.uk/news/world-asia-17054056

Wakefield, R. (2011). Critiquing the generic/specific public relations theory: The need to close the transnational knowledge gap. In N. Bardhan & C. K. Weaver (Eds.), *Public relations in global cultural contexts: Multi-paradigmatic perspectives* (pp. 167–194). New York, NY: Routledge.

World Bank. (2014). GDP. Retrieved from http://data.worldbank.org/indicator/NY. GDP.MKTP. CD?order=wbapi_data_value_2013+wbapi_data_value+wbapi_data_valuelast&sort=desc

Yao, K., & Qing, K. G. (2015, April 15). China growth slowest in six years, more stimulus expected soon. *Reuters.* Retrieved from http://www.reuters.com/article/2015/04/15/us-china-economy-gdp-idUSKBN0N52E220150415

Yu, T. H., & Wen, W. C. (2003). Crisis communication in Chinese culture: A case study in Taiwan. *Asian Journal of Communication, 13*(2), 50–64.

9   Public Relations in Europe

Copyright: Harvepino

Welcome to Europe! From the United Kingdom to Russia to Turkey, this region of about 50 countries is notable mostly for its diversity. Twenty-eight European countries have joined the European Union, pursuing greater coordination through institutions including the European Commission (which operates as a cabinet government), European Parliament, and a central bank. Nineteen European Union countries have formed a monetary union, using the euro as a common currency. Although the region is home to many advanced economies, in recent years, the Eurozone has been roiled by harrowing government debt crises in Greece and Italy and a devastating financial crisis in Spain, leaving all three countries with high unemployment rates and struggling economies.

Colin Byrne, Chief Executive Officer of the global public relations agency Weber Shandwick in the U.K., Europe, the Middle East, and Africa, says that the region's diversity means that organizations must develop campaigns for Europe on the country rather than regional level. He explains that

Germany is so different from Spain, for example. So people need to look into local cultural issues and boundaries rather than jet into London and try to fix a media plan for across Europe. Publications such as the *Financial Times, Guardian*, and *Economist* are read across the region, but they don't penetrate much beyond the upper echelons of business and opinion elites. So you need to research the most influential media in each country—and if you're a brand, social networks and bloggers, as well—because these are all local rather than regional in Europe. It's not about seeing a European market but rather a complex collection of different languages and cultures.

Public relations practice is highly developed in this region. However, across the continent, the very definition of public relations differs markedly from its roots in the United States of America. While public relations is often defined as relationship management in the U.S., van Ruler and Verčič (2004, p. 3) note that, in Europe, a distinction is not generally drawn or seen between relationships and communication. Whereas the concept of *public* relations is generally defined as relations with *publics* in the U.S., in Europe the concept is often conceptualized as communicating in the *public sphere*. Accordingly, public relations is more typically understood within the larger context of the society in which an organization operates (Holmström, 2004, p. 121). The very phrase "public relations" is widely eschewed across Europe; van Ruler and Verčič (2004, p. 3) report that "the term . . . gets more and more replaced by such terms as 'communication management' and 'corporate communication.'"

European scholars have identified four models of public relations practice:

Reflective: "to analyse changing standards and values and standpoints in society and discuss these with members of the organisation, in order to adjust the standards and values/standpoints of the organisation accordingly."
Managerial: "to develop plans to communicate and maintain relationships with public groups, in order to gain public trust and/or mutual understanding."
Operational: "to prepare means of communication for the organisation (and its members) in order to help the organisation formulate its communications. This role is concerned with services and is aimed at the execution of the communication plans developed by others."
Educational: "to help all the members of the organisation become communicatively competent, in order to respond to societal demands" (van Ruler & Verčič, 2004, p. 6).

The concept of reflective public relations is important because it stresses the need for us as practitioners to be aware of not just how we are impacting our stakeholders, but also our broader footprints within communities and how our organizations must adapt in order to keep up with changing societies. As Holmström (2004, p. 123) puts it, the practice of reflective public relations "means exposure and sacrifice in the short term in return for existence in the longer term." Practicing reflective public relations requires investigating how an organization is impacting society, engaging in dialogue and symmetrical communication with members of that larger society, understanding and responding to changing public expectations, and proactively communicating how an organization is acting as a responsible member of society (Holmström, 2004, pp. 126–128). This adds a critical new dimension to our practice, because it stresses the need for us to understand not just how our stakeholders feel today, but also how they will view our organizations tomorrow.

As the above models indicate, public relations is practiced with sophistication in Europe. According to the 2015 European Communication Monitor—a study of more than 2,200 public relations practitioners across 41 European countries—it is more common in Southern and Eastern Europe for public relations practitioners to co-produce content and platforms with media organizations (Zerfass, Verčič, Verhoeven, Moreno, & Tench, 2015, p. 25). When it comes to practicing media relations in this region, a recent study of European journalists found that, when they conduct interviews with chief executive officers, 92 percent expect their interview subject to demonstrate "outstanding knowledge of the company and market," 86 percent expect "an engaging personality," and 72 percent expect "a strong track record of performance." The worst things you can do when being interviewed by a European journalist are to exhibit "arrogant behavior," not answer key questions, and use platitudes. The study found that 64 percent of European journalists use annual reports as top sources when preparing for interviews, while 59 percent use press releases, 58 percent use previous media coverage, and just 16 percent use social media. Sixty-seven percent of European reporters prefer to conduct interviews with chief executive officers in their offices or at production sites, while 55 percent prefer restaurants and bars and 53 percent prefer telephone interviews. Interestingly, European journalists overall appear to be more willing than reporters in the U.S. to share quotes or even entire articles with sources before publishing their stories, though this varies by country. The study found that

> journalists in the U.K., Ireland, Spain, Italy and Portugal are much less willing to allow pre-publication review of quotes or articles, compared to journalists in Germany, the Netherlands, Poland and Denmark. One notable exception: While more than half of German journalists permit a review of CEO quotes, 75 percent of them draw the line at reviewing the entire article (Bulldog Reporter, 2014).

Another important factor to be aware of is the region's concern with privacy. In contrast to the U.S., for example, where free speech is more heavily prized, the European Union recognizes a "right to be forgotten," which allows individuals to request that unflattering information from the past be removed from Internet search engines.

This chapter will introduce you to the five cultural clusters in this region and profile at least one of the most important countries for public relations practitioners within each cluster.

The Anglo Cluster

The United Kingdom and Ireland fall under the Anglo cultural cluster (Gupta & Hanges, 2004, p. 191). Members of the Anglo culture are particularly known for their individualism and high performance orientation. The Anglo cluster is also characterized by low in-group collectivism and a moderate level of assertiveness, future orientation, gender egalitarianism, humane orientation, institutional collectivism, power distance, and uncertainty avoidance (Gupta & Hanges, 2004, p. 193).

The United Kingdom of Great Britain and Northern Ireland

Time zone: Coordinated Universal Time (UTC)
International dialing code: +44

When you practice public relations in the U.K., be prepared for some skepticism—and have a sense of humor.

The United Kingdom (U.K)—which includes England, Scotland, Northern Ireland, and Wales—lies off of the coast of mainland Europe. The English-speaking nation is the world's sixth-largest economy (World Bank, 2014). White, L'etang, and Moss (2009, p. 381) note that "the country, as a former imperial power, retains worldwide interests and influence, not least through its links with former dominions and colonies." The U.K. is a parliamentary democracy and monarchy and a member of the Commonwealth of Nations (known popularly as "the Commonwealth")—a group of countries that were part of the former British Empire. The U.K. is also part of the European Union, though it chose not to join the Economic and Monetary Union and therefore retains its own currency, the pound sterling—commonly known as "the pound." The U.K.'s capital city of London is a global center of finance and media.

Northern Ireland was created when Ireland was partitioned in 1921; the south became an independent state the following year. It was plagued by violence and bad blood between the mostly Protestant majority (known as unionists or loyalists) who wished to remain part of Great Britain and the mostly Catholic nationalists (also known as republicans) who favored a

Copyright: Rainer Lesniewski

united, independent Ireland. A 1998 peace agreement ended three decades of violence. In 2014, Scotland voted in a referendum not to secede and become an independent state. However, Scotland, Northern Ireland, and Wales are all governed by their own national assemblies.

In the U.K., White et al. (2009, p. 400) note that

> if there is a national culture, it is an individualistic, fretful and disputa-
> tious culture. . . . Characteristics of British social life and conversation are
> understatement and irony. As in some other cultures, people do not say
> directly what they mean, but what they say has to be interpreted—which
> is one reason why argument is seen as a way of bringing issues to the sur-
> face for resolution—or at least, clarity in disagreement. . . . The culture is
> based on robust argument: relationships are forged through argument, and
> issues, problems and their solution are clarified.

They report that, as a result, "public relations thrives, and has a large role
to play in the surfacing and clarification of arguments, and in conflict resolution." If you set up a media interview in the U.K., be prepared for tough questions; top reporters will truly grill the executives they interview! The U.K.
also has a long history of activism. Therefore, "there is, in the U.K., a strong
interest on the part of business organisations in corporate social responsibility"
(White et al., 2009, p. 399).

Byrne, of Weber Shandwick, says that "traditional media is still strong and
influential in the U.K. In our last election, broadcast media was most important; then print. Social media is becoming more important, but it is way down
the influence scale." Accordingly, the Chartered Institute of Public Relations'
2013–2014 State of the Profession Survey (2014, p. 5) found that public relations agencies and consultancies still spend nearly half (49 percent) of their
budgets (excluding staff salaries) on media relations, with just 8 percent spent
on strategic planning; 5 percent on research, planning and measurement;
5 percent on social or digital media management; 5 percent on public affairs/
lobbying; 4 percent on event management; and 4 percent on branding.

Freitag and Stokes (2009, p. 270) also note that practitioners should "be
prepared for and expect openly biased coverage in both editorial and news
content" in some of the country's sensational tabloid newspapers, which will
be described below. In 2011, it emerged that the News Corporation-owned
tabloid *News of the World*, which has since ceased publication, had illegally
hacked into the phones of British citizens in order to obtain information for
stories. London's police commissioner also resigned amidst allegations that the
publication had bribed the police.

Communicating on social media can also be challenging because of the
skepticism of U.K. audiences. Howard and Mathews (2013, p. 172) recommend that you "make sure you have your facts in hand and can back up any
claims you make. U.K. audiences react well to content that is humorous and
witty, as long as it is not offensive."

About a fifth of the world's 250 largest public relations firms by revenue
are headquartered in the U.K., including Brunswick and Grayling (Holmes
Report, 2015). The Chartered Institute of Public Relations' State of the Profession Survey (2014, p. 5) found that one of the biggest trends in the U.K.
public relations industry is currently the "expanding remit of public relations

practice," including the integration of public relations with marketing. U.K.-based practitioners also work closely with departments handling events, customer service, and social or digital media. Many practitioners are now also responsible for functions such as website design and coding, strategic partnerships, and the copywriting and design of marketing materials.

Traditionally, England was known for its class differences. White et al. (2009, p. 400) note that, today, "the culture is one of high tolerance of differences, but one in which differences are prominent, between classes and between the sexes." Accordingly, while the middle class and working class may no longer be deferential to an aristocracy, one vestige of this system is that "PR cultures continue to be based strongly on social networks and dining clubs" (White et al., 2009, p. 387). In addition, "the British respect authority and rank, so sending senior representatives will increase the likelihood of success in business matters" (Freitag & Stokes, 2009, p. 269).

Media

White et al. (2009, p. 401) note that U.K. newspapers comprise three categories:

- "Quality" newspapers such as *The Guardian* (considered to be more liberal), *The Daily Telegraph* (considered to be more conservative), *Financial Times* (the key business paper, famous for being printed on salmon-colored paper), and *The Times* (owned by the News Corporation). These papers are often referred to as "broadsheets" because of their traditionally larger size.
- "Middle-market tabloids" such as the *Daily Mail*.
- "Mass market tabloids" such as *The Sun* (owned by the News Corporation) and *Daily Mirror*.

The U.K. is also home to the major business and finance magazine *The Economist*, which famously does not print the bylines of its reporters.

As discussed in Chapter 7, the British Broadcasting Corporation (BBC)—the country's public broadcaster and the world's largest broadcasting corporation—is headquartered in London (CIA, 2014). Its flagship domestic channel is BBC One; it also operates BBC Two. The channels are funded by a license fee paid annually by U.K. television owners and are thus commercial free. Private broadcasters include the popular ITV network (Channel 3) and Sky (which was discussed in Chapter 7). Channel 4 is also a public broadcaster, but is funded through commercials as well as by government (BBC 2012c).

The BBC also operates numerous national and local radio stations, including the popular BBC Radio 2 and BBC Radio 4. Sky News Radio "supplies the national and international news, sport, business and entertainment news to almost every commercial radio station in the UK." (BBC 2012c; Sky News, 2015).

Most global media outlets have bureaus in London.

Fifty-nine percent of people in the U.K. have active social media accounts. The most popular social networks include Facebook, Twitter, LinkedIn, and Instagram (Kemp, 2015).

Practitioner Profile: Jack Lundie, Director of Communications, Oxfam Great Britain

Jack Lundie is Director of Communications for Oxfam Great Britain. Photo credit: Charlotte Ball/Oxfam

For Jack Lundie, Director of Communications for Oxfam Great Britain, public relations—or, more specifically, public engagement—is a tool that can change the world.

Jack's passion is music. After studying drama at the University of Bristol in the United Kingdom, he started working in community theatre and later became a reggae producer. In 1997, when he realized he needed a more stable job after his second child was born, he went to work for Real Adventure, a Bath, U.K.-based marketing agency, where he was a copywriter and managed the creative team working for corporate clients in fields including finance and entertainment.

Jack said that working for some commercial clients raised big questions for him about his values and personal outlook on life and what he wanted to do with it. "I realized I wanted to do cause-related work. I wanted to do something that would make a more positive and direct impact on the world."

So, in 2000, he took a position as New Media Content Manager for Comic Relief, a U.K. charity focused on fighting poverty and advocating for justice both domestically and globally. The organization's signature event is Red Nose Day, a bi-annual event on which people in the U.K. are invited to do something funny to raise money for charity (it launched in the U.S. in 2015). In the U.K., the event is covered on a special broadcast on the BBC.

Jack ended up being headhunted by his media partner. In 2003, he joined the BBC, where he helped the broadcaster's television production teams innovate in their coverage of sport. Jack later worked for the BBC as Deputy Editor of *Blue Peter*, the world's longest-running children's television program, and then as a development producer on the BBC's coverage of the 2012 Olympics in London.

In 2010, Jack joined the international children's organization Save the Children as Director of Brand and Communications. He said his proudest accomplishments there were finding powerful ways to share the stories of children around the world and the scandal of how millions of them are treated. "Powerful storytelling on an emotive subject can initiate change," he said. In particular, he commissioned a film about the plight of Syrian refugee children called "Most Shocking Second a Day Video" that has received nearly 50 million views. He also commissioned a short comedy film in defense of aid to poor countries called "What Has Aid Ever Done for Anyone?" Based on a famous scene from Monty Python's "Life of Brian" (and made with the Pythons' generous permission), he said it was influential because it "captured the imagination of decision-makers and people in power."

In 2014, Jack became a Director of Communications for Oxfam, a global movement of people fighting to end poverty in more than 70 countries. He oversees a team of 55 communicators in Oxfam Great Britain's headquarters in Oxford, U.K.—one of 17 affiliate offices around the world. Jack said that Oxfam's brand identity as an organization helping people use their own power to overcome poverty and create a world in which poverty no longer exists

is our central idea and everything has to stem from it. Bringing this identity to life, with consistency and the relevance to engage people emotionally, demands a combination of discipline and flexibility. The organization's logo never changes, and there are other parts of our identity that need to be consistent, but beyond that, brand communicators need "space for negotiation" with which to develop and adapt our communications for local audiences.

Jack explained that "as a cause, we really only communicate to further our mission, whether that's by raising awareness or bringing people into our movement, so that flexibility to adapt our brand story to resonate with local or domestic audiences is critical." As an example of cultural variance, Jack said that, in the U.K., messages that resonate most tend to be empathetic and focus on doing the right thing and preventing suffering; in Spain, as well as in Scandinavian and Latin American countries, some of the most effective messages focus on rights; in the U.S., focusing on the future or creating a better world can work well.

"These are over-simplified generalizations—which I hope are not offensive to anyone—but I'm simply observing what all communicators know, that knowing your audience is central to effective engagement," Jack said. "Messaging is about the emotions and memories you associate with it, so for content to work, it has to be culturally specific."

Latin Europe

The GLOBE study found that France, French-speaking Switzerland, Italy, Portugal, and Spain fall under the Latin European cultural cluster (Gupta & Hanges, 2004, p. 191). This region ranks high on humane orientation and institutional collectivism and moderately on assertiveness, future orientation, gender egalitarianism, in-group collectivism, performance orientation, power distance, and uncertainty avoidance (Gupta & Hanges, 2004, p. 193).

Livermore (2013, p. 43) notes that this cultural cluster has been heavily influenced by the Roman Catholic Church. He reports that

one of the most distinctive characteristics of the Latin European cluster is its paternalistic orientation. . . . This is certainly changing in the modern era across Latin Europe. People are rising up against governments and going into the streets to protest. But on the whole, some aspect of paternalism is far more prevalent in this cluster than other parts of Europe. For example, 'gentlemanliness' is still highly valued across most of the cluster.

The region also ranks moderately on power distance,

but it's more attuned to status and hierarchy than any other "Western" cluster. While Latin European cultures certainly don't emphasize Power Distance the way an African culture does, chain of command and respect for authority is much more important in France and Italy than in Germany or Britain. And there's a collective deference to the authority and teachings of the Catholic Church. Parents tend to speak more authoritatively to their children than do parents in most Western cultures today. And the governments in many of the Latin European countries are often expected to provide answers more frequently than you would find in other Western contexts (Livermore, 2013, p. 45).

Latin Europeans are known for enjoying life, especially through excellent food. Work is kept separate from family: "Latin Europeans define themselves by who they are more than what they've achieved" (Livermore, 2013, p. 46).

The GLOBE study also ranks Latin Europeans moderately on uncertainty avoidance. Livermore (2013, p. 45) notes that

> this might surprise you because we sometimes think of Italians and Spaniards as being spontaneous people who are comfortable with a great deal of chaos. But on the whole, Latin Europeans organize life around predictable structures and patterns, and prefer not to deviate from them; tradition and following the dominant norms are highly valued. Certainty isn't reached through schedules and policies, but from ascribing to the predominant religious and social norms.

The following sections will profile public relations practice in two of the most important markets in this region: France and Italy.

France

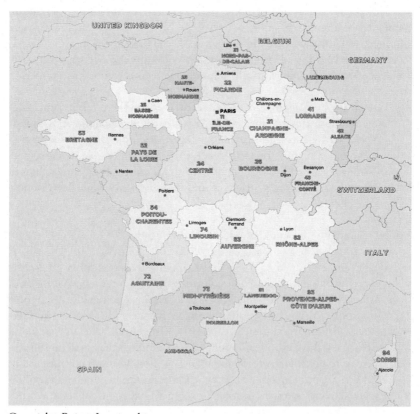

Copyright: Rainer Lesniewski

Time zone: Coordinated Universal Time (UTC) + 1:00 + 1 hour during daylight savings time
International dialing code: +33

When you practice public relations in France, be prepared to answer tough questions.

The largest country in Western Europe, France is the world's fifth-largest economy and another influential player in global affairs (CIA, 2014; World Bank, 2014). The democratic nation has both a president and parliament, its currency is the euro, and its official language is, of course, French. While the government has traditionally played a large role in the economy, many major companies have now been privatized (CIA, 2014). The French are well-known for their *joie de vivre* (joy of living) and for taking pride in their refined culture, and the country is the most popular in the world among tourists (CIA, 2014).

The practice of public relations is well-developed and sophisticated in France. Seven of the 250 largest agencies in the world by revenue are headquartered in the country, including the MSLGroup and Havas PR (Holmes Report, 2015). Carayol (2004, p. 149) notes that "some professionals have almost achieved guru status to certain company managers." French practitioners place particular emphasis on internal, brand, and product communication (Carayol, 2004, p. 145).

Christophe Ginisty, a global public relations consultant based in Paris, says that France is a demanding market because "it's very cultural to try to challenge things. The French ask why. They are always arguing, they are always discussing, they want to express their opinions. You will see this in the streets." This means that you must not expect your messages to be accepted unquestioningly. Furthermore, Ginisty says that corporate social responsibility initiatives are a must in France. "There is a lot of pressure on the market for ethical behavior," he reports. "People demand transparency."

Chinowith (2010, p. 27) describes the relationship between public relations practitioners and reporters in France as "similar to that in the United States. There is a friendly tension stemming from different goals, along with some defensiveness, but in general the relationships are cooperative." However, she notes that it is also common for journalists to approach sources directly, rather than reaching out to spokespeople to request interviews. "Journalists prefer to go directly to the source, which means the chairman and/or company president. Otherwise, it is perceived as a waste of time for them." Another challenge of working with the French press is that "French journalists . . . hate being pushed around and just want news." As a result, "many times, this means that clients have to be taught to develop meaningful and legitimate news stories."

It can also be helpful to provide French journalists with extra background information. One practitioner notes that "journalists here are very interested in cultural as well as economic success. So it is a good idea to brief them on how the company was built and what it is contributing to society overall" (Howard & Mathews, 2013, p. 175).

Lewis PR (2013, p. 23) recommends including video and/or infographics when pitching French reporters because French journalists expect creativity. "The content not only needs to be interesting and original, but visually it needs to stand out from the crowd."

Furthermore, Chinowith (2010, p. 40) reports,

> French journalists are cautious about working closely with companies and are less trusting than their American counterparts of news releases, which are often seen as promotional. There is less public concern over journalism bias, however, and policies restricting the acceptance of gifts by journalists are not as strict as in the United States.

In addition, Chinowith reports that it is not uncommon for advertising purchases to be linked to media coverage. The manager of public relations at a global manufacturing company reported that

> I've often been involved in editorial meetings in Europe where they would approach me after the presentation and say, "I would be glad to cover your story if you will buy advertising space." At first, I would think they were at the wrong meeting (Chinowith, 2010, p. 27).

Ginisty says that trust in the media has been declining in France and the country's daily newspapers reach a relatively limited audience, so it often makes sense for practitioners to consider other platforms. The French are very active on social media, and Ginisty particularly recommends trying to offer interactive experiences in this market, because "people really like to play games, to play with brands."

The nation—which is home to Evian, Chanel, Hermes, L'Oreal, LVMH and Peugeot, among others—is also one of the most "brand conscious" countries in the world (Sudhaman, 2010). Lewis PR (2013, p. 23) reports that most French people use brand websites as "key sources of information." Many global companies therefore focus particularly heavily on branding strategies for the French market (eMarketer, 2009).

Media

Agence France-Presse is the world's oldest global news agency, with 200 bureaus covering 150 countries (AFP, 2014a; AFP, 2014b). As discussed in Chapter 7, its stories run in media outlets around the globe.

Newspapers remain important, though French newspapers have low circulation numbers in comparison with other parts of Europe (Pasquier & Lamizet, 2015). Major daily French newspapers include the evening *Le Monde*, which is considered to be the country's newspaper of record, the center-right *Le Figaro*, the center-left *Libération*, *Le Parisien*, and the financial newspapers *Les Échos* and *La Tribune*. Also popular are free daily newspapers including *Metro* and *20 Minutes*, and the sports paper *L'Equipe* (BBC, 2014a; Sudhaman, 2010).

Carayol (2004, p. 136) reports that "the French are the most rapacious magazine readers." More than 97 percent of French people over the age of

The French read newspapers less than other Europeans. Copyright: Opachevsky Irina

fifteen read at least one magazine per month (Pasquier & Lamizet, 2015). The weekly magazine *Paris-Match*, known for its sensational celebrity content, is especially popular.

Nevertheless, "watching television remains the favourite leisure activity of the French" (Carayol 2004, p. 136). Television networks include the public stations France 2, France 3, France 5 (which broadcasts mostly educational programing), and France Ô (which broadcasts overseas programming), along with the privately owned TF1, Canal Plus, and M6. As discussed in Chapter 7, the publicly owned France 24 broadcasts globally in English, French, and Arabic (BBC, 2014a).

Major radio stations include the public Radio France and Radio France Internationale (RFI), along with the commercial Europe 1 (broadcasting news and entertainment), RTL (broadcasting news, general talk, and music) and NRJ (a leading music station). (BBC, 2014a).

Forty-five percent of the French people have active social media accounts. The most popular networks include Facebook, Twitter, LinkedIn, the French social networking site Copains d'avant, and Instagram (Kemp, 2015).

Italy

Time zone: Coordinated Universal Time (UTC) + 1:00 + 1 hour during daylight savings time
International dialing code: +39

Copyright: Rainer Lesniewski

When you practice public relations in Italy, be prepared to focus on the family.
Located in Southern Europe, Italy is famous for its cultural and religious heritage (and its cuisine!). Its capital city, Rome, was the capital of the Roman Empire. Vatican City—home of the pope of the Roman Catholic Church—is located in Rome, though technically an independent state. Unfortunately, Italy's more modern history has been less illustrious. Benito Mussolini established a fascist dictatorship in Italy in the 1920s, forming an alliance with

Nazi Germany. The country was defeated in World War II and established a democratic republic. Today, Italy is plagued by low growth, high unemployment, and high public debt. Part of the problem is the country's significant underground economy (CIA, 2014). Furthermore, Italy is known as a "crony society" in which connections can be more important than competence in obtaining employment—resulting in a significant drag on economic efficiency (Muzi Falconi, 2009, p. 497). There is also a substantial divide between the more prosperous and industrialized North and the country's less affluent South (CIA, 2014). Italy's currency is the euro and the official language is, of course, Italian.

The existence of a "crony society" has significant implications for the practice of public relations in Italy. First, practitioners are often hired based upon whom they know. Muzi Falconi (2009, p. 497) notes that this is especially the case in the field of public relations, because "the delicate issue of trust between a professional and his/her boss is highly relevant."

While Italy is certainly a relational society, Furio Garbagnati, Chief Executive Officer of Weber Shandwick Italy, says that practitioners within organizations tend to manage relationships between groups rather than individual relationships. "The realisation has dawned that, in order to govern a company, it is necessary to govern its relational systems, which become more complex with each passing day" (Weber Shandwick, 2010, p. 3). Since there are a small number of true decision-makers in the government, public relations practitioners typically also attempt to develop personal relationships in order to influence them (Muzi Falconi, 2009, p. 493).

Gianni Catalfamo, former head of the global public relations firm Ketchum in Italy, says that, to target the general public in Italy, "I always advise my clients to think about families." Because the family is the backbone of Italian society, "the messages that resonate are not directed towards the individual. Instead, you need to talk about the benefits for the whole family."

When targeting the Italian media, Catalfamo says that it is helpful to remember the local adage that "Italy is the country of a thousand bell towers." In other words, Italy is oriented around local communities, where most decision-making occurs, rather than its capital and national government. Targeting the many local newspapers in the country's provinces is therefore one of the best ways to reach the Italian people.

Muzi Falconi (2009, pp. 491, 498) estimates that media relations comprises about 60 percent of public relations activities in Italy—a number that has decreased in recent years, as practitioners and organizations increasingly recognize the importance of other functions, such as corporate social responsibility. Lewis PR (2013, p. 45) notes that "Italian journalists love social media: 83% use Facebook, 69% use Twitter and 38% consider social media as a source of information. It is therefore important to stay in close contact with journalists on these social media platforms." Additionally, Italian reporters cover consumer technology heavily, so pitches related to this topic are especially likely to be successful. Bernasconi (2013) notes that "bloggers in Italy have become, as in other countries, very important opinion leaders: Tech, food and mommy blogs are the biggest."

If you book an interview for one of your executives, be aware that many Italian journalists believe that their personal lives are fair game. Forty-four percent of Italian reporters say that they use chief executive officers' personal lives as a way to assess the executives (Bulldog Reporter, 2014).

Another factor that complicates public relations in Italy is the media bias of news organizations. "Usually, the owner of a newspaper is engaged in other businesses, and publishing is considered a good investment because of the attraction a newspaper has for the political and other elites, and the damage it may cause to competitors" (Muzi Falconi, 2009, p. 499). Meanwhile, the positions taken by the public broadcaster, RAI, typically "adapt to the government agenda" (Muzi Falconi, 2009, p. 493). This can make it difficult to influence the media. In media relations, as in the rest of Italian life, relationships are critical; Muzi Falconi (2009, p. 499) describes the relationship between journalists and public relations practitioners in Italy as "intense and incestuous."

Muzi Falconi (2009, pp. 495–496) notes that a further frustration for public relations practitioners in Italy is that lawyers often insist on approving communications before they are released, because the judiciary is so slow, inefficient, and archaic that organizations do everything possible to try to avoid using it.

Although the country's legacy of communism and Catholicism means that civil society has been less active in Italy than in other European countries, today Italian non-governmental organizations are increasingly active, and accordingly organizations are making greater efforts to engage them (Muzi Falconi, 2009, p. 496).

Despite all of its challenges, the field of public relations has been growing and professionalizing in Italy. Muzi Falconi and Kodilja (2004, p. 228) note that there is "a truly new awareness of the pervasiveness of the profession in every walk of Italian society. Public relations is progressively less confused with propaganda, persuasion and manipulation. Italy shows a trend towards the development of quality in relationship management." Still, a recent study found that, although senior managers in Italy appear to appreciate the value of public relations, practitioners in the country are generally not part of their organizations' decision-making processes, indicating that the field still has progress to make (Valentini & Sriramesh, 2014, p. 12).

Media

Agenzia Nazionale Stampa Associata (ANSA) is a global news wire service based in Italy. Agenzia Giornalistica Italia (AGI) is an Italian news agency focused on economic and business news.

Italian newspapers have low circulation numbers in comparison with other parts of Europe, but nevertheless remain important to public relations practice. Major daily newspapers include *Corriere della Sera, La Repubblica, Il*

Messaggero, *La Stampa*, and the business-focused *Il Sole 24 Ore*; *Panorama* is a popular weekly (BBC, 2013; Lewis PR, 2013, p. 44).

Television reaches the largest audiences in Italy (Muzi Falconi, 2009, p. 499). Television channels Rai Uno, Rai Due, Rai Tre, and Rai News 24 (which provides rolling news) are operated by the country's public broadcaster, RAI (BBC, 2013). The other free national channels are Rete 4, Canale 5, Italia 1 (all owned by Mediaset, whose controlling shareholder is former Prime Minister Silvio Berlusconi), La 7, and MTV Italia (Giomi, 2015). Satellite television provider Sky Italia, owned by the News Corporation, offers numerous packages of channels.

RAI also operates radio stations RAI 1 (the flagship national station), Radio 2 (which is entertainment focused), Radio 3 (cultural programming), and GR Parlamento (which covers Parliament). Commercial stations include Radio 24 (which covers news and business), R101 (pop music), and Radio Italia (Italian pop music) (BBC, 2013).

Forty-six percent of Italians have active social media accounts. The most popular platforms include Facebook, Shazam, Twitter, Instagram, and LinkedIn (Kemp, 2015).

Germanic Europe

Europe is also home to the Germanic countries of Austria, Belgium, Germany, the Netherlands, and the German-speaking parts of Switzerland (Gupta & Hanges, 2004, p. 185; Livermore, 2013, p. 25). This cultural cluster is characterized by high assertiveness, future orientation, performance orientation, and uncertainty avoidance; a moderate level of gender egalitarianism and power distance; and low humane orientation, in-group collectivism, and institutional collectivism (Gupta & Hanges, 2004, p. 193). Most of the people in this culture speak German, with the exception of the Netherlands, where Dutch is spoken.

The Netherlands is also an exception because, while most of the countries in this cluster tend to be competitive and "very focused on results and winning," the culture of the Netherlands is more cooperative (Livermore, 2013, pp. 30–31).

Livermore (2013, p. 30) notes that

> uncertainty avoidance is the cultural dimension that most uniquely characterizes the Germanic cluster. . . . Rules and policies are created to help reduce the chance that things will get out of control. Germanics tend to buy as many different kinds of insurance to avoid risk at all cost. Order is highly valued. . . . The Germans are masters of security and careful planning . . . the preferred way of life in the Germanic culture [is] predictable and structured.

For this reason, "punctuality is king; following schedules is one way to reduce uncertainty." The culture is also known for "rigorous thinking, insistence on quality control, and tenacity" (Livermore, 2013, p. 27).

While this group does not officially rank as being as individualistic as the Anglo cultural cluster, Livermore (2013, p. 29) argues that the Germanic cluster is ultimately more individualistic because rules are created with the intention of protecting individual rights. Employees are expected to have opportunities to raise their concerns and to pursue their own civic interests outside of the workplace.

The culture is also low context. Livermore (2013, p. 30) assures that "you can expect most Germanic people to be clear, explicit, and blunt." Business transactions tend to be more formal, at least initially. "When you're meeting someone, expect intense eye contact and a firm hand shake with a slight nod of the head—that's a typical Germanic greeting" (Livermore, 2013, pp. 30–31). Finally, unlike other cultures in which it would be inappropriate to discuss topics such as politics and faith, "Germanic people thrive on a good debate" (Livermore, 2013, p. 31).

Germany

> *Time zone: Coordinated Universal Time (UTC) + 1:00 + 1 hour during daylight savings time*
> *International dialing code: +49*

When you practice public relations in Germany, be aware of laws and expectations governing privacy.

Out of the ashes of the defeat of Nazi Germany in World War II has come Europe's largest economy and most populous nation after Russia (CIA, 2014). Following the collapse of the Soviet Union and the end of the Cold War, Western and Eastern Germany were unified in 1990. Today, Germany is a highly industrialized nation. It is a federal republic and a social market economy—"a special type of economy that pursues the synthesis of legitimized economic freedoms with welfare state ideals of social safety and social justice" (Bentele & Wehmeier, 2009, p. 418). The official language is German and the country's currency is the euro. The birthplace of carmakers including Audi, BMW, Daimler, Porsche, and Volkswagon, the country is especially known for its automotive and technology sectors (Sudhaman & Hay, 2010).

The practice of public relations in Germany has grown and professionalized significantly since the mid-1980s (Bentele & Junghänel, 2004, p. 158). Today, the vast majority of German heads of communications "work at the top hierarchical level" in their organizations and "the necessity of professional communication management is mainly unquestioned" within German organizations (Bentele & Junghänel, 2004, pp. 163–164). Bentele and Wehmeier (2009, p. 416) note that "some of the more recent trends, especially at the bigger agencies, focus on change communication (i.e., the management of communication by companies undergoing change), issues management, sustainability communication, brand public relations, corporate governance, and impression management." They (2009, p. 423) predict that, in the future, public relations

Copyright: Rainer Lesniewski

will continue to be "more differentiated and specialized" within German organizations, as practitioners specialize in particular areas, such as reputation or issues management.

The growth of the industry has been driven in part by the proliferation of private media outlets. While until the mid-1980s there was only public broadcasting in Germany, the growth of private channels has given public relations professionals more outlets to pitch and greater opportunities to select the media they target (Bentele & Wehmeier, 2009, p. 420). However, this has also complicated the practice. Bentele and Wehmeier (2009, p. 421) note that, today,

> on the one hand, it is easier to reach certain publics because of the large number of specialized media; on the other hand, it is more difficult to reach the entire population by performing classical media relations activities because the audience is much more fragmented.

Hines (2009, pp. 5–6) notes that one factor that helps is that practitioners tend to be more trusted by reporters in Germany than in other nations. "Journalists and public relations employees are more closely aligned in Germany than in many other countries, especially the UK. A credible public relations counsellor or firm is viewed as a valuable source of information by members of the media."

However, this does not mean that you should expect your messages to be accepted without question. Joerg Winkelmann, former Head of Marketing and Communications for IBM Europe, notes that

> Germans like to see both sides of the coin. They are not easily buying into a one-sided message. Consumers are exposed to a highly diverse spectrum of opinion and a wide range of national, regional, and local media that aim at capturing a broad spectrum of opinion. So as an organization, you have to be ready for a lot of journalistic scrutiny and fact checking.

Therefore, when pitching journalists, be prepared to discuss specifics. Lewis PR (2013, p. 27) reports that

> German journalists are very into facts and figures. If you want to get a journalist's attention, the best chance is if you can present a new product and talk about details such as technical features, pricing, availability and market share. You should also be able to showcase the USPs of the product or service and differentiate yourself from the competition. Last but not least, visuals such as product shots, screen shots or infographics really increase the chance for publication.

Similar to Italian journalists, 42 percent of German reporters indicate that they rely on chief executive officers' personal lives to help form assessments of them (Bulldog Reporter, 2014).

Another critical factor to be aware of when practicing public relations in Germany is the country's strict privacy laws. This means that you need to get permission from a reporter before adding him or her to your distribution list for press releases and should always include an option to unsubscribe in each of your emails (Lewis PR, 2013, p. 27). Also for this reason, Howard and Mathews (2013, p. 171) recommend that, when communicating with the German public on social media, you should "make sure you know the rules for company use of social media and explain exactly why you need any user data."

Another challenge is that German companies have traditionally been publicity shy and some of this reticence towards public relations remains. Hinner (2009, p. 45) reports that "in Germany, many business managers are still convinced that an excellent product sells itself." Hines (2009, p. 5) notes that "thus, a company might not wish to extol all of its virtues and stand out from the crowd."

The term traditionally used for public relations in Germany is *Öffentlichkeitsarbeit*; it continues to be used by government practitioners (Bentele & Junghänel, 2004, p. 162). This translates literally as "public work," and means "working in public, with the public and for the public"—with "public" having the connotation of the public sphere (Verčič et al., 2001, p. 376). The term public relations, or PR, is often used by consultants. According to Bentele and Junghänel (2004, p. 162), the term is "considered to be more modern and progressive, particularly by the younger generation." They report that

> terms such as "information" or "communication" (as in "corporate communication") are also frequently mixed with public relations. For some years now, "communication management" has been used more and more to refer to a special type of PR—namely, PR with high professional standards—or to refer to public relations in general.

Media

Deutsche Presse-Agentur (DPA), based in Germany, is a major news agency.

Major newspapers include the conservative *Frankfurter Allgemeine Zeitung*, the more liberal *Süddeutsche Zeitung*, the weekly *Die Zeit*, the tabloid *Bild-Zeitung*, and the financial newspaper *Handelsblatt* (Sudhaman & Hay, 2010). *Der Spiegel* is one of Europe's largest weekly news magazines.

Germany is home to Europe's largest television market. The public broadcaster ARD is comprised of the country's regional broadcasters, funded by annual license fees paid by citizens and corporations. Its national television network is *Das Erste* ("the first.") A different public service broadcaster, ZDF, operates a second national channel. Commercial broadcasters include n-tv and N24 (both airing "rolling news") and RTL (which operates entertainment channels). As discussed in Chapter 7, Deutsche Velle is Germany's international broadcaster and the News Corporation-owned Sky Deutschland offers subscription channels (BBC, 2012a).

ARD and Deutschlandradio both operate public radio stations, while Deutsche Velle radio broadcasts internationally (BBC, 2012a).

Thirty-five percent of Germans have active social media accounts. The most popular social platforms include Facebook, Twitter, Shazam, Instagram, and LinkedIn (Kemp, 2015).

Nordic Countries

Chilly Northern Europe is home to the Nordic countries of Denmark, Finland, Iceland, Norway, and Sweden. This cultural cluster is characterized by high gender egalitarianism, future orientation, institutional collectivism, and uncertainty avoidance; moderate humane orientation and performance orientation; and low assertiveness, in-group collectivism, and power distance (Gupta & Hanges, 2004, p. 193).

Nordic countries exhibit a "moderate level of individualism," but less so than Anglo and Germanic cultures because they place importance on the needs of the group and ensuring autonomy and individual choice for all people (Livermore, 2013, p. 15). Livermore (2013, p. 12) argues that one of the most important things to understand about Nordic culture is the Law of Jante, which derives from a 1933 novel by a Danish author, Aksel Sandemose. He explains,

> the overarching rule of Jante Law is this: "Don't think you're anything special." It's hard to overstate how strongly this idea weaves through the Nordic cultures. Modesty, equality, humility, and skepticism are all expressions of Jante Law. Everyone is on equal footing and each citizen—and society as a whole—should do whatever it can to protect that right.

Livermore (2013, p. 13) says that this explains the minimalism and functionalism that characterize Nordic dress and design. It also explains why "rich people generally dress, eat, and travel in the same style as the prosperous middle class" (Gupta & Hanges, 2004, p. 199). The countries in this cluster also "tend to be very irreligious . . . religion is something that most people don't take part in or really understand as having much relevance to real life" (Livermore, 2013, p. 17).

However, Livermore (2013, p. 15) says that what most distinguishes Nordic cultures from the rest of Europe is their "strong belief in the importance of working to live rather than living to work. Nordic culture, while certainly pursuing many business interests, is committed first and foremost to enhancing people's quality of life." Employees enjoy generous vacation and family leave policies. For this reason,

> if you're traveling to the Nordic region on business, punctuality for meetings is extremely important. Scandinavians are terribly worried about wasting other people's time. They have a limited amount of time to do their job, so efficiency is everything for the Nordic people (Livermore, 2013, p. 16).

The countries in this culture are all among the ten freest presses in the world, as ranked by Reporters Without Borders (2014).

Sweden

Time zone: Coordinated Universal Time (UTC) + 1:00 + 1 hour during daylight savings time
International dialing code: +46

When you practice public relations in Sweden, be transparent.

Sweden is a constitutional monarchy and parliamentary democracy known for its neutrality; the country has not engaged in war for about 200 years (CIA, 2014)! The capitalist country is renowned for its policies and programs to ensure the welfare of its people; citizens enjoy universal healthcare and the most generous parental leave policies in the world (Killian, 2011). Geographically large but with a small population, the country is also known for its gender egalitarianism. Swedish women hold one of the world's highest rates of seats in parliament (Inter-Parliamentary Union, 2014). Although Sweden is a member of the European Union, it has not adopted the euro. The country's currency is the krona. Its capital is Stockholm and official language is Swedish, though English is widely spoken, as well.

Flodin (2009, pp. 472, 474) reports that the demand for public relations "exploded" in the 1990s and today Sweden has one of the world's highest numbers of practitioners per capita. One study of 800 Swedish executives found that 99 percent recognized the value of public relations and the majority of Swedish practitioners are members of the dominant coalitions within their organizations (Flodin, 2009, pp. 473–474). Mattinson (2014b) notes that

> in global terms, the Swedish PR sector is a relatively small player, but by most measures it has been punching far above its weight . . . the country has developed a reputation as a hotbed of creativity as agencies such as Prime PR and Jung Relations have been showered with global awards for innovative, integrated campaigns.

One of the most significant characteristics of the practice of public relations in Sweden is the country's history of and expectations for openness with the public. The government has a long tradition of providing open access to information, and Sweden is believed to have been the world's first country to enjoy freedom of the press (Flodin, 2009, p. 477). Flodin (2009, p. 476) notes that "there are numerous opportunities for individuals, groups, and organizations to participate in public debates, and the country has a long tradition of influencing politicians and decision makers." For this reason, there has not traditionally been a significant demand for government relations in Sweden, because individuals and groups have been able to access their elected officials so readily. However, since Sweden joined the European Union in 1995, there has been increased need for practitioners who have the skills, knowledge, and contacts to influence the significantly less accessible bureaucracy of the European Parliament, European Commission, and European Council (Flodin, 2009, p. 476).

Copyright: Rainer Lesniewski

This tradition of openness also means that it is essential for practitioners in Sweden to be transparent with the press. Charlotte Erkhammar, Chief Executive Officer of the Stockholm-based strategic communications agency Kreab Worldwide, says that organizations "can quickly lose trust if they are not considered to be playing fairly or if they seem to be misleading."

It is also essential for media relations practitioners in Sweden to respond to the press rapidly. This is the case because Swedish media face intense competition, including from international outlets such as the BBC World Service and CNN International, and therefore work under tight deadlines (Flodin, 2009, p. 481). Swedish journalists are also known for their integrity (Holt, Sierra, Vaughn, Winston, & Copeland, 2013, p. 4). Lewis PR (2013, p. 73) notes that "this means PR pros need to be careful about how they phrase offers to journalists. Anything that can be perceived as a bribe or gift can easily be misunderstood."

The government subsidizes the press in an effort to ensure that each region of the country has at least two competing newspapers and more than 75 percent of Swedish adults read a newspaper daily. Still, the relatively small number of outlets in the country can make it difficult to place a large number of stories (Flodin, 2009, p. 480; Holt et al., 2013, p. 4; Weibull, Jönsson, & Wadbring, 2015). Having local spokespeople available will give you a big advantage. Lewis PR (2013, p. 73) explains that

> media in Sweden are often keen to meet with a local spokesperson, even though many companies try to get around this. When making public announcements it is important to use a local spokesperson to conduct interviews, to quote and to appear in speaking engagements with the media. Using international spokespeople is always possible, but PR results will never be as good.

Erkhammar says that she also often recommends that clients communicate directly with their stakeholders. "Sweden is not a small country, but in many situations it is possible to communicate directly with those you would like to communicate with," she says. She also notes that, more so than in other markets, the Swedish people expect to be consulted on decisions that will impact them. This is due in part to the country's corporate culture, which is non-hierarchical and allows for even junior employees to question management.

Swedish practitioners have also pioneered sophisticated online public relations strategies. Holt et al. (2013, p. 3) note that Sweden's "technology-heavy industries and tech-savvy culture have led Swedish PR agencies to quickly adopt online tools in campaigns for clients. And that has, in turn, enabled Swedish PR practitioners to move ahead of their European competitors in online sophistication." Swedish practitioners also excel at focusing on high-level strategy rather than simply execution (Mattinson, 2014b).

Swedish companies are global leaders in corporate social responsibility and are particularly proactive about monitoring and reporting on their activities

(Holt et al., 2013, p. 6). They emphasize ethical issues in their communications and often refer to themselves as "corporate citizens" (Flodin, 2004, p. 421). Because Swedish society has a proud tradition of balancing the needs of different groups in society through dialogue and consensus, the country's businesses have not traditionally contended with dramatic encounters with activists. However, Flodin (2009, p. 478) reports that this has recently changed:

Swedish companies had become used to having a dialogue with traditional nongovernmental organizations and supporting them via sponsorships. However, in the last 5 years, activists have been using tactics to grab attention such as climbing on rooftops and chimneys, trying to steal animals from fur farmers, sitting in front of machines that build new roads, sitting in trees to prevent logging, and throwing eggs at ministers. When confronted with this new form of unconventional activist tactics, baffled organizations have often been silent and refused to meet with such activists. Recently, however, corporations and government authorities have been much more open toward inviting activists for constructive dialogues. As one would expect, it is not unusual that these attempts have turned out to be unconstructive and result in dramatic attention-grabbing tactics by activists, who end up being carried away by the police.

Finally, internal communication is a particularly important facet of public relations practice in Sweden. Since 1976, employers have been required by law to communicate a range of information to their employees, including facts about the employer's finances, production, and personnel policies (Flodin, 2009, p. 477).

Media

The Swedish news agency Tidningarnas Telegrambyrå (TT) is the largest in the region.

There are about 150 Swedish newspapers. Daily papers include the largest-circulation tabloid, *Aftonbladet*, along with *Dagens Nyheter*, *Svenska Dagbladet*, and the tabloid *Expressen* (BBC, 2012b; Weibull et al., 2015).

Television is the most popular form of media in Sweden. The country's public broadcaster, SVT, operates SVT1, SVT2, SVT24 (a news channel), and SVT Europa. Private broadcasters include TV3, TV4, Kanal 5, and ZTV (BBC, 2012b).

The public broadcaster, Sveriges Radio, operates P1, which focuses on news, P2 (classical music), P3 (targeted to youth), and P4 (regionally based music). National private radio stations include Rix FM, NRJ, and Mix Megapol (BBC, 2012b).

The tech-savvy Swedes are active users and early adapters of social media (Kullin, 2011). Popular social media platforms include Facebook, YouTube, and LinkedIn; Twitter is not as influential as in other parts of the world, but is used by communication professionals and journalists (Alexa, 2014; Lewis PR, 2013, p. 73).

Case Study: @Sweden

On June 20, 2015, the Swedish tweeter of the week, Therese Larsson, posted this photo of herself in traditional Swedish attire, announcing she was "on my way to celebrate Midsummer!" The annual celebration signifies the start of summer vacation for many Swedes.

As previously discussed, Sweden has a strong tradition of openness and transparency. One initiative to promote the country takes these traits to the extreme. The Twitter handle @Sweden—developed by the advertising agency Volontaire on behalf of the Swedish Institute (a government agency that promotes Swedish culture) and the country's tourism agency, VisitSweden—turns over control of the country's Twitter handle to a different Swedish person every week. VisitSweden CEO Thomas Brühl told Mashable that "no one owns the brand of Sweden more than its people. With this initiative we let them show their Sweden to the world" (Haberman, 2012).

Their tweets provide a largely unfiltered view into the lives of the country's people. As Lyall (2012) notes,

> if there is anything to be learned from the @Sweden experiment . . . it is that there is no such thing as a typical Swede. One @Sweden posted photographs of his Christmas moose hunt. Another tartly criticized the foreign secretary. . . . Another declared that she would like to be making love, so to speak, right that very second. Another, a Muslim lawyer, discussed the ubiquity of the name Muhammad among immigrants and joked that if anyone forgot the names of her six brothers, Muhammad would do fine. And Jack Werner, the very first @Sweden, attracted thousands of followers and the nickname "the masturbating Swede" after he decided to be honest when listing his favorite leisure activities.

Volontaire's creative director says the initiative, called Curators of Sweden and launched in 2012, was designed to illustrate the country's democratic and progressive values. He told *The New York Times* that Swedes selected to tweet through the platform are merely given a "soft suggestion" to act with "dignity" and "not make a fool" of themselves (Lyall, 2012). Of course, it is precisely this level of openness that has likely attracted followers around the globe. As of June 2015, the @Sweden Twitter handle has nearly 84,000 followers, while the country's other Twitter handle, @Swedense, which is managed by the Swedish Institute, has under 35,000 followers. As discussed in Chapter 6, many experts argue that diplomacy efforts that are controlled by citizens (even if they are ultimately funded by their governments) are more credible because they are viewed as cultivating more authentic exchanges (Mueller, 2009, p. 103).

However, the potential risk is that some tweets may showcase Swedes in a negative light (one Swedish student spelled "Finnish" incorrectly in one of his first tweets) or even offend (Lyall, 2012). In 2012, a tweeter of the week named Sonja Abrahamsson drew global headlines and outrage after posting tweets about Jewish and gay people that many around the world found to be offensive, as well as a series of other bizarre posts, such as one claiming that she had put urine in her food. Even then, VisitSweden's social media manager defended the platform as essential to showcasing "the multi-faceted people that Sweden is composed of" and noted that to delete posts or ban a tweeter on the platform would constitute censorship, which is inappropriate in Swedish culture (Stoll & Heron, 2012).

Furthermore, as Wasserman (2012) notes, the controversy "raised awareness via its cringe factor." The year following its launch, VisitSweden reported that media coverage of the Twitter handle had garnered promotional attention for the country that it estimated to be worth U.S. $40 million (Ronalds-Hannon, 2013). *Forbes* noted that "if nothing else, Sweden has definitely rid itself of the reputation of 'most boring country in the world'"—an accusation leveled at the nation by the United Kingdom's *Daily Mail* six years previously (Frith-Powell, 2006; Hill, 2012).

Of course, another problem with the approach is that the lack of coordination of messaging means that the Swedish government is unable to craft and implement a purposeful strategy for the picture it will present to the world on this platform—other than, of course, one of extreme openness, tolerance, and diversity.

Eastern Europe

The cultural cluster of Eastern Europe includes Albania, Bulgaria, the Czech Republic, Estonia, Georgia, Greece, Hungary, Kazakhstan, Mongolia, Poland, Russia, Slovenia, and Serbia (Gupta & Hanges, 2004, p. 191; Livermore, 2013, p. 33).

This cultural group is characterized by high assertiveness, gender egalitarianism, and in-group collectivism; moderate humane orientation, institutional collectivism, and power distance; and low future orientation, performance orientation, and uncertainty avoidance (Gupta & Hanges, 2004, p. 193). However, these countries are also more diverse than other clusters in their politics, economies, languages, and religions (Livermore, 2013, p. 39). For example, although the Russian Orthodox Church exerts strong influence in many countries in the region, Poland and Lithuania are primarily Roman Catholic.

Livermore (2013, p. 38) notes that

> for the most part, the cluster is more Collectivist than Individualist. But the moderate Collectivist orientation across Eastern Europe is primarily directed toward one's extended family, so it's unlikely someone will behave as much as a Collectivist in the work environment as they might if they're from an Asian or Arab culture. There is, however, a communal sense of looking out for each other.

The culture is moderately competitive, "something that is not too surprising given what was required for them to survive their battles with harsh terrain and weather, emperors, and other clans;" the region has a long history of colonization (Livermore, 2013, p. 38).

However, for public relations practitioners, the most important character-istic of this region is the fact that, since the breakup of the Union of Soviet Socialist Republics (USSR)—or Soviet Union—in 1991, the states in this region have been transitioning from communism towards capitalism and democracy. Ławniczak (2004, p. 217) therefore calls the public relations prac-ticed in this region "transitional public relations." He (2004, p. 223) notes, for example, that

> the average Polish citizen, and especially older Poles, associate capitalism with unemployment, the lack of a welfare safety net, the negative con-sequences of substantial social inequalities, the negative consequences of monopolistic practices and a fear of foreign capital; the latter is believed to be part of a plan to "take over the country."

Thus, while the opening of Eastern European markets to foreign goods and investment has created many opportunities for public relations practitioners, the challenge has been to change popular perceptions of private enterprise and property (Ławniczak, 2004, pp. 222–224). Practitioners have been chal-lenged to change the views of not just the public but also of business owners, who have not understood the value of promoting their products and services and have even believed that doing so would be a bad idea because it could result in higher taxes (Ławniczak, 2004, p. 221).

The following profile, of Russia, exemplifies how poorly developed ethical codes and government control can further complicate the practice of public relations in this region.

Russian Federation

Time zone: Spans 11 time zones, ranging from Coordinated Universal Time (UTC) + 2:00 to UTC + 12:00
International dialing code: +7

When you practice public relations in Russia, be prepared to be solicited for money by reporters.

Russia is the world's largest country by landmass. About 75 percent of the country lies in Asia, with the rest in Europe—though most Russians live in the part of the country that lies in Europe (Rand McNally, 2014). Following the communist revolution led by Vladimir Lenin in 1917, the USSR was formed. Joseph Stalin ruled from 1928–1953, presiding over the imprisonment of millions of people in labor camps and the deaths of millions more as the result of famine and political purges. After World War II, the USSR and U.S. emerged as the world's two superpowers, leading to tensions known as the "Cold War." In 1991, the Soviet Union broke apart into fifteen independent states, including Russia. The privatization of businesses that followed concentrated the country's wealth in the hands of a small elite. Although many people

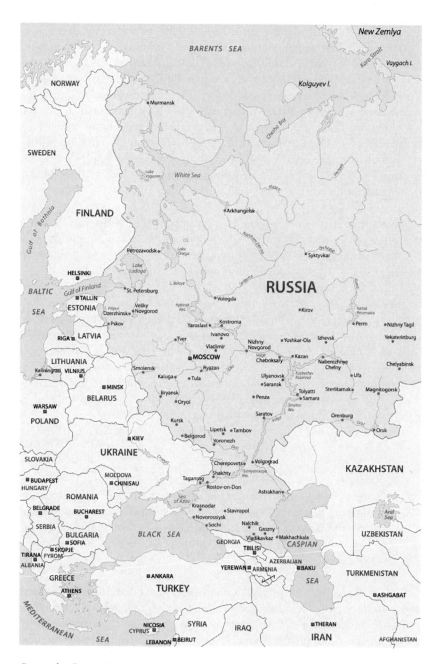

Copyright: Rainer Lesniewski

had high hopes that Russia would become a modern democracy, the U.S. government today describes the country as "a centralized semi-authoritarian state in which the leadership seeks to legitimize its rule through managed national elections, populist appeals . . . and continued economic growth" (CIA, 2014). In 2014, Russia invaded Crimea, which is widely recognized by the international community as being part of Ukraine, leading to a global crisis. The U.S. and Europe responded with economic sanctions. Russia also faces a separatist movement in Chechnya, which has resulted in violent terrorist attacks. Today, Russia is the world's ninth-largest economy, its currency is the Russian Ruble, and its official language is Russian (World Bank, 2014).

The field of public relations has been growing at double-digit rates annually in Russia (Mattinson, 2014a). However, Erzikova (2012, p. 456) found that one reason for this is that

> organizational leaders believe that having a public relations position is fashionable and a symbol [of] power—like a luxury car. Accordingly, public relations staffers are bosses' assistants whose professional behavior is regulated by the bosses' impulsive desires.

Tsetsura (2009, p. 601) notes that the country is so vast and diverse that public relations practice differs significantly in different regions of Russia. As the capital city, Moscow is Russia's hub of politics and business and therefore "a leading center for the development of public relations." However, most of the other areas of Russia "continue to struggle to inculcate strategic public relations practices in business mostly because the phenomenon is neither widely known, nor recognized, by leaders of business and government and by publics"—though this is changing (Tsetsura, 2009, p. 604).

Tsetsura (2004, p. 339) notes that Russian practitioners often use Western terms such as "press release" and "publicity" and reports that

> in media relations, Western techniques of developing and distributing press releases are quite successful when used to appeal to Moscow and St Petersburg journalists and editors, while interpersonal techniques and personal friendship as well as personal visits are more helpful in getting publicity in the media published outside of this region, such as in the European part of Russia or the Urals.

A study of practitioners across Russia likewise found that, in the richer parts of the country, public relations practice tends to be "rational and technological" and to use strategies developed in the West, while in poorer regions of the country, practitioners are more creative with their limited resources. The latter practitioners "believed 'true Russian PR' reflects 'the Russian essence'— emotionality and unpredictability" (Erzikova, 2012, p. 456).

The Russian metaregion of Central Siberia is rich in natural resources, including gas and oil. Practitioners there are involved in financial relations and lobbying. However, "their primary focus continues to be on positive publicity (press agentry model) rather than strategic public relations" (Tsetsura, 2009, pp. 607–608). In the European metaregion—in the Northern, Central, Central Black-Soil, and Southern areas of the country—business has been growing, but organizations have been reticent to practice public relations and those larger businesses that have engaged in public relations have tended to focus on publicity (Tsetsura, 2009, pp. 601, 608). The lack of economic growth in other parts of the country has hindered the practice of public relations (Tsetsura, 2009, p. 608).

Overall, practicing public relations in Russia is challenging. First, many practitioners are overtaxed and do not enjoy high standing within their organizations. Tsetsura (2009, p. 608) reports that

> although many companies can afford to have public relations practitioners, only a few actually hire more than one professional. This one person is responsible for all aspects of the public relations practices of the organization from technical aspects such as writing press-releases to conceptualizing and implementing strategic campaigns . . . because very often organizational decision makers (the dominant coalition) do not appreciate the benefits of strategic public relations management. Most senior managers consider public relations to be a technical rather than strategic function [and] one that is not so crucial to the effectiveness of the organization.

Second, it can be difficult to access and influence the press due to self-censorship by media outlets which feel financial and legal pressure from both the Kremlin (the name for the official residence of the Russian president, which is often used to refer to the country's government) and from corporations (Tsetsura, 2009, p. 613). The Russian state itself directly controls much of the country's media. Freedom House (2014) notes that

> the state owns, either directly or through proxies—including Gazprom Media, an arm of the state-owned energy giant Gazprom; and National Media Group, owned by Yuriy Kovalchuk, a close ally of [President] Putin and board chairman of Rossiya Bank, one of the largest banks in Russia—all five of the major national television networks, as well as national radio networks, important national newspapers, and national news agencies. It also controls more than 60 percent of the country's estimated 45,000 regional and local newspapers and periodicals. State-run television is the main news source for most Russians and generally serves as a propaganda tool of the government, while the newspapers and radio stations with the largest audiences largely focus on entertainment content. The government also owns RT, an international, multilingual satellite news network, which generally seeks to promote the Kremlin's take on global events.

The Russian government controls the editorial policies of state-run outlets. In Russian provinces, local governments actually pay the media to portray governors and other officials favorably (Erzikova, 2012, p. 456). While there are some independent media outlets—mostly aimed at the country's urban elite—that foster political debate, journalists criticize the government at their own risk (Freedom House, 2014). Freedom House (2014) notes that "politicians and government officials frequently use the country's politicized and corrupt court system to harass the few remaining independent journalists who criticize widespread abuses by the authorities." Reporters in the country have been subject to physical attacks and even murder. Businesses also reportedly fear advertising in media outlets that are critical of the Kremlin (Freedom House, 2014). Some businesses in Russian provinces actually choose not to pitch stories to the media because they fear that the governor will suspect that the business' leaders "want to challenge him by appearing as successful leaders" (Erzikova, 2012, p. 456).

Alexandra Konysheva, a Moscow-based Communications Manager for the Russian educational consulting company IViKO Consult, explains that

> TV networks are the most censored media [in Russia], as TV is the main news source for most Russians. Anyone, however, can watch Western channels on cable TV—which is rather affordable. So, for those who speak foreign languages, it is not a problem to watch the BBC or CNN. Newspapers are subject to government control to a much lesser degree. And online media outlets are practically completely overlooked by the government, while becoming more and more influential. Also, one can access pretty much all the Western media outlets online. Unlike China, none of the Western media web resources are blocked or have limited access. The same applies to social media, which have become an alternative source of information and platform for discussing various political topics in Russia.

Konysheva advises reaching out to the country's influential bloggers as part of any public relations strategy. "Bloggers are a strong political force and a source of information in Russia nowadays," she says. "There are bloggers that have thousands of followers and in a way are more influential than official media."

When you do pitch the Russian press, expect to be asked for payments. Paying journalists to publish information—a practice called *zakazukha* in Russian—is a widespread practice in Russia. One study by a Russian public relations firm found that more than half of Russian national newspapers and magazines would accept a payment of between U.S. $200-$2,000 to publish a press release, without even verifying the accuracy of its contents (Freitag & Stokes, 2009, p. 253).

Public relations practitioners are also notorious for their sometimes unethical practices in Russia, which has led to the notion of "black PR"—a term used to describe practices such as manipulation and deceit, typically in the context of political campaigns, in Russia, Ukraine, and Poland (Freitag & Stokes, 2009, p. 254). Of course, many scholars do not consider so-called "black PR" to be public relations, at all (Tsetsura, 2009, p. 605). Nevertheless, a major challenge is that many practitioners in Russia believe that international ethical codes of public relations are "idealistic and not practical in the Russian environment" (Tsetsura, 2009, p. 605). Tsetsura (2009, p. 606) reports that

> many Russian practitioners would readily admit that they do not always practice ethical public relations as presented in the code of ethics of the Russian Public Relations Association. They present what in their view is a plausible excuse for ignoring ethical considerations in their professional practice by citing differences in the mentality of Russian society. . . . Many of them simply say it is impossible to practice ethical public relations because nobody would pay for it.

Erzikova (2012, p. 456) likewise notes that "economic dependency, coupled with the constraints of the command system, forces practitioners to get the job done at any expense."

An additional challenge is that, given its Soviet history, there is not a tradition in Russia of information being openly and widely shared with the public, and organizations may attempt to cover up problems rather than being transparent (Tsetsura, 2009, p. 606). The Soviet legacy also means that there is not a strong history of activism in the country (Tsetsura, 2009, p. 608).

Another obstacle is Russian law. The country's media law states that reporters may not be paid to publish material, while its advertising law makes it illegal to promote products or services in the media without statements identifying the material as advertising. However, outside of the major cities of Moscow and St. Petersburg, officials of the Antimonopoly Committee so misunderstand public relations that they sometimes consider articles written based upon press releases to be "hidden advertising" and send reporters legal warnings (Tsetsura, 2009, p. 609).

Media

Russia is home to a large media. News agencies include the state-owned Tass and privately owned Interfax (BBC, 2014b).

Daily newspapers include the government-owned *Rossiyskaya Gazeta* and privately owned newspapers including *Nezavisimaya Gazeta, Komsomolskaya Pravda* and *Trud*, the business-focused *Kommersant*, and the popular *Moskovsky Komsomolets* and *Izvestia* (BBC, 2014b). The English-language *Moscow Times* is the most successful foreign language paper (Freitag & Stokes, 2009, p. 252).

Most Russians get their news from television. Russia One and Channel One are state-owned. NTV is nominally independent but is controlled by Gazprom-Media, a subsidiary of the large energy company that the *New York Times Magazine* has described as "all but a government ministry." The Magazine notes that "executives from all three companies regularly meet with

Kremlin officials" (Shteyngart, 2015). Centre TV is operated by the city government in Moscow. The privately owned Ren TV has a major regional network (BBC, 2014b).

Radio outlets include the state-run Radio Russia and Radio Mayak, along with Ekho Moskvy (which is run independently but majority-owned by the state) and the private, music focused Russkoye Radio (BBC, 2014b).

Russia is home to Europe's largest number of Internet users (Kritsch, 2014). One of the most popular online sources of news is Lenta.ru (BBC, 2014b).

Forty-six percent of Russians have active social media accounts. The most popular social networks are Vkontakte—a hugely popular platform that is similar to Facebook and is also popular in other countries in the region, such as Ukraine and Belarus—and Odnoklassniki, which helps users connect with old friends, followed by Facebook (Kemp, 2015).

References

AFP. (2014a). AFP in dates. Retrieved from http://www.afp.com/en/agency/afp-history/

AFP. (2014b). AFP in numbers. Retrieved from http://www.afp.com/en/agency/afp-in-numbers/

Alexa. (2014). Top sites in Sweden. Retrieved from http://www.alexa.com/topsites/countries;0/SE

BBC News Europe. (2012a, March 19). Germany country profile. Retrieved from http://news.bbc.co.uk/2/hi/europe/country_profiles/1047864.stm

BBC News Europe. (2012b, May 4). Sweden profile. Retrieved from http://www.bbc.com/news/world-europe-17961251

BBC News Europe. (2012c, December 18). United Kingdom profile. Retrieved from http://www.bbc.com/news/world-europe-18027956

BBC News Europe. (2013, February 13). Italy profile. Retrieved from http://www.bbc.com/news/world-europe-17433146

BBC News Europe. (2014a, January 12). France profile. Retrieved from http://www.bbc.com/news/world-europe-17299010

BBC News Europe. (2014b, November 28). Russia profile. Retrieved from http://www.bbc.com/news/world-europe-17840134

Bentele, G., & Junghänel, I. (2004). Germany. In B. van Ruler & D. Verčič (Eds.), *Public relations and communication management in Europe* (pp. 153–168). Berlin: Mouton de Gruyter.

Bentele, G., & Wehmeier, S. (2009). From literary bureaus to a modern profession: The development and current structure of public relations in Germany. In K. Sriramesh & D. Verčič (Eds.), *The global public relations handbook: Theory, research, and practice* (2nd ed.) (pp. 407–429). New York, NY: Routledge.

Bernasconi, S. (2013, August 1). Social media landscapes: Italy. *Ketchum*. Retrieved from http://kpg-digital-blog.de/social-media-landscapes-italy/

Bulldog Reporter. (2014, May 30). Global PR: Do you think your CEO is prepared to be interviewed by European journalists? Execs should expect different media practices, reports new study by PRGN. Retrieved from http://www.bulldogreporter.com/dailydog/article/pr-biz-update/global-pr-do-you-think-your-ceo-is-prepared-to-be-interviewed-by-euro

Carayol, V. (2004). France. In B. van Ruler & D. Verčič (Eds.), *Public relations and communication management in Europe* (pp. 135–151). Berlin: Mouton de Gruyter.

Central Intelligence Agency (CIA). (2014). World factbook. Retrieved from https:// www.cia.gov/library/publications/the-world-factbook/

Chartered Institute of Public Relations. (2014). *CIPR state of the profession survey 2013/14*. Retrieved from http://www.cipr.co.uk/sites/default/files/J9825_CIPR_State OfTheProfession_2014_V10_AW.pdf

Chinowith, E. (2010, July). *France*. Global Alliance for Public Relations and Communication Management. Retrieved from http://www.globalalliancepr.org/website/ sites/default/files/globalalliance/pr-landscape-france.pdf

Emarketer. (2009, May 28). Online branding with a French flair. Retrieved from http:// www.emarketer.com/Article/Online-Branding-with-French-Flair/1007102

Erzikova, E. (2012). Practitioners in Russia's provinces: Affectionate and unpredictable. *Public Relations Review*, 38(3), 454–457.

Flodin, B. (2004). Sweden. In B. van Ruler & D. Verčič (Eds.), *Public relations and communication management in Europe* (pp. 413–423). Berlin: Mouton de Gruyter.

Flodin, B. (2009). Public relations in Sweden: A strong presence increasing in importance. In K. Sriramesh & D. Verčič (Eds.), *The global public relations handbook: Theory, research, and practice* (2nd ed.) (pp. 471–483). New York, NY: Routledge.

Freedom House. (2014). *Freedom of the press: Russia*. Retrieved from https://freedomhouse.org/report/freedom-press/2014/russia#.VKCe1f8LcgA

Freitag, A. R., & Stokes, A. Q. (2009). *Global public relations: Spanning borders, spanning cultures*. New York, NY: Routledge.

Frith-Powell, H. (2006, June 20). Is Sweden the most boring country in world? *Daily Mail*. Retrieved from http://www.dailymail.co.uk/news/article-391602/Is-Sweden-boring-country-world.html

Giomi, E. (2015). Media landscapes: Italy. *European Journalism Centre*. Retrieved from http://ejc.net/media_landscapes/italy

Gupta, V., & Hanges, P. J. (2004). Regional and climate clustering of societal clusters. In R. J. House, P. J. Hanges, M. Javidan, P. W. Dorfman, & V. Gupta (Eds.), *Culture, leadership, and organizations: The GLOBE study of 62 societies* (pp. 178–218). Thousand Oaks, CA: Sage.

Haberman, S. (2012, June 12). Sweden Twitter experiment goes painfully awry. *Mashable*. Retrieved from http://mashable.com/2012/06/12/sweden-twitter/

Hill, K. (2012, June 13). Why did Sweden hand its national Twitter account over to a troll? *Forbes*. Retrieved from http://www.forbes.com/sites/kashmirhill/2012/06/13/ why-did-sweden-hand-its-national-twitter-account-over-to-a-troll/

Hines, R. (2009). German public relations. *PRism*, 6(2), 1–9.

Hinner, M. B. (2009). Culture's influence on business as illustrated by German business culture. *China Media Research*, 5(2), 45–54.

The Holmes Report. (2015). Global top 250 PR firms 2015. Retrieved from http:// www.holmesreport.com/ranking-and-data/world-pr-report/agency-rankings-2015/ top-250

Holmström, S. (2004). The reflective paradigm of public relations. In B. van Ruler & D. Verčič (Eds.), *Public relations and communication management in Europe* (pp. 121–133). Berlin: Mouton de Gruyter.

Holt, A., Sierra, A., Vaughn, D., Winston, E., & Copeland, V. (2013). *Sweden: PR country landscape*. Global Alliance for Public Relations and Communication Management. Retrieved from http://www.globalalliancepr.org/website/sites/default/files/ nolie/PR%20Landscapes/Sweden-2013.pdf

Howard, C. M., & Mathews, W. K. (2013). *On deadline: Managing media relations* (5th ed.). Long Grove, IL: Waveland Press.

Inter-Parliamentary Union. (2014, 1 November). Women in national parliaments. Retrieved from http://www.ipu.org/wmn-e/classif.htm

Kemp, S. (2015, January 21). Digital, social & mobile worldwide in 2015. *We Are Social*. Retrieved from http://wearesocial.net/blog/2015/01/digital-social-mobile-worldwide-2015/

Killian, E. (2011, August 8). Parental leave: The Swedes are the most generous. *NPR*. Retrieved from http://www.npr.org/blogs/babyproject/2011/08/09/139121410/parental-leave-the-swedes-are-the-most-generous

Kritsch, A. (2014). The state of social media in Russia. *Hootsuite*. Retrieved from http://blog.hootsuite.com/social-media-in-russia/

Kullin, H. (2011, September 8). 55 fascinating facts about social media in Sweden. *Social Media Today*. Retrieved from http://www.socialmediatoday.com/content/55-fascinating-facts-about-social-media-sweden

Ławniczak, R. (2004). The transitional approach to public relations. In B. van Ruler & D. Verčič (Eds.), *Public relations and communication management in Europe* (pp. 217–226). Berlin: Mouton de Gruyter.

Lewis PR. (2013). Global media guide. Retrieved from http://publish.lewispr.com/globalmediaguide/LEWIS_Global_Media_Guide.pdf

Livermore, D. (2013). *Expand your borders: Discover ten cultural clusters.* East Lansing, MI: Cultural Intelligence Center.

Lyall, S. (2012, June 10). Swedes' Twitter voice: Anyone, saying (blush) almost anything. *The New York Times*. Retrieved from http://www.nytimes.com/2012/06/11/world/europe/many-voices-of-sweden-via-twitter.html?_r=3&

Mattinson, A. (2014a, February 24). Postcard from Russia. *PR Week*. Retrieved from http://www.prweek.com/article/1282027/postcard-russia

Mattinson, A. (2014b, May 21). Postcard from Sweden. *PR Week*. Retrieved from http://www.prweek.com/article/1293096/postcard-sweden

Mueller, S. (2009). The nexus of U.S. public diplomacy and citizen diplomacy. In N. Snow & P. M. Taylor (Eds.), *Routledge handbook of public diplomacy* (pp. 101–107). New York, NY: Routledge.

Muzi Falconi, T. (2009). Public relations in Italy: Master of ceremonies in a relational society. In K. Sriramesh & D. Verčič (Eds.), *The global public relations handbook: Theory, research, and practice* (2nd ed.) (pp. 484–502). New York, NY: Routledge.

Muzi Falconi, T., & Kodilja, R. (2004). Italy. In B. van Ruler & D. Verčič (Eds.), *Public relations and communication management in Europe* (pp. 227–244). Berlin: Mouton de Gruyter.

Pasquier, M., & Lamizet, B. (2015). Media landscapes: France. *European Journalism Centre*. Retrieved from http://ejc.net/media_landscapes/france

Rand McNally. (2014). Q: Which continent is Russia mostly in? Retrieved from http://education.randmcnally.com/classroom/action/getABNArchive.do?showSingleAnswer=true&abnQuestionId=0042

Reporters Without Borders. (2014). World Press Freedom Index 2014. Retrieved from http://rsf.org/index2014/en-index2014.php

Ronalds-Hannon, E. (2013, August 15). @Sweden's odd Twitter experiment has been a multimillion dollar boon for tourism. *The Week*. Retrieved from http://theweek.com/articles/461071/swedens-odd-twitter-experiment-been-multimillion-dollar-boon-tourism

Shteyngart, G. (2015, February 18). Out of my mouth comes unimpeachable manly truth. *New York Times Magazine*. Retrieved from http://www.nytimes.com/2015/02/22/magazine/out-of-my-mouth-comes-unimpeachable-manly-truth.html?smid=tw-nytmag&_r=0

Sky News. (2015). Sky news radio. Retrieved from http://news.sky.com/info/radio

Stoll, J. D., & Heron, L. (2012, June 12). Sweden stands by Twitter strategy despite controversy. *The Wall Street Journal*. Retrieved from http://blogs.wsj.com/dispatch/2012/06/12/sweden-stands-by-twitter-strategy-despite-controversy/

Sudhaman, A. (2010, February 19). Focus on . . . France. *PR Week*. Retrieved from http://www.prweek.com/article/985101/focus-on-france

Sudhaman, A., & Hay, P. (2010, March 29). Focus on. . . Germany. *PR Week*. Retrieved from http://www.prweek.com/article/993161/focus-ongermany

Tsetsura, K. (2004). Russia. In B. van Ruler & D. Verčič (Eds.), *Public relations and communication management in Europe* (pp. 331–346). Berlin: Mouton de Gruyter.

Tsetsura, K. (2009). The development of public relations in Russia: A geopolitical approach. In K. Sriramesh & D. Verčič (Eds.), *The global public relations handbook: Theory, research, and practice* (2nd ed.) (pp. 600–618). New York, NY: Routledge.

Valentini, C., & Sriramesh, K. (2014). To be, or not to be: Paradoxes in strategic public relations in Italy. *Public Relations Review, 40*(1), 3–13.

van Ruler, B., & Verčič, D. (2004). Overview of public relations and communication management in Europe. In B. van Ruler & D. Verčič (Eds.), *Public relations and communication management in Europe* (pp. 1–11). Berlin: Mouton de Gruyter.

Verčič, D., van Ruler, B., Bütschi, G., & Flodin, B. (2001). On the definition of public relations: A European view. *Public Relations Review, 27*(4), 373–387.

Wasserman, T. (2012, June 12). Why Sweden was right to hand over its Twitter account. *Mashable*. Retrieved from http://mashable.com/2012/06/12/sweden-was-right-twitter/

Weber Shandwick. (2010, Autumn). *33&A third RPM*. Retrieved from http://www.webershandwick.de/download/33-3-ISSUE6-AW.pdf

Weibull, L., Jönsson, A. M., & Wadbring, I. (2015). Media landscapes: Sweden. *European Journalism Centre*. Retrieved from http://ejc.net/media_landscapes/sweden

White, J., L'etang, J., & Moss, D. (2009). The United Kingdom: Advances in practice in a restless kingdom. In K. Sriramesh & D. Verčič (Eds.), *The global public relations handbook: Theory, research, and practice* (2nd ed.) (pp. 381–406). New York, NY: Routledge.

World Bank. (2014). GDP. Retrieved from http://data.worldbank.org/indicator/NY.GDP.MKTP.CD?order=wbapi_data_value_2013+wbapi_data_value+wbapi_data_valuelast&sort=desc

Zerfass, A., Verčič, D., Verhoeven, P., Moreno, A., & Tench, R. (2015). *European communication monitor 2015*. European Public Relations Education and Research Association and the European Association of Communication Directors. Retrieved from http://www.zerfass.de/ECM-WEBSITE/media/ECM2015-Results-ChartVersion.pdf

10 Public Relations in the Middle East and North Africa

Welcome to the Middle East and North Africa—birthplace of many of the world's major religions, including Christianity, Islam, and Judaism. Like most regions, the area commonly referred to as "MENA" is characterized by enormous diversity. Crossing the continents of Africa and Asia, the region is home to people who speak numerous languages, from Arabic to French, and practice myriad religions. Many of the countries in the region—including Saudi Arabia, Iran, Iraq, and the United Arab Emirates—enjoy significant oil resources.

MENA too often makes global headlines because of volatility. In 2011, the "Arab Spring" swept the region, resulting in anti-government revolts in Tunisia, Egypt, Libya, and Syria. At the time of writing, Syria is still embroiled in a bloody, devastating civil war and the other post-Arab Spring countries experience varying levels of instability. The more than six-decade-old conflict between Israel and Palestine resulted in the deaths of more than 2,200 people during the summer of 2014 alone. A terrorist organization called the Islamic State of Iraq and al-Sham (ISIS) has gone on a violent rampage across

Iraq and Syria as well as parts of Libya, massacring and enslaving civilians and beheading foreigners. The Taliban, an Islamic fundamentalist movement, continues to menace Afghanistan and in December 2014 attacked a school in Pakistan, killing 141 people—the majority of whom were children.

Another challenge facing the region is its "youth bulge." More than half of the population of the Middle East and North Africa is under the age of 25, and the region has the highest youth unemployment rate in the world (World Economic Forum, 2014, p. 4). However, there are also signs of progress—from the prosperous and stable United Arab Emirates, which has become a global media hub, to Qatar, where, as discussed in Chapter 7, Al Jazeera has revolutionized the region's media landscape.

With the exception of Israel, the countries of this region fall under the Middle East cultural cluster. This chapter will introduce you to four countries and territories in this cluster—Egypt, Palestine, Saudi Arabia, and the United Arab Emirates—before describing Israel, which the GLOBE study classifies under the Latin European cultural cluster (Gupta & Hanges, 2004, p. 184).

The Middle East Cluster

The GLOBE study identifies the most important feature of the Middle East cultural group as the influence of the religion of Islam. The study found that the culture is characterized by high in-group collectivism; moderate assertiveness, humane orientation, institutional collectivism, performance orientation, and power distance; and low future orientation, gender egalitarianism, and uncertainty avoidance—though other researchers report the culture to be high in uncertainty avoidance (Gupta & Hanges, 2004, p. 193; Al Kandari & Gaither, 2011, p. 269). Al-Kandari and Gaither (2011, p. 268) argue that the five most salient cultural characteristics of Arabs who are Muslim are their "commitment to religion, devotion to group, recognition of hierarchical order, resistance to change/attachment to history and sense of pride."

It is difficult to overstate the influence of Islam in this region of the world. For adherents of the religion, who are called Muslims, the most important pillar of their faith is that Allah is the only god and the prophet Mohammed, who lived from roughly 570 to 632 AD, was his messenger. It is a great offense to Muslims to desecrate their holy book, the Koran, or to speak poorly of the prophet, so you should ensure that you show respect for their religion. In 2015, terrorists attacked the Paris offices of the French satirical magazine *Charlie Hebdo*, which had satirized Mohammed and Islam (as well as other religions), killing eleven people. Similarly, in 1989, after British-Indian author Salman Rushdie wrote a fictional book with a storyline that the Ayatollah Ruhollah Khomeini of Iran deemed offensive to Islam, Khomeini issued a *fatwa*—or Islamic legal decree—calling for Muslims to murder the author. Although Rushdie went into hiding and survived, the furor led to deadly protests and bookstore bombings. Of course, the vast majority of Muslims are not extremists, but you should take extra care not to offend in this region of the world.

The four other pillars of Islam require the faithful to pray five times per day (in Muslim countries, you will hear the call to prayer broadcast from places of worship, called mosques, beginning early in the morning), to give alms to the poor, to fast during the day during the holy month of Ramadan (which falls during a different time each year), and to make a pilgrimage once in their lifetimes to the holy city of Mecca, in Saudi Arabia, where Mohammed is believed to have been born and where Allah is believed to have revealed the Koran to him. The two key denominations of Islam are Sunni and Shiite. The division between the two groups dates back to a split that occurred as the result of a disagreement over who would succeed Mohammed as leader of the Muslim community.

The Koran instructs women to dress modestly, and many women in this region of the world wear a *hijab* to cover their hair and chest. In some places, it is considered inappropriate for members of the opposite sex to interact with one another unless they are relatives. The degree of freedom accorded to women varies; in Saudi Arabia, for example, it is illegal for a woman to drive a car.

It is important to note that Muslims are strictly forbidden to eat pork or drink alcohol. Inviting a Muslim to do so—or to eat before sunset during Ramadan—would be considered offensive.

While the use of religious elements in public relations campaigns is inadvisable in other cultures, in the Arab world it may be effective, given the central role that religion plays in the identities and lives of so many people in the region (Kanso, Sinno, & Adams, 2001, p. 77). Al-Kandari and Gaither (2011, p. 271) note that

> practitioners should stress that a practice accords with the teachings of Allah. A message that includes religious elements might use dramatic elements and stories, both of which are consonant with Arab culture. In addition, ordinary Arab publics might perceive receiving ideas from Muslim-Arab interests employing religion in persuasive messages more favorably than if a non-Muslim or foreigner were to disseminate such messages.

A critical factor to be aware of in this region is that Friday and Saturday are the weekend, and people do not typically work on these days—in contrast to other regions in which the weekend falls on Saturday and Sunday. This is the case because Friday is the holy day when Muslims gather for prayer.

Of course, not all countries or peoples within this region are Muslim. Rana Nejem, Founding Director of the Jordanian cultural intelligence firm Yarnu, notes that

> Arab Christians, though a minority, are very prominent, practice their religion openly in churches, and hold very senior positions in government, business, and the armed forces in different countries across the Arab world—mainly, Lebanon, Jordan, Syria, Palestine, Egypt, and Iraq.

The importance of family in the Arab world can also hardly be overstated. Al-Kandari and Gaither (2011, pp. 268–269) note that "while Americans might change their jobs and residences for better opportunities, an Arab might stay where the family is. Islam states that individuals need to band together to achieve mutual welfare." Nejem says that this stems from the influence of the region's Bedouin and tribal culture and is also characteristic of non-Muslim Arabs. Accordingly, family and social commitments are prized and work is ranked somewhat less importantly in this culture than elsewhere in the world. Livermore (2013, p. 86) reports that, in some countries, parents can actually sue their children for not taking care of them! Arab families tend to be patriarchal; "the father maintains the ultimate authority in this pyramidal flow of power. The father expects total respect and obedience as long as he is the benefactor" (Al-Kandari & Gaither, 2011, p. 269). It is still typical for women to require approval from their father or husband before undertaking activities or decisions.

The importance of the family also extends to a broader emphasis on relationships in this collectivist culture. Furthermore, because of the Islamic tradition of almsgiving, "generosity and sharing with others are very strongly held values across the Arab cluster" (Livermore, 2013, p. 83). Arabs are famous for their hospitality (Feghali, 1997, p. 353). Therefore, in contrast to individualistic cultures where public relations practitioners should stress individuality and individual benefits, messages that emphasize group benefits will be particularly effective in this culture (Kanso et al., 2001, p. 75).

In accordance with this emphasis on relationships, the personal influence model is a central feature of Arab public relations practice and people with more social ties are afforded higher social esteem (Al-Kandari & Gaither, 2011, p. 271; Curtin & Gaither, 2004). Building relationships with reporters is therefore essential to successful media relations. Allen and Dozier (2012, p. 197) report that Arab journalists prefer to view their relationships with public affairs officers (PAOs) as communal, rather than as based simply upon information exchange. "The more that Arab journalists view their relationship with PAOs as an exchange relationship, the less their satisfaction . . . and trust."

In this relationship-oriented region of the world, engaging local influencers is also a particularly effective public relations strategy. Al-Kandari and Gaither (2011, p. 271) note that

> non-Arab practitioners are encouraged to engage with Arab political, religious, tribal and social leaders. Establishing ties with leaders might be helpful, if not in achieving change in attitudes of the people they exercise power over, then in keeping those people's attitudes or actions neutral. Non-Arab practitioners must know that they need to approach those leaders with great respect, showing their importance and influence on their trusted circle. Practitioners must never show to leaders that establishing relationships with them is done with the purpose of achieving specific goals, even if it is implicitly understood by both parties. Showing

such an intention might be harmful as it shows that the relationship is built on materialistic aims.

One of the reasons why community leaders are particularly influential in this region is because Arab culture is quite hierarchical. In contrast to cultures where youth is worshiped, Kanso et al. (2001, p. 73) point out that "in the Arab culture, the advice of older people is well received by the youth. Many campaigns aimed at Arab audiences have centered on such themes as 'seek the wisdom from the elderly,' and 'the experience of last generation.'" However, Nejem says that this is beginning to change with a younger generation that is more affected by the West and technology.

Arabs take great pride in their culture's history and accomplishments. Al Kandari and Gaither (2011, p. 272) note that

> non-Arab practitioners could use Arab and Islamic history to their advantage. They could bring the history alive and correlate it with intended changes. In fact, many Arab commercials use nostalgic appeal to connect with audiences, telling them how adopting a product or an attitude will return them to the past or that it resembles the choices of their ancestors.

Connected to this pride in the past is a resistance to change. Al Kandari and Gaither (2011, p. 269) note that "people in 'strong uncertainty avoidance' cultures, like the Arab culture, prefer the conventional sets of rules and structures." Nejem reports that

> Arab countries are eager to develop and modernize, but they fear losing their identities and becoming too Westernized. So a lot of resistance to change stems from this fear of losing the Arab and Islamic identity and that the change is imposed from the outside by the West.

Yet she notes that this is not universally the case—in Dubai, for example, as will later be discussed, change is happening at breakneck speed. However, if promoting innovation or change is critical to a public relations campaign, it may take some extra work to convince audiences in this region. Al Kandari and Gaither (2011, p. 272) suggest that practitioners

> might highlight an innovation as consistent with Arab heritage and religion to ease concerns. . . . Non-Arab practitioners might draw upon the Arab heritage and Islamic teachings that change is important and that Prophet Muhammad, for example, encouraged change. For example, a verse from [the] Koran encourages change: "Allah may never bring change to people until they change themselves."

A related characteristic is the present orientation of Arab culture. Livermore (2013, p. 86) notes that, in this region, "life is approached somewhat passively," because many Arabs believe that things that happen are the will of Allah and thus cannot be controlled or changed (Al-Kandari & Gaither, 2011, p. 270). One phrase you will hear often in this part of the world is *inshallah*, meaning "God willing." Furthermore, the culture takes a polychronic approach to time. Feghali (1997, p. 366) notes that "simultaneous involvements are common. For example, if one is meeting with the manager of an office during a prearranged appointment, the manager may accept frequent phone calls, interruptions and extended visits from others at the same time."

Also, because Arabs have a great deal of pride, it is important to provide criticism very carefully. Al Kandari and Gaither (2011, p. 272) note that "in Arab culture, criticism is usually perceived as personal and harmful. Negative assessment or criticism of an Arab, especially in front of others, is degrading and considered as shameful to someone's reputation in society." Accordingly, if it is necessary to convey negative feedback, "it should be approached carefully, discreetly and behind closed doors." However, in contrast to some Asian cultures, providing public praise is appreciated. "Arabs like it if someone applauds them in front of others as it accords a higher social status to that individual" (Al Kandari & Gaither, 2001, p. 272).

Related to this concept of pride, honor is very important in Arab societies. Nejem explains that

> like other honor driven cultures, people in the Arab world place a higher value on the community as opposed to the individual. Hence, people feel they do not only represent themselves but the entire community or group they belong to. According to the situation, that group or community could be the family or tribe, the organization, or a group of people who share a specific background or status within an organization. The group becomes a support mechanism for the individual in both the good and difficult times. But the group also holds the individual accountable for his behavior, ideas, and decisions and determines whether a person's behavior is honorable or shameful.

In the Arab region, expected emotional responses can differ significantly from those in other parts of the world. For example, while U.S. audiences expect people on television news to be "emotionally cool or reserved" (as will be discussed in the following chapter), Zaharna (2005, p. 195) notes that the opposite is true in this region:

> In the Arab world, a variety of factors contribute to a preference for an emotionally expressive and engaging on-screen presence. First, because of the nature of Arab families and group social habits, television watching tends to be a group experience. It also tends to be an active experience, with the audience often commenting more than the television commentators. The physical distance between the viewers and television is not intimate but rather public, usually ten feet or more. Televisions in public

settings, such as cafes, are common with a distance of up to twenty feet. Finally, compared with the dominant Anglo-American culture, the Arab culture is more emotionally expressive and more accepting of emotional expression. This combination of group viewing patterns, group interaction, physical distance and greater emotional expression tend to favor an on-screen presence that is emotionally engaging.

Zaharna (1995) explains that the emphasis on emotion in Arab communication stems from the fact that the Arab region has a history of oral, rather than written, communication. Furthermore, the Arabic language has been used historically as a form of art—especially poetry—and as a tool for promoting Arab identity, and is believed to have been selected by Allah (God) to reveal the Koran. Therefore, whereas the purpose of communicating in the English language is often simply to share facts, in the Arabic language, "rather than viewing language as a means for transferring information with a stress on factual accuracy, language appears to be a social conduit in which emotional resonance is stressed" (Zaharna, 1995, pp. 245–246). Zaharna (1995, p. 253) notes that

> for the Arab culture, language appears to be a social tool used in the weaving of society. Emphasis is on form over function, affect over accuracy, and image over meaning. Accordingly, content may be less important than the social chemistry a message creates.

As a result of this oral and social tradition, the Arabic language is characterized by the use of repetition, heavy imagery, symbolism, and what Westerners may consider to be exaggeration (Zaharna, 1995, p. 248). The Arab culture is high-context; "much is left implicit and unstated" (Al-Kandari & Gaither, 2011, p. 268).

As a result of this expectation for emotion, people from the U.S., for example, often come across as "wooden and stiff" on Arab television. This is particularly problematic because Arabs view people who are unemotional as "not fully presenting the situation—and thus less than truthful and not credible" (Zaharna, 2005, p. 195). It is therefore critical to train foreign spokespeople to speak passionately in media interviews in this region—or, better yet, to use local spokespeople. Al-Kandari and Gaither (2011, p. 271) note that "emotional appeals are more likely to be persuasive to Arabs than logical appeals." When crafting messages for this region, you should work "to engage the imagination and feelings of the audience" (Kanso et al., 2001, p. 72).

Furthermore, because the Arab world is an oral society, printed materials are viewed differently here than in other cultures. Kanso et al. (2001, pp. 73–74) note that

> a brochure with 'style' for an American may have a single, dramatic image on the cover, lots of white space, consistency in the typeface, and balanced lines and images. In contrast, a brochure with 'style' in the Arab culture would focus more on utilizing the space to include more content.

Similarly, while in many other countries press releases are expected to include new announcements, "Arabic press releases serve more as position papers, providing background on events or ideology" (Kanso et al., 2001, p. 74).

Fawaz Al Sirri, founder of the Kuwaiti public relations agency Bensirri PR, says the true "king of the land" in this region of the world is the Arabic language. Al Sirri therefore advises practitioners to develop their messages in Arabic from the start, because it is extremely difficult to translate between Arabic and other languages (McDowell, 2012). Zaharna (1995, p. 250) explains that "trying to translate literally, or even 'thinking in Arabic and writing in English,' produces sentences that are a paragraph in length, have little or no punctuation, and abound with compound and complex sentence structures and LOTS of adjectives." The same difficulties of translation apply in reverse when attempting to translate other languages into Arabic. Al Sirri explains:

> I keep seeing really good PR pros come to town and build good communication strategies that quickly become duds because they don't translate well into Arabic, in terms of approach and content. What's even more shocking is that I keep seeing PR firms developing press content in English first, and then translating it into Arabic. Then they get disappointed when clients and editors reject their content because of poor writing (McDowell, 2012).

Furthermore, despite the common language of many Arab countries, Al Sirri cautions against adopting a unified approach for the entire region, given the diversity of its countries. He explains:

> In my home town of Kuwait for example, business editors love well-written market insights and thought leadership stories. That's because their journalists are busy covering the stock market, which is what the readers want, and therefore have less time to write in- depth articles. On the other hand, NGO, CSR, and community-engagement stories don't get much traction. Whereas in Jordan, those types of stories, including entrepreneurship stories, do go a long way and truly engage your audience. Why? That's because the national agenda is different from one country to another. The same is true for other countries in the Middle East, including Saudi Arabia where stories about human development, grand employment initiatives, and women empowerment topics are on the agenda (McDowell, 2012).

Nevertheless, as a rule, Al Sirri recommends pitching business, financial, and political stories to Arab daily newspapers—which, unlike in other parts of the world, continue to grow in circulation and to have the financial resources to cover political news. Because blogs tend to be written by younger authors and to be less well-resourced, he recommends pitching them consumer and lifestyle stories. Finally, he notes that women's discussion forums are some of the most highly trafficked websites in the region, so they should be included in public relations strategies targeted at women (McDowell, 2012).

There is a strong regional press in the Arab world, with numerous media outlets reaching a pan-Arab audience, including the broadcasters Al Jazeera, Al Arabiya, BBC Arabic, France 24, Russia Today (known in Arabic as Rusiya Al-Yaum), and Sky News Arabia (all discussed in Chapter 7). The London-based newspapers *Asharq al-Aswat* and *Al-Hayat*, controlled by the Saudi royal family, have the highest pan-Arab circulation (Freedom House, 2014d; Dubai Press Club, 2012). *Elaph* is a popular pan-Arab online newspaper, also based in London.

The region's large youth population uses social media, online videos, and mobile applications heavily, so strategies for such platforms are a must in this market (Dubai Press Club, 2012, p. 19). Studies conducted in Egypt, Morocco, Saudi Arabia, and the United Arab Emirates find that the average amount of time people in these countries spend online is now at least as high or higher than the amount of time they spend watching television (Dubai Press Club, 2012, p. 8). The most popular platforms in the region are Facebook, YouTube, and Twitter (Dubai Press Club, 2012, p. 224).

The month of Ramadan is a particularly good time to try to achieve broadcast media coverage, since television audiences increase significantly during this time (Flanagan, 2012; Keenan, 2009, p. 371). However, media censorship continues to limit the types of stories that public relations practitioners can place in the region's press. Freedom House (2014a, pp. 13, 16) ranks just one country in the region—Israel—as enjoying a free press and says that four countries in the region—Algeria, Kuwait, Lebanon, and Tunisia—have presses that are "partly free," while the remaining 74 percent of countries in the region have presses that are not free. The lack of press freedom is a legacy of authoritarian rule and the ongoing fight against terrorism and radicalization. Zayani (2005, p. 14) reports that

> in the Arab world, the media in general, and satellite channels in particular, operate under a patron who is either the government or some rich owner who in many cases is associated, in one way or another, with the ruling elite or the government. Most television systems in the Arab world are subsidized by the government partly because they need a great deal of money and partly because Arab governments have a stake in the media. Historically such monopolies go hand in hand with centralization; they help maintain a country's unity, preserve a centralized system of government and exercise control over the people. TV also serves as a propaganda tool, an extension of state power and a mouthpiece for state policies, and control of such an apparatus ensures that dissident voices do not have access to the public.

However, Nejem notes that a large number of privately owned media, including satellite television stations, radio stations, and online news portals, have recently sprung up across the Arab world—many of which are owned by businesspeople. "Censorship and control over the media varies from one country to the other," she says. "Egypt, Lebanon, and Kuwait are known for their strong and relatively professional media." Furthermore, Louay Al Samarrai, Managing Director of the Dubai-based Active Digital Marketing Communications, says that while media coverage of political and social issues is not transparent in the Arab region, business stories are generally not contentious or subject to censorship.

The GLOBE study found that Israel falls under the Latin European culture described in Chapter 9 and that countries such as Iran and Pakistan (which are both largely Muslim) correspond most closely to the Southern Asian cultural group described in Chapter 8 (Gupta & Hanges, 2004, p. 191). The next sections profile public relations in five markets: Egypt, Palestine, Saudi Arabia, the United Arab Emirates, and Israel.

Egypt

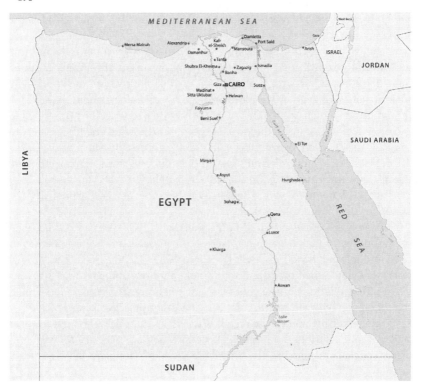

Copyright: Rainer Lesniewski

Time zone: Coordinated Universal Time (UTC) + 2:00
International dialing code: +20

When you practice public relations in Egypt, be prepared to change your plans. The most populous country in the region and a critical player in regional affairs, Egypt spans the most northeastern part of Africa and extends into Asia. The Egyptian people mostly live along the Nile River in this country that is largely made up of desert; the country borders the Mediterranean Sea in the north. Ninety percent of the Egyptian people are Muslim (predominantly Sunni), while 10 percent are Christian (predominantly Coptic) (CIA, 2014).

The country famously made peace with neighboring Israel in 1979. In 2011, Egyptians took to the streets in protest against the three-decade rule of President Hosni Mubarak, who resigned. Since then, the country has struggled to achieve political stability. Egypt elected a new president in 2012—the candidate of the Muslim Brotherhood, a large Islamic movement in the country. However, after large protests, the new president was removed in a military coup in 2013, and the military authorities cracked down violently on the Brotherhood, banning the organization and declaring it to be a terrorist group. In 2014, Egypt created a new Constitution and the former head of the Egyptian Armed Forces was elected president.

Although the country has a diversified economy—earning revenue from agricultural exports, oil, remittances from expatriate Egyptians working abroad, the Suez Canal, tourism, and aid (predominantly from the U.S.)—the majority of the Egyptian people have faced poor living conditions and job opportunities, which has fed the country's unrest (Keenan, 2009, p. 368; CIA, 2014). The political instability has, of course, further weakened Egypt's economy and made many organizations hesitant to invest in the country (CIA, 2014; Saleh, 2014). Egypt's capital is Cairo, its currency is the Egyptian pound, its official religion is Islam, and its official language is Arabic, though both English and French are widely understood among educated Egyptians (CIA, 2014; Freedom House, 2014b).

Although the privatization of businesses that began in the 1970s did open opportunities for public relations practice, the profession remains underdeveloped and misunderstood in Egypt (Keenan, 2009, pp. 365, 368). Hay (2010) notes that the "general lack of understanding of how comms works" has hindered public relations in the country. Many organizations do not understand the difference between public relations and other practices such as advertising and marketing, and "most organizations consider sales to be the primary goal of public relations, and there is little interest in or patience for programs or tactics that do not directly contribute to sales" (Keenan, 2009, p. 365). Keenan (2009, p. 365) reports that

in Egypt, public relations is often synonymous with hospitality or customer relations. The industry that is probably most associated with public relations jobs is the service industry. Hotels employ public relations directors responsible for guest services such as arranging airport transportation, hosting dignitaries, and generally putting on a 'smiling and friendly face' on behalf of the organization.

Practitioners are often not part of dominant coalitions, and organizations often do not recognize the full value that public relations can offer (Keenan, 2009, p. 366). However, things are changing. In particular, the 2011 revolution transformed the practice of public relations. Hossam Zakaria, Managing Director of the Cairo-based agency Fresh PR, says that while public relations practitioners focused mostly on media relations before the revolution, they have now branched out considerably. Because many companies seek to reach the country's large youth population, social media platforms—especially Facebook, Twitter, and YouTube—are critical. Zakaria says that bloggers have also become a critical constituency. "Before Egyptians buy anything, they read about it," Zakaria says. Therefore, when his clients launch new consumer products, he typically gives bloggers opportunities to test and write about them.

Zakaria says that, while before the revolution practitioners focused primarily on influencing three government-owned newspapers—*Al-Ahram*, *Al-Akhbar* and *Al-Jumhuriyah*—today, these papers are less trusted and the emphasis is on privately owned newspapers, especially the influential *Al-Misri al-Yawm*, *Alwatan*, and *Youm7*. However, even after the Egyptian revolution, press "censorship, both official and self-imposed, is widespread;" numerous reporters have been arrested for allegedly "insulting the president" (Freedom House, 2014b). In 2013, Egypt arrested and imprisoned three Al Jazeera journalists for what Al Jazeera (2014) calls "false charges" of helping the Muslim Brotherhood and promulgating false news, despite pressure from the White House, European Union, British Foreign and Commonwealth Office, Australian government, and more than 150 rights groups around the world to release them. *The New York Times* reports that, today, the Egyptian media continues to limit its criticism of the government; "television programs known for showing opposing views in the past three years or more have quietly gone off the air. The private Egyptian news media has spoken in virtually unanimous support of the current government" (Kirkpatrick & Thomas, 2014).

Another major problem in Egypt is that journalists often expect either to be paid outright for stories or for advertising to be purchased alongside editorial coverage (Keenan, 2009, p. 365; Hay, 2010). The Egyptian legal system is notoriously slow and inefficient and, because the Mubarak regime cracked down on dissent, there is not a history of a vibrant civil society in Egypt or a tradition of openness and transparency. Furthermore, because more than a quarter of Egyptian adults are illiterate, the population cannot be reached through print media alone (CIA, 2014).

Still, practitioners say that the practice of public relations in Egypt is on the rise. In the practitioner profile which follows, Rania Azab, Chief Executive Officer of the 4PR Group, discusses how the revolution changed the practice of public relations in Egypt—and the importance of keeping public relations plans flexible so that you can adapt with the changing country.

Media

The Middle East News Agency is state-run (BBC News Africa, 2013).

The state-owned *Al-Ahram* is the oldest newspaper in the region. Other major daily newspapers include the state-owned *Al-Akhbar* and *Al-Jumhuriyah* and the privately owned *Al-Misri al-Yawm, Alwatan, Youm7,* and *Al-Shuruq.* English-language publications include the state-owned *The Egyptian Gazette* along with *Al-Ahram Weekly* and *Daily News Egypt* (BBC News Africa, 2013; Keenan, 2009, p. 373).

The state-operated Egypt Radio Television Union (ERTU) operates domestic and satellite television networks, which include Nile News and Nile TV International. Private satellite operators include the Dream TV network, Al-Mihwar, Al-Nahar, Al-Hayat, and CBC (BBC News Africa, 2013). The most popular channels in the country are run by Al Hayat (Dubai Press Club, 2012, p. 141).

Radio outlets include the state-run Egypt Radio Television Union (ERTU), whose flagship is the General Programme Network, alongside privately owned Nogoum FM, which broadcasts Arabic pop music, and Nile FM, which broadcasts Western pop music (BBC News Africa, 2013).

Twenty-five percent of Egyptians have social media accounts (Kemp, 2015). The most popular social media platform in Egypt is Facebook Arabic, followed by Facebook English, Google+, and Twitter Arabic (Dubai Press Club, 2012, p. 144).

Practitioner Profile: Rania Azab, Chief Executive Officer, 4PR Group, Egypt

Rania Azab

Rania Azab is a Cairo-based practitioner who started her own public relations firm in 2004. Azab, who is originally from Alexandria, Egypt, studied Journalism and Mass Communication at the American University in Cairo before beginning her career in advertising. After working for two advertising agencies, she was recruited to start an advertising department at the Egyptian stock exchange, where she was unexpectedly also handed responsibility for the Exchange's public relations department. Finding her true passion there, she left the Exchange to start her own public relations agency. Today, the majority of her clients are multinational firms in the oil, transportation, and finance sectors, such as Crédit Agricole bank, Ford, and Exxon Mobil. "It's difficult to be specialized in Egypt, because the market is not developed yet," Rania says.

However, Rania says that Egyptians are beginning to better understand the true function and value of public relations. "Ten years ago, PR was throwing a party or meeting people at the airport with flowers," she remembers. "Now, especially after the revolution, it's about crisis and reputation management. Clients understand the need for PR and how important it is, but it's still not as developed as advertising."

Rania reports that Egypt's 2011 revolution also revolutionized the practice of public relations in the country. "It changed by the day," she recalls. "Social media became a monster. Everyone is using it and suddenly everything changed and organizations were exposed. There were strikes and changes in management, and organizations realized that they need to talk to their stakeholders."

Since the revolution, corporate social responsibility has become critical because "there are a lot of things to be developed in the country now." Public affairs has also become an increasingly important part of public relations practice. "Before, every major company had a partner or someone who was connected to the ruling party," she says. "After the revolution, businesses were lost about who to talk to and how things are done"—creating a huge demand for help from public relations practitioners.

Rania says that, in this "TV society," talk shows aired by broadcasters including the Capital Broadcast Center (CBC), Orbit, Al Bahr, and MBC have become extremely popular since the revolution. "Talk shows are setting the tone or the mood, so clients can easily get in a crisis overnight," she says.

> Following the revolution, there was a lot of irresponsible reporting on these shows and it was very bad, though things are getting better. Presenters have become opinion leaders and are taking sides, so you have to be very careful where you place a client, because they are highly political.

This helps explain why Rania believes it is essential for businesses operating in Egypt to get insights from local practitioners. "You have to understand the culture," she says. "It's a very special market. For example, Egyptians are very emotional people, so it is important to have the right messages. For instance, if your company is going through a tough time, you don't just go out and say 'we're laying off people because we're losing money.' This is not acceptable."

Finally, Rania says, when working in Egypt, it is important to be flexible. "We cannot do long term plans, because things change," she reports. "Sometimes, we change [our plans] monthly."

Case Study: How the Facebook Page "We are All Khaled Said" Helped Promote Egypt's 2011 Revolution[1]

Protesters gathered in Tarir Square in Cairo on January 25, 2011. Copyright: Mohamed Elsayyed

In June 2010, Wael Ghonim, a 30-year-old Google executive and online activist for Egyptian opposition figure Mohamed ElBaradei, created the Arabic Facebook page "We Are All Khaled Said" in order to protest the death of 28-year-old Egyptian citizen Khaled Said. In his memoir, *Revolution 2.0*, Ghonim (2012, p. 58) describes viewing a photograph of Said's corpse, which a friend—Dr. Ayman Nour, a political activist and former presidential candidate—had posted on Facebook. In his own words,

> it was a horrifying photo showing the distorted face of a man in his twenties. There was a big pool of blood behind his head, which rested on a chunk of marble. His face was extremely disfigured and bloodied; his lower lip had been ripped in half, and his jaw was seemingly dislocated. His front teeth appeared to be missing, and it looked as if they had been beaten right out of his mouth. The image was so gruesome that I wondered if he had been wounded in war. But by accessing Dr. Nour's page I learned that Khaled Mohamed Said had apparently been beaten to death on June 6 by two secret police officers in Alexandria.

Later, Said's mother suggested that her son was killed because he possessed a video on his mobile phone that showed local police officers dividing drugs and money for their personal possession. The Egyptian Ministry of the Interior, by contrast, claimed that Said had died of asphyxiation after swallowing an entire package of marijuana—which none of three eyewitnesses reported observing. The ministry claimed that Said was wanted for dealing drugs, possessing a weapon, sexual harassment, and evading his military service. His mother later countered the final charge by producing a certificate of Said's completion of compulsory military service (Ghonim, 2012, pp. 64–66).

For Ghonim, Said's death was emblematic of the brutality and impunity of Egyptian security forces. He therefore created the Facebook page "We Are All Khaled Said" to protest Egyptian police torture and financial corruption. The page would later become an epicenter of activity during the protests against Egyptian President Hosni Mubarak during January and February 2011. After Ghonim was captured by State security forces on January 27, 2011, the page was updated by his activist friends.

The Facebook page that Ghonim created did not initially advocate street activism, because Ghonim saw that a protest recently organized by other activists had resulted in a low turnout. As a result, he says, "we chose instead to identify online activities that we could promote, to instill a sense of optimism and confidence that we could make a difference, even if only in the virtual world for the time being" (Ghonim, 2012, p. 67). Such activities included inviting followers to change their Facebook profile pictures to an image of Said against the Egyptian flag, and to photograph themselves holding a sign reading "We Are All Khaled Said" in Arabic.

Ghonim's memoir suggests that the Facebook page slowly worked to change the views and norms of its followers, and to gradually acclimate them to comfort with greater levels of political dissent and activism. Ghonim notes that "the fact that the regime had not retaliated in any way also made it easier for many people to participate. The barriers of fear were slowly being torn down" (Ghonim, 2012, p. 69). Eventually, the movement took to the streets in a form calculated to be non-threatening to the Egyptian government. The page's followers were encouraged to participate in "Silent Stands" in which they wore black and stood together in public places to express their disproval of the handling of the Said case and police brutality more generally (Ghonim, 2012, p. 70). However, such activities did not involve demands or even, as the name of the event indicates, language to express the grievances of the participants.

While the Facebook page initially focused on the death of Said and the broader issue of police brutality, it was radicalized by the revolution that occurred in Tunisia, where after a month of protests, President Zine El Abidine Ben Ali fled to Saudi Arabia in January 2011. Ghonim writes that, prior to this time, "mention of Mubarak had been off-limits on the page. But as soon as Ben Ali fled Tunisia, this was no longer the case" (Ghonim, 2012, p. 142). Ghonim began actively calling for his followers to mobilize in the streets against the Mubarak regime.

Ghonim's Facebook page—along with those of the April 6 Youth Movement, Egypt's National Association for Change, and Kefaya—encouraged their followers to participate in massive protests that began on January 25, 2011 (Ali, 2011, p. 185). In the two weeks preceding and the initial days of the protests, 32,000 Facebook groups and 14,000 Facebook pages were created in Egypt (Ali, 2011, p. 185).

On January 28, 2011, after three days of protests, the Egyptian government cut off Internet access for five days. Ironically, this seems to have only fueled the protests. "Middle-class Egyptians, denied home Internet access, took to the streets in larger numbers than ever, many driven by an urge simply to find out what was going on" (Howard & Hussain, 2011, p. 39). More than a million Egyptians participated in protests following the Internet blackout, reflecting as much as a tenfold increase in participation compared to prior to this event (Ali, 2011, pp. 186–187). Scholars also note that Egypt lost a minimum of

$90 million as a result of the blackout and that the act of censorship harmed the country's reputation as a location for investment by technology firms and generated censure from the international community (Howard & Hussain, 2011, p. 44; Ali, 2011, p. 186). After the blackout, on the day the Internet was restored in Egypt, Facebook saw its largest number of active users ever in the nation (Ali, 2011, p.187).

On February 11, 2011, the thirty-year rule of Egyptian President Hosni Mubarak came to an end when it was announced that he would step down after just 18 days of protests on the streets of Egypt. Many believe that the reason why Egyptian security forces largely held their fire when confronting demonstrators was due to their awareness that their every move was being recorded and could be streamed to the world. While some scholars suggest that social media represented an effective tool in the revolution because Mubarak's regime did not understand it, others note that state security forces did attempt to both track activist activities online and promulgate misinformation. After activists used social media to organize a strike in 2008 as part of the April 6 Youth Movement, the Egyptian Ministry of the Interior actually established a "State Security Investigation Police for Facebook" (Alqudsi-ghabra, 2012, p. 151).

The use of social media by Ghonim and other online activists in the revolution suggests a number of lessons for other activists. First, as discussed in Chapter 5, a variety of evidence suggests that human beings respond powerfully to personal stories. Said's heartbreaking story appears to have been a powerful way of bringing Egyptian citizens together initially around a shared cause, helping to build a following for Ghonim's Facebook page. (The revolution in Tunisia was likewise catalyzed by a single, powerful story—of the self-immolation of 26-year-old fruit vendor Mohamed Bouazizi in an act of protest against his inability to support himself after municipal officials confiscated his wares.)

Initially, the "We are All Khaled Said" Facebook page seemed unlikely to ignite a revolution; in fact, in his book, Ghonim himself admits that, prior to the events in Tunisia, "my own enthusiasm was beginning to fade" (Ghonim, 2012, p. 113). This suggests that it is not enough for an online activist's idea to be powerful; its time must also have come. As discussed in Chapter 5, Kingdon (1995) argues that in order for social change to happen in the U.S., a period of "softening" must first occur to prepare people to accept change, and a triggering event is also necessary. The same appears to have been the case in Egypt. In this case, there were at least two triggering events: the death of Khaled Said and the Tunisian revolution. Ghonim appears to have gradually trained his followers to be comfortable with deeper levels of dissent so that when the political conditions became ripe for a revolution, they were prepared to take action. A thoroughly refined political radar appears to be critical to gauging the realities and possibilities present in a given environment.

However, it is also clear that social media alone is not enough to affect regime change: Iran, for example, is home to the largest Internet-using population in the Middle East (Internet World Stats, 2014). Yet attempts to use social media after the disputed 2009 election were unsuccessful despite the presence of other social media tools deemed pivotal in the case of the Egyptian and Tunisian revolutions, such as iconic video of the death of 26-year-old Neda Agha-Soltan during the protests. Likewise, the use of social media to document the massive human rights violations by the government of Syria against its own people has to date failed to terminate the rule of President Bashar al-Assad, who continues to slaughter his people with impunity. This suggests that, for social movements to be successful, a government must be concerned with its reputation, both domestically and internationally. Otherwise, it can simply murder its dissenters. There remain a few extreme, brutal modern countries—such as Syria and North Korea—where this is the case.

Ultimately, demonstrations in the *streets* led to Mubarak's downfall in Egypt. However, social media appears to have been a significant driver of the protests. The story of the "We Are All Khaled Said" page shows how powerful online storytelling, consciousness-raising (or "softening,") and capitalizing upon triggering events in an environment can help ignite social change. However, the deep political instability that has followed the revolution in Egypt also indicates that while online activism may now be able to catalyze change, it can also leave great chaos in its wake.

Palestine

Time zone: Coordinated Universal Time (UTC) + 2:00
International dialing code: +970

When you practice public relations in Palestine, be prepared to utilize interpersonal communication.

Palestine's West Bank. Copyright: Rainer Lesniewski.

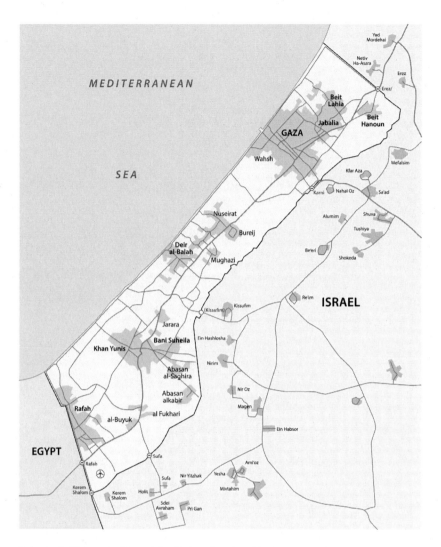

Palestine's Gaza strip. Copyright: Rainer Lesniewski

The Palestinians are a people who still seek to become a fully recognized independent nation. In 1947, the United Nations divided Palestine into Arab and Jewish states. Palestinians in the north eventually became citizens of Israel. Initially, the West Bank became part of Jordan, and Gaza came under the administrative rule of Egypt. However, since the "Six-Day War" of 1967, both the West Bank and the Gaza strip have been occupied by Israel. They are separated by the landmass of Israel, which continues to restrict the movements of Palestinians and requires that they obtain permits in order to travel between the West Bank and Gaza. As part of the 1993 Oslo Accords, it was agreed that the Palestinian National Authority would act as Palestine's government. In

2012, the United Nations gave Palestine the status of an observer state, and in 2013 the Palestinian National Authority's president signed a decree changing its name from the Palestinian National Authority to the State of Palestine. While the majority of United Nations Member States now recognize the State of Palestine, Israel and the U.S. are among the countries that refuse to do so.

The government of the State of Palestine has an elected president and legislature and a prime minister appointed by the president. In the 2006 elections, Hamas—a group that the U.S. and other nations have designated as a terrorist organization—won the majority in parliament, which led many foreign countries to suspend aid to Gaza. However, in 2014, a unity government comprised of the political parties Hamas and Fatah was formed in Gaza.

Conflict and occupation have significantly affected Palestine's economy; the World Bank (2014b) notes that "restrictions put in place by the Government of Israel continue to stand in the way of potential private investment." The majority of public relations practitioners in Palestine therefore work for the government and organizations affiliated with the government, and focus heavily on nation building. A study of government practitioners found that they are typically responsible for technical jobs including "storing newspapers and magazines," providing hospitality services (such as obtaining visas and making hotel reservations), and producing marketing materials. They struggle with insufficient funding and support (Zaharna, Hammad, & Masri, 2009, pp. 225–227).

Non-governmental organizations have traditionally been active in Palestinian society and are growing today. Public relations practice is critical to such organizations, and they tend to focus on fundraising, relationship building, and community outreach. Public relations firms grew significantly after the Palestinian National Authority was established; one of the predominant services they offer is social responsibility initiatives. Private sector practitioners tend to focus on marketing communication; while demand is on the rise, the cost of public relations means that it is often practiced only by larger organizations. Overall, the largest areas of practice in Palestine are public affairs, media relations, and corporate relations. Government, non-profit, and private sector communicators alike tend to practice mostly one-way communication. Still, "the level of professionalism and sophistication in crafting press releases and staging press conferences is on the rise, especially in the West Bank city of Ramallah" (Zaharna et al., 2009, pp. 225–238).

Television is the Palestinian people's main source of news (BBC, 2011). Zaharna et al. (2009, pp. 231–236) note that, due to the depressed economy, Palestinian media cannot survive solely on advertising revenues. Therefore, the media are dependent upon "the patronage of political sponsors" and "Palestinian public relations practitioners must be politically aware in their media relations." This also means that the Palestinian media "has not been a dominant source of credible news and information for the Palestinian people or a reliable communication vehicle for public relations activities."

For this reason, interpersonal communication plays a critical role in Palestinian public relations. This entails communication through the culture's deeply woven social networks, ranging from women's unions to mosques (Zaharna et al., 2009, pp. 236–237). Zaharna et al. (2009, pp. 237–238) note that "in the Palestinian setting, rather than generating publicity, the veracity of the viral communication and inter-connecting social networks makes 'managing the word' or reputation management more critical than 'spreading the word.'" They report that "more important than media placement, critical public relations activities include attending social functions (i.e., wedding or funeral service), sponsoring community events, and personally visiting or inviting community leaders for informal gatherings."

Media

Palestine's official news agency is the Palestine News Agency (WAFA), which reports in Arabic, English, French, and Hebrew. The private Ma'an News Agency operates with funding from Denmark and the Netherlands (BBC, 2011).

The newspaper with the largest circulation is the privately owned *Al-Quds* (which means "Jerusalem"); however, Zaharna et al. (2009, p. 234) note that because it is published in Jerusalem, it is subject to censorship by Israel. *Al-Ayyam* is a private newspaper, while *Al-Hayat Al-Jadidah* is the paper of the Palestinian government (BBC, 2011).

The government-controlled Palestinian Broadcasting Corporation (PBC) operates Palestine TV and the Palestine Satellite Channel. Hamas operates Al-Sqsa TV. Private television stations in Palestine include Al-Quds Educational TV, Al-Mahd TV, Al-Majd TV, Al-Nawras TV, and Watan TV (BBC, 2011). Palestinians in the West Bank receive Jordanian stations, while Palestinians in Gaza receive Egyptian stations, and satellite television—especially Al Jazeera—is popular (Zaharna et al., 2009, p. 235).

Radio outlets include the government-controlled PBC and the Hamas-run Al Aqsa radio (BBC, 2011).

Top social media platforms in Palestine include Facebook and YouTube (Alexa, 2015b).

Saudi Arabia

Time zone: Coordinated Universal Time (UTC) + 3:00
International dialing code: +966

When you practice public relations in Saudi Arabia, be prepared to face censorship.

The birthplace of Islam, the Kingdom of Saudi Arabia exerts enormous influence in the Arab region because it is home to the Muslim holy sites of Mecca and Medina as well as the world's second-largest oil reserves, which have produced enormous wealth for the country (OPEC, 2014, p. 22). As previously discussed, Muslims are required to make a pilgrimage, or *hajj*, to

Copyright: Rainer Lesniewski

Mecca at least once in their lives. This brings millions of people to Mecca each year. Medina, the second holiest city for Muslims, is the burial place of the prophet Mohammed. Non-Muslims are prohibited from entering Mecca or the sacred center of Medina. The desert country has become the world's nineteenth-largest economy thanks to its oil wealth and is the only country in the region that is part of the Group of 20, or G-20, major economies (World Bank, 2014a). While the government plays a major role in the economy, it is working to reduce its dependence upon oil by encouraging private-sector growth and foreign investment (CIA, 2014).

Saudi Arabia is a hereditary monarchy. Although the Kingdom did experience Arab Spring protests, they were generally small and the government responded with arrests but not the killings that occurred elsewhere in the region—as well as by offering more benefits to Saudi citizens, including funding for housing (CIA, 2014). Additionally, the government began holding elections for half of the members of municipal councils, but such positions hold little real influence in the country's governance process (CIA, 2014).

The country is known for its strict religious practices and strictures on women. Members of the government's Committee for the Promotion of Virtue and the Prevention of Vice, colloquially known as the "religious police," roam the streets enforcing Islamic law, or *Sharia*—including the separation of women and men; strict dress codes; store closings during prayer times; and prohibitions on pork, alcohol, fornication, homosexuality, and the promotion of any religion other than Islam. Punishments for infractions can be grim and severe, including public floggings and imprisonment. Saudi women are required to wear the *abaya*, a robe-like garment that covers every part of their bodies except for their faces, feet, and hands. Women are prohibited from driving and are required to obtain permission from a male guardian in order to go to the doctor or to travel (*The Economist*, 2014b). The country's capital is Riyadh, its currency is the riyal, and its official language is Arabic.

Alanazi (1996, p. 239) dates the birth of modern public relations in Saudi Arabia to the 1930s, when international oil corporations began exploring the Saudi desert. Yahya Hamidaddin, Managing Director of Adalid Public Relations, which is based in Jeddah, says that a number of initial public offerings of companies beginning around 2005 helped drive demand in the country for practitioners of financial public relations and that, more recently, companies have begun to focus on corporate social responsibility initiatives.

Al-Badr (2004, p. 204) notes that, while larger Saudi businesses "are making efforts to implement the real public relations concept and have succeeded," medium-size organizations often do not fully understand public relations, while smaller firms have not made efforts to practice public relations at all. Furthermore, he reports,

> most of the government agencies are still lagging behind. They consider public relations practice merely as services to the higher authorities of the agency, their visitors and guests; supplying newspapers, making hotel reservations, and offering escort from and to the airports, as well as preparing news releases.

However, the Saudi government does practice savvy public diplomacy. For example, the mastermind of the September 11, 2001 terrorist attacks on the U.S., Osama Bin Laden, was a Saudi citizen, as were fifteen of the nineteen hijackers who turned commercial airplanes into weapons on that day. Following the attacks, the Saudi government launched a major public relations campaign in order to improve its image in the U.S. (Zhang & Benoit, 2004).

When communicating with local audiences, Hamidaddin says that the most important thing to emphasize is an organization's long-term commitment to the country. "If you want to grab attention and build a reputation or enhance your image, the most important message is what's in it for the locals," he says. "Stress that you're here to be part of the community, not to make quick bucks and run away."

However, a major impediment to public relations practice in the Kingdom is the government's severe restriction of the press. Freedom House (2014d) reports that

according to the official media policy, the press should be a tool to educate the masses, propagate government views, and promote national unity. The government has been known to directly censor both local and international media, and journalists routinely practice self-censorship and avoid criticism of the royal family, Islam, or religious authorities.

The law prohibits the publication of any information that insults Islam (a crime punishable by death) or that might be harmful to national security or "detract from a man's dignity." Reporters are regularly imprisoned. Although the Saudi media is technically privately owned, media owners are all affiliated with the Saudi royal family (Freedom House, 2014d).

The country lacks a tradition of transparency and public debate. As Freedom House (2014d) also notes,

Saudi Arabia has no freedom of information law that provides for public access to state-held information, and does not disclose details related to sensitive topics such as government spending and allocations to the royal family. The media have been allowed to observe and report upon the functions of some state entities, such as the Shura council, but access may be arbitrarily withdrawn and is not guaranteed by law.

Content deemed inappropriate in imported foreign media—such as, for example, a woman's uncovered arms—is inked out before sale in the country.

In addition to censorship, another challenge of working with the Saudi press is the expectation of Saudi media outlets that organizations they cover positively will also purchase advertising. "Editorials are really affected by media buying," Hamidaddin says. "The departments are not separate, as in other countries."

A further challenge is that the Saudi media is not very specialized. Hamidaddin says that the country has financial, political, and sports reporters, and more recently journalists have begun to specialize in information technology, health, and tourism. However, it remains difficult to place technical or trade stories with the country's more generalist reporters.

Hamidaddin reports that, as in other countries, comments posted by the Saudi people on social media have also made companies realize that they have less control over the messages about their organizations. Social media strategies are a must for this market. Hubbard (2015) explains that

confronted with an austere version of Islam and strict social codes that place sharp restrictions on public life, young Saudis are increasingly relying on social media to express and entertain themselves, earn money and meet friends and potential mates . . . the scale of today's social media boom is staggering, with many of the country's 18 million citizens wielding multiple smartphones and spending hours online each day.

Foreign women working in Saudi Arabia should be prepared to dress modestly and should arrange to be met by a representative of the organization sponsoring their visa when they arrive in the country. The U.S. Department of State (2014) reports that women traveling alone who were not met in the airport have in the past been delayed before being permitted to board other flights or enter the country. Special enclaves have been built solely for foreigners living in the country, who often live apart from the Saudi people (Al-Badr, 2004, p. 199).

Media

The Saudi Press Agency is a state-run news agency (BBC News Middle East, 2013a).

Major Saudi newspapers include *Okaz*, *Al Riyadh*, *Al Watan*, and *Al Jazirah*. The pan-Arab, London-based newspapers *Asharq Al-Awsat* (owned by a member of the Saudi royal family) and *Al Hayat* (which is owned by a Saudi prince but is more critical of the Saudi government) are widely read in the Kingdom (BBC News Middle East, 2013a; Dubai Press Club, 2012, p. 156).

State-run Saudi TV operates networks including the news-focused Al-Ikhbariya (BBC News Middle East, 2013a). However, the most watched television channels in the Kingdom are the privately owned, Dubai-based Middle East Broadcasting Center (MBC) channels MBC 1 and MBC 2, along with Al Arabiya and Al Jazeera (Dubai Press Club, 2012, p. 159).

Saudi Radio is state-run (BBC News Middle East, 2013a). However, the privately owned MBC FM is most popular (Dubai Press Club, 2012, p. 163).

As previously discussed, Saudis are particularly avid users of social media, which *The Economist* (2014b) attributes to both the youth of the population and the censorship of the traditional press. Twenty-nine percent of Saudis have active social media accounts. The most popular networks include Facebook, Twitter, Instagram, and LinkedIn (Kemp, 2015).

United Arab Emirates

Time zone: Coordinated Universal Time (UTC) + 4:00
International dialing code: +971

When you practice public relations in the Emirates, be prepared for your news to reach audiences far outside the nation.

The United Arab Emirates is a group of seven emirates on the Persian Gulf, famous for its desert and beaches. Thanks largely to its oil wealth, the tiny nation enjoys a per capita Gross Domestic Product (GDP) that is comparable to leading Western European countries (CIA, 2014). Over just the past few decades, the country's capital of Abu Dhabi and business center, Dubai,

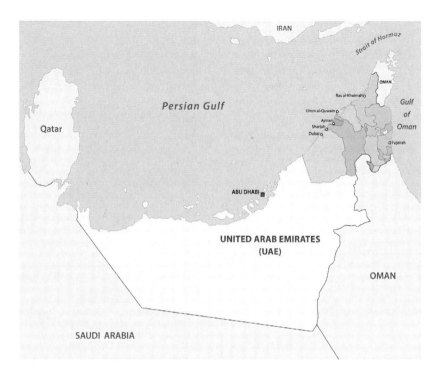

IRAN

Strait of Hormuz

Persian Gulf

OMAN

Ras al-Khaimah

Gulf
of
Oman

Qatar

Umm al-Quwain
Ajman
Sharjah
Dubai

Fujairah

ABU DHABI

UNITED ARAB EMIRATES
(UAE)

OMAN

SAUDI ARABIA

Copyright: Rainer Lesniewski

have rapidly sprung up out of the desert to become two of the world's most modern cities. The Guggenheim and Louvre museums are both opening outposts in Abu Dhabi, while Dubai boasts the world's tallest skyscraper, the Burj Khalifa, along with the Burj Al Arab, a sail-shaped hotel popularly referred to as the world's only seven-star hotel (though no such designation officially exists). Dubai is also famous for its shopping malls—including one that hosts an indoor ski resort—and manmade islands.

Each of the emirates is ruled by a hereditary leader. The seven leaders of the individual emirates are members of the Supreme Council of Leaders, which is headed by an unelected president. Political parties are banned in the country and individuals must obtain permits from the government in order to hold public meetings (Freedom House, 2014e). Emirati citizens are given an opportunity to voice concerns to their rulers in public forums known as *majlis* (Badran, Turk, & Walters, 2009, p. 203). The U.S. Central Intelligence Agency (2014) notes that, while the country did not experience an "Arab Spring," activists and intellectuals signed a petition in 2011 for increased political participation that circulated widely on the Internet; the government responded with increased infrastructure spending in poorer parts of the country and "aggressively pursued advocates of political reform."

The country's leaders are, however, widely viewed as generally benevolent, and the Emirati people enjoy a remarkable quality of life, including high-paying jobs, short workdays, and inexpensive access to education, medicine, and housing loans. However, in this society governed by *Sharia*, ultimately "there are . . . no freedoms other than those the ruler offers his 'family' or those that the head of a household offers his wife and children" (Badran et al., 2009, pp. 205–206).

Just 19 percent of the population of the United Arab Emirates is actually Emirati. Half of the population is South Asian, while 23 percent come from other Arab states and Iran (CIA, 2014). The country is widely criticized for exploiting its majority expatriate (colloquially called "expat") workers, including laborers from India and domestic workers from the Philippines who often work long hours for low wages (Badran et al., 2009, p. 205). The Emirates has attempted to diversify its economy beyond oil dependence and offers free trade zones in order to encourage foreign investment (CIA, 2014). The official language of the Emirates is Arabic, though much business is conducted in English. The country's currency is the dirham.

Dubai has become a major hub of Arab media and public relations agencies (Kirat, 2006, p. 255). In 2000, the Emirati government established Dubai Media City, a tax-free zone designed to serve as a regional hub for media. Organizations operating out of the location include the BBC, CCTV, CNN, Dow Jones, and Thomson Reuters. Major public relations firms based out of Dubai Media City include Dentsu, Havas, the Publicis Groupe, and WPP (Dubai Media City, 2015). Al Samarrai, of Dubai-based Active Digital Marketing Communications, says that unlike other regions of the world, in which organizations have different country offices, many companies conduct their public relations campaigns for the entire Arab region out of Dubai. He says that one advantage of working with the local press is that the content of major online sites based in the Emirates—including GulfNews.com, the online version of Arabian Business, and the Arabic websites of broadcasters such as Al Jazeera, CNN International, BBC World, and MBC, who have local reporters—tends to be read widely throughout the Arab region, including in Saudi Arabia, Bahrain, Iraq, and Syria. Some media outlets re-publish content from these sites verbatim, while others edit it slightly.

Much public relations spending in the Emirates is done by the government or entities linked to the government, such as the government's investment company, Dubai World (which owns assets including DP World, an international marine terminal operator) and global real estate developer Emaar Properties (Sudhaman, 2009). However, the country has also attracted corporations from around the world, creating significant opportunities for practitioners in the private sector (Kirat, 2006, p. 255).

The field of public relations has professionalized significantly in recent years. Badran et al. (2009) note that public relations was once associated with hospitality and protocol. Today, Hill (2011, p. 43) reports that the practice "runs the gamut from . . . visa assistance to highly sophisticated outreach aligned with an organization's corporate goals, and everything in between." A study of Emirati institutions found that the vast majority of their higher management executives consider public relations to be "very" or "extremely" important (Rizk, 2005, p. 393). An analysis of the websites of Emirati public and private institutions found a high degree of sophistication in their online communications, including "a high degree of commitment to openness and transparency in dealing with the general public," an emphasis on community welfare and two-way communication, and opportunities for members of the public to make direct contact with organizations (Ayish, 2005, pp. 386–387).

While the practice has become highly developed in the media capitals of Dubai and Abu Dhabi, there is still a lack of skilled practitioners outside of these cities (Badran et al., 2009, p. 203). Alongside agencies practicing modern, world-class public relations are firms which call themselves public relations agencies but perform services such as secretarial work or obtaining visas for foreign domestic workers (Ayish, 2005, pp. 382–383).

Al Samarrai says that one mistake that a lot of multinational companies that hire public relations agencies in the country make is that they develop their strategies in the U.S. and Europe and then ask local agencies to simply implement them. "It's quite sad," he says. "There's very little chance for PR agencies here in the region to be original and fresh."

He reports that Emirati and other Arab media are hungry for statistics, analysis, and information about the region specifically, and if organizations are able to find region-specific facts and figures, they will gain traction in the press. Press releases are often published verbatim (Badran et al., 2009, p. 203).

Al Samarrai says that people in the Arab region tend to be very brand conscious. Additionally, in the business-to-business and technology sectors in which he specializes, it is not possible to generate the same numbers of social media followers per dollar invested as in the U.S. and Europe, and therefore clients tend to prefer to focus on traditional media outreach. Less than 5 percent of his firm's revenue is from social and digital campaigns.

Public relations practice also remains hindered by media censorship—though, as previously discussed, Al Samarrai reports that business stories are not subject to the same types of censorship as stories about political and social issues. Freedom House (2014e) describes the country's law regulating all aspects of the press and prohibiting criticism of the government, its allies, or Islam as "one of the most restrictive press laws in the Arab world." The organization (2014e) notes that "consequently, journalists commonly practice self-censorship, and the leading media outlets frequently publish government statements without criticism or comment." While foreign media operating from the country's "media free zones"—Dubai Media City as well as others in Abu Dhabi and Ras al-Khaimah—are technically subject to the country's press law, in reality, Freedom House (2014e) reports that "the press operates with relative freedom" inside these zones.

Badran et al. (2009, p. 203) also report that "gifts and other contributions that some public relations agencies and organizations offer to media professionals in exchange for positive editorial coverage raise serious ethical questions. Anecdotal evidence exists of offers of expensive items as 'gifts' to reporters and editors."

Media

The Emirates News Agency is the country's official news agency (BBC News Middle East, 2013b).

The most widely read newspapers in the Emirates are the English-language *Gulf News* and *Khaleej Times* and Arabic-language *Al Khaleej* and *Emarat Al Youm* (Dubai Press Club, 2012, p. 166).

Dubai is home to pan-Arab broadcasters including MBC (which owns Al Arabiya), Dubai Media Incorporated (DMI) (which is owned by the government of Dubai), and Sky News Arabia (BBC News Middle East, 2013a).

Because of the large number of South Asian expats living in the Emirates, the Hindi-language HUM FM is the country's most popular radio station, followed by Abu Dhabi radio (Dubai Press Club, 2012, p. 173).

Fifty-six percent of the population has active social media accounts. The most popular social networks include Facebook, Twitter, and LinkedIn (Kemp, 2015).

Latin European Cluster

The GLOBE study officially classifies Israel as part of the Latin European cultural cluster, which you read about in the previous chapter, because the country was settled by migrants who were originally from Latin Europe (Gupta & Hanges, 2004, p. 184). As a country, Israel is characterized by high assertiveness, gender egalitarianism, and performance orientation, with moderate levels of future orientation, humane orientation, institutional collectivism, ingroup collectivism, power distance, and uncertainty avoidance (Javidan, 2004, p. 269; Ashkanasy, Gupta, Mayfield, & Trevor-Roberts, 2004, p. 304; Emrich, Denmark, & Hartog, 2004, p. 365; Hartog, 2004, p. 410; Gelfand, Bhawuk, Nishii, & Bechtold, 2004, pp. 468, 470; Carl, Gupta, & Javidan, 2004, p. 539; Kabasakal & Bodur, 2004, p. 573; de Luque & Javidan, 2004, p. 622).

Ashkanasy et al. (2004 p. 294) note that

> the Jews . . . historically preserved their tradition for generations and thus evidenced a past orientation. The family life of Ethiopian Jews, for instance, was organized around the extended family in a hierarchical structure, usually headed by an elder male, with defined gender roles. . . . The image of an ideal man in the traditional Jewish society was one of a hardworking person oriented toward showing respect for elders, preserving traditions, and maintaining self-restraint and self-control. . . . However, after the formation of Israel an alternative image of "New Israelis" evolved, with children expected to grow into adults who are strong, healthy, independent, proud, living in their own land, and adhering to the ideology of the fraternity.

Israel

Time zone: Coordinated Universal Time (UTC) + 2:00
International dialing code: +972

When you practice public relations in Israel, be prepared for your interlocutors to be blunt.

The Jewish people lived without a homeland for two millennia, enduring persecution including the Holocaust in Europe—a genocide in which about six million Jews were murdered by the Nazi regime in Germany and its territories between 1941 and 1945. As previously discussed, in 1947, a United Nations resolution partitioned Palestine into an Arab state (currently the West Bank and Gaza) and a Jewish state (modern-day Israel). During the "Six-Day War" of 1967, involving Israel, Egypt, Jordan, and Syria, Israel launched a preemptive strike after Egypt massed troops on its border, and went on to gain land that tripled the size of the country.

Modern-day Israel is the birthplace of both Judaism and Christianity. Israel continues to occupy the Palestinian territories, and the ongoing dispute over land rights is the source of tension between Israel and Palestine, which sporadically erupts into violence. *The Economist* (2014a) classifies Israel as a "flawed democracy," albeit the only one in the region (the rest of the countries in the Middle East are either hybrid or authoritarian regimes). There are free elections to the country's multi-party parliament, the Knesset, and the country enjoys a relatively robust civil society—though it is illegal to advocate for the destruction of the state (Freedom House, 2014c). Today, Israel enjoys a technologically advanced economy with major exports including diamonds, high-technology equipment, and pharmaceuticals (CIA, 2014). Though Israel professes that its capital is Jerusalem, disputes over this city are at the heart of Israel's conflict with Palestine and foreign embassies are located in the city of Tel Aviv. Israel's official language is Hebrew, though Arabic is officially used for the country's Arab minority, and its currency is the shekel (CIA, 2014).

Toledano and McKie (2007) note that early Israeli media was used to promote the cause of Zionism—the movement to establish a modern Jewish homeland—and to promote the needs of the early Israeli state, such as social integration among the immigrants who settled in Israel from around the world. However, in the 1980s, "a more pluralistic and liberalized model developed, and criticism and competition started to be perceived as beneficial to the individual and the government" (Toledano & McKie, 2007, p. 395). Though Freedom House (2014c) reports that today the Israeli media are independent and "freely criticize the government," Toledano and McKie (2009, p. 246) note the "resurrection in times of crisis" of the old model of press support for the government. Another factor that influences media coverage is that Israeli media is concentrated in the hands of a small, wealthy elite, who sometimes shape content in order to advance their other business interests (Toledano & McKie, 2009, pp. 255–256).

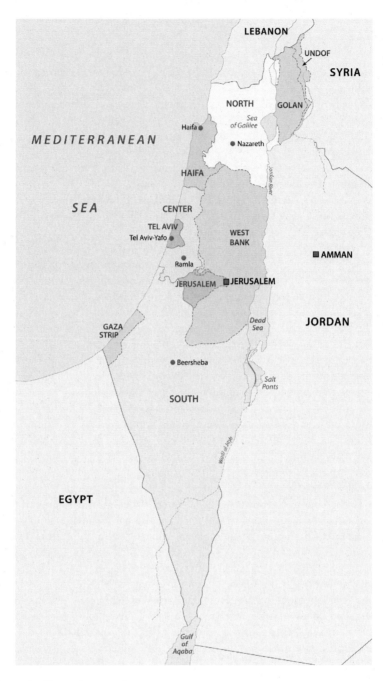

Copyright: Rainer Lesniewski

As a result of the government's privatization policy, the 1993 peace agreement with Palestine known as the Oslo accords, and the 1994 decision of the Cooperation Council for the Arab States of the Gulf to end its economic boycott of Israel, more multinational corporations began investing in the country, creating new opportunities for public relations practitioners (Toledano & McKie, 2009, p. 247). In particular, these developments and the success of the high-tech sector led many public relations firms to specialize in high-tech and investor relations (Toledano, 2013, p. 492). Fundraising and lobbying are well-established skills among Israeli practitioners, with a history dating back prior to the country's founding, when advocates raised support for the Zionist cause (Toledano, 2013, p. 492; Toledano & McKie, 2009, p. 259).

Yet Toledano and McKie (2013, p. 167) report that "the public relations function is still perceived by many Israeli managers as focused on media relations and mainly for the purpose of covering up organizational faults and for publicizing organizational achievements." Toledano and McKie (2009, p. 246) also note that "the dominant coalitions of organizations do not see public relations as a management function or practitioners as essential and equal members of the board" and most Israeli practitioners do not view themselves as the "ethical consciences of their organizations." Another challenge for practitioners in Israel is the corruption that plagues the country. Transparency International's (2014) barometer gave the country a score of just 60 out of 100 on corruption. It is not unheard of for clients to ask public relations practitioners to bribe journalists or to promulgate false information about their competitors (Toledano & McKie, 2009, p. 257). A further issue is openness; Toledano and McKie (2009, p. 252) report that "the democratic value of transparency has not been fully absorbed and the idea that the public has a right to know cannot be taken for granted."

Oren Bason, Chief Executive Officer of Israeli public relations agency All-media, which specializes in serving technology clients, says that another challenge is that there is a relatively limited number of media outlets to pitch in the country. He often advises clients to make their press releases less technical than they would be in markets such as the U.S. and Europe in order to appeal to Israel's more general press and, of course, to find local Israeli angles on their work to highlight.

Finally, if you practice public relations in Israel, be prepared for your partners to be blunt. Toledano and McKie (2009, p. 252) note that part of the culture of native Israelis is a manner of speaking called "dugri" which "involves a level of directness in speaking that would be considered rude in many other cultures."

Media

Haaretz is the country's oldest newspaper and is available in both Hebrew and English. Other major dailies include *Yediot Aharonot* and the free *Israel Hayom*, along with the English-language *Jerusalem Post* (BBC, 2014).

The Israel Broadcasting Authority is the country's public broadcaster. The country's main private television networks are Channel 2 and Israel 10 (BBC, 2014).

The Israel Broadcasting Authority also operates public radio (BBC, 2014). The technology-savvy country is particularly active on social media (Pew, 2012). Popular platforms include Facebook and YouTube (Alexa, 2015a).

Note

1   Adapted from Alaimo, K. (2015). How the Facebook Arabic page "We Are All Khaled Said" helped promote the Egyptian revolution. *Social Media & Society*, *1*(2). Retrieved from http://sms.sagepub.com/content/1/2/2056305115604854. full.pdf+html

References

Alaimo, K. (2015). How the Facebook Arabic page "We Are All Khaled Said" helped promote the Egyptian revolution. *Social Media & Society*, *1*(2). Retrieved from http://sms.sagepub.com/content/1/2/2056305115604854.full.pdf+html

Al-Badr, H. (2004). Public relations in Saudi Arabia. In K. Sriramesh (Ed.), *Public relations in Asia: An anthology* (pp. 187–205). Singapore: Thomson Learning.

Al Jazeera. (2014, December 29). Al Jazeera staff held for one year in Egypt. Retrieved from http://www.aljazeera.com/news/middleeast/2014/12/al-jazeera-staff-egypt2014 1228233546724629.html

Al-Kandari, A., & Gaither, T. K. (2011). Arabs, the west and public relations: A critical/ cultural study of Arab cultural values. *Public Relations Review*, *37*(3), 266–273.

Alanazi, A. (1996). Public relations in the Middle East: The case of Saudi Arabia. In H. M. Culbertson & N. Chen (Eds.), *International public relations: A comparative analysis* (pp. 239–256). Mahwah, NJ: Lawrence Erlbaum Associates.

Alexa. (2015a). Top sites in Israel. Retrieved from http://www.alexa.com/topsites/coun tries/IL

Alexa. (2015b). Top sites in Palestinian territory. Retrieved from http://www.alexa.com/ topsites/countries/PS

Ali, A. H. (2011). The power of social media in developing nations: New tools for closing the global digital divide and beyond. *Harvard Human Rights Journal*, *24*, 185–219.

Allen, M. R., & Dozier, D. M. (2012). When cultures collide: Theoretical issues in global public relations. In K. Sriramesh & D. Verčič (Eds.), *Culture and public relations: Links and implications* (pp. 182–201). New York, NY: Taylor & Francis.

Alqudsi-ghabra, T. (2012). Creative use of social media in the revolutions of Tunisia, Egypt & Libya. *International Journal of Interdisciplinary Sciences*, *6*(6), 147–159.

Ashkanasy, N., Gupta, V., Mayfield, M. S., & Trevor-Roberts, E. (2004). Future orientation. In R. J. House, P. J. Hanges, M. Javidan, P. W. Dorfman, & V. Gupta (Eds.), *Culture, leadership, and organizations: The GLOBE study of 62 societies* (pp. 282–342). Thousand Oaks, CA: Sage.

Ayish, M. I. (2005). Virtual public relations in the United Arab Emirates: A case study of 20 UAE organizations' use of the Internet. *Public Relations Review*, *31*(3), 381–388.

Badran, B. A., Turk, J. V., & Walters, T. N. (2009). Sharing the transformation: Public relations and the UAE come of age. In K. Sriramesh & D. Verčič (Eds.), *The global public relations handbook: Theory, research, and practice* (2nd ed.) (pp. 198–219). New York, NY: Routledge.

BBC News Africa. (2013, August 6). Egypt profile. Retrieved from http://www.bbc.com/news/world-africa-13313373

BBC News Middle East. (2011, August 31). Palestinian territories profile. Retrieved from http://www.bbc.com/news/world-middle-east-14631745

BBC News Middle East. (2013a, August 22). Saudi Arabia profile. Retrieved from http://www.bbc.com/news/world-middle-east-14703480

BBC News Middle East. (2013b, August 27). United Arab Emirates profile. Retrieved from http://www.bbc.com/news/world-middle-east-14704229

BBC News Middle East. (2014, December 2). Israel profile. Retrieved from http://www.bbc.com/news/world-middle-east-14629611

Carl, D., Gupta, V., & Javidan, M. (2004). Power distance. In R. J. House, P. J. Hanges, M. Javidan, P. W. Dorfman, & V. Gupta (Eds.), *Culture, leadership, and organizations: The GLOBE study of 62 societies* (pp. 513–563). Thousand Oaks, CA: Sage.

Central Intelligence Agency (CIA). (2014). World factbook. Retrieved from https://www.cia.gov/library/publications/the-world-factbook/

Curtin, P. A., & Gaither, T. K. (2004). International agenda-building in cyberspace: A study of Middle East government English-language websites. *Public Relations Review, 30*(1), 25–36.

de Luque, M. S., & Javidan, M. (2004). Uncertainty avoidance. In R. J. House, P. J. Hanges, M. Javidan, P. W. Dorfman, & V. Gupta (Eds.), *Culture, leadership, and organizations: The GLOBE study of 62 societies* (pp. 602–653). Thousand Oaks, CA: Sage.

Dubai Media City. (2015). Community of key industry players. Retrieved from http://www.dubaimediacity.com/join-dmc/community-of-key-industry-players

Dubai Press Club. (2012). *Arab media outlook 2011–2015.* Retrieved from http://www.arabmediaforum.ae/userfiles/EnglishAMO.pdf

The Economist. (2014a). Democracy index 2013. Retrieved from http://www.eiu.com/public/thankyou_download.aspx?activity=download&campaignid=Democracy0814

The Economist. (2014b, September 13). A virtual revolution. Retrieved from http://www.economist.com/news/middle-east-and-africa/21617064-why-social-media-have-greater-impact-kingdom-elsewhere-virtual

Emrich, C. G., Denmark, F. L., & Hartog, D. N. D. (2004). Cross-cultural differences in gender egalitarianism. In R. J. House, P. J. Hanges, M. Javidan, P. W. Dorfman, & V. Gupta (Eds.), *Culture, leadership, and organizations: The GLOBE study of 62 societies* (pp. 343–394). Thousand Oaks, CA: Sage.

Flanagan, B. (2012, August 5). Ramadan shows give TV revenue a big boost. *The National.* Retrieved from http://www.thenational.ae/business/media/ramadan-shows-give-tv-revenue-a-big-boost

Feghali, E. (1997). Arab cultural communication patterns. *International Journal of Intercultural Relations, 21*(3), 345–378.

Freedom House. (2014a). *Freedom of the press 2014.* Retrieved from https://freedomhouse.org/sites/default/files/FOTP_2014.pdf

Freedom House. (2014b). Freedom in the world: Egypt. Retrieved from https://freedomhouse.org/report/freedom-world/2014/egypt-0

Freedom House. (2014c). Freedom in the world: Israel. Retrieved from https://www.freedomhouse.org/report/freedom-world/2014/israel-0

Freedom House. (2014d). Freedom of the press: Saudi Arabia. Retrieved from https://www.freedomhouse.org/report/freedom-press/2014/saudi-arabia

Freedom House. (2014e). Freedom in the world: United Arab Emirates. Retrieved from https://freedomhouse.org/report/freedom-world/2014/united-arab-emirates-0

Gelfand, M. J., Bhawuk, D. P. S., Nishii, L. H., & Bechtold, D. J. (2004). Individualism and collectivism. In R. J. House, P. J. Hanges, M. Javidan, P. W. Dorfman, & V. Gupta (Eds.), *Culture, leadership, and organizations: The GLOBE study of 62 societies* (pp. 437–512). Thousand Oaks, CA: Sage.

Ghonim, W. (2012). *Revolution 2.0: The power of the people is greater than the people in power. A memoir.* New York, NY: Houghton Mifflin Harcourt.

Gupta, V., & Hanges, P. J. (2004). Regional and climate clustering of societal clusters. In R. J. House, P. J. Hanges, M. Javidan, P. W. Dorfman, & V. Gupta (Eds.), *Culture, leadership, and organizations: The GLOBE study of 62 societies* (pp. 178–218). Thousand Oaks, CA: Sage.

Hartog, D. N. D. (2004). Assertiveness. In R. J. House, P. J. Hanges, M. Javidan, P. W. Dorfman, & V. Gupta (Eds.), *Culture, leadership, and organizations: The GLOBE study of 62 societies* (pp. 395–436). Thousand Oaks, CA: Sage.

Hay, P. (2010, June 14). Focus on . . . Egypt. *PR Week.* Retrieved from http://www.prweek.com/article/1009753/focus-on-egypt

Hill, R. (2011). Public relations and corporate communications in the UAE. *Middle East Media Monitor, 1*(1), 43–47.

Howard, P. N., & Hussain, M. M. (2011). The role of digital media. *Journal of Democracy 22*(3), 35–48.

Hubbard, B. (2015, May 22). Young Saudis, bound by conservative strictures, find freedom on their phones. *The New York Times.* Retrieved from http://www.nytimes.com/2015/05/23/world/middleeast/saudi-arabia-youths-cellphone-apps-freedom.html

Internet World Stats. (2014). Internet users in the Middle East and the world: 2014 Q2. Retrieved from http://internetworldstats.com/stats5.htm

Javidan, M. (2004). Performance orientation. In R. J. House, P. J. Hanges, M. Javidan, P. W. Dorfman, & V. Gupta (Eds.), *Culture, leadership, and organizations: The GLOBE study of 62 societies* (pp. 239–281). Thousand Oaks, CA: Sage.

Kabasakal, H., & Bodur, M. (2004). Humane orientation in societies, organizations, and leader attributes. In R. J. House, P. J. Hanges, M. Javidan, P. W. Dorfman, & V. Gupta (Eds.), *Culture, leadership, and organizations: The GLOBE study of 62 societies* (pp. 564–601). Thousand Oaks, CA: Sage.

Kanso, A., Sinno, A. K., & Adams, W. (2001). Cross-cultural public relations: Implications for American and Arab public relations practitioners. *Competitiveness Review, 11*(1), 65–82.

Keenan, K. L. (2009). Public relations in Egypt: Practices, obstacles, and potentials. In K. Sriramesh & D. Verčič (Eds.), *The global public relations handbook: Theory, research, and practice* (2nd ed.) (pp. 362–378). New York, NY: Routledge.

Kemp, S. (2015, January 21). Digital, social & mobile worldwide in 2015. *We Are Social.* Retrieved from http://wearesocial.net/blog/2015/01/digital-social-mobile-worldwide-2015/

Kingdon, J. (1995). *Agendas, alternatives, and public policies.* New York, NY: Harper Collins.

Kirat, M. (2006). Public relations in the United Arab Emirates: The emergence of a profession. *Public Relations Review, 32*(3), 254–260.

Kirkpatrick, D. D., & Thomas, M. (2014, October 26). Egyptian media to limit criticism of government. *The New York Times.* Retrieved from http://www.nytimes.com/2014/10/27/world/middleeast/egyptian-media-to-limit-criticism-of-government.html?_r=0

Livermore, D. (2013). *Expand your borders: Discover ten cultural clusters.* East Lansing, MI: Cultural Intelligence Center.

McDowell, J. (2012, June 1). Golden rules for PR in the Middle East. *International Public Relations Association.* Retrieved from http://www.ipra.org/itl/06/2012/golden-rules-for-pr-in-the-middle-east

Organization of the Petroleum Exporting Countries (OPEC). (2014). *Annual statistical bulletin.* Retrieved from http://www.opec.org/opec_web/static_files_project/media/downloads/publications/ASB2014.pdf

Pew Research Center. (2012, January 17). Social networking popular worldwide, with Israel in the lead. Retrieved from http://www.pewresearch.org/daily-number/social-networking-popular-worldwide-with-israel-in-the-lead/

Rizk, A. (2005). Future of public relations in United Arab Emirates institutions. *Public Relations Review, 31*(3), 389–398.

Saleh, H. (2014, November 26). Egypt's hopes of attracting investment given timely boost by IMF. *The Financial Times.* Retrieved from http://blogs.ft.com/beyond-brics/2014/11/26/egypts-hopes-of-attracting-investment-given-timely-boost-by-imf/

Sudhaman, A. (2009, November 27). Focus on . . . the United Arab Emirates. *PR Week.* Retrieved from http://www.prweek.com/article/969908/focus-onthe-united-arab-emirates

Toledano, M. (2013). Israel, practice of public relations in. In R. L. Heath (Ed.), *Encyclopedia of public relations* (2nd ed.) (pp. 491–493). Thousand Oaks, CA: Sage.

Toledano, M., & McKie, D. (2007). Social integration and public relations: Global lessons from an Israeli experience. *Public Relations Review, 33*(4), 387–397.

Toledano, M., & McKie, D. (2009). The Israeli PR experience: Nation building and professional values. In K. Sriramesh & D. Verčič (Eds.), *The global public relations handbook: Theory, research, and practice* (2nd ed.) (pp. 243–261). New York, NY: Routledge.

Toledano, M., & McKie, D. (2013). *Public relations and nation building: Influencing Israel.* New York, NY: Routledge.

Transparency International. (2014). Corruption by country/territory. Retrieved from http://www.transparency.org/country#ISR

United States Department of State. (2014, November 21). Saudi Arabia. Retrieved from http://travel.state.gov/content/passports/english/country/saudi-arabia.html

World Bank. (2014a). GDP. Retrieved from http://data.worldbank.org/indicator/NY.GDP.MKTP.CD?order=wbapi_data_value_2013+wbapi_data_value+wbapi_data_valuelast&sort=desc

World Bank. (2014b, September 24). West Bank and Gaza overview. Retrieved from http://www.worldbank.org/en/country/westbankandgaza/overview

World Economic Forum. (2014, October). *Rethinking Arab employment: A systemic approach for resource-endowed economies.* Retrieved from http://www3.weforum.org/docs/WEF_MENA14_RethinkingArabEmployment.pdf

Zaharna, R. S. (1995). Understanding cultural preferences of Arab communication patterns. *Public Relations Review, 21*(3), 241–255.

Zaharna, R. S. (2005). Al Jazeera and American public diplomacy: A dance of intercultural (mis-)communication. In M. Zayani (Ed.), *The Al Jazeera phenomenon: Critical perspectives on new Arab media* (pp. 183–202). London: Pluto Press.

Zaharna, R. S., Hammad, A. I., & Masri, J. (2009). Palestinian public relations—Inside and out. In K. Sriramesh & D. Verčič (Eds.), *The global public relations handbook: Theory, research, and practice* (2nd ed.) (pp. 220–242). New York, NY: Routledge.

Zayani, M. (2005). Introduction—Al Jazeera and the vicissitudes of the new Arab media landscape. In M. Zayani (Ed.), *The Al Jazeera phenomenon: Critical perspectives on new Arab media* (pp. 1–46). London: Pluto Press.

Zhang, J., & Benoit, W. L. (2004). Message strategies of Saudi Arabia's image restoration campaign after 9/11. *Public Relations Review, 30*(2), 161–167.

11 Public Relations in North and Latin America

Welcome to my home region of the Americas! Canada and the United States of America fall under the Anglo cultural cluster, while Mexico, the Caribbean, Central America, and South America fall under the Latin American cultural cluster (Gupta & Hanges, 2004, p. 186). This chapter profiles some of the biggest public relations markets in the region: Canada, the U.S., Argentina, Brazil, Chile, and Mexico.

The Anglo Cluster

Livermore (2013, p. 22) explains that Anglo cultures (including the U.S. and Canada, as well as the English-speaking United Kingdom, Australia, and New Zealand) are particularly notable for their individualism. "The Anglo cultures are largely organized around the idea of individual rights, freedom, and responsibility," he explains. "Roman law declared that all should be equal, and the [culture] was built around this premise. Free speech is an extremely important value, which reflects [their] priority on protecting individual rights." He describes the U.S. as "the extreme version of individualism" and explains that individualism explains the culture's emphasis on maintaining personal space; people in this culture are also particularly fastidious about their personal hygiene!

Members of this culture are action-oriented and competitive (Livermore, 2013, p. 23). In this culture, "rewards tend to be based on merit and achievement [and] goals take precedence over the family bonds" (Gupta & Hanges, 2004, p. 200). Livermore (2013, p. 24) also warns, "be on time. Time is money in the Anglo world and you will be judged severely based on punctuality." Focus is on the short term. "There's very little patience for long-term, twenty-year ideas. These cultures are interested in performance that can achieve results now or in the very near future" (Livermore, 2013, p. 23). Additionally, people place strong importance on "'quid prop quo.' Anglos believe there should always be give and take. There's a reluctance to ask people for something unless there's an ability to return the favor" (Livermore, 2013, p. 23). Not only is giving gifts to a new business partner not expected here, as it would be in some other cultures, but it may actually be interpreted as a bribe (Livermore, 2013, p. 24).

The GLOBE study found that the Anglo cultural group is overall characterized by high performance orientation; a moderate level of assertiveness, future orientation, gender egalitarianism, humane orientation, institutional collectivism, power distance, and uncertainty avoidance; and low in-group collectivism (Gupta & Hanges, 2004, p. 193). The following sections profile the two Anglo countries in North America: Canada and the United States.

Canada

> *Time zone: Spans 6 time zones, ranging from Coordinated Universal Time (UTC) - 2:30 to UTC - 8:00*
> *International dialing code: +1*

When you practice public relations in Canada, be nice.

A parliamentary democracy and constitutional monarchy whose head of state remains the Queen of England, Canada stretches across a huge landmass that is rich in natural resources. These resources help drive the world's eleventh-largest economy in areas such as farming, fishing, forestry, mining, and oil and gas (World Bank, 2014b; Likely, 2009, p. 654). Although a free-market economy, the Canadian government plays a much greater role in the economy and in providing social welfare programs such as healthcare and childcare than does the country's southern neighbor, the U.S. A legacy of the country's settlement by both the British and the French, today Canada is a bilingual and bicultural nation; its official languages are English and French. The heart of French Canada is the province of Quebec. Livermore (2013, p. 41) notes that while the English-speaking parts of Canada are part of the Anglo cluster, the

Copyright: Rainer Lesniewski

French-speaking parts of Canada are characteristic of the Latin European cultural group described in Chapter 9. The country is also one of the most immigrant-friendly in the world. While the U.S. has pursued a "melting pot" approach of creating a single culture out of great diversity, Canada has instead "accepted the mosaic where each nationality preserves its own characteristics and is listened to equally in national debates" (Guiniven, 2002, pp. 398–399). Canada's currency is the Canadian dollar and its capital is Ottawa.

Johansen (2013, p. 94) reports that "today, public relations is routine within most private- and non-profit sector organizations of any size, and public relations specialists perform the same mix of managerial, strategic, and technical work as colleagues elsewhere." Public relations is practiced with sophistication in the country; PR Week (2010) notes that Canada now has a "thriving industry that has grown a strong reputation for supplying talent and innovation to the PR world at large."

Canada enjoys a free press and Guiniven (2002) finds that Canadian practitioners practice greater two-way symmetrical communication than their counterparts in the U.S. By contrast, one Canadian practitioner says, "publicity campaigns alone 'somehow seem too American, a little too garish'" (Guiniven, 2002, p. 396).

Guiniven (2002, p. 395) argues that Canada's political history of tolerance for diversity and compromise has resulted in a public relations practice that emphasizes dialogue and accommodation between different groups, such as activists and corporations, instead of confrontation. As one Canadian practitioner explains,

> we are almost programmed to enter any public issue dispute looking first for a solution, a win-win outcome, while public relations in the US seems to start from the base of "how can I beat the other guy." We tend to ascribe influence to the other side rather than to manufacture weaknesses in their arguments (Guiniven, 2002, p. 399).

Likely (2009, p. 663) notes that, because of this tradition, political communication "usually is neither extreme nor negative, and not attack-oriented."

Elissa Freeman, Principal of @elissapr communications, concurs that "any time I'm working with a client, there's never an untoward comment to make someone look lesser. Comparisons to the other brand or the other issue just don't play well here and Canadians get very indignant about that." Freeman says that a 2014 campaign in which the Canadian airline WestJet sent Santa Claus to ask people in the Dominican Republic what they wanted for Christmas and then actually surprised them by making their wishes come true epitomizes the type of approach that is received well in the Canadian market. "We tend to like things that make us feel good," she says. "That's the kind of thing that plays well here."

A man gets the horse he wanted for Christmas in this WestJet campaign, which Freeman says is a model of what works best in the Canadian market. Photo courtesy of WestJet

Another cultural element that impacts the practice of public relations in Canada is the fact that Canadians are not very deferential to authority. Likely

(2009, p. 669) notes that "from Prime Ministers to rock stars to wealthy businessmen, all 'elites' are fair game for satire and ridicule. . . . Canadians believe more in knocking high-flying 'stars' down."

Despite these differences, Freeman says that, too often, she sees organizations attempting to implement the same public relations tactics in the U.S. and in Canada. "When a company from the U.S. comes into Canada, they still must consider the cultural differences and potentially adjust their strategy," she says.

Practitioners in Canada conceptualize different strategies and messages for different groups—"not only for French Canadians, as one would expect, but also for smaller but still distinct ethnic groups" (Likely, 2009, p. 664). The strategies that will be most successful for engaging different Canadian groups can differ markedly; for example, one recent study found that Francophone Canadians read online posts by brands "just as closely as if they were from friends," while Anglophone Canadians simply skim such posts (eMarketer, 2014).

Another area of practice in which Canadian practitioners are adept is public and government affairs. *PR Week* (2010) notes that "extensive government regulation at both a national and local level means that public affairs is a mature and sophisticated practice area in the country. It is also one of the world's most tightly regulated and transparent lobbying markets."

Media

The Canadian Press (CP) is a national news agency.

Canada's major daily newspapers are *The Toronto Star*, *The Globe and Mail*, and the *National Post* (PR Week, 2010).

A major difference between the U.S. and Canada is that Canada has a tradition of public broadcasting. The national, public CBC television channel broadcasts in English, while the public Societe Radio-Canada broadcasts in French. CTV is a major English-language national broadcaster, while TVA is a major French-language national broadcaster (BBC, 2012a).

The CBC also operates the public, English-language Radio One network, as well as the culturally focused Radio Two and the external Radio Canada International. The public Societe Radio-Canada operates Première Chaîne and Espace Musique (BBC, 2012a).

Fifty-six percent of Canadians have active social media accounts. The most popular networks include Facebook, Twitter, Instagram, and LinkedIn (Kemp, 2015).

United States of America

Time zone: The continental U.S. (excluding Alaska and Hawaii) spans 4 time zones, ranging from Coordinated Universal Time (UTC) - 4:00 to UTC - 8:00
International dialing code: +1

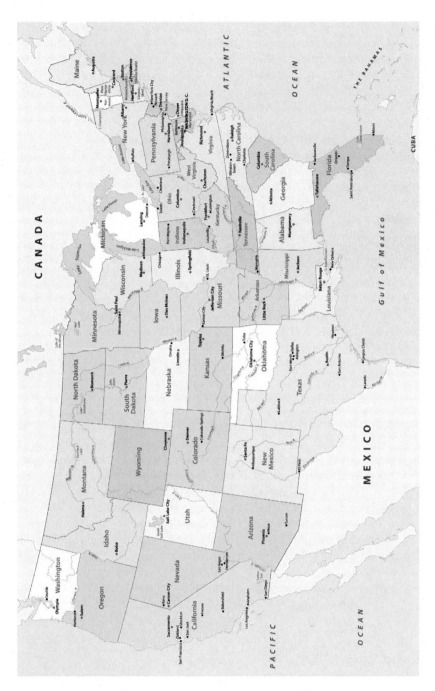

When you practice public relations in the U.S., remember to stay calm.

The world's largest economy and a mega player in foreign affairs, the U.S. is a democratic republic with a market economy (World Bank, 2014b). Nearly 80 percent of the population is white, nearly 13 percent is black, and more than 4 percent is Asian. Just over 15 percent of the population is Hispanic (which includes people of many races). The country's currency is the dollar. Although there is no official national language, most people speak English, while 10.7 percent of the population speaks Spanish (CIA, 2014). The nation's capital is Washington, D.C., though New York City is the commercial center.

The U.S. is renowned for its free press and tradition of democratic debate, which has aided the development of public relations practice. The First Amendment to the U.S. Constitution has guaranteed freedom of speech and freedom of the press since the eighteenth century. Additionally, since 1966, the Freedom of Information Act has mandated that the federal government disclose records requested by citizens (though it contains nine exemptions allowing the government to withhold certain information, such as that related to national security and personnel practices).

The country is also famous for its entrepreneurial spirit, dating back to the American Revolution, when colonial Americans declared independence from Great Britain in 1776. More than half of the 100 companies named by Interbrand (2014) as the world's most valuable brands are American. For better and for worse, the country has given the world everything from McDonalds to Mickey Mouse.

The American spirit of individualism, youth, and optimism is often reflected in public relations messages. Kanso, Sinno, and Adams (2001, p. 73) note that "American practitioners have capitalized on the youth appeal. . . . 'Think young,' 'the new generation,' 'you are as young as you feel,' and the 'natural (youthful) look' are recurrent themes." Similarly, because "Americans pride themselves on individuality," messages that work well in the United States tend to focus on individual—rather than group—benefits (Kanso et al., 2001, p. 75). Kanso et al. (2001, p. 77) also note that "age, titles, and positions are not necessarily looked upon as signs of wisdom or reasons for respect. Americans tend to be much more impressed with personal accomplishments."

One of the first things that strikes many newcomers to the U.S. is the mainstream media's focus on covering entertainment stories as opposed to global affairs. The U.S.—the birthplace of Hollywood movies—is famous for its infatuation with celebrities, and this means that the practice of public relations often includes celebrity sponsorships and endorsements.

Although many other countries have traditions of public relations that arguably date back centuries, the development and practice of public relations in the U.S. has been hugely influential globally; the Austrian immigrant to the U.S. Edward Bernays is widely regarded as the father of modern public relations. The U.S. is home to the headquarters of more than 100 of the biggest 250 public relations agencies in the world by revenue, including seven of the eight largest firms in the world: Edelman, Weber Shandwick, FleishmanHillard, Ketchum, Burson-Marsteller, Hill+Knowlton Strategies, and Ogilvy PR (Holmes Report, 2015).

A recent study of U.S. practitioners found that nearly a third act as "policy advisors" within their organizations—management positions that require researching and developing strategic plans to engage both internal and external audiences, nearly 23 percent serve as "negotiators" who participate in strategic planning within their organizations and are focused on internal and external audiences, nearly 17 percent are responsible for internal communications and are not part of senior management but support strategic planning, nearly 15 percent act as "brand officers" who are focused on marketing messages but are not part of the senior management of their organizations, and nearly 12 percent act as "press agents" who focus on the media but also engage in strategic planning and communicate internally with their management (Vieira, Jr. & Grantham, 2014, p. 65).

The concept of two-way symmetrical communication discussed in Chapter 1 was born out of U.S. scholarship (Grunig & Grunig, 1992). Although press agentry remains the most common practice in the U.S., practitioners began moving towards two-way communication in the latter part of the twentieth century (Grunig & Grunig, 2009, p. 646; Bashir & Fedorova, 2014, p. 763). Bashir and Fedorova (2014, p. 763) note that "PR organizations have become not only interested in delivering the messages to the targeted audience, but in the feedback to these messages as well." This is all but inevitable on social media.

Social media platforms including Facebook, Twitter, LinkedIn, and YouTube were all born in the U.S. More than half of the U.S. population regularly uses social networks, making the use of such platforms a major feature of public relations practice (Adweek, 2015). While there is much discussion of how social media has revolutionized the practice, Chris Nelson, Crisis Lead for the Americas at FleishmanHillard, notes that, in the U.S., while many people may now get their news through social media platforms, the news stories that are shared on platforms such as Twitter are still predominantly created by the traditional media. "The international news networks are still the leaders in content creation, which is why they dominate the sharing in social channels in the U.S., especially during crises," he says. Therefore, traditional media relations remain an extraordinarily important part of public relations practice.

Nevertheless, because most reporters are now on social media, pitching reporters on social media platforms is becoming more common. Lewis PR (2013, p. 81) recommends, "don't use Direct Messages (DM), as most reporters dislike receiving them. Instead, follow trending conversations and interact intelligently to connect with reporters or influencers who might just be on the other end of the conversation." They also note that, because U.S. reporters are often overwhelmed by the deluge of information they receive, no matter what medium you are using to pitch, it is important to do your homework before-hand to understand the types of stories that individual journalists cover and whether and how your ideas will be appropriate for their audiences.

In contrast to the Arab world, it is important to prepare your spokespeople to remain cool and collected during media interviews—no matter what their interviewers may ask. As Zaharna (2005, p. 194) explains,

> according to the American model, losing composure is the equivalent of losing objectivity. Losing objectivity makes one's argument and facts sus-pect and, ultimately, undermines one's credibility. Thus, to be an effective persuader in the American context, one should control the visual display of strong emotions. Rapid hand movement or animated facial expressions are discouraged. Instead, American officials tend to manipulate their voice tone or volume and language—either using sarcasm or understatement—to express anger.

Also in contrast to Arab cultures, religious appeals should generally be avoided in public relations campaigns. Kanso et al. (2001, p. 77) note that "while religion is very important to many Americans, it is both private and personal. It should not . . . be used as a selling point."

Finally, when practicing public relations in the U.S., be aware of local regu-lations. Under the Foreign Agents Registration Act of 1938, U.S. citizens who work for foreign governments are required to register with the U.S. Depart-ment of Justice and provide the agency with details of their work. Practitioners working in investor relations must follow the regulations of the U.S. Securities and Exchange Commission, while lobbyists must register with the U.S. Con-gress and practitioners working on political campaigns must be mindful of laws regulating campaign contributions (de la Moriniere, 2006, p. 14).

Media

Major national newspapers include *The New York Times* (discussed in Chap-ter 7), *Washington Post*, and *Los Angeles Times*, all of which have been accused of having a liberal bias, along with *USA Today*, which has been found to be more centrist (Sullivan, 2005). The economics and finance-focused *Wall Street Journal* is generally conservative in its editorial stances. There are also regional newspapers across the country.

National television broadcasters are ABC, NBC, and CBS; they compete with the cable news networks CNN (which, compared to broadcasters such as the BBC, is more sensationalist), the liberal MSNBC, and the conservative FOX news.

The country's public broadcaster is National Public Radio; Clear Channel is the country's largest source of commercial radio, with more than 1,200 sta-tions across the nation (BBC News, 2012f).

Fifty-eight percent of the U.S. population has active social media accounts. The most popular social networks include Facebook, Twitter, Instagram, and LinkedIn (Kemp, 2015).

Case Study: ALS Ice Bucket Challenge

The Ice Bucket Challenge raised millions of dollars to fight ALS. Copyright: Marcos Mesa Sam Wordley

In the summer of 2014, individuals living with Amyotrophic lateral sclerosis (ALS)—a disease that attacks the brain and spinal cord and is popularly known as "Lou Gehrig's Disease"—started a grass-roots campaign along with their families and other supporters to raise money for the ALS Association, a U.S. organization that fights the disease. As part of the "ALS ice bucket challenge," participants filmed themselves dumping a bucket of ice water over their heads during the hot summer months, and at the end of their video named other people whom they challenged to do the same and/or to make a donation to the ALS Association within 24 hours. The campaign went viral at an astonishing pace. In just one month, the organization raised $100 million from more than 3 million donors—a 3,500% increase over the same period the prior year, which represented four times the organization's annual budget (ALS Association, 2014a; Diamond, 2014). "We have never seen anything like this in the history of the disease," Barbara Newhouse, President and Chief Executive Officer of the ALS Association, said (ALS Association, 2014b).

High-profile individuals who dunked and/or donated include U.S. President Barack Obama, Facebook co-founder Mark Zuckerberg, Microsoft co-founder Bill Gates, and celebrities including Oprah, Matt Damon, and Justin Timberlake.

It is notable that the campaign began organically—it was not a public relations strategy dreamed up in an ALS Association boardroom. The organization's spokesperson, Carrie Munk, told the Associated Press that

> one of the big take-aways is the power of individuals who are so tightly connected to a cause can really make a difference. I'm pretty sure that if any company or any nonprofit had all of the public relations dollars in the world to come up with a campaign, we never would've seen this kind of success (Rancilio, 2014).

What lessons can public relations practitioners learn from the success of this campaign? First, of course, it was a fun summer activity. Participants likely also got a "helper's high" from participating in the good cause. Ironically, the element of pain involved in being soaked in ice water likely contributed to the popularity of the Challenge. Christopher Olivola of Carnegie Mellon University and Eldar Shafir of Princeton University have found that people will donate more money if they are asked to do something that is physically painful or difficult, such as running a marathon—a phenomenon dubbed the "martyrdom effect." Olivola said that people may derive more meaning from an experience "if blood, sweat and tears are involved" (McGugan, 2014, p. 36).

Another factor that helped the campaign go viral was the use of "social tagging." As Allen (2014) explains,

> the Ice Bucket Challenge became viral because of the simple rule that dictated that you have to nominate three of your friends to take the challenge after you. It's such a simple concept that I'm sure marketers everywhere are kicking themselves that they didn't think of it.

Cline (2014) noted that video is now the "medium of choice on social media" and the campaign capitalized on this and on the use of hashtags such as #IceBucketChallenge and #StrikeoutALS, which are now critical to use in social media campaigns.

Sander van der Linden, a social psychologist who studies attitude change, said that the 24-hour deadline likely also fueled the success of the Challenge, because "people like setting goals, and they like achieving goals." Therefore, "when you make people set specific goals, they become more likely to change behavior" (McGugan, 2014, p. 36).

Of course, the opportunity that it gave do-gooders to publicize their support for the cause on their social platforms undoubtedly also played a role. As *The New York Times Magazine* put it, "the challenge fed our collective narcissism by allowing us to celebrate with selfies or videos of our drenched faces and bodies on Facebook and Twitter" (McGugan, 2014, p. 36).

For this reason, some observers saw the campaign as a vain gimmick rather than an expression of genuine national commitment to fight the disease, and noted that dumping water does not cause participants to learn about the disease or engage in the fight against it in a substantive way. Many experts are therefore skeptical of whether campaigns such as the ice bucket challenge are successful in building long-term support for organizations. In an influential 2010 article in the intellectual U.S. magazine *The New Yorker*, for example, Gladwell argued that individuals will take action inspired by requests on social media only if they are asked to do things that are relatively easy. He argued that people are recruited to engage in the kind of activism that requires true sacrifice and makes a major difference—such as, for example, the African-American college students in the U.S. who risked their lives in the 1960s to protest the country's racial segregation—only by people with whom they are very close. In reality, the ice bucket challenge required relatively little sacrifice by participants.

Another big problem with such campaigns is "funding cannibalism." Griggs (2014) has noted that "because people on average are limited in how much they are willing to donate to good causes, if someone donates to one organisation, they will likely donate less to other charities. One good deed often displaces another."

While the degree to which the campaign translates into long-term support for the Association and fighting the disease remains to be seen, it is unquestionable that the campaign raised an enormous amount of awareness and funds, leaving practitioners across the nation and around the world wondering how to come up with the next Ice Bucket Challenge—and how to engage such social media supporters over the longer term.

The Latin America Cluster

Latin America is the term used to describe the part of the Americas where mainly Spanish and Portuguese are spoken—namely, Mexico (which is in North America), Central and South America, and the Caribbean.

Latin American countries inherited their languages from their Spanish, Portuguese, English, French, and Dutch colonizers. Spanish is the most widely spoken language in most of Latin America, with the major exception of Portuguese-speaking Brazil, which accounts for half of the population and geographic size of South America (Sharpe & Simoes, 1996, p. 291). Additionally, English is spoken in Belize and Guyana, Dutch is spoken in Suriname, and French is spoken in French Guiana. Spanish, French, English, and Dutch are also spoken in the islands of the Caribbean, along with local creole languages that reflect European and African influences. As a result of their colonial history, the people of Latin America are also very diverse, with populations of indigenous people and descendants of European colonizers and black slaves varying by country. Montenegro (2004, p. 112) notes that

> Venezuela, Brazil, and Colombia have a very mixed population, whereas Bolivia, Mexico, Peru, Guatemala, and Ecuador have large indigenous populations. Argentine and Chilean societies are predominantly of European descent. Southern Brazil is shaped by the large numbers of German and Italian immigrants who settled in the area; whereas the north is shaped by the Portuguese sugar cane plantation owners and their slave descendants.

Latin America is characterized by high in-group collectivism; moderate levels of assertiveness, gender egalitarianism, humane orientation, and power distance; and low future orientation, institutional collectivism, performance orientation, and uncertainty avoidance (Gupta & Hanges, 2004, p. 193). The culture has been heavily influenced by Roman Catholicism; today, 69 percent of Latin American adults are Catholic (Pew, 2013). Livermore (2013, p. 53) notes that

> Latin American cultures are very Collectivist, but their collectivism is primarily oriented around the family. There's less devotion to institutional groups like workplaces or community organizations than what you might find in other Collectivist cultures. There's certainly some loyalty to the church and religious groups, but the primary source of identity is the family. To many Latin Americans, the family is everything. There's fairly low trust of those outside one's family network.

The concept of family extends beyond the nuclear family. Gupta and Hanges (2004, p. 186) note that "the family's boundaries are guided by *compadrazgo* (i.e., coparenting), in which a child's godparents move beyond friendship to formalize a closer bond to the family in the baptismal ceremony."

Relationships are "the glue that makes life happen in this part of the world" (Livermore, 2013, p. 55). Montenegro (2004, p. 112) notes that

> all professional activities in Latin America are built on personal relationships. It is very important to get to know someone at a personal level. . . . Latin Americans, in general, need to have face-to-face contact with the person with whom they are dealing.

As a result, "a closer relationship with employees is required."

Eunice Lima, the São Paulo-based Director of Communications and Government Affairs for the global aluminum company Novelis, says the same is true with the press. "It's quite different from other parts of the world," she says. "We have more focus on building relationships. It's very personal."

Additionally, their low future orientation means that "Latin American societies tend to enact life as it comes, taking its unpredictability as a fact of life, and not overly worrying about results. There is less concern with institutional collective goals than with family bonds" (Gupta & Hanges, 2004, p. 199). Accordingly, people in Latin America tend to place less priority on work than other cultures and to place greater priority on enjoying life. Livermore (2013, p. 54) notes that "family trumps work. In fact, supervisors are often expected to attend the family functions of employees and to give special consideration to what happens to the family if an employee is fired."

Montenegro (2004, p. 117) describes the culture as "more present-oriented or past-oriented than future oriented. As a result, government decrees may not take place today, but perhaps tomorrow. Business meetings may not start on time, but will take place later on." As discussed in Chapter 2, an absolutely critical cultural factor to be aware of when working in Latin America is the society's polychronic approach to time. As one government affairs practitioner explains, "if someone says, 'Let's do this tomorrow at 10 a.m.,' at 10:05 in the U.S. we're late. In Brazil, a week later we're not late; we're just getting talking" (Judd, 2011, p. 17).

Although the GLOBE study ranks Latin America low in uncertainty avoidance, Livermore (2013, p. 53) reports that Latin Americans are actually more averse to uncertainty than many other cultures:

> This seems like a contradiction with the laid-back, "que serà serà" Latino ethos. But change and uncertainty are avoided far more in Latin America than they are among the dominant cultures of North America. However, the Latin American response to uncertainty is very different from that of the Germans or Japanese, who also have High Uncertainty Avoidance. Latinos are less likely to use laws, schedules, and policies to achieve certainty. Instead, they rely upon their religion and their family networks to attain certainty. Your best security lies in having someone you can trust to take care of you.

Latin Americans' emphasis on the family and social class also means that "status differences are accepted, and paternalism is the prevailing hierarchical arrangement" (Montenegro, 2004, p. 116). Despite its GLOBE ranking, Montenegro (2004, p. 110) and Livermore (2013, p. 53) describe high power distance in Latin American culture; the more senior executives are the decision-makers.

Although the region was ruled by many dictatorships in the 1970s, democratic governments began to take root in the following decade (Montenegro, 2004, p. 111). The practice of public relations in Latin America expanded considerably following the end of military governments in Argentina, Brazil, Chile, Paraguay, Peru, and Uruguay in the 1980s and the development of free market economies in the 1990s (Montenegro, 2004, p. 105). The profession remains less developed in Central America, where economic growth has been hindered by civil wars, poverty, and natural disasters in countries including El Salvador, Honduras, and Nicaragua, but the practice of public relations is expected to expand in this region as trade increases (Montenegro, 2004, p. 106).

Still, the region suffers from high levels of poverty, inequality, and crime; Montenegro (2004, p. 117) notes that "class antagonism has created an enormous mistrust between the poor and the rich, resulting in kidnappings and robberies of members of higher social levels." This certainly complicates the practice of public relations. For example, Leslie Gaines-Ross, Chief Reputation Strategist for the global public relations firm Weber Shandwick, says she learned on a recent trip that some heads of Latin American corporations do not want their pictures posted online because they fear becoming the victims of crime.

When you practice public relations in this region, be careful not to view Latin America as a monolith. The major divide is between Portuguese-speaking Brazil and the mainly Spanish-speaking rest of the region, but even among Spanish-language countries, there are significant differences. Serge Giacomo, Head of Communications and Institutional Relations for GE in Latin America, recommends, "the more local you are, if you can actually be a Peruvian in Peru and a Colombian in Colombia, that's the best." He says that, in the past, many companies based their Latin American communications in Miami, Florida, in order to avoid having to choose between Argentina, Brazil, or Mexico, the three major markets in the region. Today, GE has a Portuguese-speaking spokesperson based in Brazil; the decision of whether to locate the company's spokesperson for the rest of Latin America in Mexico or Argentina was complicated. Giacomo says that his colleagues feared that, because Argentinians speak with a distinctive accent,

> if the colleague in Argentina needed to talk to journalists in Colombia, they would not be able to engage in a positive conversation—so we went for Mexico because although it is far away it doesn't have a strong sense of competition with the other countries.

Still, Giacomo, who is based in São Paulo, Brazil, says he must be careful to be sensitive to members of his team in other parts of Latin America who "think it's a sort of neocolonialism and Brazil may be perceived as trying to take over and have everything done here." For example, to avoid deciding whether team conference calls should be conducted in Spanish or Portuguese, he and his colleagues speak English.

A major problem in this region is the restriction of press freedom. Freedom House (2014a) reports that only 2 percent of Latin Americans live in media environments that are free. Rueda (2012) notes that "one of the greatest threats to press freedom in Latin America comes in the form of shady criminal groups like Mexican drug cartels or Colombian paramilitaries who harass and sometimes murder journalists that report on their activities." Political corruption also leads to government restrictions on the press. For example, Freedom House (2014c) notes that, since coming to power in 2013, Venezuelan President Nicolás Maduro has "hampered the opposition media by arbitrarily fining outlets, enforcing licensing requirements without respecting due process rights, and excluding certain outlets from access to public information." In Ecuador, meanwhile, the government of President Rafael Correa continues to charge critical journalists with crimes; in 2014, it brought an $80 million lawsuit against an opinion editor and columnist of the newspaper *El Universo* for an opinion piece that was critical of how the government handled a police uprising in 2010 (Freedom House, 2014b). Paraguay, Brazil, and Mexico were among the world's deadliest countries for journalists in 2014 (Committee to Protect Journalists, 2014).

Another factor that influences press coverage in the region is the ownership of media outlets. Montenegro (2004, p. 113) notes that, in Latin America, "most leading mass media outlets are family-owned. Thus, these media are likely to be influenced to some extent by the interests of the family in question."

Television and radio are the predominant forms of media in the region. Montenegro (2004, p. 107) explains that "radio and television, with their great proportion of entertainment content, such as *telenovelas* (soap operas), draw immense audiences, whereas newspapers are read more by the highly educated and those interested in politics."

Latin America is currently experiencing increased citizen consciousness and activism, with anticorruption protests sweeping countries including Brazil, Chile, Guatemala, Honduras, and Mexico (Malkin, 2015). A dynamic that often surprises practitioners who are new to the region is social expectations of businesses. Giacomo says that, in this part of the world,

a company is perceived as a public entity, so journalists and the general public can and will summon a company to take action on things totally unrelated to the business. For example, if you are a company that operates in the Amazon, the population may say that we'd like you to take action on something that is totally up to the government to do, but you're strong and rich, so help us. It doesn't mean they trust you more, maybe there's no trust; it's just that you can do it, it's about having the means.

Finally, Latin American public relations theory differs from other parts of the world. The Latin American School of Public Relations focuses on the role of public relations in society. Molleda (2000, p. 513) explains that "the public relations practitioner is seen as a change agent or the conscience of the organization." This emphasis "reflects a more active society that is experiencing political and economic transformations in an era of privatization, deregulation, increased social inequalities and market integration." The aim of the profession is seen as being to promote human well-being, community interests, social progress, understanding, integration, and consensus among groups (Molleda, 2000, pp. 519–520). The following sections profile public relations in four of the region's key markets: Argentina, Brazil, Chile, and Mexico.

Argentina

Time zone: Coordinated Universal Time (UTC) - 3:00
International dialing code: +54

Before you practice public relations in Argentina, figure out how local politics is impacting your client or organization.

Argentina is Latin America's third-largest and the world's fifteenth-largest economy (World Bank, 2014a). The country achieved independence from Spain in 1816 and has been heavily influenced by immigration from Europe, especially from Italy and Spain. Argentina was ruled by a military junta beginning in 1976—a period during which many thousands of people were killed or "disappeared"—but returned to democracy in 1983. Today, it is a federal republic (CIA, 2014). Although the country has been plagued by recent economic instability—including a 1998–2002 crisis which resulted in high unemployment and riots and caused the nation to default on its debt—the country is rich in natural resources and is one of the world's major exporters of food, including beef (World Bank, 2014a). Argentina's official language is Spanish, its currency is the Argentine peso, and its capital is Buenos Aires. Ninety seven percent of the population is white (predominantly Italian and Spanish) and three percent is mestizo (mixed white and Amerindian), Amerindian, or of other ancestry (CIA, 2014).

Argentina boasts a particularly well-developed public relations industry. Montenegro (2004, pp. 113, 124) reports that "local companies understand the importance of communicating their messages effectively to the public" and also "understand public relations as the management of relations with key publics" (Montenegro, 2004, pp. 113, 124). Another study confirms that the Argentinian public relations industry is notable for its breadth and diversity of services (CPRPRA, 2012, p. 15). One practitioner says that the traditional press agency is literally disappearing in Argentina, as agencies strive to add

value through new services, such as digital and social media strategies and campaigns (IMAGEN, 2010, pp. 66–68).

However, Allan McCrea Steele, Chief Executive Officer of Edelman in Latin America and President in Argentina, says that, in recent years, the government's willingness to intervene in businesses and heavy restrictions on foreign imports have significantly impacted the practice of public relations in the country. "The first thing you need to do when practicing public relations in Argentina is have an open mind," McCrea Steele says. "Argentina has a fast-changing political, economic, and social environment and experiences a crisis every ten years, so just imagine doing business here."

In particular, McCrea Steele says that the government's willingness to intervene significantly in the economy and businesses has made companies fearful of communicating publicly. Businesses are instead inclined to cover up any problems that they have, because they are afraid that otherwise the government will step in. As a result, "businesses only want to talk about their products and services—nothing else," he says. Furthermore, the government has heavily restricted foreign imports, and local businesses lack access to foreign currency; as a result, many foreign products are not available in the country. "All the public relations initiatives today are really only Argentinian businesses talking about products," McCrea Steele says.

McCrea Steele says that the country's political and economic situation has driven significant demand for government relations practitioners, since local political officials have the power to issue waivers to individual companies allowing them to import. "It's not straight lobbying, but building bridges with public officials who can make decisions," McCrea Steele says. He says that it is difficult, but not impossible, to obtain such waivers.

He also says that the current crisis has made it harder to pitch stories to the mainstream Argentinian press. "There is less room for news in the dailies because everyone is focused on politics, so it's hard to place stories about products," McCrea Steele says. However, he says that, because corporate executives are so reticent to speak to the media because of the political climate, any time a senior official is willing to do so, there will be big demand from the press. McCrea Steele also says that because many multinational corporations have left the country and foreign investment is so greatly needed, any foreign investment in the country will generate significant media coverage. He says that

> it is needed so badly that whenever any client makes an investment, no matter how large or small, that is big and they can leverage that, not just for media coverage but also to get something from the government, like approval for additional imports or tax reductions.

Despite the present difficulties of practicing public relations in Argentina, McCrea Steele has hope for the future and says that the current crisis has only strengthened the skills of local practitioners. "We can't currently implement some modern practices because the market doesn't allow it," McCrea Steele says. "But Argentina has some of the best P.R. practitioners in the region, because we live and operate in a crisis mode, so we're adaptable, flexible, open-minded, and extremely creative."

Media

Argentinian news agencies include the state-run Telam and privately owned Diarios y Noticias and Noticias Argentinas (BBC, 2012b).

Major daily newspapers include *La Prensa* (the country's oldest newspaper), the popular *Clarín*, the conservative, respected *La Nación*, the tabloid *Crónica*, the business-focused *El Cronista*, the left-wing *Página/12*, and the English-language *Buenos Aires Herald* (BBC, 2012b).

Television networks include the leading national networks El Trece (Canal 13), owned by the media conglomerate Grupo Clarín; Telefe (Canal 11), owned by Grupo Telefe; the popular Canal 9; America (Canal 2); and the state-run Canal 7, which broadcasts educational and cultural programming. Grupo Clarín also owns the cable/satellite channel Todo Noticias (BBC, 2012b).

Popular radio outlets include Radio Mitre (owned by Grupo Clarín), Radio América, Radio Continental, the music-focused Los 40 Principales, and the state-run Radio Nacional, which broadcasts cultural programming (BBC, 2012b).

Argentinians are some of the most avid users of social media in the world. Sixty percent of Argentinians have active social media accounts, and they spend 4.3 hours per day on average on social media—leaving them tied with the Philippines for the most time of any users in the world. The most popular social networks include Facebook, Twitter, LinkedIn, and Instagram (Kemp, 2015).

Brazil

> *Time zone: Spans 4 time zones, ranging from Coordinated Universal Time (UTC) - 2:00 to UTC - 5:00*
> *International dialing code: +55*

When you practice public relations in Brazil, be prepared to make a lot of local friends.

Far and away the largest country in Latin America by both size and population, Brazil is the world's seventh-largest economy and was the first nation in the region where public relations was practiced (World Bank, 2014b; Ferrari, 2009a, p. 710). The gargantuan country is also, of course, one of the "BRICS"—the term used to describe Brazil, Russia, India, China, and South Africa, whose economies have become increasingly powerful. The world's largest coffee producer, Brazil achieved independence from Portugal in the nineteenth century and was ruled by a military junta beginning in 1964, until its return to democracy in the 1980s (ICO, 2015). Somewhat isolated from its

Copyright: Rainer Lesniewski

Spanish-speaking neighbors by the fact that its official language is Portuguese, Brazil is now an important country for multinational corporations because of its recently expanded middle class and "buy now, pay later culture," which drives consumerism (Molleda, Athaydes, & Hirsch, 2009, p. 727; Magee, 2014). Brazil is a federal republic; its currency is the real and its capital is Brasilia, though its commercial capital is São Paulo (CIA, 2014). The country is notable for its great diversity, including people with indigenous, European, African, and Asian roots whom Molleda et al. (2009, pp. 738–739) describe as a "very friendly people" who have "a great passion for life."

In 1967, Brazil became the first country to license public relations professionals. Practitioners are required to have a degree from a recognized university in communication with a focus on public relations and to be licensed by a regional council, although there has been a lively debate in recent years about updating the law (Molleda et al., 2009, p. 732). However, Brazilian practitioners say that the law does not stop some people from practicing without a license (Molleda & Athaydes, 2003, p. 271). One Brazilian practitioner explains that many people who work in public relations simply call themselves communicators, both in order to skirt the law and because the term "public relations" is often confused with the job of being a hostess in Brazil.

Because of the importance of relationships in Latin American society, the personal influence model of public relations prevails in Brazil. Fabio Cavalcanti Caldas, Director of External Affairs for the oil company Shell in Latin America, says that "it is unbelievable how you can get so many things by being close to people." Relationships are built at the local level in Brazil; as discussed in Chapter 4, in this country, a Brazilian who is from a different city will be greeted as a foreigner.

Andre Morais, an institutional relations specialist who works in government affairs for the Brazilian telecommunications company Oi, warns that Brazil is home to so many different cultures that dramatically different public relations strategies are needed in different parts of the country. Lala Aranha, President of Rio de Janeiro's regional chapter of CONRERP, Brazil's council of public relations professionals, likewise notes that

> in other parts of the country, people speak the language with a different accent, they have different local expressions, they even use verbs in a different way, though these differences are now narrowing because of the web. That is why it's so important to think globally but act very locally.

The south of Brazil is significantly richer than the country's north, and unlike in countries such as the U.S. where the middle class may live in suburbs outside of major cities, the areas surrounding Brazil's cities tend to be poor. Paulo Henrique Soares, the Rio de Janeiro-based Head of Communications for the Brazilian mining company Vale who is profiled in this chapter, explains that, "in Brazil, you only live outside a city if you don't have a way out of there."

Claudia Afflalo, Rio de Janeiro-based Communications and Media Relations Supervisor for the oil company Chevron, says that, in recent years, consumer companies have increasingly begun to recognize the economic contributions of low-income people and begun conducting public relations campaigns in the *favelas* (a Portuguese word for slums). Angela Giacobbe, Manager of Communication and Sustainability for the Brazilian maritime and port logistics company Wilson, Sons, says that strategies that tend to work particularly well in poorer communities, where illiteracy remains a problem, are using soap opera celebrities, television, and radio. Soares reports that some companies literally go door-to-door in the favelas. In such communities, relationships are especially important. Giacomo, of GE, explains that

> outside of a city, it becomes really personal. The top management of your company needs to be part of the same circle as the mayor and local

officials, the local elite, and even the priest. In order to work with those audiences, you need to belong; you need to be part of the same group.

Hugo Godinho, Executive Director of the Brazilian communication holding company Grupo In Press, which is part of the Omnicom Group, says that even low-income Brazilians are remarkably well connected online, and many Brazilian companies selling consumer products use paid content on Facebook in order to segment and deliver different messages to different audiences in the country. Indeed, social media strategies are a must for this hyper-connected country. As Soares explains, "We are very social and we have moved into social media with our socialness." Giacobbe says that "unless you have mainstream, massive products, you need online influencers, viral campaigns, and social media to get people talking."

However, Caldas, of Shell, says that the traditional media is still paramount here. "Media is the main stakeholder in Brazil, and it influences all others. In Brazil, you are dead without the media." Afflalo says that a major difference between media relations in Brazil and in countries such as the U.S. is that, in Brazil, public relations professionals do not typically serve as spokespersons for their companies. "Here in Brazil, reporters expect that when something important happens, the President or C.E.O. will speak," she says.

Ana Juliao, Executive Vice President of the Rio de Janeiro office of Edleman Significa, which is part of the global public relations firm Edelman, says that Brazilian journalists generally expect more interviews—and more facts—than in other places. "In other parts of the world, practitioners send a lot of statements to the press, but here we give more interviews," she says. Juliao reports that most Brazilian journalists do not speak English with enough fluency to conduct an interview and will expect interviews to be conducted in Portuguese. She also says that, "with press releases in English, you find a lot of adjectives, but here journalists are more demanding and want hard facts, so information needs to be more precise than general." There is significant demand in the Brazilian press for content such as fresh studies and analysis (Judd, 2011, p. 27).

Another reason why you will need local help crafting your messages for Brazil is because, in this high-context society, certain things are just understood by locals. Flavio Oliveira, a global public relations consultant from João Pessoa, Brazil, says that "you have to know the background and the context before you craft your message, because there are so many assumptions that Brazilians make about the meaning of things."

Giacobbe says that another successful public relations strategy in this country is partnering with Brazil's ultra-popular soap operas, which cause the country's streets to empty during final episodes and are exported to countries around the world, including Portugal, Angola, and China. Giacobbe says that product placement on such shows has been found to promote effective brand recall and many soap operas have also partnered with non-profit organizations pro-bono in order to deliver messages on social issues such as adoption, cancer, and missing persons.

Brazilians are socially and environmentally conscious—the country is, after all, home to the majority of the Amazon rainforest. Cristina Schachtitz, Executive Vice President of Edelman Significa, says that when companies enter the Brazilian market, they should be prepared to talk about their local impact. "What Brazilians want to hear now is how this new business, this project, this investment is going to impact our country," she says. "Not only that the company is coming and that the C.E.O. wants to talk to you. Maybe 20 years ago, just being an American company would be good enough, but not now."

Finally, internal communication with employees is emphasized in Brazil (Molleda & Ferguson, 2004, p. 346). Soares says that

> in internal communications, we talk about the pride of working for a company. There is a Portuguese expression that you put on the jersey of the company you work for. In Brazil, there is a passion and a sense of belonging to your company that we have found doesn't exist elsewhere. So employees play a very important role in a communication strategy and in everything we do we must ensure that employees are impassioned and well connected to our brands.

Media

Brazilian news agencies include the state-owned Agencia Brasil and privately owned Agencia Globo and Agencia Estado (BBC, 2012c).

Major daily newspapers in Brazil include *Folha de S. Paulo*, *O Estado de S. Paulo*, *O Globo*, *O Dia*, *Correio Brazilense*, and the financial newspaper *Valor Econômico* (BBC, 2012c).

Rede Globo, owned by Grupo Globo, is one of the world's largest television networks. Other major television networks are TV Band, Sistema Brasileiro de Televisao (SBT), TV Record, Rede TV, TV Brasil (operated by EBC, which is state run), and the public TV Cultura (BBC, 2012c).

Major radio networks include Globo Radio, Radio Bandeirantes, Radio Nacional (operated by state-run EBC), and the public Radio Cultura (BBC, 2012c).

Forty-seven percent of Brazilians have active social media accounts. The most popular social networks include Facebook, Twitter, Instagram, and LinkedIn (Kemp, 2015).

Practitioner Profile: Paulo Henrique Soares, Head of Communications, Vale, Brazil

Paulo Henrique Soares is the Rio de Janiero, Brazil-based Head of Communications for Vale, the world's third-largest mining company. Paulo

Paulo Henrique Soares

has spent his entire twenty-year career working in communications for Vale and says his longevity working internally within the organization is one of the keys to his success.

Paulo studied communication at the Pontifícia Universidade Católica in his home state of Minas Gerais, Brazil, where he later returned to earn his master's degree. Upon graduating from college in 1995, he began his career as a Communication Analyst for Vale in Carajás, Brazil, where he was responsible for hosting visitors (including clients, members of the community, and other stakeholders) to Vale's operations. He was later promoted to the job of Communication Coordinator for the company in São Luís, Brazil, before returning to his hometown of Belo Horizonte, Brazil, to manage communications for several different mines and railroads, as well as community affairs. In 2002, Paulo moved to Rio de Janeiro to serve as General Manager of Communications for the company, where he has remained, with the exception of another year-long stint in Belo Horizonte in 2009. In 2014, he was promoted to Head of Communications for Vale.

Paulo says that the benefit of working for a single organization for so long and handling public relations internally, as opposed to through an agency, is that

> I have lived the history of the company for the past twenty years, and that makes a big difference. I know the problems and hope to know the right solutions. I know the issues. I know the people and that makes a big difference.

Contrary to the perception that he says some people have that working for the same organization for so long would be boring, Paulo says,

"By moving around, I have been exposed to a lot of different experiences, cultures, and challenges and learned a lot." Paulo also keeps his skills and contacts up to date by serving as Director of the Rio de Janeiro chapter of Aberje, the Brazilian Association for Business Communication.

When Paulo began working for Vale in 1995, it was a $6 U.S. billion, state-owned company with 15,000 employees. Today, Vale is a $35 billion U.S. private organization with 120,000 employees. Paulo handled public relations during the firm's privatization in 1997 and as it has purchased companies in Australia, Canada, Indonesia, and New Caledonia and started projects in Mozambique, Chile, Oman, and Peru.

When working in different countries, one of the most important lessons that Paulo has learned is that there is no alternative to communicating—correctly—in local languages. "It's so obvious, but it is incredible how many people make mistakes," he says. "Companies still think that everyone speaks English, or they don't want to spend the time and money to translate, but they are wrong." Paying attention to local dialects is just as important. For example, even though Portuguese is spoken in both Brazil, where Vale's headquarters are based, and in Mozambique, all of Vale's communications written in headquarters for audiences in Mozambique are adjusted by a local staff member, so that the language sounds local.

Beyond language, Paulo says that he approaches all of Vale's international communications by considering two lenses. "Brands and companies are perceived by stakeholders through a lens on top of a lens," he says. "There is the country's culture, and then there is the company's culture to consider on top of that."

In his home country of Brazil, Paulo says that maintaining relationships is one of the most important components of success. "In Brazil, you need to know people in order to interact," he says. "If I call and I don't know a person, he or she will answer me, but knowing a person is key and important. Personal relationships are the key to success. This is part of our Brazilian culture."

Chile

Time zone: Continental Chile is on Coordinated Universal Time (UTC) - 3:00. International dialing code: +56

When you practice public relations in Chile, start by thinking about Mrs. Juanita.

The BBC (2012d) describes Chile as "one of South America's most stable and prosperous nations." Chile achieved independence from Spain in the nineteenth century. The country was ruled by the Marxist government of Salvador

Copyright: Rainer Lesniewski

Allende from 1970–1973, followed by the right-wing military dictatorship of Augusto Pinochet until 1990, when a president was elected. Free market policies were implemented beginning in the 1980s, opening up opportunities for public relations practitioners within organizations that now compete in a globalized economy (Ferrari, 2009b, p. 752). The country's major industries include mining—it is the largest producer of copper in the world—and telecommunications (BBC, 2012d; Hay, 2010; PR Week, 2012). Although all of Latin America is heavily influenced by the Roman Catholic Church, this is especially the case in Chile, which did not legalize divorce until 2004, making it the last country in the Western Hemisphere to do so (Ferrari, 2009b, p. 757; Rohter, 2005).

Nearly 89 percent of the population is white and non-indigenous, while over 10 percent are of indigenous origin (CIA, 2014). The country's currency is the peso, its official language is Spanish, and its capital is Santiago.

Ferrari (2009b, p. 763) reports that large organizations in Chile have in-house public relations departments, but many medium and smaller organizations still do not. However, "the profession is not fully understood and is confused with the activities practiced by journalists" and journalists continue to constitute a large number of the country's public relations practitioners (Ferrari, 2009b, pp. 749, 764). Nevertheless, a recent study found that the majority of Chilean practitioners see long-term strategy as being important to their roles, alongside activities such as promoting change within their organizations and more short-term work such as generating news—suggesting that the field is maturing (Mellado & Barría, 2012, p. 449).

Today, Chile is experiencing "a citizen moment, a moment of change of traditional power in politics, companies, and media," according to Pamela Leonard, General Manager of Hill+Knowlton Strategies in Chile. Leonard reports that "today, citizens have a lot of power and are really the influencers." She says that this is revolutionizing the way that public relations is practiced in the country by placing greater importance on corporate social responsibility and responding to the demands of citizens—a trend that she notes is also happening in Mexico and Spain. "Companies today have to take time to get to know the expectations of the public—not only their clients, consumers, and partners, but also citizens," Leonard says. "What are their wants, their worries in general? What values are they defending now?" She says that it is also important for organizations to communicate how their activities and presence will benefit "Mrs. Juanita"—a Chilean expression for the average person.

Leonard says that the most effective public relations strategy in Chile is fostering "intimate conversations" with local audiences. In particular, she says that Chileans are eager to hear human stories behind their brands. "Even when you're talking about your brand, you have to talk about the people behind your brand," she says. "Chileans want to hear from the mom who uses Pampers. I don't want to hear the C.E.O. taking about [corporate social responsibility] because it's not really emotional. That's what we do—we are storytellers for the brands." She also advises her clients to consider original and emotional actions to surprise consumers, such as guerilla marketing tactics or partnerships to contribute to social causes.

Leonard also recommends crafting local content for Chilean audiences. She says that, too often, multinational companies will have a single spokesperson for the entire Spanish-speaking world, yet the nuances of the language are different in Chile than in other countries, and these organizations are therefore "losing opportunities to connect with our people." One tactic that she says works well is using local Chilean celebrities or influencers as brand ambassadors, both because they are seen as credible and because this approach usually results in significant media coverage. Because social media has such a huge penetration in Chile, social strategies are also essential.

Finally, Leonard warns companies to be respectful when operating in Chile. She says,

Because we are a little country in the south of a very poor region, when multinationals come here, they often say that they are a big company and they think our country has potential. In the 1990s, that kind of speech was wonderful. Today, it doesn't work and it feels a little arrogant. Today we feel very connected with the rest of the world and very different from the other countries of our region. We are part of the O.E.C.D., so we feel like we are on the same stage with the big companies.

Media

Major daily newspapers in Chile include the influential, conservative *El Mercurio*; its competitor, *La Tercera*; the conservative, evening *La Segunda*; the government-owned *La Nacion* (which is now exclusively an online outlet); and the business-focused *Diario Financiero*, which publishes on weekdays only (Ferrari, 2009b, p. 750; BBC, 2012d). *The Santiago Times* is published in English.

Major television outlets include the National Television of Chile, which is state-owned but commercially funded, along with the privately owned Canal 13, Chilevisión, Megavisión, and Red TV (BBC, 2012d).

Radio outlets include the news-focused Radio Cooperativa and music-focused Radio Horizonte, along with Pudahuel FM, Bio Bio La Radio, and El Conquistador FM (BBC, 2012d).

Chileans are active on social media platforms, including Facebook and Twitter (Heim, 2011).

Mexico

Time zone: Spans 4 time zones, ranging from Coordinated Universal Time (UTC) - 5:00 to UTC - 8:00
International dialing code: +52

When you practice public relations in Mexico, be prepared to do a lot of local radio interviews.

The southernmost country in North America, the federal republic of Mexico is the world's ninth-largest and Latin America's second-largest economy (World Bank, 2014b). Its capital is Mexico City, its currency is the peso, and nearly 93 percent of the population speaks Spanish (CIA, 2014). Sixty percent of the Mexican population is mestizo, while 30 percent is predominantly or fully Amerindian and 9 percent is white (CIA, 2014).

Mexico's indigenous people came under the domination of Spain in 1519. The Spanish were overthrown in 1821, the French unsuccessfully attempted

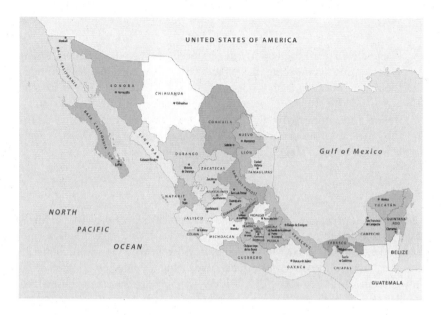

Copyright: Rainer Lesniewski

to colonize the country four decades later, and beginning in 1911 several fac-
tions fought for control of the country for three decades. From the 1930s to
2000, a single political party ruled the country. The 2000 presidential election was seen as marking the federal republic's transition to true democracy;
the privatization of the economy has also bolstered the public relations sector (Rebeil, Montoya, & Hidalgo, 2009, p. 686). However, in spite of these
events, Mexico continues to be plagued by one of the world's highest rates
of income inequality and high rates of crime and violence; the lack of jobs
leads many of both the country's poorer and more educated citizens to emi-
grate (Rebeil et al., 2009, pp. 686, 691–692). The country's economy is heavily dependent upon remittances from such migrant workers, as well as on oil
exports (BBC, 2012e).

The North American Free Trade Agreement, which took effect in 1994,
significantly boosted Mexico's public relations industry. "New and more
sophisticated ways of doing public relations were introduced at a greater
speed than before, given the presence of more and more diverse multinational corporations demanding communication and public relations services"
(Rebeil & Herrera, 2012, p. 168). As one practitioner explains, "Mexican
companies are looking for investors abroad, and they are much more aware
today that their corporate reputation will impact their ability to attract capital" (Long, 2004, p. 51).

However, while appreciation and understanding of the field is growing, the President and Chief Executive Officer of Burson-Marsteller Mexico says that

> there is still a long way to go. It is still common to find that those responsible for communication remain secluded from the decision-makers or are invited to join the discussion too late. Most of the time, they are seen as operational employees, those who take pictures, write or organise events, but not as strategic partners capable of contributing to the business (Valladares, 2014).

Today, three-quarters of the Mexican people live in cities (Rebeil et al., 2009, p. 685). The practice of public relations remains concentrated in urban areas and touristic centers of Mexico, while

> smaller-scale cities continue to practice public relations within the paradigm of the *old concept*, which basically refers to the public relations practice being conceived as inter-personal attention and services provided by ways of *being nice* or *agreeable* to clients, based upon the belief that those attitudes will favor sales, bring new business opportunities, and create a good image or the promotion of persons, organizations, or projects. Therefore, public relations clients hire people who demonstrate this disposition to *be friendly*, instead of strategic communicators and public relations experts (Rebeil & Herrera, 2012, pp. 172–174).

In this Latin American country, personal relationship building with reporters and clients is, of course, essential (Howard & Mathews, 2013, p. 176). Adriana Garza, a public relations practitioner from Monterrey, Mexico, explains that

> Mexicans do business socially. It is always about the drink, lunch, or dinner, and that is how most of the deals close. It's part of the business culture, not only in P.R. but in general. There is a term called "viernes chilango" which means that every Friday people leave the office at 3 p.m. for long lunches and drinks with clients and coworkers.

Personal influence, or *palanca*, is also critical for getting jobs and contracts (Pineda, 2010, p. 16).

Furthermore, as is the case elsewhere in Latin America, media ownership is concentrated in the hands of a small number of firms. When a story is pitched on behalf of a company, media owners may take account of factors such as their current or potential future business relationships with the company when deciding whether or not to run the story; overall, media coverage is often slanted to advance the interests of powerful owners (Rebeil et al., 2009, pp. 695–697).

Mexican public relations practitioners report that corruption remains part of the country's culture and that reporters view them with suspicion and mistrust

(Molleda & Moreno, 2008, p. 156). Although payment for stories does still occur in Mexico, one practitioner describes the practice as an "endangered species." (Rebeil et al., 2009, p. 696; Long, 2004, p. 50). Garza explains that "we call those payments under the table *mordidas*, but things are changing, and every year they happen less and less. However, relationship building with reporters is always about 'what can you do for me in the future.'"

There are a significant number of media outlets with wide diffusion across Mexico. High rates of illiteracy often lead practitioners to eschew print media when attempting to reach broader audiences. Although radio has the highest penetration of any medium, the large number of radio stations has resulted in very segmented audiences, and therefore practitioners often turn to television in order to achieve the widest possible reach for their messages (Molleda & Moreno, 2006, p. 106). However, Jorge Acosta, a partner in the Mexico-City-based public relations firm Alterpraxis, says that, too often, he sees both the Mexican government and corporations in Mexico focus their efforts on gaining media coverage in a handful of media outlets based in urban centers. While such outlets are useful for reaching thought leaders, Acosta says that "it doesn't really get to most of the population. To really reach the Mexican people, you need to do interviews on local radio stations across the country."

Another reason why local interviews are important is because Mexico is such a diverse society, making segmentation critical (Rebeil et al., 2009, p. 692). Garza explains that "because there is such a wide range of 'small cultures' and socio-economic groups, you can never target Mexico as a whole. You have to regionalize. The north is different from the Caribbean, from the Pacific, from the center."

Additionally, be prepared for reporters to editorialize. Rebeil et al. (2009, p. 695) note that "media news programs are strongly oriented towards providing opinions and editorial contents rather than straight information. Anchormen and ladies provide evaluations and opinions as they read the news in front of the TV cameras and radio stations." Garza concurs that

> there are very powerful anchors and reporters who have their own opinions, and their influence can change elections easily. Joaquin Lopez Doriga of Televisa and Carmen Aristegui of CNN en Español are good examples. They have very strong opinions and Mexicans trust them because they question government, politicians, and corporations.

Garza also says that Mexico is experiencing a period of heightened citizen activism similar to what Leonard described in Chile. "Mexicans are starting to speak up against their government," she says. "They are disappointed and tired and they are demanding more."

Finally, when developing public relations campaigns, consider the Mexican people's sense of humor. Garza says that

> Mexicans are known to have a great sense of humor, and there is no catastrophe that can befall Mexicans that within hours will not be converted

Carmen Aristegui is one of Mexico's most influential journalists. Photo courtesy of CNN en Español

into a humorous anecdote. It takes five seconds for people to create memes about a negative event. We make fun of ourselves, our families, and our stereotypes, but if someone from a different country makes a joke about our country, that will backfire. However, if you understand Mexican humor, which as a foreigner requires getting local help, then it is 95 percent certain that your campaign will be a success.

Media

Notimex is a state-run news agency in Mexico, while El Universal is a private news agency.

Reforma is "the most influential newspaper in the capital—and perhaps in the country." (Long, 2004, p. 47). Other major dailies include *El Norte*, *Excelsior*, and *El Universal*.

The country's two television giants are Televisa and TVAzteca, both of which have national networks and local stations. Canal Once is a public television broadcaster, focused on educational and cultural programming, while public broadcaster XEIMT-TV, on channel 22, is focused on cultural programming (BBC, 2012e).

Radio outlets in the country include the public broadcaster Instituto Mexicano de la Radio (IMER) and the news network W Radio (owned by Televisa). Grupo ACIR, MVS Radio, and Grupo Radio Centro operate stations across the country (BBC, 2012e).

Forty-six percent of Mexicans have active social media accounts. The most popular social networks include Facebook, Twitter, Instagram, and LinkedIn (Kemp, 2015).

References

Adweek. (2015, January 12). Infographic: Who's really using Facebook, Twitter, Pinterest, Tumblr and Instagram in 2015. Retrieved from http://www.adweek.com/news/adver tising-branding/new-social-stratosphere-who-using-facebook-twitter-pinterest-tumblr-and-instagram-2015-and-beyond-1622

Allen, K. (2014, August 27). How the ALS ice bucket challenge could change PR for nonprofits. PR Daily. Retrieved from http://prdaily.com/Main/Articles/17156.aspx

ALS Association. (2014a). ALS ice bucket challenge—FAQ. Retrieved from http://www.alsa.org/about-us/ice-bucket-challenge-faq.html

ALS Association. (2014b, August 12). ALS ice bucket challenge takes U.S. by storm. Retrieved from http://www.alsa.org/news/archive/als-ice-bucket-challenge.html

Bashir, M., & Fedorova, M. (2014). Conglomeration among the top American public relations agencies: A case study. Public Relations Review, 40(5), 762–771.

BBC News US & Canada. (2012a, February 1.) Canada profile. Retrieved from http://www.bbc.com/news/world-us-canada-16841120

BBC News. (2012b, May 29). Argentina country profile. Retrieved from http://news.bbc.co.uk/2/hi/americas/country_profiles/1192478.stm

BBC News. (2012c, August 14). Brazil country profile. Retrieved from http://news.bbc.co.uk/2/hi/americas/country_profiles/1227110.stm

BBC News. (2012d, August 14). Chile country profile. Retrieved from http://news.bbc.co.uk/2/hi/americas/country_profiles/1222764.stm

BBC News. (2012e, September 4). Mexico country profile. Retrieved from http://news.bbc.co.uk/2/hi/americas/country_profiles/1205074.stm

BBC News. (2012f, November 2). United States profile. Retrieved from http://www.bbc.com/news/world-us-canada-16757497

Central Intelligence Agency (CIA). (2014). World factbook. Retrieved from https://www.cia.gov/library/publications/the-world-factbook/

Cline, J. (2014, August 25). The ALS ice bucket challenge is NOT a social media success. The Cline Group. Retrieved from http://www.theclinegroup.com/2014/08/25/als-ice-bucket-challenge-social-media-success/

Committee to Protect Journalists. (2014). 60 journalists killed in 2014/motive confirmed. Retrieved from https://www.cpj.org/killed/2014/

Consejo Profesional de Relaciones Públicas de la República Argentina (CPRPRA). (2012). Investigación de mercado de las relaciones públicas. Retrieved from http://www.rrpp.org.ar/archivos/Investigacion%20de%20mercado%202012.pdf

de la Moriniere, G. L. (2006). United States PR country landscape 2006. Global Alliance for Public Relations and Communication Management. Retrieved from http://www.globalalliancepr.org/website/sites/default/files/nolie/PR%20Landscapes/US-2006.pdf

Diamond, D. (2014, August 29). The ALS ice bucket challenge has raised $100 million—and counting. Forbes. Retrieved from http://www.forbes.com/sites/dandiamond/2014/08/29/the-als-ice-bucket-challenge-has-raised-100m-but-its-finally-cooling-off/

eMarketer. (2014, April 4). In Canada, social media usage is a tale of two languages. Retrieved from http://www.emarketer.com/Article/Canada-Social-Media-Usage-Tale-of-Two-Languages/1010746

Ferrari, M. A. (2009a). Overview of public relations in South America. In K. Sriramesh & D. Verčič (Eds.), The global public relations handbook: Theory, research, and practice (2nd ed.) (pp. 704–726). New York, NY: Routledge.

Ferrari, M. A. (2009b). Public relations in Chile: Searching for identity and imported models. In K. Sriramesh & D. Verčič (Eds.), The global public relations handbook: *Theory, research, and practice* (2nd ed.) (pp. 749–766). New York, NY: Routledge.

Freedom House. (2014a). Freedom of the press 2014. Retrieved from https://freedomhouse.org/sites/default/files/FOTP_2014.pdf

Freedom House. (2014b). Freedom of the press: Ecuador. Retrieved from https://www.freedomhouse.org/report/freedom-press/2014/ecuador

Freedom House. (2014c). Freedom of the press: Venezuela. Retrieved from https://freedomhouse.org/report/freedom-press/2014/venezuela

Gladwell, M. (2010, October 4). Small change: Why the revolution will not be tweeted. *The New Yorker*. Retrieved from http://www.newyorker.com/magazine/2010/10/04/small-change-3

Griggs, I. (2014, September 4). The big debate: Do ice bucket challenge-type campaigns produce long-term engagement? *PR Week*. Retrieved from http://www.prweek.com/article/1310781/big-debate-ice-bucket-challenge-type-campaigns-produce-long-term-engagement

Grunig, J. E., & Grunig, L. A. (1992). Models of public relations and communication. In J. E. Grunig (Ed.), *Excellence in public relations and communication management* (pp. 285- 325). Hillsdale, NJ: Lawrence Erlbaum Associates, Inc.

Grunig, J. E., & Grunig, L. A. (2009). Public relations in the United States. In K. Sriramesh & D. Verčič (Eds.), *The global public relations handbook: Theory, research, and practice* (2nd ed.) (pp. 621–653). New York, NY: Routledge.

Guiniven, J. E. (2002). Dealing with activism in Canada: An ideal cultural fit for the two-way symmetrical public relations model. *Public Relations Review, 28*(4), 393–402.

Gupta, V., & Hanges, P. J. (2004). Regional and climate clustering of societal clusters. In R. J. House, P. J. Hanges, M. Javidan, P. W. Dorfman, & V. Gupta (Eds.), *Culture, leadership, and organizations: The GLOBE study of 62 societies* (pp. 178–218). Thousand Oaks, CA: Sage.

Hay, P. (2010, September 28). Focus on: Chile. *PR Week*. Retrieved from http://www.prweek.com/article/1030467/focus-on-chile

Heim, A. (2011, July 21). Stats from Chile: The internet is young and social. Retrieved from http://thenextweb.com/la/2011/07/21/stats-from-chile-the-internet-is-young-and-social/

The Holmes Report. (2015). Global top 250 PR firms 2015. Retrieved from http://www.holmesreport.com/ranking-and-data/world-pr-report/agency-rankings-2015/top-250

Howard, C. M., & Mathews, W. K. (2013). *On deadline: Managing media relations* (5th ed.). Long Grove, IL: Waveland Press.

IMAGEN. (2010). El cambio seguro. Retrieved from http://www.relacionespublicas.com/recursos/uploads/rankings/000002.pdf

Interbrand. (2014, October 9). Interbrand's 15th annual best global brands report. Retrieved from http://interbrand.com/en/newsroom/15/interbrands-th-annual-best-global-brands-report

International Coffee Organisation (ICO). (2015, January). Exporting countries: Total production. Retrieved from http://www.ico.org/prices/po.htm

Judd, E. (2011). *O momento mágico: Managing public affairs in Brazil*. Washington, DC: Foundation for Public Affairs. Retrieved from http://pac.org/files/Final%20Brazil%20Report.pdf

Johansen, P. (2013). Canada, practice of public relation in. In R. L. Heath (Ed.), *Encyclopedia of public relations* (2nd ed.) (pp. 93–97). Thousand Oaks, CA: Sage.

Kanso, A., Sinno, A. K., & Adams, W. (2001). Cross-cultural public relations: Implications for American and Arab public relations practitioners. *Competitiveness Review*, *11*(1), 65–82.

Kemp, S. (2015, January 21). Digital, social & mobile worldwide in 2015. *We Are Social*. Retrieved from http://wearesocial.net/blog/2015/01/digital-social-mobile-worldwide-2015/

Lewis PR. (2013). *Global media guide*. Retrieved from http://publish.lewispr.com/globalmediaguide/LEWIS_Global_Media_Guide.pdf

Likely, F. (2009). A different country, a different public relations: Canadian PR in the North American context. In K. Sriramesh & D. Verčič (Eds.), *The global public relations handbook: Theory, research, and practice* (2nd ed.) (pp. 654–675). New York, NY: Routledge.

Livermore, D. (2013). *Expand your borders: Discover ten cultural clusters*. East Lansing, MI: Cultural Intelligence Center.

Long, R. K. (2004). The other "new" Mexico: Public relations accelerates the move to a legitimate democracy. In D. J. Tilson & E. C. Alozie (Eds.), *Toward the common good: Perspectives in international public relations* (pp. 43–62). Boston, MA: Pearson.

Magee, K. (2014, January 22). Postcard from Brazil. *PR Week*. Retrieved from http://www.prweek.com/article/1228136/postcard-brazil

Malkin, E. (2015, June 12). Wave of protests spreads to scandal-wary Honduras and Guatemala. *The New York Times*. Retrieved from http://www.nytimes.com/2015/06/13/world/americas/corruption-scandals-driving-protests-in-guatemala-and-honduras.html?_r=0

McGugan, I. (2014, November 16). Bucket racket: What science tells us about the strange reasons we give to charity. *The New York Times Magazine*, 34–36.

Mellado, C., & Barría, S. (2012). Development of professional roles in the practice of public relations in Chile. *Public Relations Review*, *38*(3), 446–453.

Molleda, J. C. (2000). International paradigms: The Latin American school of public relations. *Journalism Studies*, *2*(4), 513–530.

Molleda, J. C., & Athaydes, A. (2003). Public relations licensing in Brazil: Evolution and the views of professionals. *Public Relations Review*, *29*(3), 271–279.

Molleda, J. C., Athaydes, A., & Hirsch, V. (2009). Public relations in Brazil: Practice and education in a South American context. In K. Sriramesh & D. Verčič (Eds.), *The global public relations handbook: Theory, research, and practice* (2nd ed.) (pp. 727–748). New York, NY: Routledge.

Molleda, J. C., & Ferguson, M. A. (2004). Public relations roles in Brazil: Hierarchy eclipses gender differences. *Journal of Public Relations Research*, *16*(4), 327–351.

Molleda, J. C., & Moreno, Á. (2006). Transitional socioeconomic and political environments of public relations in Mexico. *Public Relations Review*, *32*(2), 104–109.

Molleda, J. C., & Moreno, Á. (2008). Balancing public relations with socioeconomic and political environments in transition: Comparative, contextualized research in Colombia, Mexico, and Venezuela. *Journalism & Communication Monographs*, *10*(2), 115–174.

Montenegro, S. L. (2004). Public relations in Latin America: A survey of professional practice of multinational firms. In D. J. Tilson & E. C. Alozie (Eds.), *Toward the common good: Perspectives in international public relations* (pp. 102–125). Boston, MA: Pearson.

Pew Research Religion & Public Life Project. (2013, November 13). Religion in Latin America. Retrieved from http://www.pewforum.org/2014/11/13/religion-in-latin-america/

Pineda, J. J. (2010). Mexico PR country landscape 2010. *Global Alliance for Public Relations and Communication Management*. Retrieved from http://www.globalalliancepr.org/websiite/sites/default/files/nolie/PR%20Landscapes/Mexico-2010.pdf

PR Week. (2010, May 10). Focus on . . . Canada. Retrieved from http://www.prweek.com/article/1001914/focus-oncanada

PR Week. (2012, April 6). Global: Focus on . . . Chile. Retrieved from http://www.prweek.com/article/1125706/global-focus-chile

Rancilio, A. (2014, August 22). Ice bucket challenge may change nonprofit world. *Associated Press*. Retrieved from http://news.yahoo.com/ice-bucket-challenge-may-change-nonprofit-world-144539005.html

Rebeil, C. M. A., & Herrera, B. M. V. (2012). Public relations in Mexico: Culture and challenges vis-à-vis globalization. In K. Sriramesh & D. Verčič (Eds.), *Culture and public relations: Links and implications* (pp. 163–181). New York, NY: Taylor & Francis.

Rebeil, C. M. A., Montoya, M. D. C. A., & Hidalgo, T. J. A. (2009). The public relations industry in Mexico: From amateurship to the construction of a discipline. In K. Sriramesh & D. Verčič (Eds.), *The global public relations handbook: Theory, research, and practice* (2nd ed.) (pp. 676–703). New York, NY: Routledge.

Rohter, L. (2005, January 30). Divorce ties Chile in knots. *The New York Times*. Retrieved from http://www.nytimes.com/2005/01/30/weekinreview/30rohter.html?_r=0

Rueda, M. (2012, May 19). How governments threaten press freedom in Latin America. *ABC News*. Retrieved from http://abcnews.go.com/ABC_Univision/News/elected-governments-threaten-press-freedom-latin-america/story?id=19204522

Sharpe, M. L., & Simoes, R. P. (1996). Public relations performance in South and Central America. In H. M. Culbertson & N. Chen (Eds.), *International public relations: A comparative analysis* (pp. 273–297). Mahwah, NJ: Lawrence Erlbaum Associates.

Sullivan, M. (2005, December 14). Media bias is real, finds UCLA political scientist. *UCLA*. Retrieved from http://newsroom.ucla.edu/releases/Media-Bias-Is-Real-Finds-UCLA-6664

Valladares, A. (2014, July 10). Postcard from Mexico. *PR Week*. Retrieved from http://www.prweek.com/article/1302921/postcard-mexico

Vieira, Jr., E. T., & Grantham, S. (2014). Defining public relations roles in the U.S.A. using cluster analysis. *Public Relations Review*, 40(1), 60–68.

World Bank. (2014a). Argentina overview. Retrieved from http://www.worldbank.org/en/country/argentina/overview

World Bank. (2014b). GDP. Retrieved from http://data.worldbank.org/indicator/NY.GDP.MKTP.CD?order=wbapi_data_value_2013+wbapi_data_value+wbapi_data_valuelast&sort=desc

Zaharna, R. S. (2005). Al Jazeera and American public diplomacy: A dance of intercultural (mis-)communication. In M. Zayani (Ed.), *The Al Jazeera phenomenon: Critical perspectives on new Arab media* (pp. 183–202). London: Pluto Press.

12 Public Relations in Sub-Saharan Africa

The Sub-Saharan African Cultural Cluster

Sub-Saharan Africa is a region on the rise. The cultural cluster, which includes approximately 50 African countries located south of the Sahara desert, is growing more prosperous, more populous, and more stable. Africa's economy as a whole has been growing at the second-fastest rate on earth, surpassed only by East Asia. Sub-Saharan African countries are growing even faster than the continent overall, and their Gross Domestic Product (GDP) is expected to increase by 6.9 percent annually through 2019. The growth is being driven by increased prices for commodities the region supplies, such as oil and minerals, as well as by the manufacturing, telecommunication, transportation, and wholesale and retail trade sectors (Leke, Lund, Manyika, & Ramaswamy, 2014).

Sub-Saharan Africa is also growing more stable. By 1980, most countries in the region had achieved independence from their European colonizers. However, colonizers had in some places actually fostered ethnic tensions among the peoples of the region in order to strengthen their own hold on power, and the national borders that were drawn post-colonization often did not reflect the communities of peoples who actually lived in particular areas. The region suffered from repressive regimes and political instability (CFR, 2015; Fisher, 2013). However, things are getting better. By the late 2000s, African civil wars were half as common as they were in the mid-1990s, wars had become smaller in scale, and mass killings of civilians were on the decline (Straus, 2012, p. 179).

The region's population and consumer base is also growing rapidly. Africa is already the world's second most populous continent. Barrett (2012) notes that, because the population of Africa as a whole is expected to double, from 1 billion to 2 billion, by the year 2030,

> corporations, brands, and agency networks are . . . eyeing up the region and deciding how to invest to exploit these new opportunities in the future . . . By 2050 there will be 1.3 billion consumers on the continent—and that's a market no global brand or agency network can afford to ignore.

Despite the region's poverty, already, more than 100 million African households have discretionary income to spend (Leke et al., 2014). This is a major boon for public relations. Skinner and Mersham (2009, p. 285) predict that public relations in Africa will grow even faster than the continent's economy overall. The global public relations agency Burson-Marsteller, for example, reported in 2012 that it had received more inquiries about Africa in the previous year and a half than it had in the prior two decades (Barrett, 2012; Skinner & Mersham, 2009, p. 243). Skinner (2013, p. 18) notes that

> while a few governments see public relations as a propagandist tool, quite a number of public and private sector businesses are considering effective public relations as essential for spreading their message across a terrain occupied by a multiplicity of media.

Many major global advertising firms have recently entered the market and started buying up smaller digital, marketing, and public relations agencies in order to offer integrated services to their clients (Wiener, 2014).

Yet, despite these exciting and promising developments, Sub-Saharan Africa continues to face major challenges. Africa is a continent that enjoys vast natural resources, but in too many Sub-Saharan countries, this wealth has fueled bitter conflict and enriched a tiny, corrupt elite while the majority of the population has lived in poverty. Today, 48 percent of Sub-Saharan Africans still live on less than U.S. $1.00 per day, a third of Sub-Saharan Africans are undernourished, and a third lack access to safe drinking water (United Nations, 2014, pp. 8, 12, 43). Sub-Saharan Africa continues to be plagued by diseases, including malaria and HIV/AIDS, and by a lack of infrastructure such as adequate roads and transport systems, which hinders trade and travel among countries in the region (Skinner & Mersham, 2009, pp. 265–266). This means that corporate social responsibility is especially important in this region. Skinner and Mersham (2009, p. 267) note that when "organizations are exploiting Africa's commercial opportunities—either as a market or as a source of raw materials and resources—the need to act as good global corporate citizens is drawn into sharp relief." African practitioners themselves focus heavily on social issues. A survey of practitioners in Sub-Saharan Africa found that public relations is practiced with a "societal perspective" in the region. Practitioners

> show a high concern for societal issues, which motivates continuous dialogue between the organisation and society. This illustrates that the PR practitioners have a responsibility towards the organisation and to society, because the success of an organisation depends on adapting to the norms, values and expectations of society for socially responsible behaviour by the organisation. In this process, society learns to trust the organisation (Van Heerden & Rensburg, 2005, p. 85).

Another huge challenge for the region is illiteracy. A shocking 60 percent of Africans are illiterate, which means that public relations practitioners must often find alternatives to print media (UNESCO, 2011). Radio has the broadest reach in Africa and newspaper distribution outside of major cities is often limited (Mersham, Skinner, & Rensburg, 2011, p. 197). Mobile phones are ubiquitous in Africa; by 2012, there were more mobile phone users in Africa than in the U.S. or European Union. The World Bank and African Development Bank (2012, p. 13) note that, in some African countries, more people have access to mobile phones than to clean water. In this region, phones are used for everything from conducting financial transactions to communicating via SMS.

Word of mouth is also critical in this region, because Sub-Saharan Africans avidly communicate and share information orally. Mersham et al. (2011, p. 197) note,

> Western civilisation and its penchant for automation often appears designed to reduce face-to-face interaction with others to an absolute minimum—in Western cities it is possible, even commonplace, to find one's way across the city on public transport, buy a load of groceries and get a take-away meal on the way home without ever speaking to another human being. This is hardly possible in any African city.

Additionally, indigenous forms of outreach remain important. Alzoie (2004, p. 245) notes that

> Africans hold consultations, dialogues, and conflict resolutions with each other as a way of promoting mutual understanding and resolving issues.

Other forms of African public relations include visits, gift giving, festivals, sports events, intermarriage, and the use of town criers and dispatchers to relay messages.

However, the diversity of the region, from the Anglophone countries of the east to the Francophone nations of the west, means that no single public relations approach can work for the entire region—or even necessarily for an entire country (Barrett, 2012; Skinner & Mersham, 2009, p. 275). All twenty of the most ethnically diverse countries on earth are located in Africa; many are home to a great multiplicity of ethnic groups, tribes, and languages (Fisher, 2013). Solly Moeng, Managing Director of the Cape Town, South Africa-based reputation management firm Don Valley, who is profiled below, explains that "there's no such thing as one appropriate, Africa-wide strategy. We're all African brothers and sisters, but, in reality, the idea of a pan-African identity is more aspirational than real." Merham et al. (2011, p. 203) also note that as the Chinese and other governments and corporations invest more heavily in Africa, public relations practitioners will have a role to play in mediating between partners who have cultural differences; for example, "practitioners will be challenged to develop communication approaches and skills to resolve the discordance between the Chinese business-as-business practice and the prevailing African orthodoxy of business-as-a-social cause on the continent."

The GLOBE study found that the Sub-Saharan African cultural cluster is also characterized by high humane orientation and moderate assertiveness, future orientation, institutional collectivism, in-group collectivism, gender egalitarianism, performance orientation, power distance, and uncertainty avoidance (Gupta & Hanges, 2004, p. 193). One of the major characteristics of this cultural group is the importance placed on relationships. Sub-Saharan Africans see themselves as deeply interdependent with other people, nature, and the transcendent and are "deeply religious" (Livermore, 2013, pp. 74–75). As part of the philosophy of *Ubuntu*—literally, "I am because we are"—Africans see themselves as their brothers' keepers (Livermore, 2013, pp. 73–74; Skinner & Mersham, 2009, p. 286). For this reason, they value inclusiveness, negotiation, tolerance, and transparency (Mersham et al., 2011, p. 196). Despite the GLOBE study's ranking of the culture as moderately collectivist, Livermore (2013, p. 77) argues that "collectivism is so vital to their psyche that it's difficult to conceive of being a person apart from the larger group." For this reason,

who you are is far more important from the African perspective than what you do. Individuals typically identify themselves in light of their extended families, and there isn't the same concern for efficiency and achievement among many of the countries in this cluster as there is elsewhere in the world. Africans often say to Westerners, "You have the watches. We have the time." There's a much more relaxed, laid-back approach to life (Livermore, 2013, p. 78).

Therefore, Livermore (2013, p. 79) advises, it is important to engage in small talk and inquire about a business partner's family before getting down to business. Furthermore, you should emphasize cooperation and concern for local communities. Livermore (2013, p. 77) reports that

> businesses that go into Africa presenting a value proposition by appealing to competitive instincts are unlikely to be successful. Success and results are valued, but the way to get there is through cooperation. International businesses that want to develop a presence in Africa are often expected to give money to a village project or some other aid and development initiative.

Sub-Saharan Africans are also high-context communicators—yet another reason why local expertise is critical when working in this region of the world (Livermore, 2013, p. 77).

Another huge challenge for practitioners is a common expectation among African journalists to receive payments for coverage. This concept is known as "brown envelopism" because the money is typically given in brown envelopes. Skjerdal (2011, p. 137) reports that

> from Maseru to Marrakech, Dar es Salaam to Dakar, the brown envelope is spreading like an Arab Spring in newsrooms across the continent. In Cameroon it is known as gombo, in Ghana as soli, in Liberia as gatu, in Nigeria as kola, in Ethiopia as buche, in Tanzania as mshiko—and the list goes on and on.

Skjerdal says that while the envelopes are often described as stipends to cover reporters' costs of traveling to cover events, in reality they represent payment for coverage. Of course, part of the problem is that African journalists are often paid little for their work; in some instances, the only payments they receive for their stories are those that they obtain from their sources. However, this complicates the practice of public relations considerably. When I worked for the U.S. government and our Deputy Treasury Secretary spoke in Togo's Parliament, a U.S. embassy press officer actually drove around town picking up journalists and bringing them to the Parliament building, as it was the only way to get them to cover the event!

Another challenge for practitioners representing African organizations is the continent's poor overall reputation. Mersham et al. (2011, p. 202) note:

> Africa has not always been fairly and evenly treated in the world's communication media. . . . Africa continues to be stereotyped as "the dark continent," backward and barbaric, referred to as "the world's basket case" by the world's media. Africa is portrayed "as a land of pestilence, disease, war and calamity . . . flagrant corruption, and incompetent leadership" . . . Whereas Africa's failures and conflicts are regularly exposed (and need to be revealed), equally, the authentic efforts made by African states to

overcome these and other problems, usually against formidable odds, remain largely ignored.

A challenge for practitioners is to overcome these stereotypes by sharing such success stories and convincing the world of the region's increasing stability, which can help drive the tourism and investments the region still desperately needs.

Merham et. al (2011, pp. 198–199) argue that an African theory of public relations can move the field away from the West's "self-first, profit-at-all-costs, market-driven" approach, and towards a more communitarian approach that will be successful in "establishing and maintaining the balanced relationships necessary for organisations to thrive over the long term."

While some have argued that the field of public relations remains "significantly under-developed" in this region (Skinner & Mersham, 2009, p. 279), Akpabio (2009, pp. 361–362) notes that there is evidence that many Africans practice public relations with sophistication—from using symmetric communication to acting as members of dominant coalitions—and that "Africa has kept pace with global public relations practice through multinational corporations, local affiliates of global public relations consultancies and through the personal efforts of practitioners and academics."

If you practice in this region, the website of the Pan Africa Media Research Organisation, www.pamro.org, will be a valuable resource. The organization offers country reports outlining top media outlets and media penetration in African nations. As discussed in Chapter 7, BBC World Service radio is one of the best ways to reach a large pan-African audience. Other outlets that reach a pan-African audience include South Africa's public broadcaster, the South African Broadcasting Corporation (SABC); the entertainment-focused Ebonylife TV; the business-focused Bloomberg Africa and CNBC Africa; and the French-language Africa 24 (Ferreira, 2015).

The following sections profile public relations practice in four of the region's most important markets: Ghana, Kenya, Nigeria, and South Africa.

Ghana

Time zone: Coordinated Universal Time (UTC)
International dialing code: +233

When you practice public relations in Ghana, be aware of the expectation for *soli*.

In 1957, Ghana gained independence from Britain, becoming the first country in Sub-Saharan Africa to be free of colonial rule. A period of military rule ended in 1992, when the country became a constitutional democracy. Although English is the official language, Ghana is home to numerous ethnic groups which speak a multiplicity of local languages (CIA, 2014). The country's economy is based upon services, agriculture, and natural resources,

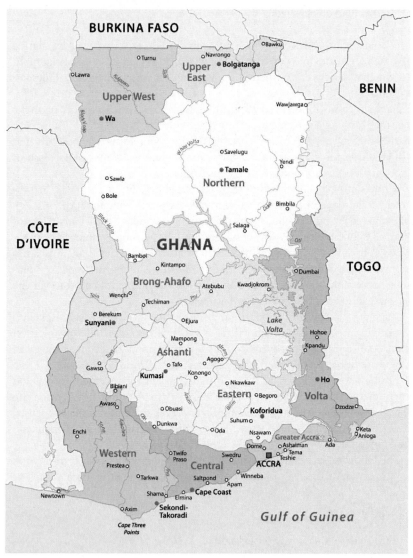

including oil and minerals such as gold (CIA, 2014). An offshore oil field discovered in 2007, called Jubilee, has provided a major boost to the country's economy (Freedom House, 2014b). The country's capital is Accra and its currency is the cedi.

Wu and Baah-Boakye (2007, p. 31) note that

> with its record of political stability as well as consistent and relatively successful economic performance, Ghana has been considered both as an

oasis of peace amidst conflicts in the West African region . . . and a model of economic progress in Africa.

The country's economic reforms and 1995 decision to allow private owner-ship of the previously state-controlled media have had a major impact on the practice of public relations. A study of public relations practitioners in Ghana found that, prior to these reforms, the majority of their public relations efforts were directed towards influencing the government or public officials, who controlled much of society—a situation common in poor countries (Blankson, 2004, p. 307). Today, however, "the independent media operations are serving as self-appointed watchdogs of the government and organizations by exposing organizational fraud, abuses, negligence of duty, and social irresponsibility" (Blankson, 2004, p. 314). Blankson (2004, p. 314) notes that "the growth in the private sector business and in mass media in Ghana created a critical discerning public and advocacy groups who demanded more information and accountability from organizations"—forcing public relations practitioners to respond. The multiplicity of media outlets has also given practitioners impor-tant new platforms for disseminating their messages.

Faith Senam Ocloo, Executive Director of the Accra-based E'April Public Relations, which specializes in serving startups in the fashion, beauty, and life-style industries, says that garnering coverage in the traditional media remains critical for Ghanaian practitioners, though social media is becoming increas-ingly important. Because Ghanaians are already bombarded with advertise-ments on social media, Ocloo suggests starting an interesting conversation on social media with a catchy hashtag first and then introducing your brand. For example, she notes that in 2014, a local beverage company called Kasapreko launched a successful campaign using the hashtag #whatif, asking Ghanaians what would happen in different scenarios.

Ocloo says that it is also helpful for local celebrities to endorse brands because it generates significant attention and media coverage—but convinc-ing them to do so can be tricky, because local celebrities often demand signifi-cant payments in return, since signing on to one brand precludes them from opportunities to endorse competitors. For example, when Ocloo worked on a new product launch in Ghana for Unilever in late 2014, she attempted to sign on local celebrities, but the company ultimately decided that the prices demanded by such local personalities were too high.

In 2001, the Ghanaian Parliament passed a law which allows only members of the Institute of Public Relations, Ghana (IPR) to practice public relations in the country (Pratt & Adamolekun, 2008, p. 32). A study of Ghanaian prac-titioners found that they practice two-way communication more commonly than one-way communication. Their most frequent role within their organi-zations is acting as cultural interpreters, which the authors note is likely due to the fact that Ghana is a multi-cultural society and international trade is becoming increasingly important in the country. Unsurprisingly, in this col-lectivist culture, the second most common model of public relations prac-ticed in Ghana is the personal influence model. This "suggests that Ghanaian public relations practitioners are good networkers. They help their organizations and clients socialize and communicate with key publics in order to build good relationships with them" (Wu & Baah-Boakye, 2009, p. 84).

Further evidence of the sophistication of Ghanaian practitioners comes from another study, which found that 81 percent of private sector practitioners and 93 percent of public sector practitioners use a moderate, high, or very high amount of research in their work (Aggrey, 2009, pp. 412–413). Another study found that most Ghanaian practitioners enjoy decision-making power within their organizations (Wu & Baah-Boakye, 2007, p. 34). However, Ocloo says that the majority of local businesses in Ghana do not fully understand or appreciate the value of public relations, and therefore do not hire full-time practitioners—giving global brands which attempt to compete with local businesses, and almost always do have public relations teams, a distinct advantage.

Another challenge for practitioners is that the practice of brown envelopism—colloquially known as *soli*—is "commonplace" in Ghana. A survey of Ghanaian reporters found that they "perceived the practice as customary" (Kasoma, 2009, p. 25). For example,

> a male reporter for a private radio station who received 200,000 cedis (about US $20) at a press conference by a mining company said that receiving *soli* from news sources "helps relieve the journalist of financial difficulties but should not in any way affect how the journalist reports. But it is also true that taking money from a news source makes it difficult to write against them" (Kasoma, 2009, p. 28).

Reporters indicated that they "found themselves drawn to reporting the type of news that attracted brown envelopes"—namely, reporting on politics and business (Kasoma, 2009, p. 27).

Additionally, Freedom House (2014b) reports that the government will "occasionally" harass and arrest journalists who report on politically sensitive topics. Political corruption and a weak rule of law still remain a problem for businesses trying to operate in the country (Freedom House, 2014b). The CIA (2014) notes that the Ghanaian government "faces challenges in managing a population that is unhappy with living standards and that perceives they are not reaping the benefits of oil production because of political corruption."

Media

The Ghana News Agency is state-run (BBC, 2013a).

Major newspapers in Ghana include the state-owned *Daily Graphic* and *The Ghanaian Times* and the privately owned *The Ghanaian Chronicle* and *Daily Guide* (BBC, 2013a).

The country's public television broadcaster is the Ghana Broadcasting Corporation. Other broadcasters are TV3, Metro TV, and UTV (BBC, 2013a; PAMRO, 2013).

Radio remains the most popular form of media in Ghana, though it is increasingly being challenged by television. The Ghana Broadcasting Corporation operates state-run radio channels; private stations include Peace FM, OK FM, OMAN FM, and Adom FM (BBC, 2013a; PAMRO, 2013).

Ghana has an "exploding social media presence;" Facebook is especially popular (Issaka, 2012).

Kenya

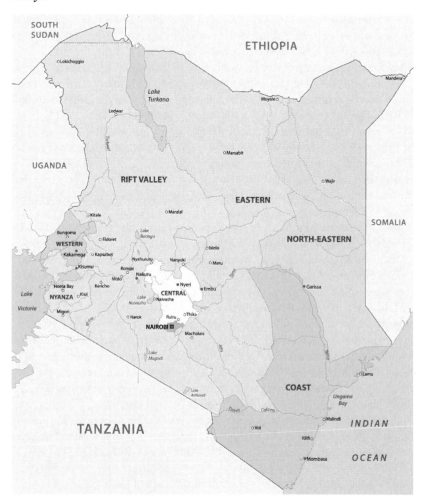

Copyright: Rainer Lesniewski

Time zone: East Africa (UTC + 3:00)
International dialing code: +254

When you practice public relations in Kenya, be prepared to adopt different strategies for the country's many diverse communities.

The Republic of Kenya gained independence from Britain in 1963. A multi-party political system established in 1992 led to improved freedom of speech and media liberalization, boosting the public relations industry considerably (Mbeke, 2009, p. 320). However, charges of vote rigging in the country's 2007 election spawned two months of violence in which as many as 1,500 people were killed. The African Union mediated a power-sharing arrangement in 2008 and in 2010 the country created a new constitution. Still, the country suffers from poor infrastructure, corruption, violence, and an unemployment rate of about 40 percent (CIA, 2014). About 6.1 percent of the adult population is infected with HIV (Avert, 2014).

The tourism sector is vital to Kenya's economy, drawing global travelers in particular to the country's game reserves and to visit the Masaai people, a semi-nomadic ethnic group who live near the game reserves (Mbeke, 2009, p. 308). However, recent acts of terrorism—including a 2013 incident in which gunmen killed more than 60 people at an upscale shopping mall in the capital city of Nairobi—have hampered tourism, and businesses operating in the country continue to have security concerns (Mattinson, 2013). The country also has a large agriculture sector, exporting tea, coffee, and flowers, and is a business hub within East Africa and the region more broadly (Mattinson, 2013). Though English and Kiswahili are Kenya's official languages, the country's 42 ethnic communities speak numerous indigenous languages (CIA, 2014; Mbeke, 2009, p. 307). Kenya's currency is the shilling.

Mbeke (2009, pp. 317–381) reports that political reforms and economic liberalization undertaken in the 1990s have resulted in "a more open society, a more aggressive consumer culture, a vibrant and dynamic media scene, a huge and fairly influential civil society and a rather litigious populace" which have caused a "seismic shift" in public relations practice. Practitioners in Kenya have grown more professional and strategic, with the country even coming to rival South Africa, which is currently the hub of public relations practice in Sub-Saharan Africa (Mattinson, 2013). Many practitioners work for the myriad United Nations agencies and international non-governmental organizations based in Nairobi (Mbeke, 2009, p. 317).

A survey of Kenyan practitioners found that they enjoy a very high level of support from managers within their organizations, but that a lack of understanding of the definition of public relations leaves them "carrying out functions that lack clarity, some of which may not be in line with the profession" (Tikolo, 2011, pp. 7, 20). Also as a result of this lack of understanding,

the industry has continued to be defined based on the amount of media coverage provided to clients. This has had the effect of keeping PR and communications at the rudimentary press agentry level, with events taking up a lot of the activities carried out to create a buzz around brands (Tikolo, 2011, p. 7).

Mbeke (2009, p. 325) reports that about 80 percent of the country's media content is placed by public relations practitioners.

A 2012 study of Kenyan practitioners found that the most common model they practice is the personal influence model. Kiambi and Nadler (2012, p. 506) note that "practitioners play a pivotal role in helping organizations and clients socialize and build good relations with key publics." The second most common model practiced in Kenya is acting as cultural interpreters, which the authors attribute to the growth of international trade and the internationalization of the country.

One practitioner notes that Kenyan society is very friendly, so media interviews tend to be less aggressive than in Europe (Mattinson, 2013). However, communicating with the country's many different ethnic groups poses challenges for practitioners (Mbeke, 2009, p. 323).

Kentice Tikolo, Managing Director of the Nairobi-based public relations firm Impact Africa, who worked on the Uwiano campaign profiled in this chapter, says that the country's cultural diversity means that a "one size fits all" approach will never work in Kenya. It is essential to tailor your strategies to local peoples—and to be particularly sensitive to the languages, literacy rates, and lifestyles of different communities.

For example, in Western Kenya, a form of dance called *sukuti* is very popular, and therefore Tikolo recommends crafting songs containing your messages, to which local peoples can dance. Meanwhile, in coastal Kenya, women tend to wear a form of colorful clothing called *khanga*. Poetic messages are often written on their garments. To promote a World-Bank-funded project aimed at encouraging environmentally sustainable practices, Tikolo gave out free clothing to local women, with messages about the importance of conservation written on the *khanga* garments. Because television tends to reach only urban populations while nearly every Kenyan household has a radio, Tikolo often works with local opinion leaders and places them on radio programs in which they speak local languages. She says that talk shows are also particularly popular in Kenya. "We don't have a homogeneous culture," Tikolo says. "It's critical that you do stakeholder mapping so you accurately reach who you are targeting."

Although Kenya's new constitution did strengthen freedom of speech and the press, a law passed in 2013 gives the government the power to levy "potentially crippling" fines against the press for violating a code of conduct. Reporters are occasionally harassed for reporting critical stories, which sometimes leads to self-censorship (Freedom House, 2014c). Brown envelopism is another challenge. "An allowance is almost now expected when a reporter comes to your function," says Tikolo. A study of Kenyan journalists and editors found that each one could provide examples of the practice, and that reporters are paid both to cover stories and also to refrain from reporting on negative stories. For example, one investigative journalist discovered that faulty cement was responsible for building collapses. "That story never got out. That investigative reporter now drives a very expensive car" (Helander, 2010, p. 535).

Media

The Kenya News Agency is state-owned (BBC, 2014).

Major newspapers include the *Daily Nation* and *The Standard* (BBC, 2014).
The Kenya Broadcasting Corporation is state-owned, with channels in both
English and Swahili (Mbeke, 2009, p. 325). Other major television broadcast-
ers include Citizen TV, the Kenya Television Network, and NTV (BBC, 2014;
PAMRO, 2013).

The Kenya Broadcasting Corporation also operates radio stations in English,
Swahili, and numerous indigenous languages (BBC, 2014). Other radio broadcasters include Radio Citizen, Kameme FM, and Inooro (PAMRO, 2013).

Kenyans are very avid users of social media; Facebook and Twitter are especially popular (Kaigwa, 2013).

Case Study: Kenya's Uwiano Platform for Peace

People gather at a mobile cinema in Western Kenya as part of the Uwiano
campaign. Photo courtesy of the Uwiano Platform for Peace

Youth at a peace march in Mwiki, Nairobi County. Photo credit: UNDP Kenya/
James Ochweri

In 2007–2008, Kenya suffered what has been described as "its worst humanitarian crisis since independence" when the perception that its 2007 presidential election was rigged led to widespread violence and fueled ethnic hatred (IRIN, 2008). As IRIN reported,

> in the days immediately after the results were announced, gangs of youths blocked Kenya's main roads and set fire to hundreds of homes of perceived "outsiders." In all, more than 1,200 people were killed and some 600,000 displaced into temporary camps, with an equal number seeking refuge with friends or relatives. Agricultural activity was seriously hampered as farmers moved away from their fields, posing long-term risks for the country's food security.

In the aftermath of this violence, the Kenyan government, United Nations, and non-profit groups came together to create the "Uwiano Platform for Peace." The partnership was led by the country's National Steering Committee on Peace Building and Conflict Management, National Cohesion and Integration Commission, Independent Electoral & Boundaries Commission, United Nations Women, the United Nations Development Programme, and Peace and Development Network Trust (PeaceNet) Kenya—an organization established by Oxfam Great Britain, the Mennonite Central Committee, and the Anglican Development Desk in order to help victims of ethnic violence. Uwiano is a Swahili word meaning "cohesion." The goal of this campaign was to ensure peace during the country's 2010 referendum on a new constitution, as well as during the country's general election in 2013.

Kentice Tikolo, Managing Director of the Nairobi-based public relations agency Impact Africa, was hired to work on the campaign. Tikolo said that outreach at the grassroots level was the key to this campaign's success. As part of the campaign, mobile cinemas were set up in rural areas of Kenya and in the slums of major cities. "There is no access to movies in these villages, so this was very attractive," Tikolo said. "We got a high turnout and maximum attention." In between the movies and election-related documentaries shown in these temporary cinemas, audiences listened to jingles with messages about the importance of peace and how to vote, since it was the first time that Kenyans voted electronically. Another way that the campaign got the message out was by erecting billboards along the sides of the mobile cinemas, listing an SMS number that Kenyans could text if they saw a disruption of peace.

Since mobile phones have very high penetration in Kenya, the campaign partnered with Safaricom, the country's largest mobile technology provider, to give a free number, 108, that people could text if they saw any threats to peace. Kenyans could also send messages of peace for free. The number was also publicized through infomercials in the country's electronic and broadcast media (UNDP, 2014). Patterson Siema, Head of Communications for the United Nations Development Programme in Kenya, said this ability to communicate with the Kenyan people in real time was critical. "If you look at mainstream media—TV, newspapers, radio—they do not have the immediacy and interactivity you get from mobile solutions," he said.

The campaign also used roadshows to reach people across the nation. "We took the opportunity to have people speaking local languages to spread our message of peace," Tikolo said. As part of the roadshows, representatives of the campaign went out to talk to local communities, giving away free collateral such as t-shirts and sun visors. Celebrities and well-known musicians also went along and performed. In all, the "peace caravans" reached more than a million Kenyans in 107 market places and towns (NSCPBCM, 2014, p. 15).

The campaign also organized peace marches and set up peace tents across the country where citizens could access information about peace and conflict. Fashion shows were hosted in slums, during which designers spoke about peace. Famous athletes spoke about the importance of peace during sporting events. Through a partnership with Google, the fashion shows and sporting events were also shared on Google Hangouts, broadening their reach. Google also provided free digital advertising to the campaign; the advertisements featured famous Kenyan athletes testifying to the importance of non-violence.

Other partners working with Uwiano helped train journalists on how to responsibly report on the elections and partnered with the media to create public service announcements about peace that ran on television during the country's presidential debate (UNDP, 2014). Grants were provided to help civil society organizations in districts across the country organize public meetings and other events to help build trust and promote reconciliation between people of different ethnic groups (NCIC, 2013).

Despite isolated incidents of violence, Kenya's 2010 referendum and 2013 election were largely peaceful. Tikolo credited the campaign's grassroots outreach with contributing to the stability. In particular, she believes the messages were effective because the campaign "smuggled in" messages about the importance of peace while osten-sibly teaching people how to vote electronically and offering free forms of entertainment that appealed to local communities.

Siema also said the campaign's success was due to the way in which numerous organizations coordinated with one another to send a unified message to the country. "A communications campaign can-not be run in isolation," he said. "People need to be given information from different sources, and this means that campaigns must speak to each other." In fact, the volume of platforms utilized by the campaign made it difficult to ignore. A report analyzing the campaign found that "there was an overwhelming message of peace, which was later described as having been 'over-evangelized.' Clearly, the multiple sources of the messages had the desired impact. . . . The entire coun-try was put under 'peace-siege.'" (NSCPBCM, 2014, p. 17).

Nigeria

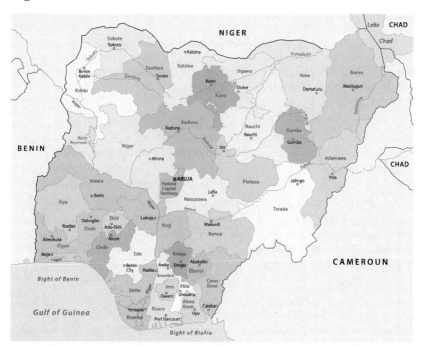

Copyright: Rainer Lesniewski

Time zone: West Africa (UTC + 1:00)
International dialing code: +234

When you practice public relations in Nigeria, be prepared to pitch the print press. You'll find Nigerians reading the newspaper in some rather unexpected places.

Africa's most populous nation and largest economy is home to more than 250 ethnic groups (CIA, 2014; World Bank, 2014). Nigeria won independence from Britain in 1960 and became a republic in 1963. After almost 16 years of military rule, in 1999 Nigeria adopted a new constitution and transitioned peacefully to a civilian government. However, the West African country continues to be plagued by ethnic and religious tensions and is menaced by Boko Haram, a militant Islamist movement that has kidnapped and killed thousands of citizens (CIA, 2014). The three ethnic groups that are predominant in Nigeria are the Hausas (in the country's North), Yoruba (in the West) and Ibo (in the East) (Amaeshi, Adi, Ogbechie, & Amao, 2006, p. 87). Half of the Nigerian people are Muslim, while 40 percent are Christian and 10 percent hold indigenous beliefs (CIA, 2014). The agricultural sector, dominated by small farms, employs the majority of Nigerian workers (Koper, Babaleye, & Jahansoozi, 2009, p. 298). The country's capital is Abuja, its official language is English, and its currency is the naira.

Although Nigeria enjoys great oil wealth, the country is plagued by corruption, insecurity, lack of infrastructure, poor management, a weak judicial system, and great inequality, leaving 62 percent of the Nigerian people in extreme poverty (CIA, 2014; Mago, 2012, pp. 108, 111). Outrage that the extraction of oil from the Niger Delta has not improved the quality of life of local peoples and has resulted in environmental degradation has led to attacks on petroleum facilities and kidnappings of oil workers.

Amujo and Melewar (2011, p. 2) argue that Nigeria's business sector—in areas including banking, insurance, telecommunications, manufacturing, mines and power, oil and gas, and more—is underserved by public relations agencies and that the country presents significant business opportunities for foreign firms. Recent economic reforms have made Nigerian businesses more competitive and opened the economy to foreign investment (Koper et al., 2009, p. 298). The country has been named, along with Mexico, Indonesia, and Turkey, as one of the "MINT" countries that will become increasingly important in the global economy (Maduegbuna, 2014).

Claudine Moore, Global Director of Corporate Communications and Marketing for the Heirs Holdings Group, a Lagos-based, pan-African investment firm, says that the sheer size of the market makes Nigeria "so central and full of opportunity." In particular, Moore says, "the Nigerian population is very aspirational and when it comes to luxury items, the appetite is huge."

Moore says that newspapers are particularly important in this market. "Because traffic in Nigeria, especially in big cities such as Lagos, is so atrocious, you can end up spending four hours a day in traffic," Moore says. "Vendors walk through the streets weaving through traffic, holding newspapers, and there's also this culture of newspaper stands, where people will crowd around reading the newspapers." As a result, "to get on the front cover of a Nigerian newspaper is a huge coup and a great way of getting your message out." Moore says that the quality of newspaper reporting "can vary drastically," though "there are publications like the *Premium Times* popping up that are making the newspaper industry step up its game."

Moore says that one good way to get on the front cover of Nigerian newspapers is to provide media outlets with dynamic pictures. She has found that Nigerian papers favor pictures with larger numbers of people, so her trick is to try to get at least three people into the shot. Moore says that, unlike in other parts of the world, often a newspaper's main headline and picture will be about two entirely different topics.

Because radios are cheap to obtain in Nigeria, radio has huge penetration in this nation. Television is also important. Nigerian television tends to focus heavily on politics because, as Moore says, "Nigerians love to talk politics." However, she says that it is important to remember to target not only the country's two main television networks—Channels TV and Africa Independent Television (AIT)—but also pan-African media outlets such as Bloomberg Africa, CNBC Africa, and Africa 24 for French speakers, because they enjoy large audiences in Nigeria. Additionally, Moore advises pitching bloggers who enjoy large followings, such as Linda Ikeja and Bella Naija. She also warns that the negative gossip blogger sphere in Nigeria across corporate, celebrity, and general business news is robust and active. She recommends building relationships with bloggers and being prepared to address online attacks.

Indigenous forms of outreach may also be called for in Nigerian public relations campaigns, because more than half of the adult population is illiterate (UNICEF, 2013). Koper et al. (2009, pp. 295–296) note that Nigeria has a large oral tradition, and that, in rural areas, community leaders are hugely influential:

> Oral tradition in Nigeria depends on special custodians of tradition and culture to remind the people of what happened in the past to predict what could happen in the future. . . . They exist in all the tribes or ethnic groups in the country and relate past events with the political happenings of today alongside advice on how to deal with issues. . . . The praise singers are known to use all sorts of imagery to convey their messages . . . including the drum language, gong language, masquerade dances, and puppet theatre. . . . The rural population to a very large extent relies heavily on the opinion of the traditional rulers who by virtue of the oral culture have an influence upon them. . . . A group of people or a whole community can change their mind overnight through the sending of emissaries under cover from the traditional rulers by the use of oral communication.

Another practice that is central in Nigeria is corporate social responsibility. Amaeshi et al. (2006, p. 92) found that, among Nigerian businesses, "the emphasis is more on community involvement, less on socially responsible employee relations and almost non-existent in relation to socially responsible products and processes."

A law passed in 1990 gives the Nigerian Institute of Public Relations the power to decide the skills and knowledge that practitioners must have and requires practitioners to register with the Institute and to abide by a code of conduct (Pratt & Adamolekun, 2008, pp. 31–32; Amujo & Melewar, 2011, p. 9). A study of Nigerian practitioners found that, although registration is difficult to enforce in practice, they believe that the law has boosted their prestige, legitimacy, and recognition (Molleda & Alhassan, 2006, pp. 67–68). Another recent study found that members of the Nigerian public do believe that the messages promulgated by public relations practitioners are credible—though they also believe that practitioners are more loyal to their clients than they are to the public interest (Olatunji, 2014, pp. 470–471).

However, the challenges to working in this country are significant. In addition to security concerns, another obstacle is the practice of brown envelopism. Ekeanyanwu (2012, p. 521) reports that

> in Nigeria, many journalists attend political and various events expecting to receive not necessarily scoops, but cash-filled brown envelopes. Local and international observers monitoring ongoing elections warn that the practice is threatening to corrode Nigeria's fledgling democracy because positive publicity is usually reserved for the highest givers.

While the Nigerian Constitution guarantees freedom of the press and the country enjoys a "lively" media, Freedom House (2013) notes that

> state security agents occasionally arrest journalists, confiscate newspapers, and harass vendors, notably when journalists are covering corruption or separatist and communal violence. Local authorities frequently condemn those who criticize them, and cases of violence against journalists often go unsolved. Sharia (Islamic law) statutes in twelve northern states impose severe penalties for alleged press offenses. Media outlets have also been the victims of terrorist attacks.

Furthermore, Koper et al. (2009, p. 293) note that state-run media are often seen as being less independent in Nigeria than in other countries because they are "integrated into the mainstream of government decision-making bodies to avoid misrepresentation of the government's intentions," unlike other public broadcasters such as the BBC.

Media

The News Agency of Nigeria is state-run (BBC, 2013b).

Major newspapers include *This Day*, *The New Telegraph*, *The Guardian*, *The Punch*, and *The Daily Independent* (BBC, 2013b).

Television broadcasters include the state-run Nigerian Television Authority and the privately owned Channels Television, Africa Independent Television (AIT), Minaj TV, and Silverbird TV (BBC, 2013b).

Radio broadcasters include the Federal Radio Corporation of Nigeria (FRCN) and its external service, Voice of Nigeria, as well as the privately owned Ray Power and Freedom Radio (BBC, 2013b).

Seven percent of Nigerians have active social media accounts (Kemp, 2015). Facebook is especially popular (BBC, 2013b).

South Africa

Copyright: Rainer Lesniewski

Time zone: South Africa (UTC + 2:00)
International dialing code: +27

When you practice public relations in South Africa, be prepared to focus on your social impact.

Modern-day South Africa sits on land occupied by the Dutch East India Company in 1652 and later by the British. Beginning in 1910, the British and the Afrikaners (descendants of Dutch settlers) together ruled the Union of South Africa. In the country's 1948 election, the National Party won power and began a policy of apartheid (racial segregation), under which the country's white minority was separated from and favored over the black majority. Opposition to this policy was led by the African National Congress (ANC), which was banned and declared to be a terrorist organization (CIA, 2014; Rensburg, 2009, p. 336). Internal protests—sometimes violent—against the regime, along with boycotts, sanctions, and divestments by numerous countries, the United Nations, and businesses, led to elections in 1994 in which the previously imprisoned ANC leader Nelson Mandela was elected president.

South Africa enjoys significant natural resources (including diamonds and gold), along with modern infrastructure, a well-developed legal system, and established sectors in areas including communications, energy, finance, and transport. The Kruger National Game Park draws tourists from around the world. However, South Africa also has one of the highest rates of inequality in the world and a 25 percent unemployment rate, which is especially high among black youth (CIA, 2014). Despite significant recent reductions, 45.5 percent of South Africans still live in poverty (Mbatha, 2014). The diverse country has eleven official languages, including IsiZulu, IsiXhosa, Afrikaans, and English, but English is used in government and business (CIA, 2014; Rensburg, 2009, p. 329). South Africa's legislative capital is Cape Town and its currency is the rand. The GLOBE study found that white managers in South Africa exhibit characteristics of the Anglo cultural cluster, while black South Africans fall under the Sub-Saharan African cultural cluster (Gupta & Hanges, 2004, p. 191).

The country enjoys a well-developed public relations industry and is widely perceived to be the country in Sub-Saharan Africa "in which corporate communications and public relations can most easily be managed, and where they can be most effective in reaching specific audiences with specific messages" (Skinner & Mersham, 2009, p. 283). In South Africa, public relations is "increasingly recognized as an essential component of organizational and business activities" (de Beer & Mersham, 2004, p. 325). Skjerdal (2011, p. 138) also reports that it is "the only place [in the region] where brown envelopes are not a common problem." Most major global agencies have a presence in the country, as South Africa is seen as "the Gateway to Africa" (Skinner & Mersham, 2009, p. 279; Wiener, 2014).

Kate Thompson-Duwe, Managing Director of the Cape Town-based Amplicon Group, says that

> people have a misperception that we're behind the rest of the world, and certain platforms are a bit behind for economic reasons, but the way we communicate is more exciting and cosmopolitan purely because of the many languages and influences we have.

The diversity of South African audiences makes segmentation critical. "There's no such thing as how to communicate in Africa. It's about who you want to communicate with and the message you want to portray," Thompson-Duwe says.

For example, Merle O'Brien, a former President and Fellow of the Public Relations Institute of Southern Africa, says that in the country's townships—

which are informal settlements outside of major cities where people of pre-dominantly non-white racial groups reside—

> people buy on a daily needs basis as they are paid daily, and you don't have tarred roads for public transport and have to walk or use the taxi, so the kind of value proposition you would make in Europe just doesn't work here. Stressing product functionality and quality in your messages is key to success. People can be reached on the social platforms such as WhatsApp and Mixit which they use to communicate.

In the country's suburbs—which are still predominantly white, affluent areas—O'Brien says that "people use smartphones and take buses, so the chan-nels for communication are completely different."

In rural parts of the country, Thompson-Duwe says,

> you have to be there. You need to communicate first with, and then via, the community leaders. They will not only act as your conduit, but also inform you on the correct message. The rural communities aren't inter-ested in what is being portrayed to city dwellers; they require their own specific communication that pertains to their lifestyles and their needs.

Themba Ngada, Head of Marketing for the City of Cape Town, says that, as discussed in Chapter 4, the chief of a village is all-important in such places. "If someone wants to interview me and I live in a village, they must talk to the chief first," he explains. "Short of bringing a proper gift for a chief, which would be a goat or a sheep, a bottle of brandy will do, as this is good currency in rural Xhosaland."

While newspapers are available in urban areas, Faith Muthambi, Minister of Communications for the South African Government, says that face-to-face communication remains the best way to reach rural South Africans. "Com-munity meetings are the most efficient communication tool" in such areas, Muthambi says. She explains that

> you can't use Facebook because we have a problem with broadband. That's changing, but for now the best mechanism is direct contact. People like to see their leaders, ordinary people sitting under the tree. That's one thing that our communities love.

Muthambi says that radio is also a great medium for reaching South Afri-cans in rural areas. Folk media—including theatre, puppet shows, poetry, and music—are also used, especially to promote social causes (Rensburg, 2009, pp. 345–346).

Modern South African practitioners are also heavily focused on digital strat-egies. Wiener (2014) notes that, today, the number of mobile phones in South Africa is larger than the country's population, which has caused a "dramatic shift" among practitioners to provide integrated services, including digital communication.

Thompson-Duwe says that influencer engagement strategies, in which thought leaders are asked to share SMS messages and content on social platforms such as WhatsApp, can be particularly effective for reaching the country's segmented audiences. "It's like an old school, word of mouth campaign," she says. "You develop key messaging that you want people to share and it's about accessing their networks and ensuring it's done in an authentic way so that it's not seen as a branded campaign." However, Thompson-Duwe says that this also requires educating clients that they will not be able to fully control their messages. "We guide the conversation, but we need to allow it to be authentic," she says.

However, O'Brien says that

> in Africa, you have to lose your concept of what an influencer is, because this continent is so hybrid. Township influencers may not be educated, with money, but may be at the forefront of what's hot and what's not. Its stature, not economics, that makes a township influencer. Or, you could have a client that wants to reach cognac connoisseurs. We may not have cognac connoisseurs, but you can help a local person who wants to be one to become one.

For this reason, Thompson-Duwe says that it is important to educate clients that "in South Africa it may not mean that an influencer has 100,000 followers. It may mean that 100 members of your target audience listen to the person. It could just be someone who is well-connected."

Lesley Schroeder, Managing Partner of the South African research and communication strategy firm Fuller Insight, says that while influencers can be rewarded, for example, with access to events, it is often unnecessary to pay them because "influencers want to be people who are respected and considered to be thought leaders, so by giving them good content, you are helping them, too."

Patrick Collings, Director of Strategy for the Amplicon Group, says that developing compelling content for clients is therefore an important part of influencer strategies. For example, for one client which develops luxury real estate in Cape Town, Amplicon writes content about city living, highlighting local parks and strong schools in an effort to change perceptions that the best schools are in the city's southern suburbs. The stories do not mention Amplicon's client, and often even mention the client's competition. "We try to create an ecosystem that allows users to find the information themselves," Collings explains. "It's a much richer and more concrete connection."

Another preeminent characteristic of public relations practice in South Africa is its focus on corporate social responsibility. Today, it is expected that large organizations will devote money to community projects (de Beer & Mersham, 2004, p. 330). Steyn (2009, pp. 517, 529) has identified a reflective strategist role played by South African practitioners which she reports "rests on three pillars: environmental scanning, organizational stakeholders and societal issues" and is rooted in the African culture of collectivism. Steyn (2009, p. 529) reports that

> focused on strategic reflection, the reflective strategist acts as a coordinating mechanism between organization (business, government, or nonprofit) and environment, providing management with an outside (societal) perspective, assisting them to reflect on the organization's position in the bigger context with the aim of balancing organizational goals with the well-being of society (the collective interest/common good). By spanning the organizational boundary, gathering information by means of environmental scanning, transmitting this information to management, and providing it as input to the strategy formulation process, the reflective strategist enlightens management on societal/stakeholder values, norms, and expectations for socially and environmentally responsible behavior. Management is also influenced to state the organization's position, practice two-way communication, and build trusting relationships with stakeholders about issues of strategic importance.

Holtzhausen (2005, p. 414) likewise reports that "South African organizations seem to be aware of the ability of the environment to decide their survival" and accordingly practice corporate social responsibility, for which they are often rewarded with positive media coverage. Moeng, of Don Valley, also notes that the government has created industry-specific codes for Broad Based Black Economic Empowerment (BBBEE), under which companies are expected to procure goods and services from local businesses and promote diversity in their staff and management structures. If a company does not comply, they will not receive support or business from the government.

Activist groups also "have direct access to the media, and their causes are often taken up and supported by the mass media in the country" (Rensburg, 2009, p. 345).

South Africa's Constitution provides for freedom of the press, and Freedom House (2014a) notes that the right is "generally respected in practice," though "journalists and media houses are occasionally threatened with legal action or charged as a result of their work, particularly when reporting on prominent political or business figures. Prosecutions and indictments are rare, however."

Fay Davids Kajee, a practitioner based in Cape Town, also notes that because newsrooms in traditional media outlets are today staffed by more junior reporters and suffer from staff shortages, it is critical that you only pitch stories that are well-crafted and newsworthy. However, "shortage of staff in the newsroom can work to your advantage, as a well-written story is appreciated and often used in its entirety" (Howard & Mathews, 2013, p. 176).

Rensburg (2009, pp. 334–335) reports that public relations departments in South Africa are called various names, including corporate communications and public affairs, but "the term public relations is still the most acceptable and most often used term in this country." A study of South African

practitioners found that they practice four culturally specific models of public relations: a Western dialogic model, which involves identifying points
of conflict between an organization and publics and advocating internally
for change to rectify problems; an activist model, in which practitioners
attempt to change the attitudes and behaviors of their organizations; an
Ubuntu model, in which practitioners promote harmony and reconciliation
and advocate for marginalized publics; and an oral communication model, in
which practitioners use mediums such as theatre, proverbs, song, and dance
to communicate with publics (Holtzhausen, Petersen, & Tindall, 2003).
Practitioners working for the government and in the industrial, manufacturing, and mining sectors often act as cultural interpreters between their organizations and their myriad stakeholders (Tindall & Holtzhausen, 2011, p. 90).

Media

The country's national news agency is the South African Press Association.

Major newspapers include the *Mail & Guardian*, *The Star*, *The Sowetan*,
Business Day, and the Afrikaans-language *Beeld* (BBC, 2012).

The state broadcaster, the South African Broadcasting Corporation
(SABC), operates several television channels. Private broadcasters include
e.tv and M-Net (BBC, 2012).

The SABC operates numerous domestic radio stations, as well as the external Channel Africa. Private radio broadcasters include YFM and 702 Talk
Radio (BBC, 2012).

Twenty-two percent of South Africans have active social media accounts. The
most popular platforms include Facebook, Twitter, and LinkedIn (Kemp, 2015).

Practitioner Profile: Solly Moeng, Managing Director, Don Valley, South Africa

Solly Moeng is Managing Director of Don Valley, a corporate reputation
management firm based in Cape Town, South Africa.

Born in Soweto in Johannesburg, South Africa, Solly studied linguis-
tics and French at the University of the Witswatersrand in Johannesburg and later earned his master's degree in French at the Université de
Franche-Comté in Besançon, France. He started his career as a marketing and communication officer for the South African Tourism Board in
Canada from 1995 to 1998. When he started the job, the apartheid era
had just ended. "I was part of the first generation of black South Africans to officially represent South Africa abroad," Solly says.

In 1998, Solly returned to South Africa with the Tourism Board. The
following year, he began a new job as Marketing and Communication
Manager for the National Botanical Institute (now called the South

Solly Moeng

African National Biodiversity Institute), which manages a network of national botanical gardens. He later returned to work for the country's tourism board as country officer for the U.S., based in New York.

Returning again to South Africa in 2003, he worked for a French construction company and for CapeNature, an organization that works to promote biodiversity in South Africa's Western Cape Province. In 2006, he started Don Valley, his own corporate reputation management firm. He has consulted for a variety of organizations in the oil and gas, nuclear, tourism, retail, and logistics sectors and is working on his Ph.D. at the University of Cape Town, researching how the nuclear industry uses the media as part of its crisis communications. His clients have included Chevron and Woolworth's, a high-end local retailer.

Solly says that the most important aspect of practicing public relations in South Africa is increasingly stakeholder engagement. "There was a time when your stakeholders were limited to your customers and shareholders," he remembers. "Now, it's everyone. You have to understand local and global sensitivities, as well as political considerations."

Today, Solly asks his clients, "where do you see yourselves in the next five or ten years and what people matter in order to get you where you're going?" He then works with his clients to "ensure they have the right people as friends, who will support them with independent voices."

In this country that prizes corporate social responsibility, Solly advises his clients that messages about socioeconomic development are important. "People want to know that you give back, that you're not just taking," he says. "Giving back to your community can be a big boost to your brand."

However, he warns that it is important that such messages be crafted appropriately. "You must be sensitive to how you communicate," he says. "For example, today race is still a big issue and that can impact how you talk about things. You have to understand the local nuances."

References

Aggrey, K. (2009). Do public relations in Africa use research? A comparison of public and private organizations in Ghana. *African Communication Research*, 2(3), 397–418.

Akpabio, E. (2009). African public relations and the mainstream of global practice. *African Communication Research*, 2(3), 351–366.

Alzoie, E. C. (2004). Public relations exigencies in a developing democracy: A case study of Nigeria's fourth republic. In D. J. Tilson & E. C. Alozie (Eds.), *Toward the common good: Perspectives in international public relations* (pp. 239–254). Boston, MA: Pearson.

Amaeshi, K. M., Adi, B. C., Ogbechie, C., & Amao, O. O. (2006). Corporate social responsibility in Nigeria. *Journal of Corporate Citizenship*, 24, 83–99.

Amujo, O. C., & Melewar, T. C. (2011). Contemporary challenges impacting on the practice of public relations in Nigeria (1990–2011). *Prism*, 8(1), 1–20.

Avert. (2014, July 18). HIV and AIDS in Kenya. Retrieved from http://www.avert.org/hiv-aids-kenya.htm

Barrett, S. (2012, March 30). Africa: The final PR frontier. *PR Week*. Retrieved from http://www.prweek.com/article/1279681/africa-final-pr-frontier

BBC News Africa. (2012, August 22). South Africa profile. Retrieved from http://www.bbc.com/news/world-africa-14094861

BBC News Africa. (2013a, September 12). Ghana profile. Retrieved from http://www.bbc.com/news/world-africa-13433793

BBC News Africa. (2013b, September 12). Nigeria profile. Retrieved from http://www.bbc.com/news/world-africa-13949549

BBC News Africa. (2014, December 2). Kenya profile. Retrieved from http://www.bbc.com/news/world-africa-13681344

Blankson, I. A. (2004). Public relations in emerging democracies: The case of Ghana. In D. J. Tilson & E. C. Alozie (Eds.), *Toward the common good: Perspectives in international public relations* (pp. 300–319). Boston, MA: Pearson.

Central Intelligence Agency (CIA). (2014). World factbook. Retrieved from https://www.cia.gov/library/publications/the-world-factbook/

Council on Foreign Relations. (2015). Africa's conflict zones. Retrieved from http://www.cfr.org/world/africas-conflict-zones/p14543

de Beer, A. S., & Mersham, G. (2004). Public relations in South Africa: A communication tool for change. In D. J. Tilson & E. C. Alozie (Eds.), *Toward the common good: Perspectives in international public relations* (pp. 320–340). Boston, MA: Pearson.

Ekeanyanwu, N. (2012). The Nigerian press, brown envelope syndrome (BES) and media professionalism: The missing link. *Journalism and Mass Communication*, 2(4), 514–529.

Ferreira, T. (2015, May 22). DStv extends SABC News channel into Africa. *Channel 24*. Retrieved from http://www.channel24.co.za/TV/News/DStv-extends-SABC-News-channel-into-Africa-20150522

Fisher, M. (2013, May 16). A revealing map of the world's most and least ethnically diverse countries. *The Washington Post*. Retrieved from http://www.washingtonpost.com/blogs/worldviews/wp/2013/05/16/a-revealing-map-of-the-worlds-most-and-least-ethnically-diverse-countries/

Freedom House. (2013). Freedom in the world: Nigeria. Retrieved from https://www.freedomhouse.org/report/freedom-world/2013/nigeria

Freedom House. (2014a). Freedom of the press: South Africa. Retrieved from https://freedomhouse.org/report/freedom-press/2014/south-africa

Freedom House. (2014b). Freedom in the world: Ghana. Retrieved from https://www.freedomhouse.org/report/freedom-world/2014/ghana-0

Freedom House. (2014c). Freedom in the world: Kenya. Retrieved from https://www.freedomhouse.org/report/freedom-world/2014/kenya-0

Gupta, V., & Hanges, P. J. (2004). Regional and climate clustering of societal clusters. In R. J. House, P. J. Hanges, M. Javidan, P. W. Dorfman, & V. Gupta (Eds.), *Culture, leadership, and organizations: The GLOBE study of 62 societies* (pp. 178–218). Thousand Oaks, CA: Sage.

Helander, E. (2010). A critical view of the Kenyan media system through the perspective of the journalists. *African Communication Research*, 3(3), 521–542.

Holtzhausen, D. R. (2005). Public relations practice and political change in South Africa. *Public Relations Review*, 31(3), 407–416.

Holtzhausen, D. R., Petersen, B. K., & Tindall, N. T. (2003). Exploding the myth of the symmetrical/asymmetrical dichotomy: Public relations models in the new South Africa. *Journal of Public Relations Research*, 15(4), 305–341.

Howard, C. M., & Mathews, W. K. (2013). *On deadline: Managing media relations* (5th ed.). Long Grove, IL: Waveland Press.

IRIN. (2008, January 7). In-depth: Kenya's post election crisis. Retrieved from http://www.irinnews.org/in-depth/76116/68/kenya-s-post-election-crisis

Issaka, S. (2012, August 12). The rise of social media in Ghana. *The African Business Journal*. Retrieved from http://www.tabj.co.za/features/aug12_features/the_rise_of_social_media_ in_ghana_by_sharifah_issaka.html

Kaigwa, M. W. (2013, December 13). Kenya at 50: How social media has increased the pace of change. *The Guardian*. Retrieved from http://www.theguardian.com/global-development-professionals-network/2013/dec/13/kenya-social-media-mark-kaigwa

Kasoma, T. (2009). Development reporting as a crumbling tower? Impact of brown envelope journalism on journalistic practice in Zambia and Ghana. *Global Media Journal*, 3(1), 18–32.

Kemp, S. (2015, January 21). Digital, social & mobile worldwide in 2015. *We Are Social*. Retrieved from http://wearesocial.net/blog/2015/01/digital-social-mobile-worldwide-2015/

Kiambi, D. M., & Nadler, M. K. (2012). Public relations in Kenya: An exploration of models and cultural influences. *Public Relations Review*, 38(3), 505–507.

Koper, E., Babaleye, T., & Jahansoozi, J. (2009). Public relations practice in Nigeria. In K. Sriramesh & D. Verčič (Eds.), *The global public relations handbook: Theory, research, and practice* (2nd ed.) (pp. 289–305). New York, NY: Routledge.

Leke, A., Lund, S., Manyika, J., & Ramaswamy, S. (2014, August). Lions go global: Deepening Africa's ties to the United States. *McKinsey & Company*. Retrieved from http://www.mckinsey.com/insights/globalization/lions_go_global_deepening_africas_ties_to_the_united_states

Livermore, D. (2013). *Expand your borders: Discover ten cultural clusters*. East Lansing, MI: Cultural Intelligence Center.

Maduegbuna, N. (2014, October 25). Postcard from Nigeria. *PR Week*. Retrieved from http://www.prweek.com/article/1316559/postcard-nigeria

Mago, M. (2012). Nigeria, petroleum and a history of mismanaged community relations. In K. Sriramesh & D. Verčič (Eds.), *Culture and public relations: Links and implications* (pp. 105–123). New York, NY: Taylor & Francis.

Mattinson, A. (2013, December 19). Postcard from Kenya. *PR Week*. Retrieved from http://www.prweek.com/article/1225138/postcard-kenya

Mbatha, A. (2014, April 3). South African poverty rate drops as government expands welfare. *Bloomberg News*. Retrieved from http://www.bloomberg.com/news/2014–04–03/south-african-poverty-rate-drops-as-government-expands-welfare.html

Mbeke, P. O. (2009). Status of public relations in Kenya. In K. Sriramesh & D. Verčič (Eds.), *The global public relations handbook: Theory, research, and practice* (2nd ed.) (pp. 306–327). New York, NY: Routledge.

Mersham, G., Skinner, C., & Rensburg, R. (2011). Approaches to African communication management and public relations: A case for theory-building on the continent. *Journal of Public Affairs, 11*(4), 195–207.

Molleda, J. C., & Alhassan, A. D. (2006). Professional views on the Nigeria Institute of Public Relations' law and enforcement. *Public Relations Review, 32*(1), 66–68.

National Cohesion and Integration Commission (NCIC). (2013). UWIANO platform for peace. Retrieved from http://www.cohesion.or.ke/index.php/programmes/uwiano-platform-for-peace

National Steering Committee on Peacebuilding and Conflict Management (NSCPBCM). (2014). Implementation of the UWIANO communication strategy final report.

Olatunji, R. W. (2014). As others see us: Differing perceptions of public relations in Nigeria among practitioners and the general public. *Public Relations Review 40*(3), 466–472.

Pan African Media Research Organisation (PAMRO). (2013). *PAMRO country reports: Africa rising: The role of audience media research in emerging markets*. Retrieved from http://pamro.org/country-reports-2/

Pratt, C. B., & Adamolekun, W. (2008). The People's Republic of China and FAPRA: Catalysts for theory building in Africa's public relations. *Journal of Public Relations Research, 20*(1), 20–48.

Rensburg, R. (2009). Public relations in South Africa: From rhetoric to reality. In K. Sriramesh & D. Verčič (Eds.), *The global public relations handbook: Theory, research, and practice* (2nd ed.) (pp. 328–361). New York, NY: Routledge.

Skinner, J. C. (2013). Africa, practice of public relations in. In R. L. Heath (Ed.), *Encyclopedia of public relations* (2nd ed.) (pp. 15–19). Thousand Oaks, CA: Sage.

Skinner, C., & Mersham, G. (2009). The nature and status of public relations practice in Africa. In K. Sriramesh & D. Verčič (Eds.), *The global public relations handbook: Theory, research, and practice* (2nd ed.) (pp. 265–288). New York, NY: Routledge.

Skjerdal, T. S. (2011). Brown envelopes and professional paradoxes in African journalism. In G. Berger (Ed.), *Media in Africa: Twenty years after the Windhoek Declaration on press freedom* (pp. 137–138). Cape Town: Media Institute of Southern Africa.

Steyn, B. (2009). The strategic role of public relations is strategic reflection: A South African research stream. *American Behavioral Scientist, 53*(4), 516–532.

Straus, S. (2012). Wars do end! Changing patterns of political violence in Sub-Saharan Africa. *African Affairs, 111*(443), 179–201.

Tikolo, K. L. (2011, June 30). *Public Relations Society of Kenya draft report on the practice of public relations in Kenya: Future growth prospects*. Retrieved from http://www.prsk.co.ke/images/status_survey_pdf/status_survey.pdf

Tindall, N. T., & Holtzhausen, D. R. (2011). Toward a roles theory for strategic communication: The case of South Africa. *International Journal of Strategic Communication*, 5(2), 74–94.

UNICEF. (2013, December 27). At a glance: Nigeria. Retrieved from http://www.unicef.org/infobycountry/nigeria_statistics.html

United Nations. (2014). *The Millennium Development Goals report 2014*. Retrieved from http://ww.un.org/millenniumgoals/2014%20MDG%20report/MDG%202014%20English%20web.pdf

United Nations Development Programme (UNDP). (2014). Uwiano platform: A multi-stakeholder strategy for peaceful elections. Retrieved from http://www.undp.org/content/kenya/en/home/operations/projects/peacebuilding/uwiano-peace-platform-project/

United Nations Educational, Scientific and Cultural Organization (UNESCO). (2011). *Literacy initiative for empowerment (LIFE)*. Retrieved from http://www.unesco.org/new/fileadmin/MULTIMEDIA/FIELD/Dakar/pdf/Info%20sheet%20LIFE%20in%20Africa%202011.pdf

Van Heerden, G., & Rensburg, R. (2005). Public relations roles empirically verified among public relations practitioners in Africa. *Communicare*, 24(1), 69–88.

Wiener, E. (2014, November 18). Postcard from South Africa. *PR Week*. Retrieved from http://www.prweek.com/article/1322435/postcard-south-africa

World Bank. (2014). *GDP*. Retrieved from http://data.worldbank.org/indicator/NY.GDP.MKTP.CD?order=wbapi_data_value_2013+wbapi_data_value+wbapi_data_valuelast&sort=desc

World Bank & African Development Bank. (2012). *The transformational use of information and communication technologies in Africa*. Retrieved from http://siteresources.worldbank.org/EXTINFORMATIONANDCOMMUNICATIONAND-TECHNOLOGIES/Resources/28 2822–1346223280837/MainReport.pdf

Wu, M. Y., & Baah-Boakye, K. (2007). A profile of public relations practice in Ghana: Practitioners' roles, most important skills for practitioners, relationship to marketing, and gender equality. *Public Relations Quarterly*, 52(1), 30–36.

Wu, M. Y., & Baah-Boakye, K. (2009). Public relations in Ghana: Work-related cultural values and public relations models. *Public Relations Review*, 35(1), 83–85.

Acknowledgments

The author (right) takes notes during a focus group in São Paulo, Brazil. Photo courtesy of Susan Alaimo

It may take just one village to raise a child, but it took many to write this book. I am grateful to the people in every corner of the globe who helped me along the way.

Thank you to Suzanne Phelps Chambers, who first asked me to write a book and connected me with my outstanding editor, Linda Bathgate. I have been privileged to work with an editor who has published so many of the seminal texts in public relations and immediately saw the value in this project. Special thanks as well to crack editorial assistants Stephanie Gorman and Nicole Salazar and former editorial assistant Ross Wagenhofer.

I am especially grateful for the extraordinary support I received at Hofstra University while writing this book. Thank you to the Provost's office (and to the National Center for Suburban Studies) for my Faculty Diversity Research and Curriculum Development Grant and to Dean Evan Cornog for my Lawrence Herbert School of Communication Research and Development

Grants, which helped fund my focus groups in Brazil and South Africa. Thanks to Dean Cornog as well for supporting my speaking engagement at the 2015 World Communication Forum in Davos, where I met many of my interview subjects. I am also grateful to Vice Provost Cliff Jernigan; Vice Dean Dwight Brooks; Vice President Melissa Connolly; Department of Journalism, Media Studies, and Public Relations Chair Carol Fletcher; former Associate Chair Mary Ann Allison; and Associate Director of Public Relations Neena Samuel for their never-ending support of my work. Thank you to my public relations colleagues Suzanne Berman and Jeff Morosoff for connecting me with interview subjects; to my graduate research assistants Marissa Slattery and Andrew Manning; to my student aide Rachael Durant; and to the Hofstra librarians for cheerfully fulfilling my requests for hundreds of articles and books.

Thank you as well to the American Political Science Association (especially the wonderful Betsy Super) for helping fund my focus groups through a grant from the Edward Artinian Fund for Publishing, and for their years of support for my research.

I am indebted to Cristina Schachtitz at Edelman Significa and Paulo Henrique Soares at Vale for hosting my focus groups in São Paulo and Rio de Janeiro, as well as to Ana Juliao, Andre Morais, Ariane Sefrin Feijó, and Flavio Oliveira for help organizing the focus groups in Brazil. Thank you as well to Kate Thompson-Duwe at the Amplicon Group for hosting my focus group in Cape Town, and to Solly Moeng for bringing the South Africa group together.

Thank you to the organizers of the World Communication Forum in Davos (especially Yanina Dubeykovskaya and Valentina Atanasova) and the Social Media Strategies Summit in New York, where I got many great ideas for this book. Special thanks as well to IAU College in France for hosting me as a Resident Fellow in the summer of 2014, where I researched the case study in Chapter 8 on the public relations strategies of the Bordeaux wineries.

Thanks to Harlan Loeb and Cailly Morris at Edelman for connecting me with so many of their colleagues around the world for this project. Thanks as well to Sarah Dumbrille, Williams Ekanem, Villi Wee Lee Geow, Jill Hamburg Coplan, Marielle Legair, and Sarah Wincott for sharing valuable sources and literature. Thank you to Robin Straus, Fraser Seitel, Helio Fred Garcia, and Mark Pearson for sage advice and to Dr. Basilio Monteiro, who first gave me the opportunity to develop my course in international public relations at St. John's University. Thanks to my mom, Susan Alaimo, and my brother, Peter Alaimo, who first proposed that I write this book.

Finally, of course, I am deeply grateful to my interview subjects around the world, whose brilliant insights informed this book. Thank you to Allan McCrea Steele in Argentina; Louise Nealon in Australia; Claudia Afflalo, Lala Aranha, Fabio Cavalcanti Caldas, Mateus Furlanetto, Angela Giacobbe, Serge Giacomo, Hugo Godinho, Paulo Henrique Soares, Ana Juliao, Eunice Lima, Andre Morais, Flavio Oliveira, Cristina Schachtitz, and Rodrigo Soares in/from Brazil; Elissa Freeman in Canada; Pamela Leonard in Chile; Maggie Chan, David Croasdale, Holly Zheng, and Chen Liang in/from China and

Hong Kong; May Hauer-Simmonds from Ecuador; Rania Azab and Hossam Zakaria in Egypt; Christophe Ginisty in France; Jennifer Stapper and Joerg Winkelmann in Germany; Faith Senam Ocloo in Ghana; Sujit Patil in India; Indira Abidin in Indonesia; Oren Bason in Israel; Gianni Catalfamo in Italy; Ross Rowbury in Japan; Rana Nejem in Jordan; Kentice Tikolo and Patterson Siema in Kenya; David Lian in Malaysia; Jorge Acosta and Adriana Garza in/from Mexico; David Brain in New Zealand; Claudine Moore in Nigeria; Alexandra Konysheva in Russia; Yahya Hamidaddin in Saudi Arabia; Patrick Collings, Aloy Gowne, Faith Muthambi, Solly Moeng, Themba Ngada, Merle O'Brien, Lesley Schroeder, and Kate Thompson-Duwe in South Africa; Jim Morris in South Korea; Beatriz Alegría Carrasco from Spain; Charlotte Erkhammar in Sweden; Louay Al Samarrai in the United Arab Emirates; Colin Byrne, Richard Lewis, and Jack Lundie in the United Kingdom; and Rowan Benecke, Pete Borum, Pam Didner, Leslie Gaines-Ross, Glenn Goldberg, Ahna Hendrix, Sheri Herrmann, R.P. Kumar, Rich Kylberg, Harlan Loeb, Sabrina Lynch, Chris Nelson, Cassandra Olivos, Devi Thomas, and Ekaterina Walter in the United States.

Thank you as well to all who granted me interviews for my case study in Chapter 8 on how top Bordeaux wines are promoted in China: Virginie Achou-Lepage, Aline Baly, Philippe Castéja, Didier Frechinet, Hervé Gouin, Pierre Lurton, Amy Mumma, Xavier Planty, and Christophe Salin in France and Henry Ho, Thomas Jullien, Thibault Pontallier, and Damon Yuen in Hong Kong.

To my friends, old and new, gracias, obrigado, 谢谢, شكراً, merci, danke, धन्यवाद, terima kasih, תודה, grazie, ありがとう, asante, спасибо, ngiyabonga, 고맙습니다, tack, and thank you.

Kara Alaimo, Ph.D.
New York, September 1, 2015

About the Author

Dr. Kara Alaimo is Assistant Professor and Associate Chair in the Department of Journalism, Media Studies, and Public Relations at Hofstra University in New York. She also consults on global communication campaigns and designs customized employee training programs for companies on how to adapt public relations messages and strategies for different global markets.

From 2012 to 2013, Dr. Alaimo was Head of Communications for the Secretariat of the United Nations Secretary-General's High Level Panel on the Post-2015 Development Agenda, a group of heads of state and other eminent thinkers convened to recommend the world's next plan for ending extreme poverty and achieving sustainable development. In 2011 she was appointed by U.S. President Barack Obama as Spokesperson for International Affairs in the U.S. Treasury Department, where she communicated global economic diplomacy initiatives, including America's bilateral economic relationships; engagement in multilateral institutions including the G-20, World Bank, and IMF; and international monetary, trade, development, environmental, and energy policy. In this capacity, she also served as media adviser to Jim Yong Kim during his successful 2012 campaign for the World Bank Presidency. Dr. Alaimo also previously served as Press Secretary of the Peter G. Peterson Foundation, Global Media Coordinator for the United Nations Millennium Campaign, and as a spokesperson for New York City economic development initiatives during the administration of Mayor Michael R. Bloomberg.

Dr. Alaimo earned her Doctor of Philosophy, Master of Philosophy, and Master of Arts degrees at the City University of New York and her Bachelor of Arts with honors at New York University (NYU). She is a member of the board of the World Communication Forum in Davos.

Her research on international and political public relations has been published in academic journals including the *International Journal of Communication, Journal of Communication Management, Journal of Public Affairs, Case Studies in Strategic Communication*, and *Social Media & Society*. She has also contributed to industry publications including *PRWeek, The Public Relations Strategist, Public Relations Tactics, The Bulldog Reporter, Ragan's PR Daily*, and the *World Communication Review*.

To read more of her work, visit her website at www.karaalaimo.com and follow her Twitter handle, @karaalaimo.

Index

Note: Page numbers in italics indicate tables